National Institute for Social Work

Growing up in Groups

Barbara Kahan

London: HMSO

ISBN 0 11 701843 0

The view expressed in this report is that of the author, and do not
necessarily reflect the views of the Department of Health.

Further information regarding this and other NISW titles may be
obtained from:

National Institute for Social Work
5 Tavistock Place
London
WC1H 9SS
Telephone: 071 387 9681

Contents

PART TWO: LIVING AWAY FROM HOME IN GROUPS

Preface

This book springs from the work and discussions of a large multidisciplinary group drawn mainly from health, education and social services. Their common bond was deep concern for the welfare of children and young people living in groups away from home and belief in the benefits of such group living for some children and young people. Their primary aim was to define a common core of good practice which could be adopted wherever the children might be - in children's homes, boarding schools, therapeutic communities and hospitals. "Growing up in Groups" is the first attempt in Britain to do this.

For many years cooperation between services in the interests of children and young people has been the subject of recommendations of research studies, teaching of good practice and public policy. Changes in social services in 1968 in Scotland and in England and Wales in 1970 were major statutory steps in that direction. Synthesis of policy between central and local government, however, continues to be a desirable aim, widely supported but difficult to achieve and practice still demonstrates a need for greater collaboration and common acceptance of good practice. This book is a contribution towards achieving these aims.

'*Growing up in Groups*' expresses the need for consensus on the principles which should underpin the welfare of children living away from home in group settings and the common core of good practice complementary to them. It also identifies the need for practitioners to have easier access to source material which describes the theory, knowledge and skills required to carry out the tasks expected of them, and background information about how services for children and young people relate to each other. Training and good management are seen as essential corollaries to the principles and practice.

Readers will find much to compare and contrast in the good practice brought together in the book and, like the group whose work preceded it, may discover that practitioners in different services often have much more in common than is usually assumed.

A great many people have contributed in various ways to this book. They include Dame Gillian Wagner who gave support to an initiative on behalf of children following her report '*A Positive Choice*'; Daphne Statham, Director of the National Institute for Social Work, who provided administrative support as well as professional participation;

and the Department of Health which provided funding. Very special thanks are due to certain individuals: Mark Davies, formerly Secretary to the Warner Committee, who carried out an initial analysis of the group's material and produced a first framework for the report; John Rowlands, Social Services Inspector, who undertook major consultative and drafting work; and Audrey McLeod, Personal Assistant to Daphne Statham, who produced the text from many drafts with great patience, good humour and commitment. In the production of a book of this kind there are many people who assist by generously giving and checking information, providing statistics, suggestions and quotations. They are too numerous to name but they will know who they are and that we are grateful to them.

As Chair of the group, editor and part author of the book, I accept responsibility for any shortcomings.

Barbara Kahan.

PART ONE

BACKGROUND AND PRINCIPLES

1 Introduction

'So widespread is the misconception that children in care are blameworthy that ultimately they come to accept this stigma themselves'.

R Page and G Clarke (Editors) 'Who Cares: Young People in Care Speak Out' – NCB 1977

'You say you are in care and lots of people feel sorry for you.....'.
'When you say you are in a children's home people think you have done something wrong....'.

Young People in Care in the 1990s

'Boarding school teaches you to tolerate people's differences and to fit into society quickly......'.
'You make friends and it teaches you discipline.....'.

Boarding school pupil in response to Wagner Children's Group inquiry

1.1 Who is this book for?

The Aim of this book is to provide a resource for staff working in residential settings with children and young people, whether they be children's homes, boarding schools, health service units or other settings in which children and young people are looked after in groups. It is particularly relevant for those in the 'front line' – residential social workers in children's homes, teachers and care staff in boarding schools, nursing staff in hospital psychiatric units for adolescents, – in fact anyone who has regular 'caring' responsibilities for children in residential settings. It is also for those with overall managerial responsibility for establishments, heads of homes, head teachers, doctors in charge of health service units and senior nurses. The authors hope these front line people, particularly those in children's homes, will recognise clearly that the importance and complexity of their task is appreciated and valued in what we have written. This task and the care they give the children have been undervalued for too long. It is part of our purpose to try to redress that balance.

This book is also for managers whose work is outside the residential establishments. The task they undertake is complex and important to those for whom they are accountable. By helping to develop good management structures and systems, they can give support to front line staff to ensure they use their skills and experience effectively. Local authority inspection units – monitoring the provision of responsive and protective environments for children and young people who are accommodated will, we hope, find much in the book to assist their understanding of the services they inspect. It will also, we believe, be of value to elected local authority members, trustees and others on governing bodies of residential homes, schools and hospitals. It is their responsibility to support and monitor the delivery of good services and, through their role in representing the public, from an informed position, exert pressure on professional managers if necessary.

It is a substantial book, not one to be read at a sitting, nor necessarily in entirety by every reader, although those who achieve this will gain a broader view of the subject than they can currently find elsewhere between two covers. In order to make it easy for those who want to find a particular topic eg. children's rights, the need to physically restrain children, sex education or support for staff, we have provided a table of contents which pinpoints these, and others, in great detail. In many instances the page number for the material the reader is seeking will be immediately apparent.

In addition, for readers who work in the different settings discussed, children's homes, schools, hospitals, we offer suggestions on how to obtain substantial information and assistance by selection of parts of the book. The following examples demonstrate this:-

(a)   A newly appointed member of staff in a children's home might begin with Chapter 6: 'The Common Core' (in total), followed by Chapter 5: 'The Physical Environment'. Chapter 4: 'Rights and Responsibilities' will also be important as will Chapter 8: 'Protecting the Welfare of Children and Young People'.

(b)   A newly appointed house master in a boarding school might turn first to part of Chapter 9: 'Boarding Schools (Maintained and Independent) or 'Boarding Special Schools'; then to Chapter Six: 'The Common Core', reading particularly the parts dealing with Caring (6.2) and Behaviour (6.3). Chapter 7: Arrival and Settling In: Leaving and then Chapter 8: 'Protecting the Welfare of Children and Young People' would carry him through immediately important areas of good practice from the first day in his new job; Chapter 5: 'The Physical Environment' would provide useful background to the others.

(c)   A manager/principal officer in a local authority, responsible for children's homes should find time to read Chapters 1 to 4: 'Background and Principles', 'Who Lives in Residential Settings?', 'The Legal and Political Background and 'Rights and Responsibilities'. Chapters 11 and 12, 'Training and Management Issues – 'The Buck Stops Here'' could helpfully follow. Then, if the manager is not going to read the whole book, Chapters 5 to 8 will be important; 'The Physical Environment', 'The Common Core', 'Arrival and Settling In: Leaving' and 'Protecting the Welfare of Children and Young People'.

(d)   A Governor of an EBD Special school might start with Chapters 2 and 4: 'Who Lives in Residential Settings?' and 'Rights and Responsibilities' then go on to Chapters 9, 11, and 12: 'Boarding Schools and Therapeutic Communities', 'Training' and 'Management Issues: 'The Buck Stops Here''. We would hope s/he might then want to read Chapter 6: 'The Common Core'.

(e)   A nurse in a psychiatric hospital might begin with Chapter 10: 'Medical and Health Settings' then go on to Chapter 2: 'Who Lives in Residential Settings?', Chapter 4: 'Rights and Responsibilities and Chapter 6: 'The Common Core'.

(f)   A Diploma in Social Work student should read it all!

1.2 Growing up in groups: Aims and objectives

The aim of this book, as we have said, is particularly to provide a resource for staff working in residential establishments. We have tried to do this by examining good practice in a variety of settings and identifying what each can learn from the others. It is not official 'guidance'; its use is voluntary; it is intended to provoke discussion, not provide definitive statements or prototype models. It emphasises good practice which would be common to all settings and which relates to children and young people of all ages.

This common core incorporates good 'caring' practice; the physical environment; management issues; staffing issues; and issues of children's rights. We discuss common themes and consider issues relating to specific types of establishments, including those regulated by the *Children Act 1989*, particularly children's homes. This is against the background that children have a right to effective intervention in their lives, both to remedy their wrongs and to provide them with services.

Our intention is to encourage cross-fertilisation of ideas. Each type of residential setting has positive and negative features. Good practice exists in all the areas we have considered. As long as legal requirements are met in any establishment, there is scope for different groups of staff to learn from one another. If readers develop some of the ideas and good practices of others working in different sectors, and apply them in their own establishments, we believe they will enrich good practice generally and broaden understanding of children and young people and their needs.

1.3 Children and young people growing up in groups: Origins of this book

The majority of children and young people in Britain, rich or poor, are brought up at home with their own families. There are some, however, who live in group settings for all or part of each year. Boarding school education is a positive choice for some families and has been so for centuries. In recent times some children board in schools because their parents are abroad or they are members of one parent families. Some children whose own parents cannot care for them are accommodated in children's homes or other care establishments; sick children experience hospital life; some children with special physical, emotional, educational needs or behaviour problems, live in therapeutic communities, special boarding schools, or establishments for group control and treatment of young offenders.

The reasons why they do not live at home range from parental choice or circumstances to educational, physical, emotional and mental health considerations; from protection of children themselves to protection of the public from their behaviour. The children live in establishments which are large and small; religious and secular; therapeutic and penal; educational and health provision; specialised and eclectic groups; short term or long term provision; for single or mixed sexes; and for different age groups. The adults looking after the children include qualified teachers, doctors, nurses, social workers, psychologists and large numbers of unqualified, though in many cases experienced, staff.

Residential group living for children and young people has been debated for many years, particularly, though not exclusively, within social services. Its use has waned and waxed, and waned again, depending on fluctuations of professional and political theories and fashions, and changing pressures in national resources. The care aspect of group living is greatly underestimated and undervalued, unlike special skills associated with it such as medicine and teaching. This is, perhaps, because it is often regarded as an extension of ordinary child rearing which has also traditionally been undervalued and taken for granted. In psychiatric units for young people with mental health problems, ordinary day-to-day childhood needs sometimes receive lower priority than medical needs. In boarding schools, where teaching may be of high quality, the quality of care outside the classroom may not always be of matching quality. Although a pastoral approach is part of the school programme, individual schools vary in the emphasis given to it and it is often provided by staff with no special training for the task. In children's homes, young offenders' institutions and other special provision, staff dealing with very serious needs and problems are frequently untrained and inadequately supported.

The common factor in all situations in which children and young people live in groups away from home has been that childhood and developmental needs frequently receive less than adequate recognition and provision. Standards vary from good or reasonable to inadequate or poor, and occasionally scandalous. There has been no commonly accepted good minimum standard throughout the country. In addition, in some residential settings, such as children's homes, management which is essential in achieving high standards of care, has been weak and bureaucratic.

1.3.1 Home Life – 1984

In the early 1980s the need for good standards of residential social services for adults was specifically recognised for the first time in the *Registered Homes Act 1984*, which regulated the establishment and conduct of private and voluntary homes. This Act, primarily concerned with homes for adults, also applied to homes for children with disabilities. To support implementation of the legislation, the Government set up a working party to produce a code of practice for residential care. The Code, published in 1984 under the title '*Home Life*', identified certain basic rights for

> '*all who find themselves in the care of others*'.

These were **fulfilment, dignity, autonomy, individuality, esteem, quality of experience, expression of emotional needs, opportunities for making choices and taking risks.**

The Secretaries of State for Social Services and for Wales, in their joint foreword to the Guidance, said it had:-

> '*striven towards the good rather than simply defined the acceptable...... These establishments are home for people who live in them and the standards of management and care determine the whole quality of their lives*'.

1.3.2 Independent Review of Residential Care – 1985

Shortly after '*Home Life*' was published, the Secretary of State for Health and Social Services set up an independent review of residential care. At that time there was wide agreement that residential services, particularly in the statutory sector, were in a demoralised state. They were too often used as a service of last resort and had low status within the range of other services. In her introduction to the *Review Report* in 1988, the Chairman, Lady Wagner, described how she and her colleagues had changed their view of their task while they worked, moving from their

> *'original premise that, with suitable modification and adjustments, the (residential) sector as it was constituted, could be adapted and improved to meet changing needs'*

to one which led them to recognise that only by seeing residential services as *'A Positive Choice'* (the title they chose for their report) could necessary changes be achieved. Their recommendations were applicable in the statutory, voluntary and private sectors and they believed they would also have an impact on housing, education and health services. (The work and findings of the Wagner review team are discussed at greater length in Chapter 3 of this book).

1.3.3 *House of Commons Select Committee on Social Services: Report on Children in Care – 1983/1984*

While the Wagner Committee was sitting, the Government – responding to the House of Commons Select Committee on Social Services' investigation *'Children in Care'* (1983/1984) set up a review of child care law. The Select Committee referred to the resulting White Paper *'The Law on Child Care and Family Services'* (Cmdn 62) and welcomed its statement that

> *'residential services for children and young people should not necessarily be seen as a mark of failure either on the part of the family or of those working to support them'.*

1.3.4 *Report of the Independent Review of Residential Care* *'A Positive Choice' – Report of the Wagner Committee Published 1988*

Following the publication of *'A Positive Choice'*, Lady Wagner and the National Institute for Social Work set up the Wagner Development Group to pursue active implementation of the Report's recommendations. A number of initiatives were taken. One of these was the decision to carry out further work to promote the interests of children as a special group needing residential care. Requests from residential child care services had urged that attention be given to the specific contribution they make and how the report's recommendations could be applied to them. The task was defined initially in the following terms:-

'to produce an equivalent of 'Home Life' for children identifying good practice and providing a useful tool for managers and practitioners, for staff development and for users and their families;

to provide a resource for whoever might, in the future restructure 'Home Life', which would ensure that the specific needs of children would be taken into account and that any revised publication would benefit from the principles which underpinned the Wagner Review of Residential Care.'

It was decided that the project should not be restricted to residential settings in social services (ie. children's homes) but should include boarding schools (omitted from the Wagner Review but highlighted in their Report), health settings, and others in which children and young people spend time living in groups away from home. *'Bridges Over Troubled Waters'* (published by the Health Advisory Service in 1986 and concerned with services for disturbed adolescents) had already demonstrated the importance of greater uniformity of good practice in various residential services.

To achieve the task, a multidisciplinary steering group was established, with representation from the whole of the UK. It included representatives of local authorities, voluntary organisations, education and health services, research, therapeutic communities, the National Institute of Social Work (NISW), the National Children's Bureau (NCB), the Central Council for Education and Training in Social Work (CCETSW), the Association of Directors of Social Services (ADSS), the Social Care Association (SCA) and the National Association of Young People in Care (NAYPIC). Members of the Department of Health, Northern Ireland and Welsh Office Social Services Inspectorates, the Scottish Social Work Services Group and an Inspector from Her Majesty's Inspectorate of Schools acted as observers. (Those who participated are listed in Appendix I). Barbara Kahan, Chair of the National Children's Bureau and co-author of *'The Pindown Experience'* agreed to chair the group. Daphne Statham, Director of NISW, acted as its administrator. The Department of Health welcomed the proposal and made a grant in support of the project.

The work of the Group took place during a period of unprecedented activity and concern with child care issues, and with residential care in particular. Resulting from the review of child care law, the *Children Bill* had been drafted and was the focus of extensive debate and consultation. It received Royal Assent in November 1989 and the *Children Act 1989* was implemented on 14 October 1991. Between Royal Assent and implementation, the Department of Health drafted many volumes of

Guidance and Regulations, as well as other supporting material. These were drafted, put out for consultation, and later published.

The Children Act 1989 has been hailed as the major child care legislation of this century. In drawing together a wide range of legal provisions, and in stressing the wholeness of a child's personality, characteristics and needs, it has given a clear signal that a more unified approach to children's needs is required wherever they may be cared for away from home. Our book is in tune with this unified approach in its emphasis on a common core of care.

Our initiative created a forum where the worlds of social services child care, special education, adolescent psychiatry and public schools sat around a table and explored their common ground. There was some concern that the key purpose of the venture -the production of a supportive asset for staff in children's homes – might be deflected by too much attention to boarding schools. This did not happen but the path through such a complex field was sometimes difficult. Some of the shared experience is important to acknowledge. First, those from the social services world were struck by the confidence of those who spoke for the mainstream boarding school world. This was not arrogance or superiority – it was simply assurance. They were confident about their place in the scheme of things. They were confident enough to explore with child care colleagues the more difficult areas of child care and willing to acknowledge their own problems with indiscipline. This contrasted with the sense of marginalisation, bewilderment, and sometimes betrayal, of representatives from the child care sectors. They had strong personal convictions that what they were doing was right and necessary but they were not confident that the rest of the world saw their work as they did. Two cultures met at the discussion table. The world of education saw boarding as a highly desirable experience for children, which conferred advantages persisting throughout their lives. The world of social services, by contrast, saw residential care as a fate from which children needed to be protected – one which would be detrimental to their life chances. But when these two cultures sat down and talked to each other, there were wide areas of common ground. Extremes of privilege and under-privilege had so much in common when talking about means; but such contrasting outcomes when comparing ends. The central tenet of this book is that it need not be like this.

The two cultures had met before during the events and negotiations which led to Sections 87 and 63 of the *Children Act 1989*. These sections gave social workers authoritative access to the world of public schools. These provisions have not been without their tensions, but it is notable that some prestigious establishments have positively embraced social services departments' inspections and, rather than resisting or playing down their importance, have seen the advantages and recognised that there are important things to be learned from the world of child care and welfare.

What did the child care system have to learn from education in their task of caring for and controlling young people whose views and expectations of the world were likely often to be very different from many children in boarding schools? Some of the assets of the education world which emerged in our discussions, and which could be usefully translated into residential child care, were as follows:

(i)   A reliable, longish term time scale of engagement with a child.

(ii) A strong sense of the developing child and an in-built sense of attainment targets and progress.

(iii) Confidence that staff and child know the direction in which they are going.

(iv) A capacity to impart useful knowledge and skills to the child.

(v)   Belief in the value of organised time.

(vi) A celebration of the work of creative activity.

(vii) A strong sense of culture and spiritual elevation.

(viii) A powerful sense of child centredness.

(ix) Willingness to capitalise on tradition.

(x)   Positive parental perceptions.

Several of these features match the five factors discussed in research carried out by the Dartington Social Research Unit (see Chapter 6.3.2). Clearly, running a local authority child care residential service is different in many respects from running a prestigious boarding school; but to misquote William Booth *'why should the public schools have all the best tunes?'* What this book suggests is that just as the *Children Act 1989* has required the boarding schools to learn from child care, so there are attitudes and ideas in the boarding schools which, if translated across, could be of great advantage to children and young people in the public care.

1.3.5 *Growing up in Groups: A Common Core of Care*

What then is the book which has developed from the process described above? It is a response from a multi-disciplinary group to readers of the Wagner Report *'A Positive Choice'*. They wanted more work to be done on practice with children and young people. The Department of Health, which partially funded the work, looked for a hand book which would help staff carry out the requirements of the *Children Act 1989* and its regulations; which would fill out the Departments's own guidance and address practical issues of everyday care of children and young people.

Representatives from a wide spectrum of experience and knowledge came together to support the task. They rapidly found that they had no doubts about the common ground between them and their common interests in meeting the needs of children. There were differences, some obvious, some more subtle, between different residential settings and perceptions of the tasks. These generated great complexities in discussion and in the early stages it sometimes felt as though the group had bitten off more than it could chew. As the task developed, however, recognition of its importance grew. Some of the complexities of the task find expression in the book itself. It has, for example, elements of repetition in certain chapters. This was unavoidable because common issues had to be discussed in different contexts. A further aspect of the complexities is that some issues are dealt with in greater detail than others, where it is assumed that existing publications are available to provide what is needed.

The book does not offer cut and dried answers to the many difficult problems it acknowledges. It offers experience, information, ways of looking at problems, and suggestions based on widely acknowledged good practice. It also encourages wider recognition of the importance of the residential work skills, and the dangers of under-supporting those who carry out the work with children and young people. We hope it will be a text which can be used in learning and training activities within staff teams caring for children, but also in training activities in colleges, management courses, social work and other professional training. The group which worked together on the preliminary thinking for the book were fully convinced of the need for its emphasis on the core of good practice which should characterise all residential group care of children and young people.

2 Who Lives in Residential Settings?

2.1 Introduction

In this Chapter we look at background information concerning the residential sector. We consider who lives in residential settings – numbers, ages, gender, ethnic composition and circumstances – and the general needs of children and young people, including those of some special groups. Finally we consider the value that life in a residential setting has for children.

2.2 Statistics in 1992

2.2.1 Numbers

It is a curious fact that there are no accurate comprehensive national statistics about children and young people living away from home in various kinds of group settings. For example, in 1992 estimates of the numbers in boarding schools for children with special educational needs vary between 20,000 and 33,000. The best estimates of independent and maintained boarding school places are 115,000 and 5,700 respectively, whereas the numbers in NHS psychiatric units are difficult to ascertain with any precision. Even in relation to children's homes the latest estimate results from a survey conducted for the *Warner Enquiry*[1] in March 1992 ie. 11,300 children and young people looked after in 1300 children's homes. Further small groups totalling about 680 children and young people were estimated to be in secure settings, ie. penal institutions, youth treatment centres, and secure units provided by local authorities. In addition children and young people spend periods of time in NHS hospitals and mental nursing homes but there is little information about these totals. Very recently it has emerged that an unknown but significant number of young people are looked after in privately run homes for fewer than three children, which are not required in law to register as children's homes.

It must also be borne in mind that even the figures given above are not static. In *'Child Care Now'* (1985), Jane Rowe noted the surprisingly large flow of children and young people through children's homes in the

---

1 'Choosing with Care' – The Warner Inquiry 1992, HMSO

course of a single year. This 'through flow' is belied by the figures quoted above which refer to a 'snap shot' on a single day and give no indication of numbers of relatively short-term placements which take place in children's homes in particular. Figures quoted for boarding schools are likely to be more static since children and young people normally stay in one establishment for the whole academic year, rather than moving from one school to another at shorter intervals.

The statistical information above is summarised in the following table.

Type of Provision	Number of Units	Number of Places
Boarding Schools		
'Mainstream'	1000 approximately	115,000 approximately
'Special'	n/k	20,000-
		33,000 (estimates)
'Maintained'	80	5,700
Children's Homes (estimated March 1992)		
Local Authority	950	7,800
Voluntary*	170	2,000
Private*	180	1,500
(*includes homes registered under the Registered Homes Act 1984)		
NHS Psychiatric Units	48	535
Penal institutions, secure units, etc	n/k	650 approximately
Other (Nursing homes, mental nursing homes, other NHS , etc)	n/k	n/k

2.2.2 Ages

Children and young people living in residential settings vary in age from birth to over 18 years old. The very youngest may be in a children's home through an emergency admission to care; in medical settings because they suffer from a severe illness or disability; or because they are with their mothers in a residential setting. The oldest, 16 and above, may be in boarding schools; in children's homes prior to returning home or moving towards independent living in the community; in long-term health facilities; in penal establishments as a result of criminal proceedings in a court.

Statistical information, as we have said, is incomplete and sometimes misleading, as in the static versus the 'through flow' situation. The most up-to-date estimates of age groupings in 1992 were also those resulting from the study of children's homes commissioned for the Warner Inquiry. This showed that the average age of children and young people in children's homes was about 14, although there were more 16 year olds than any other age group. Department of Health figures show that the proportion of children in residential care aged 16 or over has increased from 22% in 1980 to 31% in 1990. However, in responding to the Warner Committee survey, a number of children's homes reported the **average** age of residents to be under 13, and a few to be under 10. Some children's homes look after very young children (as young as 3 months); occasionally in others, there are adults (ie, aged over 18). Thus the picture in children's homes in 1992 was of an overwhelmingly adolescent population – from mid to late teens – but with a small number of much younger and much older children and young people in residence.

The picture in boarding schools is much clearer. Schools generally accommodate particular age groups – usually 7 or 8 to 12 or 13 years old in preparatory groups, and 12 to 18 years in senior schools. A substantial number of schools are 'all age', with children from as young as 5 or 6 at admission. The older age groups, ie. 12 or 13 up to 18, are the largest groupings. In the younger age group, exceptionally, children as young as 3 may be boarders. Most maintained boarding schools look after children aged 10 or 11 and above, although a very small minority take children as young as 8.

In residential special schools, about half accommodate children across the age range (i.e. from both the under-11 and the over-11 age groups). About 40% take the older group only, and a very small minority take under 12 years old only.

2.2.3 Gender

Department of Health statistics show that in 1990 58% of residents in children's homes in England and Wales were male. The Warner Inquiry survey showed that only 11% of children lived in single sex homes, with about twice as many boys as girls in such homes. The overwhelming majority of children's homes were providing care for boys and girls together.

Within the boarding school sector, excluding residential special schools, currently there are approximately 280 boys' schools, 190 girls' schools and 500 mixed schools. The pupils divide into 62% boys and 38% girls.

In residential special schools boys outnumber girls by 72% to 28%. The majority of these schools (58%) cater for both sexes, although 36% are boys-only schools. Only 6% of schools look after girls only.

2.2.4 Ethnic Groups

There are no national statistics on the ethnic composition of the child residential population. Some local authorities and voluntary organisations collect and monitor information on ethnic groupings of children and young people they look after in order to improve planning and delivery of services. However, research on children in local authority care, particularly *'Child Care Now'*, suggested that children of mixed parentage were over-represented in local authority accommodation, and that children from Asian families were slightly under-represented. Black children appeared to enter residential care at a younger age than other ethnic groups, but remained for shorter periods.

Cumulative impressionistic information derived from HMI inspections suggests that the numbers of black or Asian children in independent boarding schools are small. Most of them are foreign nationals, mainly from Hong Kong and West Africa. Those from Hong Kong represent a significant proportion of the total.

2.2.5 Family Backgrounds

Research findings on the backgrounds of children being 'looked after' under the *Children Act 1989* are that the majority come from backgrounds which could be described as financially and environmentally poor, with a high proportion from one-parent families. Bebbington and Miles, in a study of 2,500 children admitted to care[2], (either 'accommodated' or 'in care' under Children Act terminology) reported the following:

- a quarter were living with both parents;

- almost three-quarters of their families received income support;

- only one in five lived in owner-occupied housing;

- over one-half were living in 'poor' neighbourhoods.

The survey commissioned by the *Warner Inquiry* asked all children's homes what proportion of children **the staff believed** to have been sexually abused before entering residential homes. The figure which resulted was around one-third. Although this figure cannot be confirmed, it indicates the staffs' perception of the problems the children had already endured before they began to look after them. Bebbington and Miles attempted to determine the probability of a child being cared for by a local authority, based on the contributory factors which they identified. They constructed the following table for two children of similar age but different circumstances:

2 Bebbington A, Miles J, 'The Background of Children who enter Local Authority Care' The British Journal of Social Work, Volume 19, No.5, October 1989. Quoted in PATTERNS AND OUTCOMES IN CHILD PLACEMENT, HMSO (1991)

Child A	Child B
No dependence on social security benefits	Household head receives income support
Two parent family	Single adult household
Three or fewer children	Four or more children
White	Mixed ethnic origin
Owner occupied home	Privately rented home
More rooms than people	One or more persons per room
Odds of Admission to Care: 1 in 7,000	**Odds of admission to care: 1 in 10**

This is not the place to discuss the influence of material and other deprivation and poverty on the later life-chances of young people in children's homes as compared with those in boarding schools. Staff, however, particularly those working in social services care, need to take into account that many children and young people in care lack the support of relatives, stable homes, and financial assistance which are often available to other children. In consequence, the children's need for the staff's support, comfort and advocacy will be much greater.

The family backgrounds of children in most independent boarding schools are likely to be very different although it would be wrong to assume that all children and young people in boarding schools come from affluent middle-class families and that none of them has been abused. Around one-fifth of pupils (boarding **and** day pupils) in independent schools receive some help with their fees. Help for about two-thirds of these children is provided by the school; slightly less than one-third receive help through the Government's Assisted Places Scheme, although this scheme does not provide assistance with boarding fees; and a small minority are helped by local authorities. A number of schools have foundations that pay for places for children whose parents would not be able to afford to do so. Others are closely tied to particular religious or ethnic groups whose pupils pay very low fees, their places being supported by local (or international) religious or ethnic groups. Many children and young people in boarding schools come from families where their parents no longer live together. In addition, in some boarding schools, a significant number of pupils are placed because they have a Statement of Special Educational Need under the provisions of the *1981 Education Act*. Some of these pupils are local education authority placements. Although the families of boarding school children are not all 'well off', they are unlikely to suffer the degree of poverty which is characteristic of many children being cared for by local authorities.

2.3 The needs of children and young people

From conception to adulthood, children and young people pass through well known patterns of growth and development, although the age at which they reach any particular stage may vary considerably within the broad overall sequence. Allowance has to be made for such individually different rates of growth and development in providing for children and young people living away from home.

Every child has the right to protection, as far as possible, from damaging events, circumstances and influences, so that he or she can attain full potential as an adult. Chapters 4 and 8 discuss in greater detail the way in which these rights can be safeguarded and promoted.

Whatever their ages, or the settings in which they are being looked after, children and young people have common needs. The most important of these are for physical comfort, shelter, warmth and food; a stable environment to live in and to feel safe and secure; protection from abuse and ill-use; proper health care; education and the opportunity to fulfil their potential; personal privacy and space; association with, and the opportunity to make friends with children and young people of their own age; to feel valued by other people, particularly those who are significant to them like parents or substitute parents. They also need clear boundaries, consistency in the care they receive and effective benevolent control. Beyond this, specific needs of particular groups of children and young people may differ, depending on physical, mental and emotional needs and individual backgrounds.

Having identified a 'common core' of needs, there must clearly be a common core of good practice which is applicable in the care of children and young people living away from home in groups, to ensure that these needs are met as effectively as possible. In the following chapters, aspects of the common core are considered in detail. Of course, each type of residential setting will also have unique elements of good practice which may not apply to any other setting. For example, the needs of a severely disabled child in a medical setting will differ from those of a healthy seventeen year old in a major independent boarding school. In the following sections we look at some of the groups of children and young people who may have specific needs which require particular understanding.

2.3.1 *Children and Young People with Particular Needs*

Every child or young person in a residential setting is an individual. Each one is where s/he is because of unique circumstances. Each child has a unique personality, and individual needs and wants. There is no such thing as a 'typical' child or young person in any of the settings with which we are concerned.

However, there are groups of children and young people who can be identified as having particular needs which must be considered when caring for them. This is not to say that they should be treated as 'special cases" all the time. The aim should be care for them in a way which is sensitive to all their needs, including the need to be an ordinary child or young person. Sometimes they will be living in a setting especially designed for them and others like them; but more often than not they will live in mixed groups with other children and young people who have a wide range of needs. It is as important to avoid stereotyping and pigeonholing them under categories of 'problems' as it is to ensure that their needs are met adequately and with sensitivity.

We discuss below some of the groups who may need particular attention and identify some considerations to be borne in mind when looking after them. The general message we wish to convey, however, is that the care of children and young people with particular needs should be **integrated** into the whole package of care provision and good practice. They are first and foremost children and young people, and should never be categorised solely in terms of their 'difference' from other people. In *'Residential Care for Children, A Review of the Research'*, Bullock, Little & Millham, 1993, HMSO, the point is made that an effective residential centre would develop an approach which integrated several theories which, in themselves, are appropriate to the task and aims. Part of the value of residential care, they argue, lies in the breadth of its approach.

CHILDREN FROM DIFFERENT ETHNIC GROUPS AND CULTURES

There are no available statistics as yet but any group of children and young people living in a residential setting is likely to include some from a range of ethnic groups and cultures. They need help and encouragement to develop understanding and retain pride in their cultural heritage and to feel comfortable about their origins. In addition, as far as practicable, their specific linguistic and religious needs have to be met. Department of Health guidance makes this an explicit requirement when a local authority is considering an appropriate placement for a child, and this should be seen as good practice in all residential settings. How far children and young people are empowered in this way will depend on good practice, and more about how the best results can be achieved can be found in Chapter 6.

Regrettably, as in our larger society, some staff and children have racist attitudes towards people from different ethnic groups or cultures. Racism – apart from being morally abhorrent – affects everyone, particularly the victim, and may influence many aspects of his or her life. Good practice means taking a firm stand against racism and staff, particularly managers, have a duty to take positive action both to prevent it as far as possible, and to deal with it whenever it occurs. Dealing with issues of race and racist attitudes can be complex, confusing and, at times, painful for all concerned. It is not surprising that staff often feel bewildered and confused, and white staff working in a staff group committed to anti-racism may find themselves having to confront their own largely unconscious, but underlying prejudice. This is a necessary experience which they have to face honestly but which need not render them ineffective in working with black children. It may, however, lead to lack of confidence and sometimes result in 'paralysis' which is not in the children's interests. Managers need to take steps to equip these staff with the knowledge and skills which will give them confidence. Sometimes staff may feel they are being asked to work outside their normal practice or to give preference to a particular group. This is not so. Good practice means meeting the needs of all individuals, whoever they are, by caring for them and being their champions whenever necessary.

CHILDREN AND YOUNG PEOPLE FROM OTHER COUNTRIES

Children from other countries, living in groups away from home, include refugee children and others whose families have sent them to the United Kingdom, usually to receive education. In addition to the important ethnic and cultural considerations (referred to above) they are likely to experience some special problems. Chief among these is the fact that they have left their country of birth. In doing so refugee children may have had extremely traumatic experiences and may also be in 'limbo" concerning their legal status. The majority of children and young people from other countries who are in the United Kingdom to receive education, are likely to have come from relatively affluent families Nevertheless they may find it difficult to come to terms with living in a strange country for the first time. They will need special help to enable them, where appropriate, to keep in contact with their homes, and to maintain the religion and culture of their family and home country. In addition, English may not be their first language, and some may speak, or read, little or no English. Adequate and prompt provision should be made for English teaching as well as maintenance of their own language. Provision may include tuition to help them learn English; provision of appropriate reading materials, both in English and in their own language; and making contact with others in the community who speak the same language, and can help them maintain it and befriend them. Meanwhile, staff need to be sensitive and understanding about their language difficulties and ensure that other children are too.

In recent years unaccompanied refugee children from several parts of the world have been received into the UK. For some of these children a positive decision was made that they would best be cared for together in residential homes. The evidence suggests that, in spite of the extreme trauma which they experienced before they arrived, sensitive care and attention to their cultural, educational and personal needs given by residential staff have enabled them to recover and have set them on their way to satisfactory adulthood. They have gained strength from being kept together with their brothers and sisters and others who shared similar experiences. They have not had to face the fragmentation of family and cultural loyalties and continuity which would probably have happened in different types of care. Family unity has been sustained over years of separation and in spite of language differences most of the children and young people have been relatively successful educationally, some going on to higher education, including university.

Many children from other countries are educated in boarding schools in the UK. Their numbers fluctuate as economic and social circumstances change. Currently, significant numbers of pupils from Hong Kong are in independent schools, probably outnumbering all the other nationalities put together.

VERY YOUNG CHILDREN

We described earlier the wide range of ages of children being looked after in residential settings. It is usually the case, although not always, that different establishments look after specific age groups; a boarding school may take children from 5 or 6 years old and upwards, while most young people in children's homes are in their 'teens. Some schools, in particular preparatory schools, concentrate on children under the age of 12 or 13. A few residential special schools look after children under the age of 11 or 12. Staff in these settings need a great deal of skill and experience of looking after younger children. Where there are very young children (for example, aged 5 to 7, or even younger) it is important that their accommodation and care is related closely to their needs. They are very different even from 8 year-olds and the younger the age the greater the need for nurturing care. This will inevitably entail higher staffing ratios, a different distribution of staff duties during the day, more and different play facilities and daily routines. It is also important that staff in establishments where the children's ages range so widely should take special care to provide for the equally wide range of age-related needs.

CHILDREN AND YOUNG PEOPLE WITH DISABILITIES

There are no annually collected statistics of children and young people with disabilities, although various estimates are made from time to time. The Council for Disabled Children at the National Children's Bureau, published in *Children Act News, Issue 10, October 1993* an estimate of at least 46,050 such children in some form of residential school or communal provision. They may be accommodated and educated in a variety of settings, including mainstream services, as well as in special facilities. Some are in 52 week placements in residential education, some in small residential homes in the independent sector for young people aged 16 or over. The NHS, in principle, has ceased to provide residential or social care for children with disabilities, and long stay hospitals have ceased admissions although there is evidence of their continuing use, in some areas, for respite care for adolescents or young adults. Although there are no figures for NHS residential services, 1989 figures suggested that about 3000 children with learning disabilities were in respite or other NHS provision. The Children's Hospice Movement accommodates some children with major physical disabilities, severe health problems or terminal illnesses. There have been no studies of children with disabilities who belong to ethnic minorities in residential care, but black families are generally under-represented in most respite care schemes. Whilst family based respite care schemes have developed apace it is clear that residential care continues to be used to meet the needs of children who because of complex disabilities are likely to present difficulties in providing care for them.[3]

HOMELESS YOUNG PEOPLE

Homeless young people inevitably have very special problems. By the time they come to live in a residential setting they are no longer technically homeless, but the severe difficulties which they have had to face while living rough in the past may result in serious problems which staff need to understand. Foremost among these may be health problems which have developed in consequence of their circumstances. Homeless people suffer an abnormally high incidence of certain illnesses, in particular respiratory problems, and conditions caused by poor diet, lack of proper hygiene facilities, poor sleep, cold and damp.

In '*A Lost Generation*', Abrahams A and Lobstein T, 1993, National Children's Home, Action for Children, the seriousness of the problems can be clearly seen. Amongst the key findings concerning the 120 young people interviewed in thirteen locations across Scotland, England and Wales were the following:

(i)   38% had experienced foster care and 48% residential care.

(ii)   Due to lack of money 1 in 3 of all those living independently had eaten only one meal, or no meals at all, during the previous 24 hours.

(iii)   As a group, disproportionately high numbers had recently been ill compared with others of their age; 41% had dental problems, 35% skin disorders, 27% asthma, 56% nose/throat/chest

---

3 Information provided by Philippa Russell, the Director of the Council for Disabled Children – National Children's Bureau

infections and 35% allergies. In addition, they could not afford glasses when they needed them.

(iv)   Their financial situations were so grave that high proportions said, in certain circumstances, they would be prepared to try to make ends meet by illegal means.

Some homeless young people turn to prostitution to survive on the streets. When they cease to be homeless they may want to continue the practice in order to earn money. Apart from other health problems, they may have a high risk of sexually transmitted diseases. They may also be disruptive because their previous experiences have made them more streetwise than the other young people in the group they have joined. Staff will need to get to know them and, by their understanding and practical help, assist them to adjust to a different way of life. Their understanding will need to include recognition that the experiences which the young people have had, have engendered feelings of desperation and forced them into choosing a way of life which formerly they would have rejected. Survival in this way of life has also inevitably brought strong feelings of self determination which mean that immediate change is not likely to be possible and that rehabilitation will be a slow process of negotiation and compromise, often one step forward and two steps back. If the pace is forced the young people will just leave and nothing will have been gained.

Staff time and patience may have to be greater than usual since the young people's harsh experiences may have destroyed all trust and confidence and made them confrontational and challenging. Hostels can present staff with very complex management tasks, different from many other residential settings and those who work in them need to be supported and helped in their difficult task.

2.4 The value of living in a residential setting

As we briefly discussed in Chapter 1, educationalists' views of the residential experience and the perspective of the child care world have at times appeared dramatically opposed. The former have celebrated the merits of group living in boarding schools as providing a positive experience which can confer life long advantages. A strongly held child care view has stressed the essential importance of family life (the child's own or a substitute) to the extent that efforts have been exerted to avoid using residential care in any circumstances but as a last resort.

'...... There is often a big organisational divide between residential and field work in social services departments. Perhaps even more telling, many social workers in the field regard it as one of their primary objectives to keep people out of residential establishments wherever possible. Yet a person who leaves home for another place remains the same person, with the same human needs and the same emotional links with family or local community. The services provided to people living in their own homes and those provided to people living permanently in residential establishments are not fundamentally different in kind'.

The Barclay Report – 'Social Workers: Their Role and Tasks' 1982, Chapter 4: Social Work in Residential and Day Services, para. 4.3

These views represent two cultures which have been totally separated and opposed. This book seeks to demonstrate that such a view is not only unrealistic but is also destructive and deprives some children and young people of services which they need and from which they can benefit.

Many parents have traditionally chosen boarding education for their children, some of whom may be as young as seven or eight years old, occasionally even younger. They believe that a group living environment away from home offers a better opportunity to concentrate on education and activities, free from the distractions of home and neighbourhood. They also believe that the experience of group living engenders independence and confidence in dealing with their peers and with situations which will be of great assistance to their children in making their way in the world after school. Many children, though not all, take the same view and may carry friendships with them from their school days throughout the rest of their lives. Their confidence is there for all to see, and any analysis of groups of 'top people' provides evidence of the assistance which their schools have been to them in their subsequent careers. This may be so even when the reasons for the children going to boarding school include family problems such as divorce, separation or illness which in poorer families might have led to local authority care.

Other children have a need for boarding education because their parents live abroad or may have to move at regular intervals because of their work. Families in the armed services often come into this category. Children as young as five may board in these circumstances, and may present staff with a very special set of needs. A recent development is the growth in weekly boarding, whereby children board at school during the week and return to their families for weekends. This has become more common as the practice of both parents working has grown. Parents in these circumstances may be using boarding to avoid creating 'latchkey" children.

The children who live in social services group care, whether local authority, voluntary or private, are there because for some reason their families **cannot** look after them at home. As we have indicated, some professional beliefs amongst social services staff, unlike education, have led, for many years, to the view that living in a group is less beneficial, even damaging, as an alternative to living in a domestic environment ie. a foster home, if a child cannot be in his or her own home. This view has been held despite there being little support from research that outcomes for children living in foster families are better than those for children in residential care. Risks to children, including physical and sexual abuse, exist in foster homes as well as in residential care. Recently, the high incidence of breakdown in foster homes, the emphasis on children's and parents' choice, and the results of extreme neglect of residential care, have all led to a re-evaluation of its importance, its role and its positive aspects. For many years however, it has been seen as second best and its use has often carried a stigma with it. This has been reinforced by the professional perceptions just described. Whilst children living in boarding schools have been encouraged by parents, teachers and society, to feel positive about themselves in that setting, children in children's homes and the staff who have cared for them have often been made to feel like 'second class citizens', undervalued and unable to view positively the life they have lived together. This has happened in spite of the facts established by research, (eg. *'Children's Homes'* Berridge D, 1985, Blackwells) and experience, that some children's homes provide very good care and positive experiences, giving children confidence, self-reliance and a 'sense of belonging', while some boarding schools have been characterised by poor child care practice and unsatisfactory education. *'After Grace – Teeth'* by Millham, Bullock and Cherrett, 1975, demonstrated that the more benign the regime the better the outcomes, and vice versa. The scandals which have rocked group care have occurred in schools, children's homes, and health establishments. They have not been confined to any particular type of setting and experience demonstrates that abusers – emotional, physical and sexual – can be found anywhere. What needs to be acknowledged for the majority of children and young people is that, whilst group care may be a first choice, for children in care in particular it will be natural for them to wish they could be at home but this may also be true of other forms of care.

Residential care can provide a valuable home for children, enabling them to grow to their full potential in a safe and caring setting. For some children and young people it is to be preferred to living with a foster family and many young people express a preference for it. Some young people find that a foster placement represents a challenge to their loyalty to their natural family. Even when not able to live in their own home, a residential placement may thus be preferred as it represents less threat to the concept of their own family. In addition, brothers and sisters can stay together and their parents also experience less rivalry with other adults while often being able more easily to maintain contact. Where children and parents express a preference for residential care, as under the Children Act they are entitled to do, the choice of this placement is likely to be more successful, even though the choice may not seem ideal, than a placement which is resisted from the outset. The professionals involved have a duty to convey to parents the advantages of different placement options but to insist upon one in the face of parents' and children's contrary wishes is likely to be counterproductive. What is certain is that residential care should never be seen as a last resort, only to be used when all else has failed. It should be recognised as providing part of a spectrum of care which will be of greater or lesser benefit to a child, depending on their individual needs. Unfortunately, the disproportionate emphasis on foster placements by some social services departments can lead to a series of unsuccessful placements (foster breakdowns). In *'Children's Homes'*, Berridge found that 6% of the children in the homes he studied had ten or more placements before arriving at their current home[4]. Another result of over-emphasis on fostering is that the length of stay of a child in residential care is very short, as social workers attempt to find more 'appropriate' foster placements. Thus the blind belief that residential care can only be second best can lead to damaging instability and uncertainty in the lives of children and young people. As long ago as 1946 the *Curtis Report* noted that:

> *'Children undergoing several changes of foster parents are often worse off than if they had never been boarded out at all',*

and concluded that:

> *'...it would be wrong, in view of....the risk to the child where the [foster] home is less than satisfactory, not to develop...an alternative form of compensation for the loss of a normal home life.'*[5]

This view has been echoed in research and reports ever since. The research commissioned by Warwickshire County Council from the National Children's Bureau (*'Closing Children's Homes – An End to Residential Child Care?'* David Cliffe with David Berridge, National Children's Bureau, 1991) to evaluate their policy of closing all their own children's homes, indicated that amongst the prices paid for doing so

4 'Children's Homes', Berridge D (1985), Basil Blackwell
5 The Report of The Care of Children Committee (1946) HMSO Cmnd 6922. (Paragraph 461)

were that some children had no choice as to where they might be looked after, and children's moves while in care were higher then the national average. The instability of some children's lives, as a result of this policy, was regarded by the researchers as 'unacceptable". In addition, a proportion found their way into residential care in spite of everything. There have also been some indications in the press that adopters of children with serious emotional or developmental difficulties have, in later years, not been able to maintain their care and have felt resentful and defeated at being asked to take on a burden the full weight of which they felt they had not been enabled to appreciate at the time. At least one case of adopters seeking to 'unadopt' on these grounds was being tested in the courts whilst this book was being written.

This argues for continued provision of high-quality residential care, catering for children and young people who cannot remain with their families, and yet for whom substitute family care, or other alternative provision (such as boarding school) is not an acceptable, practicable or appropriate alternative. We suggest that some children might have a less traumatic life if this need were to be recognised from the beginning, rather than having to suffer continuing uncertainty as attempts to foster them break down, sometimes many times, with the consequent serious damage to their self-regard and confidence which such experiences inevitably produce. The contrast between this situation and the long term stability of boarding education is highlighted in Chapter 1.

Social services authorities and agencies should also recognise that placements need not be 'all or nothing'. A boarding school placement, for example, could provide an option for local authorities which, if combined with support for the child's family or a long term foster placement, could create a supportive family life with good educational opportunities. Placing authorities need to be flexible rather than dogmatic in their approach, looking to the needs of an individual child rather than basing decisions on what is either traditionally available to them, what suits financial policies which have been adopted for general, not child care, reasons, or what current professional doctrines or fashions dictate.

The similarity of essential elements in group life for children and young people in boarding schools and children's homes can be clearly seen in an analysis of *'what constitutes good 'family' provision'* contained in a review of maintained boarding schools carried out by HMIs in 1988. This Report brings together the importance of good accommodation providing adequate space for personal and private needs as well as communal activities; sensitivity to boarders' circumstances and feelings away from home; equal opportunities; creation of a *'homely, friendly atmosphere'*; good contact with external agencies such as educational welfare officers, social workers, psychologists; case conferences; complaints systems; promotion of pupils' personal and social development; pupils' involvement in decision making about their own welfare and their life in their own school house. All of these features are characteristic of good practice in children's homes.

Recognising that life in a residential setting can be as valuable and rewarding for young people looked after by a local authority, as boarding school life is for children placed there by their parents or by education departments, may be an essential first step in providing the stability and security children in care need to develop their full potential in adulthood. We regret that we have to record a not uncommon view among some professional staff that children should not be allowed to stay long enough or have a sufficiently good environment that they actually come to enjoy living in a residential home. Such a view is misjudged, thoughtless, insensitive and damaging both to children and their staff, and evidence of a very narrow approach to the welfare of children in the public care. It may, in part, be related to misunderstanding of well known research by the Dartington Social Research Unit, '*Lost in Care*' Millham and others, Gower, 1986, in which it was demonstrated that if a child remained in care for as long as six weeks they were likely to remain for a much longer period. This referred to being in care in whatever form of accommodation, but it seems sometimes to have led to somewhat indiscriminate attempts to prevent children from staying in residential care 'too long'. It should be clear that the longer a child stays in local authority accommodation may represent greater need. It is also true that inadequate planning may be the cause.

Finally, it is important to note that many children and young people who live or have lived in residential care are able to tell us that they have found it a positive and rewarding experience. In their evidence to the Wagner Inquiry, the National Association of Young People in Care (NAYPIC) argued, not untypically, that

> '*some young people prefer a children's home and choose not to be fostered; some young people find families, either their own or an alternative, difficult to cope with but can and do settle in a children's home; some young people simply need 'time out' of a family because of a crisis or difficulties coming to a head'.*

Young people gave similar evidence to the House of Commons Select Committee on Social Services during their investigation of '*Children in Care*' in 1983–1984, and in the early 1990s they continue to voice the same views through publications, conferences and seminars.

Although living in residential care is not always a rewarding time for children and young people nor, regrettably, are many other experiences such as broken foster placements, failed adoptions or rejecting own homes. In many instances it is rewarding and efforts must be made to ensure that, for those children who experience it, it is so for as many as possible.

3   The Legal and Political Background

3.1 Introduction

There is a large body of law and international agreements which concerns the status of children in general and those living away from home in groups in particular. In this chapter we consider first the United Nations Convention on the Rights of the Child, which was ratified (with certain formal reservations) by the United Kingdom in December 1991. The convention provides a series of statements on the minimum standards of human rights to which all children are entitled. Against this international background we next consider the Acts of Parliament and other legislative provisions which govern the care and treatment of children living away from home in groups in the United Kingdom.

The Children Act 1989 provides the legal basis for provision of children's homes in England and Wales, for promotion and safeguarding of the welfare of children in boarding schools and for children living for extended periods in other settings such as hospitals. We have assumed that many readers, particularly those concerned with children's homes will already be familiar with the principles and much of the *Children Act*. These are therefore considered only briefly. (For those who are not familiar with the Act, we have provided a note of relevant publications in APPENDIX 2). Scotland and Northern Ireland have separate legislation which is similar but different in certain respects from the legislation for England and Wales. (Information is given on this Legislation in the main text and in APPENDIX 3). While the book was in preparation, a Scottish White Paper, Scotland's Children, Proposals for Child Care Policy and Law, was presented to Parliament in August 1993, Cmnd. 2286. This would, if embodied in statute, make major changes, some of which would reflect the principles of the *Children Act 1989*.

Finally, we consider a number of reports arising from enquiries into bad practice. These make recommendations on the care children receive whilst living away from home in groups, and are relevant to the content of this book.

The principles laid out in the *United Nations Convention* apply to all children in all settings, and should underpin the work of anyone concerned with the care of children and young people. It is important that all staff are familiar with them and understand that the United Kingdom has committed itself to those principles.

Although, in the main, the *Children Act 1989* and most of the reports discussed, address practice in children's homes and boarding schools, we see no reason why the principles they have established and their recommendations for better practice could not be adopted in other residential facilities. All settings have common features and good practice in children's homes is likely often to be good practice in schools, hospitals and nursing homes.

3.2 International provisions

3.2.1 The United Nations Convention on the Rights of the Child

The United Nations Convention is a public avowal by all signatory countries that children are especially vulnerable and are entitled to receive special consideration. Its underlying ethos is to listen to and respect the voice and needs of the child. The Convention represents an important and significant step forward. For the first time **all** currently defined rights of children – from their right to protection to their right to self-expression – have been brought together into a single and internationally agreed document. This is intended to help improve the lives of children throughout the world. Because they are important, we have included certain sections in this chapter.

PRINCIPLES

The UN Convention on the Rights of the Child comprises a series of articles which apply to everyone under 18. Underlying these are three basic principles:

NON-DISCRIMINATION

All the rights in the Convention must apply to all children without discrimination whatever the colour of their skin; their religion; language; disability; opinions or family background (Article 2).

BEST INTERESTS

Any adult responsible for making decisions about a child must always consider their best interests. All organisations, including the Government, courts, local and health authorities, must give priority to considering what is best for those children. (Article 3).

THE CHILD'S VIEWS

Children have the right to be consulted on all matters concerning them. Their views must be taken seriously. They must be allowed to discuss their opinions in court or in any official proceedings affecting them (Article 12).

CIVIL AND POLITICAL RIGHTS

These cover the rights of children to take part in society and to follow their own interests. They describe a child's right to be an active member of society and to be involved in matters of importance to them.

NAME AND NATIONALITY AT BIRTH

Everyone is entitled to a name at birth and to acquire a nationality. No child must be left stateless because they cannot take a parent's nationality (Article 7).

FREEDOM OF EXPRESSION

Children have the right to express what they think and feel through speech; writing; drawing; dress or style, as long as they do not affect other people's rights by doing so. They must be allowed information about things of interest to them (Article 13).

FREEDOM OF THOUGHT, CONSCIENCE AND RELIGION

Although it is a parent's duty to give guidance, children are free to choose their own religion, beliefs and opinions as soon as they are capable of making choices – and this right must be respected (Article 14).

MEETING OTHER PEOPLE

Children have the right to join organisations and to take part in meetings, peaceful marches and demonstrations, so long as by doing so they do not infringe other people's rights (Article 13).

PRIVACY

All children should have personal privacy, including personal letters and personal phone calls (Article 16).

ACCESS TO INFORMATION

Children must be allowed access to a wide range of information – both at home and from abroad. The Government should encourage the media to produce interesting and useful material for children, making sure that they take account of the language needs of children whose first language is not English (Article 17).

PROTECTION FROM ABUSE

Violence to children is unacceptable in any form – physical and mental. So are neglect, exploitation and abuse. Active steps must be taken to protect children from abuse (Article 19) and any child who has been violently treated must be helped to recover (Article 39).

It is a child's right not to be unjustly punished nor locked up unlawfully. If they are locked up, they must be treated with respect and given both legal assistance and a fair hearing without delay (Article 39).

BREAKING THE LAW

Any child who comes into conflict with the law must be presumed innocent until found guilty. They must be provided with legal advice and representation. Their treatment should take account of their age and they should not be humiliated nor degraded. Court proceedings should be avoided whenever possible and detention and imprisonment considered only as a last and very temporary resort (Articles 37 & 40).

ECONOMIC, SOCIAL, CULTURAL AND PROTECTIVE RIGHTS

These cover the child's rights to proper standards of physical care, education and health:

RIGHT TO LIFE

Children have a right to life and to the best possible opportunities to develop fully (Article 6).

LIVING STANDARDS

Every child has the right to a decent standard of living – and this includes being fed, clothed and adequately housed. The Government must help parents reach this standard (Article 27). Every child is entitled to benefit from social security (Article 26).

DAY-TO-DAY CARE

A vital message in the Convention is that children should receive proper day-to-day care. Though a child's parents are mainly responsible for this, some may need support such as child care services (Article 18). If it is impossible for a child to live with their family, they must be properly looked after by another family or home. When choosing this new home, the child's race, religion, culture, language and need for stability must all be considered (Article 20). Any child being looked after away from home – whether in a boarding school, long stay institution or hospital – must also receive proper care (Article 3).

SEPARATION FROM PARENTS

Children should not be separated from their parents against their will. If this has to happen, the child, their parents and anyone else with an interest should have the right to put their case forward in a court of law. The law must also protect the best interests of any child who is adopted – whether from the same country or abroad (Article 21) and governments must protect children from being illegally taken out of the country.

DISABLED CHILDREN

Disabled children must be helped and encouraged to take an active and independent part in everyday life (Article 23).

A HEALTHY ENVIRONMENT

Children have the right to live in a safe and healthy environment and to be taught the dangers of pollution. They should understand the importance of hygiene and know how to prevent accidents (Article 24).

HEALTH AND HEALTH CARE

Proper health care is essential for children to grow and develop. This means the Government must try to reduce child mortality, provide proper care for mothers when they give birth and promote children's health through community health services and education (Article 24).

EDUCATION

Education should be both compulsory and free up to primary school level at least, and a range of secondary school education should be available. For children with the ability, higher education should also be provided. Schools should encourage the development of a child's skills and personality, teach them about their own and other people's rights and prepare them to live responsibly in a free mixed society (Article 29).

LEISURE
Every child is entitled to rest and play and to have the chance to join in a wide range of cultural and artistic activities (Article 31).

PROTECTION FROM EXPLOITATION
The Government must protect children from being exploited by others. This includes protection from work that could be dangerous or affect their education, from drugs, from sexual abuse and from being abducted or sold (Articles 32–35).

ARMED CONFLICT
The armed forces are not allowed to recruit children under 15 years old and must give priority to older children when recruiting up to the age of 18 (Article 38). In Britain, the minimum ages are 16 for young men and 17 for young women.

The UK Government ratified the Convention on 16 December 1991. This means that, except in certain limited areas where the Government has entered reservations, the United Kingdom has undertaken to comply with the articles of the Convention. By doing so, it committed itself to ensure that our laws and the way we treat children in this country should meet the standards laid down in the Convention. Anyone who is responsible for a child should be aware of these standards and try to ensure that they are promoted and met.

Upon signature:

> 'The United Kingdom reserves the right to formulate upon ratifying the Convention, any reservations or interpretative declarations which it might consider necessary'.

Upon ratification:

(a)   The United Kingdom interprets the Convention as applicable only following a live birth.

(b)   The United Kingdom interprets the references in the Convention to 'parents' to mean only those persons who, as a matter of national law, are treated as parents. This includes cases where the law regards a child as having only one parent, for example where a child has been adopted by one person only and in certain cases where a child is conceived other than as a result of sexual intercourse by the woman who gives birth to it and she is treated as the only parent.

(c)   The united Kingdom reserves the right to apply such legislation, in so far as it relates to the entry into, stay in and departure from the United Kingdom of those who do not have the right under the law of the United Kingdom to enter and remain in the United Kingdom, and to the acquisition and possession of citizenship, as it may deem necessary from time to time.

(d)   Employment legislation in the United Kingdom does not treat persons under 18, but over the school leaving age as children, but as 'young people'. Accordingly the United Kingdom reserves the right to continue to apply Article 32 subject to such employment legislation.

(e)   Where at any time there is a lack of suitable accommodation or adequate facilities for a particular individual in any institution in which young offenders are detained, or where the mixing of adults and children is deemed to be mutually beneficial, the United Kingdom reserves the right not to apply Article 37(c) in so far as those provisions require children who are detained to be accommodated separately from adults.

(f)   In Scotland there are tribunals (known as 'children's hearings') which consider the welfare of the child and deal with the majority of offences which a child is alleged to have committed. In some cases, mainly of a welfare nature, the child is temporarily deprived of its liberty for up to seven days prior to attending the hearing. The child and its family are, however, allowed access to a lawyer during this period. Although the decisions of the hearings are subject to appeal to the courts, legal representation is not permitted at the proceedings of the children's hearings themselves. Children's hearings have proved over the years to be a very effective way of dealing with the problems of children in a less formal, non-adversarial manner. Accordingly, the United Kingdom, in respect of Article 37(d), reserves its right to continue the present operation of children's hearings.

Moreover, the instrument of ratification by the United Kingdom of Great Britain and Northern Ireland contains the following declaration:-

> '......[The Government of the United Kingdom reserves] the right to extend the Convention at a later date to any territory for whose international relations the Government of the United Kingdom is responsible ....'

3.2.2 Other International Instruments

As a rule, **instruments** referred to as 'declarations, principles, guidelines, standard rules and recommendations' have no binding legal effect.

International **treaties**, which are referred to variously as 'covenants, protocols or conventions' are binding under international law for those states that are party to them.

THE UNITED NATIONS

Other treaties include the *Universal Declaration of Human Rights*, the *UN Declaration on the Rights of the Child*, the *International Covenant on Economic, Social and Cultural Rights*, the *International Covenant on Civil and Political Rights*, *The Convention Against Torture* and the *Convention on the Elimination of Racial Discrimination*.

The Covenants and Conventions are binding under international law. Before ratification we ensure that our domestic law fully complies with the treaties' provisions. However, such treaties are not generally incorporated into domestic law as such, and are not therefore justiciable in UK courts.

THE COUNCIL OF EUROPE

The *European Convention on Human Rights* covers primarily civil and political rights. The Convention is legally binding on States parties to it and any citizen – child or adult – who believes that his or her rights have been violated can petition the *European Commission of Human Rights* in Strasbourg. If the UK is found to be in violation of the Convention, financial compensation can be awarded and sometimes it is necessary to amend UK law. However, the Convention organs cannot directly overturn decisions of courts in the UK. *The European Social Charter (1961)* covers social and economic rights. However, it does not include the right of individual petition.

3.3 Legislation in the United Kingdom

3.3.1 The Children Act 1989

The Children Act 1989, which came into force on 14 October 1991, is wide ranging in its scope and has important implications for almost everyone involved in the care of children and young people, including those looked after in residential settings in social services, education and health services.

PRINCIPLES OF THE ACT

The Act embodies a number of key principles. They were summarised in *'The Care of Children – Principles and Practice in Regulations and Guidance'*, HMSO 1990. In total they numbered forty two, of which the following were particularly relevant to the work undertaken for this book. The first selection relate to children:-

- Children and young people and their parents should all be considered as individuals with particular needs and potentialities.

- Although some basic needs are universal there can be a variety of ways of meeting them.

- Children are entitled to protection from neglect, abuse and exploitation.

- A child's age, sex, health, personality, race, culture and life experience are all relevant to any consideration of needs and vulnerability and have to be taken into account when planning or providing help.

- The development of a working partnership with parents is usually the most effective route to providing supplementary or substitute care for their children.

- Family links should be actively maintained through visits and other forms of contact. Both parents are important even if one of them is no longer in the family home and fathers should not be overlooked or marginalised.

- Wider families matter as well as parents – especially siblings and grandparents.

- Continuity of relationships is important and attachments should be respected, sustained and developed.

- Change of home, care giver, social worker or school, almost always carries some risk to a child's development and welfare.

- Every young person needs to develop a secure sense of personal identity and all those with parental or caring responsibilities have a duty to offer encouragement and support in this task.

- Since discrimination of all kinds is an everyday reality in many children's lives, every effort must be made to ensure that agency services and practices do not reflect or reinforce it.

- Children's long term welfare must be protected by prompt, positive and proactive attention to the health and education of those in both short and long term care.

- Young people's wishes must be elicited and taken seriously.

- As young people grow up, preparation for independence is a necessary and important part of the parental role which child care agencies carry for young people in long term care.

There were also principles concerning the way agencies and 'systems' work which were closely related to our task. Amongst them were the following:-

- The various departments of a local authority (eg. health, housing, education and social services) should cooperate to provide an integrated service and range of resources even when such cooperation is not specifically required by law.

- Care givers are entitled to have appropriate information about any child or young person placed in their charge and have a duty to keep this confidential.

- Letters and documents which are sent to parents and young people should be written in language which is fully comprehensible to them.

- Planning is a crucial responsibility for all agencies providing services to children and their families.

- Care givers – whether parents, foster carers or residential staff – need both practical resources and a feeling of being valued if they are to give of their best.

- Appropriate training should be provided for carers.

CHILDREN'S HOMES

The Children Act provides a new framework which encourages openness in the conduct of children's homes. It requires that complaints procedures should be in place and that all children's homes should be regularly inspected. Among the requirements for **all** children's homes (including those in the voluntary and private sectors) the following provisions indicate the essential framework.

- Each home must provide a written statement of its purpose and function.

- There should be adequate standards of accommodation and staffing.

- The use of corporal punishment, deprivation of food and drink, requirement to wear inappropriate clothing and deprivation of sleep are prohibited.

- Those responsible for homes are required to maintain detailed records of sanctions used.

- The authorities responsible for children in homes are required to ensure that a written care plan for each child is prepared, and to consider arrangements for contact with family, for aftercare, and for health and education.

- There should be six-monthly reviews for each child looked after, involving children and their families with notification to parents (where reasonably practicable) of the result of the review.

- There should be an annual medical examination for each child looked after, and parents should be consulted about major decisions affecting the child's future.

The guidance which accompanies the *Children's Homes Regulations* emphasises the need for proper management and supervision of homes and the need for staff to receive proper training.

BOARDING SCHOOLS

There are two sections of *The Children Act* which relate directly to boarding schools, Sections 87 and 63.

Under Section 87 of the Act, proprietors of independent boarding schools have a duty to safeguard and promote the welfare of the children accommodated in their schools. Local authority social services departments are required to determine whether the children's welfare is being safeguarded and promoted. If it is considered that a proprietor has failed to safeguard and promote any child's welfare, the social services department must notify the Secretary of State for Education.

When the *Children Act 1989* was first implemented, under Section 63, independent schools accommodating 50 or fewer boarders and not approved for special education under Section 11(3)(a) of *The Education Act 1981*, were required to register as children's homes with the local authority social services department in whose area they were situated. Such schools were then subject to the provisions of the Act and Regulations as they affect the welfare of children accommodated in private children's homes.

During the time that this book was being written, Section 63 of the *Children Act 1989* was amended through Section 292 of the Education Act which was put into force on 1 January 1994. This amendment was accompanied by amendments to the Regulations, *The Children (Homes, Arrangements for Placement, Reviews and Representations) (Miscellaneous Amendments) Regulations 1993*, and by a Local Authority Circular, LAC(93)24.

Broadly the effect of the amendment is to require only those independent schools who regularly accommodate pupils during the school holidays to register as children's homes. This is expressed in terms of four or more children being accommodated for more than 295 days in a year. The amendments to the Regulations have the effect that various provisions of the Children's Homes Regulations do not apply to independent schools which are children's homes according to the amended Section 63 of the *Children Act*, recognising the difference between children's homes that are boarding schools and those that are not, and because it would have been inappropriate for all pupils to be subject to the requirements of the *Children Homes Regulations* irrespective of how frequently they return to the care of their parents. Schools registered as children's homes must be run in accordance with guidance set out in Volume 4. Local authorities can refuse to register if they are not satisfied that the principles and practices expected in the *Children Homes Regulations*, and the associated guidance, are being applied to these children.

The circular expects that schools which are in future registered as children's homes will apply Section 87 (Volume 5) standards to the welfare of pupils who **do go home** for their holidays, but for children who remain accommodated during holidays, standards required for children living in children's homes will be applied.

Under Sections 61 and 62 of the Act voluntary organisations (including non-maintained special schools) are required to safeguard and promote the welfare of children accommodated by them. Social services departments are required to satisfy themselves that this duty is being carried out and, in addition, have the responsibility to visit children who are being looked after, in the interests of their welfare.

3.3.2 Other Relevant Legislation

EDUCATION LEGISLATION

The legislation relevant to the welfare of children in boarding schools is contained in five Acts:-

(i)   *The Education Act 1944*

(ii)   *The Education Act 1981*

(iii)   *The Children Act 1989*

(iv)   *The Registered Homes Act 1984*

(v)   *The Education Act 1993*

Each of these Acts has generated regulations which are amplified by circulars and other guidance.

An independent school is defined as any school at which fulltime education is provided for five or more pupils of compulsory school age, and which is not a school maintained by the Local Education Authority, a grant maintained school or a special school not maintained by an LEA. These latter are commonly referred to as non-maintained special schools.

In 1992 there were 81 such schools in England and Wales. They are **not** covered by Section 87 of the *Children Act 1989* but by Sections 61 and 62.

Some independent schools set out to provide wholly or mainly for pupils with special educational needs (SEN). These schools may apply for the approval of the Secretary of State to admit pupils for whom a local education authority maintains a Statement of Special Educational Needs. The placement of such pupils may be funded either by the LEA or social services department alone, or jointly by both agencies. An LEA requires specific consent from the Secretary of State to place a pupil with an SEN statement in a non-approved independent school. Social services departments do not have to seek consent, but have a duty under Section 28 of the *Children Act 1989* to consult their LEA before providing accommodation for children for whom they are responsible.

Every independent school in England must be registered with the Department for Education or with the Welsh Office Education Department in Wales. Initially, registration is provisional and only denotes that the school has complied with statutory requirements to notify the Department for Education or Welsh Office Education Department of its existence. It will then be inspected by OFSTED Inspectors as many times as necessary for them to be able to recommend final registration to the Department for Education.

Under section 1(6) of the *Registered Homes Act 1984*, an independent school with 50 or fewer boarders under 18, which is not approved under Section 189 of the *Education Act 1993* for the placement of pupils with special educational needs but provides personal care for children with disability or mental disorder, must register with the local social services department as a residential care home.

Pupils under 16 spending more than two weeks at school during school holidays, will be treated as if they were privately fostered.

The diagram overleaf outlines the main sections of the *Children Act 1989* affecting boarding schools.

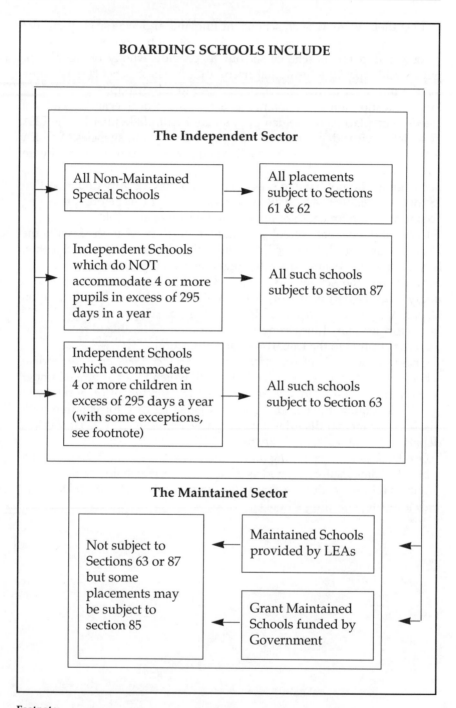

BOARDING SCHOOLS INCLUDE

The Independent Sector

All Non-Maintained Special Schools	→	All placements subject to Sections 61 & 62
Independent Schools which do NOT accommodate 4 or more pupils in excess of 295 days in a year	→	All such schools subject to section 87
Independent Schools which accommodate 4 or more children in excess of 295 days a year (with some exceptions, see footnote)	→	All such schools subject to Section 63

The Maintained Sector

| Not subject to Sections 63 or 87 but some placements may be subject to section 85 | ← | Maintained Schools provided by LEAs |
| | ← | Grant Maintained Schools funded by Government |

Footnote:
Independent schools for pupils with statements of special educational need, approved under Section 189(1) of the Education Act 1993, subject to Section 87.

THE REGISTERED HOMES ACT 1984

This Act, together with the associated *Residential Care Homes Regulations*, governs care homes and nursing homes run by private and voluntary organisations. These provide for those who need to be cared for because of disability. Disabled children who need residential care will be accommodated in a home registered under the *Registered Homes Act 1984*, rather than the *Children Act 1989*. Disabled children looked after in local authority accommodation however, will live in community homes under the same legal arrangements as other local authority children's homes. The *Children Act* concept of accommodating children, with its emphasis on partnership and agreement with parents, should allow disabled children to be cared for in exactly the same legal framework as all other children in need. The separate basis for registration of homes for disabled children may in time prove to be unnecessary.

THE MENTAL HEALTH ACT 1983
CHILDREN AND YOUNG PEOPLE IN PSYCHIATRIC HOSPITALS AND UNITS

Children and young people may be admitted to a psychiatric hospital or young people's psychiatric unit under a section of the *Mental Health Act 1983* or, as is more usual, on a voluntary and 'informal' basis. In certain circumstances it may be necessary to obtain an assessment and treatment order designated by a court under the *Children Act* or wardship legislation. Careful consideration of the appropriate legislation is required if treatment is thought to be necessary especially if the child and/or parent or guardian are against admission or unable to make sure that it takes place. As with adult patients, if compulsory admission is being considered, care is necessary to ensure that assessment and treatment are both required and are in the best interests of the child. It must also be clear that it cannot be provided in another context where it could be undertaken by mutual agreement.

The criteria laid down in the Act are first, the patient must be suffering from a mental disorder as defined by the *Mental Health Act*. Second, the disorder must be of a nature or degree which makes admission to hospital appropriate. Third, medical treatment must be necessary for the health or safety of the patient or for the protection of others. Compulsory admission should only be considered when the patient's current mental state, together with reliable evidence of past experience, indicates a strong likelihood that s/he will change their mind about informal admission prior to actual admission, with a resulting risk to the patient's health or safety or risk to other persons. It is left to the doctor's clinical judgement to determine whether these criteria are satisfied.

- When children, whether under the age of 16 or not, are detained under the Mental Health Act the conditions for such detention do not vary from those applicable to adult patients.

- When children are admitted informally under the age of 16, parents should give consent to admission. However, where it is decided the child is capable of making a decision for him/herself parents have no right to compel their child to be admitted or to keep their child in hospital on an informal basis against his/her will. Equally, if a child wishes to receive treatment, is of sufficient maturity and capable of understanding the implications of such treatment, then a parent cannot deny them that treatment even if they are under 16 years of age. Legislative support for any treatment should be sought under the *Mental Health Act* or *Children Act* legislation to ensure that both the child's interests are met, and the children's and parents' rights respected. A person must be 16 years or older to be received into guardianship under Section 7 of the *Mental Health Act*.

- For young people aged 16 or over, admission and treatment can only take place informally with their consent. However, a recent judgement in relation to treating a patient over the age of 16 with anorexia nervosa has raised the possibility of compulsory treatment without recourse to the *Mental Health Act* but with the backing of the High Court.

A Code of Practice on the Mental Health Act 1983 was first published in 1990, and revised in August 1993.[1] Although the Act applies to all age groups, the Code of Practice includes a chapter on specific issues relating to young people. The section on consent to treatment is of particular importance, and all staff who have to consider issues of consent to treatment should be aware of the guidance.

3.3.3 Scottish Legislation

The main legislation in the education, mental health and social work services in Scotland is separate from the rest of the United Kingdom. Many Acts and regulations referred to in this book do not apply to Scotland. For example, *The Children Act 1989* has no standing in Scotland apart from those sections concerning registration of day care services for young children. Details of the main legislation is set out in APPENDIX 3.

Despite the different legislative base as well as the important and unique role of Children's Hearings, it can be said that many of the principles of health, education, and social work practice in Scotland are consistent with those of other parts of the United Kingdom. Comprehensive regulations were introduced in 1988 covering residential child care. These require a statement of functions and objectives to be prepared and reviewed regularly for all children's homes. Residential

1 THE MENTAL HEALTH ACT 1983: CODE OF PRACTICE (1993). Department of Health and Welsh Office. HMSO

schools are registered by HM Inspectors of Schools and inspected by them. As already explained at the beginning of the chapter, a Scottish White Paper was published in August 1993 making proposals for future policy and legal changes.

> 'This White Paper describes the action which the Government are taking to improve child care across a wide range of services .... These commitments will be pursued in four ways. Firstly, by ensuring that all those involved pay careful attention to the views of those receiving the services, particularly children; secondly, by defining, assessing and reviewing the standards achieved and developing new standards; thirdly, by encouraging innovation and initiative in the development of new service approaches; and fourthly, by taking additional steps to safeguard children's interests.'

Of particular concern in pursuing these objectives the White Paper lists:

- listening to children;
- complaints procedures;
- research;
- improvement of management;
- training;
- strategic planning;
- the role of inspection.

THE GOVERNMENT'S

> 'decisions for change and reform across the range of child care services .... not only respond to recommendations made in a number of important reports which have appeared since late 1990, they are designed to provide a coherent programme for development, based on recognition of the responsibilities of parents, the rights of children and clear principles for the care of children'.

CONCLUDING, THE WHITE PAPER ADDS:

> 'The Government are seeking to make child care more sensitive to the needs of children and their families and to provide for the proper exercise of rights – including the right of the child to be heard'.

3.3.4 Northern Ireland Legislation

There has been an integrated structure for social services in Northern Ireland since 1973. At the time of writing four Health and Social Services Boards provide services which are run by local authorities in the rest of the United Kingdom.

Northern Ireland also has its own legislation which is similar to that in England and Wales. The main law is the *Children and Young Person's Act (NI) 1968*. Twelve parts and eight schedules cover both welfare and criminal justice. Part 7 deals with the treatment of children in care including the duty of the Boards to provide children's homes and hostels and the accommodation of children in voluntary homes. Part 8 governs registration of voluntary homes and empowers the Department of Health and Social Security to make regulations about their conduct.

The need for change in child care law has long been recognised, and a review group was set up in 1976, under the Chairmanship of Sir Harold Black. It reported in 1979 and was followed by a number of consultative papers. The most recent of these (September 1989) proposed that Northern Ireland law should follow closely the provisions of *The Children Act 1989* in England and Wales.

The proposed *Children (Northern Ireland) Order* will bring together public and private law relating to children including those with disabilities in a single statutory framework and will form an integral part of the community care reforms for the Province. On the public law side the Order will replace the welfare provisions of the *Children and Young Persons Act (NI) 1968*. In broad terms the proposed Order will:

- make the welfare of the child the first consideration in decisions affecting his or her future care and upbringing;

- emphasise parental responsibility for bringing up children while ensuring that statutory agencies are there to help when needed;

- ensure that the views of children, parents and other significant people in children's lives are taken into consideration in decisions affecting them;

- promote family relationships by encouraging partnership between parents and statutory services, and more use of voluntary arrangements;

- reduce the level of compulsory intervention in family life where children are in care, and give parents improved rights of access;

- introduce more effective arrangements for protection of children in emergencies which will allow parents to challenge quickly any action taken;

- introduce new jurisdictional arrangements aimed at ensuring children's cases are dealt with quickly and at the most appropriate level of court.

The proposed Order is expected to become law in 1994 and be brought into operation at a later date.

3.4 Inquiry Reports

3.4.1 1988 – The Wagner Report: 'A Positive Choice'

In Chapter 1, we looked at the background of the *Wagner Report*, which, in itself forms the background to this book. The Review team experienced difficulty when they came to write their Report

> *'wanting to establish general principles and yet wishing to recognise the differing social needs of children, adults and very old people.'*

Whilst they were carrying out the Review, the Audit Commission published a report *'Making a Reality of Community Care'*. This commented adversely on policy towards the private residential sector which at that time was mainly for elderly people. The Nye Bevan Lodge Inquiry was published and *'shocked the public'* with its revelations about the care of elderly people. National concern in 1986/1987 was focused on elderly people rather than other groups.

Representations were made to the Wagner Review team that boarding schools, which accommodated far greater numbers of children than children's homes, should be considered by them as well as social services' residential child care. However, their terms of reference precluded this and, in the event, like *'Home Life'*, their report concentrated primarily on adults.

It did, however, make some important recommendations concerning children in care, particularly in relation to complaints procedures; advocacy; educational and health needs; needs of ethnic minorities; keeping siblings together; and adequate accommodation for young people leaving care. They also recognised that:

> *'children's needs differ from those of other groups, because for them the whole purpose is satisfactory growth and development. In their case to separate issues of accommodation from services and care is not really possible as it is with adults – except perhaps for those young people who are at the threshold of adult life.'*

The Review shared the concern expressed in some of their evidence at the

> *'lack of any national child care strategy or overview'*,

the result being that there was no consistency in policies nor in levels of provision and standards across the country. In addition, they considered there was a pressing need to examine relationships between health, education, juvenile justice and the personal social services.

'Demands for residential care inevitably partly reflect pressures on schools, courts, and the preventative services concerned with children.'

In this context they believed it was significant that large numbers of children were placed in boarding schools because of emotional, behavioural or family problems. A relatively small number found their way into the penal system because of offending or anti-social behaviour. They also noted that increased emphasis upon foster care had led to marked reductions in the number of residential establishments catering for children whose own parents could not look after them. Financial as well as professional considerations had contributed to this, although the financial argument had become less strong, since properly supported foster care had not proved to be the cheap alternative to residential care which it had been assumed to be.

In addition, foster home breakdowns had been

'disconcertingly high in some authorities.'

Residential services had borne many of the consequences of this and had been used as a last resort without being organised and resourced to meet the tasks required of them. Many managers and field workers were ambivalent towards residential services with

'debilitating effects on residential staff and damage to their charges.'

Voluntary agencies were caught up in this situation since they could not afford to maintain residential facilities if social services departments did not take them up. The review commented that all these developments had created a climate of uncertainty, damaging to the well-being of children in care and the staff who cared for them.

3.4.2 1991 – The Pindown Experience and Protection of Children

Although concerned with the management of children's homes and bad practice in a particular local authority, the *Pindown Report* became the force which shifted the 'logjam' and brought about action nationally in relation to residential child care. Its publication created shock waves which greatly heightened awareness in central and local government in particular, and made a new beginning possible.

The *Pindown Inquiry* in 1991 carried out by Allan Levy QC and Barbara Kahan, documented unacceptable practices in children's homes in Staffordshire. Control was exercised over children through a regime of quasi-behaviour modification which deprived them of their liberty and subjected them to social isolation, humiliation and oppression. As well as recommendations directed solely at the local authority, the report made a number aimed at improving residential child care nationally, particularly in management, training and the protection of children.

The immediate impact of the *Pindown Report* was to cause the Secretary of State for Health to require a review of residential child care in England by Sir William Utting and, subsequently, similar reviews in Wales and Scotland took place. It acted as the catalyst for an upsurge of interest and concern in the whole field of residential child care, and national demand for improvements in the way children in these homes are looked after.

3.4.3 1991–1992 – The Utting Report, the Welsh Office and the Skinner Report 1992

These three reports – *Children in The Public Care* (Utting), *Accommodating Children* (The Welsh Office) and *Another Kind of Home* (Skinner) – are grouped here because, taken together, they form a broad and far reaching statement about the position of residential child care in England, Wales and Scotland in 1991–1992, and what was required to improve it. They demonstrate a powerful consensus calling, among other measures, for recognition that residential child care should no longer be seen either as 'second best' or as a 'last resort', to be used only after other types of placement have failed. Instead they emphasise that it has a crucial and essential role within the range of services available for children and young people. Other strong messages emerge from these three reports; the particular need to plan children's residential care within a coherent framework of **all** children's services, and the need for proper management, inspection and monitoring of the service provided by children's homes. *The Utting and Skinner Reports* also emphasise the need to secure more professionally-qualified staff in children's homes.

These three Reports set the national agenda. Their major recommendations, taken and acted upon together, would go far towards raising the professional and public status of the service. Their common message – all published within just over a year – was that the time was right for residential child care to enter a new phase; to be seen as an integral, essential and valuable part of services for children; for staff who work in it to be given full recognition; and for training and support to be provided for their difficult and demanding job.

1991 – THE UTTING REPORT: 'CHILDREN IN THE PUBLIC CARE'

Sir William Utting, formerly Chief Inspector of Social Services, was asked by the Secretary of State for Health to review *'all matters bearing upon residential care'* and in particular the programme of action affecting residential care which was to be introduced by the *Children Act* in October 1991. The Report confirmed serious concerns about the state of residential child care services in England. It strongly commended the *Children Act* in paving the way for a better future, if properly implemented. It argued that although extra resources were necessary, they were not the answer to all problems. Attitudes to residential services needed to be radically changed.

The report made 36 recommendations, the main requirements of which were as follows:

- The need for many more trained and qualified staff, including a requirement that all those in charge of residential units should be qualified.

- Improved inspection.

- Greatly improved management.

- A planned approach to residential care.

Some of these recommendations were acted upon quickly, ie:

- An initiative to enable all heads of homes to be professionally qualified by 1995 was taken and grants were given to both statutory and voluntary sectors for this purpose.

- An expert group was set up by CCETSW and the Department of Health to consider the residential child care content of the Diploma in Social Work. The Group published its report entitled *'Setting Quality Standards for Residential Care'* in 1992;

- Guidance was issued on inspection of children's homes; drawing up children's service plans; and permissible forms of control in children's residential care.

A number of other recommendations have required a longer time scale for implementation but progress on many has been made, in the context of subsequent initiatives including the publication in 1992 of the report *'Choosing with Care'* and the six sets of guidance[1] on educational issues, including the *Education of Children Looked After* issued jointly by the Department for Education and the Department of Health.

1991 – THE WELSH OFFICE REPORT: 'ACCOMMODATING CHILDREN'

This report which drew on a survey of Welsh children's homes was undertaken by the Social Services Inspectorate in Wales and Social Information Systems Limited. It found that many children's homes had ill-defined functions; that they were not properly integrated into the spectrum of services; that homes management needed strengthening, acknowledging the important managerial role of heads of homes. It also recognised that many homes were required to carry out tasks for which

---

1 "PUPILS WITH PROBLEMS": DFE Circulars 8/94 to 13/94 27 May 1994

they had not originally been intended and for which they were neither properly staffed nor equipped. In consequence, outcomes were often unsuccessful.

The report's main recommendations echoed many of those in the *Utting Report*. Especially important was the need to plan provision of residential child care within a strategic framework, and as part of a range of provision. In summary, its recommendations address the following areas:-

- Achieving a match of needs and provision, particularly in relation to children with very difficult behaviour.

- Identifying and developing good practice.

- Staffing the service to enable it to achieve good standards.

- Finding and maintaining suitable buildings in which to provide residential child care.

- Achieving a monitoring system which enables managers to evaluate performance.

1992 – THE SKINNER REPORT: 'ANOTHER KIND OF HOME'

This review of residential child care in Scotland by Angus Skinner, Chief Inspector of Social Work Services for Scotland, was accompanied by an analysis of relevant research. The Report reiterated many of the concerns expressed in the Utting and Welsh Office Reports. It begins with a statement of the importance of recognising the beneficial role that residential child care can play in the lives of many children and young people, and the need to integrate it into the mainstream of child care services as a

> *'positive means of meeting the needs of particular children, not simply as a last resort'.*

The report concluded that many homes and residential schools were failing to provide the environment and care needed by the children and young people placed in them.

There were 66 recommendations, many of which reinforced those in the Utting and Welsh Office reports. They set an agenda for action to ensure continuous and sustained improvement in the care of children in residential units in Scotland. Eight major principles underpinning good practice in residential child care were spelled out. They focused on:-

(a) Individuality and development

(b) Rights and responsibilities

(c) Good basic care

(d)   Education

(e)   Health

(f)   Partnership with parents

(g)   Child-centred collaboration

(h)   A feeling of safety

These principles provide a valuable framework for further development of standards and tools for quality assurance. In recognising the challenge inherent in the task of caring for children and young people, the report calls for better recruitment practices; increased training opportunities, including induction training for all staff; and more effective management, planning and supervision. A central theme of the report is the importance of listening to and taking seriously the views of children and young people. This has been echoed in the White Paper *Scotland's Children* referred to above in 3.3.2.

3.4.4 1992 – The Howe Report 'The Quality of Care'

This Report of the *Residential Staffs Inquiry*, chaired by Lady Howe, was concerned with staff working in homes for adults and children. Its broad recommendations on staffing and management were for:-

- more devolution of responsibility to managers of homes;

- more emphasis on supervision and training;

- better support for staff in stressful environments;

- better relationships between field and residential social workers and their tasks;

- external managers to be experienced and knowledgeable in residential work;

- systematic management training;

- improved career development opportunities for staff.

It also supported the system of National Vocational Qualifications (NVQ) as a framework for building a better trained and more professionally qualified workforce in residential care.

3.4.5 1992 – The Warner Report – 'Choosing with Care'

The Warner Inquiry was established by the Secretary of State for Health at the end of 1991 following the trial and conviction of Frank Beck and others at Leicestershire Crown Court for offences committed against children and young people in children's homes. Norman Warner, formerly Director of Social Services for Kent, chaired the Committee of

Inquiry, which had nine other members drawn from the private, statutory and voluntary sectors.

The Committee was asked to examine selection and recruitment methods and criteria for staff working in children's homes and to recommend practicable improvements; to consider management and other issues relevant to the protection of children and young people; and to comment on the support and guidance needed by staff in children's homes.

The Report contains 83 recommendations, about half of which are concerned with improving the way in which employers in the local authority, voluntary and private sectors recruit, select and appoint staff in children's homes. The rest are addressed to employers and to central and local government. They aim to improve training, staff support and management in children's homes.

The Report looked in detail at the methods currently used by employers in selecting staff to work in children's homes. It recommended that the range of techniques used should be widened to achieve a more complete analysis of applicants' previous experience and qualifications, suitability as people, previous employment and criminal record, if any. In some local authorities misapplication of equal opportunities policies was found to be leading to practices which made adequate inquiry difficult or impossible. In consequence, unsatisfactory appointments could be made, and frequently were. The Inquiry Report recommended that discussion, inquiry and checks of the backgrounds and experience of applicants be much more thorough and wide ranging and that applicants undergo much more rigorous testing at selection.

The Committee also looked at other aspects of staff management in children's homes. Important recommendations concerned the need for regular documented supervision sessions between staff and their managers, and annual appraisal of all staff. They also considered training needs of staff, and the professional support that should be available to staff, particularly from other services such as health and education.

Many recommendations, like others referred to above, reinforced the *Utting Report*. Although the *Warner Inquiry* was only looking at children's homes, its proposals, particularly on staff selection and recruitment, could, with benefit, be adapted for use in most settings where staff are looking after children and young people living in groups.

3.4.6 1992 – Ty Mawr Community Home Inquiry

This Inquiry into a number of incidents of self-harm and suicide in the Ty Mawr Community Home in Gwent was conducted by Gareth Williams QC, assisted by John McCreadie. It concluded that the home should close as soon as possible and severely criticised senior management in the Social Services Department, which it blamed for poor practice. It also criticised the role of elected members' involvement in staff appointments. In relation to their overall approach, it recommended that the local authority should

'care for its own employees'.

3.4.7 1992 – The Castle Hill Report: Practice Guide

This Report was published by Shropshire County Council following conviction in 1991 of the Principal of Castle Hill Special School, Ludlow, for offences against children in his care. The report provides details of the joint investigation carried out by Shropshire Social Services Department and the West Mercia Constabulary and describes some of the dynamics and interpersonal pressures characteristic of situations in which sexual abuse in residential settings can occur.

Shropshire County Council was asked to publish the Report by the Department of Health and Department for Education. They considered it provided a good model of joint working between the agencies involved, and insight into particular difficulties faced during investigation of organised abuse. Others facing similar situations could benefit from Shropshire's experiences.

3.4.8 1992 – The Review of Malcolm Thomson's Employment by Sheffield City Council

This independent review, conducted by Sheila Poupard and Malcolm Jordan, inquired into how Malcolm Thomson, an officer in charge of a children's home who was subsequently convicted of sexual offences against young people in his care, had been supervised and managed. The review concluded that the 'central feature.... was a combination of a powerful and manipulative individual and a management system that was both over confident and failed to listen or observe'.

Young people were frightened and powerless in a regime that was

'unbelieving and insensitive'.

In its way it reinforced some of the messages of the national reports reviewed above.

3.4.9 1993 – The Leicestershire Inquiry

The Report of the *Leicestershire Inquiry* carried out by Andrew Kirkwood QC was published in February 1993. It had been established at the same time as the *Warner Inquiry* (see above). It examined specifically events leading up to the recruitment of Frank Beck, and management failures which enabled him to abuse children in his care for 13 years.

The Report did not make recommendations but provided a detailed and chronological analysis of management failures in Leicestershire Social Services department during the period of Frank Beck's employment. Among these failings it noted that:-

- There was inadequate scrutiny of Beck's original application for employment, some details of which had been falsified. Recruitment and selection techniques, in general, were incapable of obtaining adequate information about applicants' previous education and careers.

- Successive senior social services managers had inadequate professional knowledge of child care and, in consequence, relied on what they believed to be the 'expertise' of Frank Beck and other residential staff.

- Professional supervision of the so-called 'therapies' practised by Beck and his staff was inadequate or non-existent and this allowed abusive regimes to flourish.

- Managerial oversight of Beck's activities as a whole was inadequate, thus allowing him to continue them unchecked. Management systems were incapable of effectively monitoring and checking on staff's behaviour and day to day work.

- Frequent complaints by children and young people were not investigated but ignored, and systems for dealing with complaints were inadequate.

This report also endorsed powerful messages from the *Pindown, Utting, Howe* and *Warner Reports*.

3.5 An essential message

Starting with the *Pindown Experience* the Reports reviewed here make it abundantly clear that, although good residential staff are essential to the well being of children in group care, they cannot be expected to be sufficient in themselves. *The Pindown, Leicestershire, Sheffield* and *Warner Reports* in particular emphasize the crucial role of external senior managers in achieving good residential care.

One conclusion from these Reports is that there appears to be a disjunction between a general management approach applied to many other aspects of service delivery and the professional, vigilant and knowledgeable management needed in the specialist field of residential care. Another conclusion is that the managers who have responsibility for residential child care have frequently lacked the knowledge and experience necessary to carry out their important task. They have also been less than vigilant about the influence of 'charismatic' characters such as Frank Beck and Tony Latham who have implicitly or explicitly encouraged deviant behaviour. Their apparent immunity from consequences has then discouraged 'whistle blowers'. In such circumstances, a range of minor deviancy eg. wrongful use of resources, money and time, can become inextricably confused with more serious issues such as child abuse ranging from intimidation to sexual abuse, and because deviancy appears unchallenged, staff who do not identify with the deviancy nevertheless face serious risks if they wish to complain.

In spite of the disastrous happenings in some areas, these Reports make clear that the need for good residential child care remains and that, for some children and young people, it is a first choice. It can offer supportive but not demanding relationships, space for brothers and sisters to be together, regular contact with parents, choice within a peer group and growing up space for those who do not wish to join a family other than their own. However, because it is essential, it requires the achievement of high standards and user satisfaction.

4   Rights and Responsibilities

4.1 Introduction

In this chapter we consider the rights of children and young people living in residential settings. Children's rights are now a familiar and much discussed concept. We have already seen the significance of the *United Nations Convention and the Children Act 1989* in this context and, later in this chapter, we look in more detail at some of the rights they identify. We also look at the limits of those rights, the responsibilities which accompany them and how the rights and responsibilities of staff interrelate with them.

A 'right' can be described as simply freedom to choose whether or not to do something, often where there is a clash of interests or when different people's needs conflict with each other. When we talk about 'rights' however, we are often talking about two specific kinds, '**rights of action**' and '**rights of recipience**'.[1] **Rights of action** include freedom to choose whether or not to do something; for example the right to worship in a particular faith, or the right of a young person to complain about the way he or she is treated. **A right of recipience** is the right to be provided with a particular service; a good example for children and young people is the right to education. These rights are often 'granted' under legislation. Some may be given to a particular group of people, for example children and young people who have a right to a statement of special educational need, under Section 7 of the *Education Act 1981*. Some rights of recipience can be expressed in the negative; for example, the right **not to be** abused or ill-used; or the right **not to be** locked up unless certain legal conditions are satisfied.

With rights come **responsibilities** or duties. This is often, but not always, true with children and young people. For example, all children in residential settings have the right to make complaints and for their complaints to be listened to, examined by an independent person, and acted upon if valid. The corollary is that children and young people should use complaints systems responsibly, and not make complaints which are unjustified or unfair. Some rights **do not** impose responsibilities on children and young people. The right to protection

---

1 'The Spiritual Rights of the Child', by John Bradford, p.5

from abuse is an absolute right, and it is the duty of those who look after them to ensure that it is jealously protected.

Children's rights have developed mainly over the course of the present century. Many are new and the majority which children and young people enjoy have only recently been codified under the *United Nations Convention* internationally, and the Children Act 1989 in England and Wales. The Scottish White Paper *'Scotland's Children'* published in August 1993 as proposals for child care policy and law, combines children's rights, adult responsibilities and child care principles in a framework for change. It is important that staff who care for children and young people in residential settings are aware of these rights. Some rights are particularly important when children are living away from home, and we talk about these later in the chapter. In particular the right of children and young people to be heard is crucial. All too often in the past people living in what were traditionally thought of as 'institutions' have not been listened to. It is now a legal requirement to listen to children and young people, to consult them about any action which may affect the quality of their life, and actively involve them in all decisions about where and how they are looked after. The phrase *'ascertain the wishes and feelings of the child'* or a variation of it, occurs in several places throughout the Act in relation to the duties of courts and authorities looking after children. This will mean going beyond simply granting rights to children and young people; it will mean giving them more power over their own lives and increasing their opportunities and expectations of acting responsibly. This realignment of rights, powers and responsibilities of children does not undermine either the responsibilities or authority of staff. We discuss this in more detail later in this chapter and elsewhere in the book.

4.2 Parental rights and children's rights

The Children Act 1989 introduced the new concept of 'parental responsibility'. This is defined in the Act as 'all the rights, duties, powers, responsibilities and authority which, by law, a parent has in relation to a child and his property' (section 3(1)).

Parental responsibility is only lost when a child is adopted. When a child is looked after by a local authority, parents share responsibility and this continues even when a Care Order is made by a court, unless the responsibility is specifically removed by an additional order. Parental responsibility is thus an important concept when considering the rights of a child. It is also possible that a parent's views and duties may be in conflict with the wishes of the child.

This concept leads naturally to the question of the age and competence of children and young people to make decisions about their own lives. The legal position derived from judgements in respect of Gillick v. West

Norfolk Health Authority 1985 and Re v. R in 1991 suggests that a parent's authority gradually attenuates with the child's increasing age and competence. This means that, in general, the older a child the more rights he or she has, and the fewer the parents have. However, a recent Court of Appeal decision[2] held that parents or others with parental responsibility, including a local authority which has a care order, or the courts, may overrule a 16-18 year old, in extreme cases, when s/he withholds consent to medical treatment, for example where life is threatened.

Thus, when children or young people are looked after by a local authority, parents retain their responsibility even when a court order has been made, and partnership with parents is increasingly part of local authority social work with children. Staff working in residential settings, however, have to exercise responsibility on a day-to-day basis. Inevitably they have to make many decisions about how far children may exercise their own judgement. In general, children should be given the benefit of the doubt, so long as this does not damage the wellbeing of others and so long as they are capable of understanding the consequences of the decisions they make. Helping them to do so is part of the skill of residential staff.

A child's right to be consulted does not mean that those with parental rights and responsibilities surrender them in favour of the child's right to choose. A child does not have a right to exercise unfettered choice under the *Children Act 1989*. We stress this point because we are aware that many staff in homes and schools feel their authority has been undermined to a point where they cannot exercise proper control. This is not so. A child does, however, have a right to be consulted and taken seriously, and we offer some suggestions as to how child care practice can balance adult responsibility with children's rights to be consulted.

First, staff need to take trouble to ensure that children have been properly consulted. In major decisions, this may be part of the planning and reviewing process and children should be asked explicitly whether they feel they have had the opportunity they require to put their point of view. The importance of this can be stressed by making a special point of communicating directly with children. Staff will then be able to judge whether the children are being reasonable in their expectations of consultation.

If staff believe a child *has* had every reasonable opportunity to express a view, they can then make a judgment about whether the child's wishes are consistent with the views of those with parental responsibility about how best to promote his welfare. It may be that the child's wishes are not precisely those of the adults but, nonetheless, are not unreasonable. In such circumstances there may be real advantages in going along with the

2 (Re J(1992)3. WLR.758)

child's wishes and so demonstrating respect for his/her sense of self determination. Staff can demonstrate their own parental-type responsibility and concern by making sure the child knows and understands their opinions and the reasons behind them, endorsing the merits or pointing out the disadvantages of the child's own decision, whilst making a positive point out of the child's reasonable choice. No one can be absolutely sure what is right and respecting a child's 'good enough' judgment is likely to bolster his or her self esteem.

If, on the other hand, a child's choice is not reconcileable with careful and well thought out judgments of those with parental responsibility to promote his/her welfare, then the adult carers' views must prevail. This may mean that a great deal of talking has to be done with the child, particularly if major decisions for the future are involved. Time spent in this way should be viewed positively, however, because it is of the essence of parental support for a young person growing up.

If after all the talking and reasoning agreement cannot be reached, there may have to be a confrontation. Although this consumes a lot of energy and may, for a time, be disruptive, confrontation is an appropriate and, for older children sometimes an essential, part of the exchange between carer and child. It is one way in which a balance between parental responsibility and children's rights is struck. If the young person still refuses to accede to staff expectations and, in practice, staff cannot impose their will, the issue may then become a problem of control.

For the purpose of considering rights and responsibilities, it is valuable to distinguish between a member of staff's authority stemming from their responsibilities and rights, and the practical problems of control. A carer does not need to feel that authority counts for nothing simply because, at a particular time, there are difficulties of enforcing compliance. They **can** take a longer term view, as parents often have to do with young people living at home.

There will be occasions where staff must stop young people taking action which could harm themselves, others or property. This might occur for example when a young person attacks another, or is intent on leaving home or school against the wishes and advice of staff. Physical restraint may be justified if it can be shown that, unless it is applied, there is a demonstrable risk that injury will occur to the child or others or property will be seriously damaged. In most homes or schools these occasions will be rare. The *Children Act 1989* and associated guidance make clear prohibitions on the use of restraint, and staff should use and understand this guidance, in order to make sure they do not encroach on children's and young people's rights. The Department of Health issued *Guidance on Permissible Forms of Control in Children's Residential Care* on 28 April 1993. This supplements the Guidance in Volume 4. Control of children and young people is considered in more detail in Chapter 6.

In boarding schools the parental role is clearly shared between teachers and care staff and parents who have chosen to entrust their children to them. The partnership has the nature of an informal contract in which parents effectively delegate some of their powers and responsibilities to the school when the child is first sent there. Staff act in *loco parentis* but do not assume full parental responsibility themselves. On a day to day basis their responsibility has much in common with children's homes staff.

4.3 Rights under the Children Act 1989 and other legislation

4.3.1 *The Children Act*

The 1989 Children Act enshrined a number of children's rights in law. For the most part these apply to children and young people 'looked after' by social services departments. Those rights in *The Children Act* which apply to residential child care could generally, as a matter of good practice, apply in all residential settings, whether regulated by the Act or not. An exception would be the right to have an independent visitor. This is formulated in relation to the duties of social services departments to certain children and their personal circumstances. It would not apply to the great majority of children and young people in boarding schools. Other rights, however, could be easily assimilated into other settings, particularly the right to complain; to be heard; to have a child's race, culture and religion respected; the right to contact with family and friends; and the right not to be locked up, unless certain legal conditions are satisfied.

Residential establishments, other than children's homes, need to be aware of this right not to be locked up. The methods of control and discipline they use should **never** include locking children up as part of regular practice. The *Secure Accommodation Regulations 1991* require that not only social services community homes but also health, education and certain other residential establishments must obtain a court order before they can restrict children's liberty for aggregated periods in excess of 72 hours.

4.3.2 *The Right to see Files*

Under the *Access to Personal Files Act 1987* children and young people have a right to see files which contain information about them. Staff need to be aware of this legislation too, and to make sure that children are told precisely what information they are entitled to see. They should be able to counsel them, if they ask to see files, in understanding how they might feel and what sort of information they may see. They should never prevent them from seeing papers, including case files, which they are entitled to see, although they will need to take into account their age and level of understanding. Children may be aware of what is in their files because staff have discussed their progress with them in the course of their daily life. There should be no surprises and an open approach should be taken in dealing with requests. Managers will need to give staff training opportunities in report writing and record keeping, including avoidance of stigmatising language such as 'delinquent' or 'uncontrollable'. Records should be as objective as possible, noting children's achievements, 'good days' and positive developments of all kinds, as well as traumatic events and negative behaviour. They should be written in a style accessible to children and avoid unnecessary professional terms or jargon.

SOCIAL WORK FILES

Under the *Access to Personal Files Act 1987* and the *Access to Personal Files (Social Services) Regulations 1989*, a child of adequate understanding who is being looked after or has been looked after by a local authority has a right to see what is written on their file. If staff believe that seeing a file would in some way harm a child, or divulge information from or about a third party without their consent, they do not have to let the child see it but, if they are not allowed, an explanation must be given to the child. If the child is not satisfied with the explanation, s/he can use the complaints procedure as a first line of appeal.

HEALTH FILES

Since 1 November 1991, young people over 16 have had the right to see their health records. These include records kept by doctors, dentists, nurses, opticians, child psychologists, psychotherapists and speech therapists. (Access to Health Records Act 1990). Health authorities have discretion to allow children younger than 16 to see their records if they are capable of understanding them. Information held on computer, under the *Data Protection Act 1984*, Section 21, can be seen by younger children if they have sufficient understanding. Application to see health records must be made in writing and the applicant may inspect the record or extract and be supplied with a copy. Access may be modified or withheld if, in the record holder's opinion, serious harm may be caused to the physical or mental health of the patient or any other individual. A child, if thought by a health professional to be capable of understanding what an application is about, can prevent a person with parental responsibility from seeing the record. Records about physical or mental health of an individual made in connection with crime investigation do not come within the Act. It is the view of some doctors that there is lack of clarity in the situation which may only appear after legal challenges have been made. Particularly in child mental health files, information from different parties concerned with a child may be recorded. Some children want their views kept confidential from parents and vice versa. Sometimes parents who are separated do not want their expressed views to be available to their ex. partners. Health professionals should record clearly to whom each record may be confidential. Similarly, health authorities need to recognise that health records may contain information which demands careful checks to be made before release is granted of all the contents contained within notes. These complex and sensitive issues are not always well understood within bureaucratic contexts.

EDUCATION FILES

Since 1 September 1990, young people over 16 have had a right to see their education records. Records on computers are covered by the *Data Protection Act 1984*. Manual records are covered by the *Education (School Records) Regulations 1989*. Attainment and reporting to parents are covered by the *Education (Individual Pupils Achievements, School Records and School Curriculum) (Amendment) Regulations 1992* which extend the *Education (Individual Pupils Achievement) (Information) Regulations 1990*.

4.3.3 The Right to Complain

FROM THE POINT OF VIEW OF CHILDREN

> "Its all right as long as we know how to use them and we know what happens."
> "I think its pretty good but its too slow. It should be hurried."
> "We should be told of the progress of a complaint."
>
> *Comments on complaints systems by young people in care*

The right to complain is now a legal requirement for children in residential settings, but before discussing it, it is important to put it in the context of general communication. If there is good communication between staff and children, and appropriate ways are provided through which problems can be ventilated as a matter of course, most issues which might be seen as complaints can be dealt with as part of the day-to-day process of caring. This provides the opportunity for staff to demonstrate their capacity to be\ fair and just and to handle criticism openly. It also helps young people to develop the skills of being appropriately assertive and of effective negotiation. This desirable situation, however, does not provide adequately for all occasions when a child may wish, or need, to complain, and the law now fills this gap. Resorting to complaints procedures first (unless the complaint is serious) before more informal but nonetheless legitimately accepted methods are tried, can imbalance the problem.

Under *The Children Act 1989* (and in the Scottish White Paper *Scotland's Children* proposals), any child has a right to complain about services provided by the local authority looking after them. For this purpose, local authorities are required to set up complaints procedures which include an independent element. The Act also requires voluntary and private organisations running children's homes and looking after children not in local authority care to establish analogous complaints procedures. The *Children Act* guidance dealing with the welfare of pupils in independent schools also expects these schools to have effective procedures and practices for dealing with complaints as part of the proprietors' duty to promote and safeguard the welfare of pupils. In independent schools parents will generally be brought into the procedure at an early stage, or may initiate the complaint themselves, since they may be the first people to whom the child complains.

It would be prudent for all residential establishments to take the trouble to establish a readily available and effective system for dealing confidentially with complaints from children and young people for whom they are responsible. This is especially important where local authority social services departments have placed children in schools or homes some distance from their home area. It is difficult to use a complaints procedure which is remote, and to which easy access is not available and it needs to be remembered that Section 23(7)(a) requires children to be accommodated as close to home as possible.

A home or school where good practice is encouraged will have an ethos that is open, trusting and supportive of the children and young people and complaints and grievances are likely to be sorted out long before any formal procedure needs to be invoked. In such a situation the existence of a written complaints procedure will not cause problems for staff and is also unlikely to be abused by the children. It will be very much accepted as a normal part of the democratic working of the establishment and discipline system at large.

Children and young people should be made aware of the complaints procedure as soon as they start living in the home or school. Volume 4 of *The Children Act Guidance and Regulations* requires that:

> *'every child in a home should be provided with an information leaflet that includes the telephone number of someone independent of the home whom the child can contact if he has any problems'.*3

Many local authorities, schools and homes already produce literature explaining how children and young people make a complaint. This should be general practice. The literature, in the form of a short, easily-

---

3 Volume 4, paragraph 5.16

read booklet should explain what complaints procedures are for; how to make a complaint; the processes which will operate when a complaint is made; what will happen if the complaint is upheld; and who to go to for help. It should also include telephone numbers and addresses of people and organisations whom the child can contact for help and advice. These include organisations such as Childline, the Children's Legal Centre, the Advice and Advocacy Service for Children, NSPCC Child Protection Line, the Children's Society Advocacy Unit, Black and in Care, the Who Cares? Magazine Advice and Information Service, the Samaritans and any local children's ombudsman service. APPENDIX 4 gives details of how these organisations can be contacted. Although Childline's Boarding School Line has been discontinued, the Childline number is still available to boarders in schools. In addition, some local authority social services departments run their own help lines, and pupils in boarding schools should be told of these where they exist locally. Many organisations provide cards with important telephone numbers for children and young people, so that they are readily available.

Information about the complaints system should be provided when children arrive at a home or boarding school. It should be backed up by discussions of complaints procedures, making a point of explaining them to children and young people with reading difficulties, visually disabled children or those with learning difficulties. Questions about the procedures should be encouraged. Staff members could carry out the task of explaining and leading discussion, but consideration should also be given to inviting someone from outside the home or school to talk to the children and young people. A person who acts locally as an 'independent element' in the procedure might be ideally placed to do this, and would be likely to inspire confidence in the complaints service.

Although children and young people will probably first discuss a problem with a carer or their parents, some who wish to complain may find it hard to do so without outside help. They may have particular problems which make it difficult for them to express themselves, or they may be nervous of the consequences of making a complaint. Access to independent advocates or other adults outside the establishment will help to give them confidence and they should all know that help is available from outside organisations and individuals. Where appropriate, they should be helped to get in touch with people who could help them put their case. Boarders in schools which have day pupils may find that older day pupils (who may be prefects or mentors) will be the first to whom they can talk. All pupils, day or boarding, need to know about and understand complaints procedures, how they work, and why they are important.

Homes and schools should also make sure that it is possible for children and young people to discuss their circumstances in confidence with someone outside if they wish to do so. This may be the beginning of a formal complaint, or it may be simply that a child is feeling lonely and wants to talk to someone outside the home or school. To help them do this they need access to a telephone where they cannot be overheard by staff or other children. They should also be provided with money or phonecards to help them use it. They should not have to ask staff for these whenever they wish to use the telephone. So that the system is not abused, it may be helpful to have a telephone which uses phonecards, and then provide phonecards regularly. Some boarding schools have found that a small room, with a frosted glass window which allows staff to see without having to listen at the door, works well. Some have installed old GPO red telephone boxes on the school campus which serve the purpose well and add an element of fun.

Staff should never discourage children or parents from making a complaint. Instead it may be helpful to encourage them to do so as a way of 'clearing the air'. As we have said earlier, many issues can be resolved, and never become formal complaints, if staff and children live together with mutual trust and respect. Staff must, therefore, be prepared to listen to children and young people individually and in groups; to respect their views; to take action where necessary; and to explain why they are not taking action if they are not going to. Often grievances will be about what is seen as unfair treatment. One young person may feel that he or she is being criticised more than others, or that they are not being allowed to watch their favourite television programme. In such cases staff must first look at adult practices critically: are the grievances justified? If so, what can be done about them? A child with a grievance should be kept informed of what is being done at all stages, and where possible should be involved in discussions with staff and other residents about resolving the problem. It may be helpful, with the consent of the aggrieved young person, to ask other young people to comment and offer solutions, and agree a course of action. The involvement of everyone at an early stage in resolving problems, may help to prevent escalation and make it more likely that matters will be satisfactorily resolved.

FROM THE POINT OF VIEW OF STAFF

The explicit right of children to complain understandably leaves staff with a heightened sense of vulnerability to unfair or false allegations. Openness in caring, and ready opportunities for gripes and grouches to be voiced, will create an atmosphere in which misunderstandings and insensitive staff responses to children are identified and dealt with before becoming serious issues. Working in such an environment, however, demands a high degree of staff maturity. Managers can help new staff who are not familiar with this way of working to adjust to it by good induction and straightforward descriptions of 'how we handle things around here'.

Managers also have a responsibility to make sure that staff are protected from occasional untrue or malicious allegations by children against staff. Although it must be made easy for children to voice a complaint and allegations must be taken seriously, this need not mean that children making a serious complaint have the power to cause immediate suspension of a staff member. Employers may need to examine their personnel policies to ensure that practices which are intended to safeguard the proper interests of staff are commensurate with children's rights to complain. An allegation must be weighed up at the outset and a judgment made about what needs to be done in investigating it. It may not be necessary to suspend the person concerned unless this is the only way to ensure that alleged abuse of children, if true, could not recur; or that the staff member's presence at work would seriously inhibit the investigation; or that the allegation, if proven, is so serious that it would lead to dismissal or prosecution.

If it is necessary to suspend a member of staff, employers can give support by allocating a more senior person, not in direct line management, to act as a confidential 'next friend'. This person can then help the staff member organize advice and representation and act as a link between him or her and employers at a time when communication is inevitably formal and likely to be strained.

4.3.4 The Right to be Heard

Within a general framework of parental responsibility, the *Children Act 1989* gives children and young people who are being looked after by a local authority the right to have their wishes and feelings considered and taken into account when plans are being made for their future. **The principle that children and young people have a right to be listened to can, and should, be extended to every residential setting and should include everyday life as well as plans and reviews**.

If children and young people are to be allowed to exercise this right, a change of attitude will be required in some establishments which have traditionally relied solely on staff to make decisions about the care of children and young people. However, any home or school is likely to be a happier place for children and young people if they are committed to it. This commitment is difficult to gain if they feel remote from those who make decisions about them, and powerless to change anything. Such regimes breed resentment, which can then lead to problems within the group, especially with discipline.

There are two ways in which homes can make sure children are listened to. First by having someone to talk to who they can rely on to lend a sympathetic ear, or be a shoulder to cry on. That person must also be respected. Respect is most readily gained if they feel the person they talk to can 'deliver'; that they can listen to a problem and take action to remedy it. This is an essential part of the care staff's task. In boarding schools a tutor or favourite teacher or even an older pupil may be the best person.

The second way is by establishing meetings to allow residents in the home or school to discuss common issues, and to speak collectively. Such meetings must be legitimised by and conducted within the general framework of adult authority in the home or school. The exact format of such meetings will vary and should, as far as possible, be related to what young people themselves wish to have. **Staff members should be involved in small numbers, primarily as enablers, but on the clear understanding that their authority remains and will be asserted if necessary**. Such circumstances might include determined attempts to gain control by a minority, or dissident group; group discussion being used to express unacceptable discrimination; or stirring up action against democratic methods of decision making or 'house rules' agreed between staff and young people.

Holding effective meetings is likely to be made easier by clearly defining rules for their conduct eg. election of officers, setting up agendas, recording discussions and decisions, and fixing regular times and dates for meetings so that everyone concerned knows what to expect. Having established a structure, there should be as free as possible a choice of issues for discussion, the group itself setting limits. Issues might include, for example, the physical state of the building; daily living routines; quality of food and meal times; methods of control and discipline; contacts with the local community. **Once issues have been raised and discussed, there must be clear ways of taking them forward**. This could mean that young people may want to appoint representatives to meet with staff and negotiate change, or express views on behalf of others.

This is not a recipe for anarchy! Encouraging children and young people in residential care to take responsibility for aspects of their everyday life is, after all, similar to what happens in many ordinary families. It also provides, through group discussion and activity, early experience in democratic responsibility and how to influence other people, important lessons for adult life. In addition, decisions reached in this way, eg. in relation to methods of control and discipline are more likely to result in their acceptance and, consequently, a calmer and steadier atmosphere in the group so that education, care and treatment can take place in a climate of relative stability.

When young people have genuinely contributed to important decisions affecting their lives, they are likely to show disapproval of those in their peer group who subsequently break rules which have been agreed. This can be much more effective than threats of sanctions and punishments by adults.

PUPILS LAY DOWN THE LAW ON DISCIPLINE
"............ the Schools Minister, said extensive guidelines to be issued before Christmas would advise head teachers and governors that school rules were far more effective when pupils felt they shared "ownership" and had helped to write them"

Home News: The Times, December 9, 1993

Every young person has a right to be listened to and experience demonstrates that they usually have something to say which is worth hearing and may help adults in their task of caring for them.

4.3.5 *The Right to Contact With Others*

Children and young people living away from home need to have contact with those people who are most important to them – parents, brothers and sisters, relatives and friends. Nurturing relationships with families and friends is essential to maintain stability and continuity in their lives; and to promote a feeling of being valued by others. Contacts with adults not known to their family may need to be checked out, at the school's or home's discretion, and schools will have various regulatory systems for permission to visit and have visitors. In some settings there are particular risks of contact being abused. For example, children who have been sexually abused may sustain an unhealthy contact with their abusers, or young people in secure accommodation may seek to undermine the security of the establishment. In these circumstances a compromise will be needed which allows a child's right to contact to be exercised in such a way that a degree of oversight reduces the likelihood of such abuse without an unacceptable sacrifice of privacy.

The *Children Act 1989*, and the Scottish White Paper proposals, recognise this and ensure that children being looked after by a local authority have a right to contact with their family unless it would be harmful, in which case the local authority must obtain a court order forbidding contact. We believe that this right should be recognised in every other setting. In most cases, for example in boarding schools, this is not a problem since the majority of pupils go home for the holidays and, increasingly often, at weekends as well. There are always some pupils, however, who, for various reasons, have little contact with their families. This may be particularly true of pupils from other countries. It is also true that a few children, regrettably, find home less welcoming and reassuring than school and do not **wish** to return.

Children and young people in other settings may have less frequent contact with their families than those in boarding schools. Breakdown of family life may have been the cause of their coming into a residential setting. Others may have been neglected by their families, or have no wish for contact because of previous unhappiness or insecurity. If it is not in a child's interests to do so, or it is strongly against his or her wishes, contact with parents will not be helpful and a child has a right to refuse it.

In general however, staff should promote children's right to contact with their families and other adults who are important to them. Keeping up to date with family circumstances is important and, where appropriate, staff should discuss family contacts and any difficulties which might arise with other professions. Equally, residential staff have a key role in identifying when contact is causing distress and is detrimental to a child's welfare. There are occasions when contact should be seen as an opportunity to work with families. A distinction may need to be drawn between contact which is at an ordinary human level of keeping in touch and contact which is used as part of a total process of therapeutic care. This latter will be very much part of the life of a mental health unit, but is less so in residential care. Visits by parents and other family members are opportunities for feedback and information sharing between staff, young people and families. In addition, if relationships are fraught, more formally arranged contact meetings can be opportunities to resolve difficulties. As we have highlighted in the chapter on training, residential workers not only need the skills to work with individuals, but also with the families as well. Too often the skills are missing and the opportunities for effective change are missed. Partnership means more than simply including parents in decision making.

Above all, the overall environment in a home or school should encourage family contact, unless it is clearly not in a child's interest. This may mean being flexible about internal organisation and timetables so that visits are not made difficult; making it possible for visitors to stay overnight (particularly if they have to travel a long way); providing comfortable spaces where parents and their children can meet privately; enabling visitors to participate in the daily routine, if they and their children wish to. Ultimately, though, it must be a child's own decision whether contacts with the family take place. The staff's role is to ensure that the child can have contact if s/he wishes and if it is not against the child's best interest.

4.3.6 *The Right to Health*

> "Childhood is a period of foundation laying....... Health and education together are seen by most parents as the vital constituents of their children's future lives. If the education and health of children in care are appropriately valued by public agencies, even short episodes in care could make a valuable contribution to strong foundations for adult life"
>
> *Kahan, B – "The Physical and Mental Health of Children in Care", Child Care Research, Policy and Practice 1989*
>
> "Arising from the evidence in the Inquiry and research which supports it we consider that the health of children in care is an aspect which should receive more attention nationally".
>
> *Levy A, Kahan B – "The Pindown Experience and the Protection of Children"*
>
> "I think at my age, 17, we should be allowed to make our own appointments and go when we think we should. I don't think we should be made to go."
>
> *Young person in care commenting on medical examination*

There are two aspects to children and young persons' right to health care. First is their right to health education and health promotion. This should involve information and education on a range of health issues; the overall importance of leading a healthy life; healthy eating; adequate exercise and sleep; sex education and personal relationships; safe sex; the hazards of smoking, alcohol and substance abuse; the specific health needs of some minority ethnic groups. These topics are likely to form part of the educational curriculum, and care staff may not, therefore, need to provide this education themselves. However, they need to know whether, and how, these issues are being addressed in the schools the children attend. It will be helpful for staff to take the same care as a good parent would, discussing issues with children and young people, helping them with the questions they want to ask, and encouraging them to lead a healthy lifestyle. It is also important that someone has responsibility to ensure that sex education has taken place. Some of these issues are discussed in more detail in Chapter 6.

Some staff may feel ill equipped to deal with health issues and support from local health and education personnel may not be readily available. If this is so, staff need to urge senior managers to negotiate better support for them from education and health authorities.

The second aspect of the right to health care is that all children should have full and appropriate access to health services. The Secretary of State for Health has a duty under Section 1 of the *National Health Service Act 1977* to provide a comprehensive health service for everyone, and children living in residential settings have the same entitlement to these services as all other children. This is especially important since many children and young people in residential establishments, including children's homes and residential special schools, are likely to have particular health needs eg. for psychiatric, psychological and therapeutic services. NHS support should be available to help provide balanced assessments and to ensure that a wide range of therapeutic services is available. The *Warner Inquiry* found that NHS support to children's homes is not consistently available at the high standard needed, and there is good reason to believe that residential special schools may be in a similar position. Where specialist provision is good, this seems often to be as a result of local agreements between the NHS and those running the home or school. Delay in assessing and treating children with mental health and related problems is unacceptable: it can lead to more or increased problems, or result in long periods of treatment subsequently. It may also mean that children are excluded from school or have to receive forms of treatment which would not otherwise have been required.

4.3.7 The Right to Education

"I was encouraged by my link worker to go to school"
"I think I am encouraged to go to college"
"I have missed loads and loads of schooling. I want home tutoring"
"I passed into grammar school....I misbehaved (and was suspended). It was all this moving about (in care)"

"Answering Back" – Report by Young People Being Looked After on the Children Act 1989, The Dolphin Project 1993

> "We recommend that there should be a named person at senior management level with responsibility for ensuring that care and attention is given to the education, career development and working life of children in care ....
> .... The named person should provide an annual report .... giving particular attention to:-
> (a)   educational achievements of children in care;
> (b)   changes in the schools they attend as a consequence of care placement;
> (c)   special educational needs;
> (d)   involvement in further education;........"
>
> *Levy A, Kahan B – "The Pindown Experience and the Protection of Children",*
> *Recommendations 23.12 and 23.13*

All children and young people have a right to education. It is compulsory up to the age of 16. After that age attendance is optional, although local education authorities must provide an education service for young people over 16. Children in residential settings have the same entitlements to education as other children. This is not a concern for most children and young people in boarding schools, who are there for educational purposes. The situation may, however, be different in children's homes. In their report, the *Warner Committee* stated:

'we have found that too often these children – many of whom need special help as a result of their behavioural problems, or previous non-attendance at school – are receiving little or no education. ... We recognise that because of their particular problems, children in homes can be disruptive for schools, or will play truant.'

Increasing exclusions from school were causing concern nationally at the time we were writing this book. In some children's homes a high proportion of the residents had been excluded. They were not receiving adequate, if any education, although local education authorities are obliged to provide a full range of services to children in residential care, at the same standard as if they were in mainstream schools.

Care staff have an important role to play in the education of children and young people. They can help them by creating a stimulating environment in which their natural inquisitiveness and proper development are encouraged. In this respect children's homes may learn much from boarding schools, where pupils are not only encouraged to do homework, but leisure activities have a broadly educational slant, without making the children feel they are being forced to learn. Higher educational expectations of children in local authority care are needed to enable them to achieve their educational potential. Sadly, all too often staff give up on the education of children in their care, which has frequently been punctuated by truancy, expulsion and changes of schools. If this is so, it is all the more important to make extra efforts to improve the children's educational prospects, and not allow them to despair about their future. Where homes are under additional pressure because of exclusions from school, senior managers and local politicians have a duty to make proper arrangements to provide education drawing upon the expertise of educational professionals and through them trying to ensure that the individual educational needs are identified and a degree of stability and progression is built into children's educational experience. Care staff should not have to feel that everything is being left to them.

Nonetheless, care staff can play their part. The Social Research Unit at Dartington found that the acquisition of 'instrumental skills' by children was associated with more positive outcomes from a period in residential care (see Chapter 7 – Short Term Guests). Opportunity for learning through activity is the cornerstone of an educational approach to the upbringing of children. As w said in Chapter 1, staff in children's homes could benefit from adopting a similar philosophy.

Time can then be regarded as a resource which can be translated into achievement. It does not have to be regarded as a 'stretch' to be got through. Care staff can contribute to the children's education by planning and programming events and opportunities. Suggestions that a visit be made to a museum, or that people go for a walk in the country, or watch a play on the TV may be met with a negative response from some young people but this should not diminish the importance of providing these opportunities for learning.

Some children being looked after in children's homes will have had a very impoverished quality of cultural life. This is a good reason why a period of living in a home should endeavour to extend their experience. Staff may be disappointed if their attempts are rejected, but this is not a reason to stop. It is worthwhile to go on trying even if only some children benefit.

Although education is recognised as important in relation to employment, earning capacity and general progress in adult life, its crucial effect on communication between one person and another, is not always understood. We discuss communication again in Chapter 6, particularly in the context of relationships between children and young people and those caring for them. Here we try to show the enormous handicap of lack of basic education in a wider context.

Recently an inquiry into suicides in Feltham Young Offenders' Institution was carried out. (*Suicides in Feltham – A Report by the Howard League, 1993*). In the report the backgrounds of the four young men concerned, aged 15, 18, 19 and 20 years old, are described. The 15 year old, who suffered from epilepsy, had spent periods in care. Letters from him and from the 19 year old, whose life had suffered many tragic losses, are included in the report as evidence. The major characteristic of both is their desperate attempts at communication. Yet, in both instances, they have no grasp of written English, as indicated by the following verbatim extracts from letters:-

'How are you Mum and Dad

hop you are well

kan you seder me pictures of you all.....

hop you and Dad + kids are oh ritt....I hop Loo seds blue will sed a letter to me But I will wipitup and pot it in the bin.....

Love you all

By God bless you all'

and

'Hi Mary

I will put a forn nuber on this letter for you to rin if you what to tank to me

.....Sory A but...the writing i hope you can mike out My writeing.....as you no i coninot ask no won to bob Anne tin for in here so piles will you com to see me or rin me.....I rout to Mammy and Bigann and Hilen and got know anser form dem so I bout no if will write to dem a gen or what......

I love and miss yous a lot'

The letter ended with a drawing of a face with tears running down it and the words 'this is me Ha Ha.'.

Lack of vocabulary, lack of ability to communicate in words, whether spoken or written, is a constant source of embarrassment and frustration in a culture in which words are the universal coinage. It can impoverish personal relationships, handicap the individual in a great range of situations every day and restrict ability to think because words are lacking as tools to use. Each year that passes in a child's life makes the problem more difficult to resolve and no opportunities should be missed to help children and young people to increase their capacity to use words in communicating. It is now well known that children with specific learning difficulties have a higher chance of developing behaviour problems if their learning problems are ignored. In addition families can feel the burden of blame for their child's behaviour quite disproportionately at times. The key factor in the development of behavioural problems may, in fact, be educational and less to do with family relationships.

Ensuring that children and young people's rights to receive proper health care and education are respected is a task which will often fall to staff in residential establishments. In many instances, only they will be in a position to tell when a youngster needs a particular service. We discuss the role of managers in ensuring that the full range of services is available in Chapter 12. Staff in day-to-day contact with children and young people need to be confident enough to inform management when needs are not being met, and to continue to apply pressure until the situation improves. It is the task of elected members and senior managers, as well as staff working with children, to take their needs and rights as seriously as they would their own children's. Parenting is the nature of the task.

"I wish I had stayed at the same school because every children's home I went to I changed school. One day I woke up and thought "I am not getting anywhere". The teacher said "you are a no hoper, you will leave school with nothing"... but..."
Young person who was in care; is now at college [Dolphin Project]

"I am going to get a degree. I'll stay at it as long as it takes....I'll get it ..it's my ambition"
Young person in care

"Answering Back" – Report by Young People Being Looked After on the Children Act 1989, The Dolphin Project 1993

In answer to the question:-
"Has boarding education been advantageous academically?"

[Wagner Group – questionnaire to boarding school pupils]
A boarder replied:-

"Yes, boarding produces an all round academic environment in which I find it much easier to apply myself and achieve the best results possible."

PART TWO

LIVING AWAY FROM
HOME IN GROUPS

5 The Physical Environment

5.1 Introduction

Most of us associate being at home with feeling comfortable, and at ease. This arises from a combination of familiarity, sense of security and physical comfort. Some children and young people, particularly those who come to be looked after by local authorities, have experienced poor accommodation, poverty and environmental stress and little physical comfort, even if they had some emotional security. Whatever children's prior experience, while they are living in groups away from home, their physical environment is of great importance. The buildings and their surroundings, the state of decoration, furnishings and equipment, the use of space and children's opportunities to personalise their own space, are all important in helping them to settle down and make the best use of the experience as a whole.

Some shades of opinion suggest the children's environment should not be of the high standard advocated by government guidance and professional thinking, because this will unsettle them and make it difficult for them to return to the poorer standards from which they came. Such a view serves only to condemn children to conditions which contributed to their need to be looked after. The standards advocated are a deliberate recognition of both children's and staff's needs in the circumstances. First, the children's need for care is the reason for their being looked after. There is also an element, as we suggest in various contexts in this book, of compensating to some extent for the high degree of deprivation experienced by most children and using their care experience to help them forward. Second, it would not be feasible to ask staff whose task is to care for children, to do so in circumstances which were less than adequate for their proper care. In this chapter, therefore, we consider some of the issues involved in ensuring that children and young people can be cared for in a comfortable and pleasant setting. This is not to say that the standard of the physical environment can compensate for an inadequate human environment – although conversely, it is remarkable how a positive staff group can make an otherwise unpromising physical environment work, at least to a reasonable extent. Equally, even if a home or school is attractive and well maintained, staff cannot afford to relax in their other tasks. However, a good environment can make the caring task much easier and managers should be aware of the costs – financially and in terms of care – of having to manage a poor quality environment housing lively and energetic children and young people.

5.2 Buildings

'...... Substandard buildings with poor decor are unacceptable; the residential unit managers should be in control of their own resources for decor and furniture, and the furniture should be of a good household standard'.

'...... Each home needs to provide space for school work etc, and staff support for educational attainment; there needs to be a budget for books, and other educational and leisure aids should be around and available'.

'....... All children's homes should have plants and other household decorations and should take a flexible approach to animals......'.

Extracts from Checklist for Practice – Welsh NAYPIC – Annex 3, Part IV in 'Accommodating Children' – Social Services Inspectorate, Welsh Office and Social Information Systems Limited, 1991

Children and young people are no different from older people in being significantly influenced by the physical condition of buildings in which they spend long periods of time. Having to live in unpleasant, poorly maintained, cold or badly decorated surroundings will signal to them that those with responsibility have little respect for them as individuals. This is likely to lead to loss of self respect in themselves as well as a loss of respect for those in authority. This, in turn, may have consequences for behaviour and discipline.

The remarks in this section relate, in the main, to relatively small settings such as children's homes, where the main function is to provide a home for children and young people. Many boarding schools are often very large by comparison and it may be difficult to achieve the home-like atmosphere which is often possible in establishments with only about 10 children and young people. This difficulty is overcome, to some extent, by division of schools into 'houses', where pupils can be cared for in smaller groups. Within the 'houses' efforts can then be made to achieve a 'homely' atmosphere. Many boarding schools are situated in relatively pleasant locations, with large and well maintained buildings. However, as evidence to the *Warner Inquiry* indicated, there are also some in poorly maintained and poorly decorated buildings. Others, particularly residential special schools, may be in purpose-built buildings, which may suffer similar problems to some purpose-built children's homes, ie.

designs, materials and furnishings achievable within the lowest estimates. They also lack the interesting, even if sometimes difficult to maintain 'nooks and crannies', spacious rooms and 'atmosphere', which characterise many older buildings. The same may be true of some purpose built hospital units.

Children's living accommodation should be attractive, suitable for its purpose and free from health and safety hazards. Individual residents should have some privacy, adequate facilities for study and as wide a range of leisure activities as possible, including quiet pursuits.

It is not possible to make general rules about suitable buildings and, as we have implied above, purpose-built does not necessarily mean good. Flexibility is an important feature in any building. This may be best achieved by having a larger number of smaller rooms adaptable for various purposes rather than a few large rooms. Temporary partitioning does not generally provide 'homely' group living, although it may sometimes be useful. Staff, regrettably, are often handicapped by having little control over either their physical working environment or its location. For children's homes this may change if the recommendations made in some of the reports reviewed earlier are adopted, eg. that there should be greater delegation of budgets to managers in charge. This would enable them to get minor repairs and decorating carried out locally, rather than having to wait for headquarters to arrange it. A home or school would feel much more like home to the residents if there were a sense of being in control of their immediate environment. It is particularly important that responsibility for decoration of a home belongs to the people who live and work there.

This does not mean that a rough and ready do-it-yourself policy should be accepted. Mending windows, fixing locks and other minor repairs need to be done well, otherwise the results may not only look makeshift, but also be inefficient. Such tasks, as well as painting and decorating, are usually best done by professionals locally. Devolved budgets would facilitate this quickly and without fuss. There may be some occasions when young people themselves carry out some small repair and decorating jobs, eg. in their own bedrooms. What is important is that boarders and children and young people in children's homes and schools are encouraged to take an interest in the state of their building, eg. reporting broken locks and windows and other deficiencies to the head of their home or house. This would fit in with moves towards independence for older children and help them to take responsibilities within their community and for their own lives.

Staff should never feel embarrassed because they seek good standards and want the children to live in a clean, well-decorated environment. On the contrary, they should be expected to set good standards in the home or school house and any residential staff member or teacher who believes that to do so is an unacceptable infringement of children's rights should listen to what the children and young people themselves say. Young people in boarding schools and children's homes have made it very clear that they do not like living in homes which do not show concern and regard for them by being maintained in a good and pleasant condition.

It is a part of 'home making' for staff to make sure that there are pot plants, pictures, books, magazines and newspapers in the home; that a cup of tea spilt over a carpet is treated with the same urgency as it would be in a domestic household. Concern to take care of furniture, to mop up spills and other messes is part of good child care. It says

> *'I am concerned that you should live somewhere nice'.*

If the home or school feels austere, neglected or cold, and the furniture is not like furniture found in ordinary households, then staff have a duty to make their voices heard. It should not be like that. Senior managers, head teachers, visiting elected members or governors should be told that conditions are not good enough and that the children and young people are entitled to something better. They may not have realised how far conditions have deteriorated and a meeting with staff and young people might help better understanding.

Regrettably, the fact that a home or school is well furnished and in good decorative order is not an insurance against any damage by resident children and young people. Every so often, they are likely to cause damage, accidentally or otherwise. However, there is sound experience which shows that a policy of restoring a home to good order quickly, does not result in endless expenditure, and that an attractive and well maintained home is much less likely to be damaged than a scruffy and neglected one. The way damage is handled may also be a good expression of the real aims of the home – therapeutically, administratively or punitively. Participation in choice of colour schemes and furniture can help young people to have a sense of 'ownership' which will lead to care for their environment. It will also help to develop an increasing awareness of environmental quality in children and young people so that they can learn to value and understand the creation of a 'good home' as part of their growing up process.

5.2.1 Bedrooms

Bedrooms are important living areas which ought to be available for use for many hours out of every day, not just for sleeping in but also for homework, day dreaming and peace and quiet from the group. They are often the only personal space a child or young person has and should be kept clean, pleasantly decorated and well furnished. Even if they are shared, there should be scope to personalise individual areas by provision of pin boards for posters and photographs and shelves or other spaces for 'treasures' and books collected by children. Because of limited storage space, it may be necessary to restrict each young person's amount of clothes, but there should be adequate personal storage for all clothing and other items such as suitcases and holdalls. If children have to share a room, their personal minimum equipment needs to include wardrobe space, a chest of drawers/desk with lockable drawers and a chair. This standard should be applicable to schools and homes.

The question of whether doors should be lockable, by whom, and who needs to hold keys must be looked at in the context of individual children's needs and behaviour and the ethos and function of a home or school. In boarding schools it is unusual for bedrooms or dormitories to be lockable. This might be difficult to arrange when there could be 500 or more boarders, but individual houses could have separate keys and size need not prohibit privacy of this kind. Some children and young people in children's homes, residential special schools and psychiatric units may have a history of self-mutilation or drug abuse. Staff will need to discuss with others such as parents, health workers and social workers, whether they can allow them to have keys to their bedrooms. Wherever possible, the children should be given the benefit of the doubt, and if there is no reason to believe they are likely to damage themselves, then they can reasonably be allowed keys. Staff will need to have master keys. We have already discussed the importance of privacy, and whether doors are lockable or not, staff will need to respect the right to privacy before entering bedrooms, or using their master keys.

When children have to share bedrooms, territory is important and they may need support in protecting their own space. It is also valuable for them to be responsible for keeping it tidy and for some, if not all, of the cleaning. However, young people are not all naturally tidy, nor are all adults, and while encouraging tidiness within reasonable limits, it is not good practice to allow tidiness to become a staff fetish.

5.2.2 Bathrooms and Toilets

The strong views of children in boarding schools about bathrooms and toilets are quoted in Chapter 6, 3.2.20 and 3.2.21 in particular. Their views are likely to be echoed in other children's establishments. Bathrooms and toilets should be warm, well-ventilated and comfortable places to be. They should also be lockable. In general, and particularly in smaller establishments such as children's homes, bathrooms are likely to resemble those in a domestic household with no more than one toilet, one bath and/or shower and one washbasin in a washing and toilet area. Although these guidelines go beyond those in the *Schools Premises Regulations 1981*, (in the process of being revised) adopting them as good practice and as a target for achievement would help to avoid an 'institutional' character in boarding schools facilities. Where this is not possible, and we recognise there may be problems in many boarding schools, showers can be privately curtained where there are, for example, more than one shower in a bathroom. Rows of showers or baths open to common view, or toilets with ill-fitting or broken doors are unacceptable in any residential establishment. As we have discussed in Chapter 6, (3.2.20) even if common facilities are the general rule after games lessons, there should be a choice of common facilities or private cubicles.

5.2.3 *Common Room and Living Rooms*

If at all possible, common and living rooms should resemble those in domestic households, large or small. Again, this is relatively easy to achieve in children's homes, but may be more difficult in boarding schools. They should be comfortably furnished with adequate sitting facilities, and varied to suit the age-range and gender-mix of residents. A choice of rooms will be needed to allow for quiet activities, such as reading, talking to friends, playing board-games, and model-making, as well as more energetic activities such as table-tennis and pool. It is advantageous for there to be accommodation where boys and girls may mix socially, but also allowing them, particularly where there is a mixed age-range of younger and older children, to withdraw from each other when they wish.

Watching television is probably the most common leisure activity for children and young people. It is also likely to be the activity which causes most dispute between them and with adults. Even in the smallest children's homes, of say six or seven residents, more than one television would be valuable to prevent disputes over which programmes to watch. Similarly, more than one living or common room would allow for quiet and 'noisy' activities. As in many ordinary households, in a small home, the dining room can double-up as a living room, if suitably furnished.

5.2.4 *Kitchens – Large and Small*

The kitchen is an important focal point in any group life and children and young people need the experience of contact with the kitchen, food preparation and sharing food with adults. Necessary hygiene requirements in 'institutions' sometimes conflict with giving children access to kitchens and also with the provision of 'homely' kitchens where people can socialise. In large groups, such as boarding schools, 'homely' kitchens may be provided by kitchenettes in house groups where children can have free access, when the main large kitchen is out of bounds. In children's homes, nowadays, groups are usually sufficiently small for the kitchen to be an integral part of the group's life as it is in an ordinary household. Whatever the situation, all children and young people who are old enough to understand the dangers, need access to 'kitchens' where even the youngest can help make hot drinks with their carers, eat biscuits or snacks and talk with each other and the adults. Older children also need this interaction and increasing responsibility under appropriate supervision according to age and maturity, for cooking snacks and looking after themselves. Teenagers need access to a washing machine and ironing facilities, not only because it may be immediately useful in caring for their clothes, but also because it is an important step in learning life skills necessary to meet the challenges of living independently.

5.2.5 *Dining Rooms, Meals and Meal Times*

Provision of food is the most fundamental expression of caring and it is impossible to create a good living environment if children and young people do not enjoy their food. So the first thing to get right in a place where children live in a group is enjoyable food eaten in a convivial atmosphere. Meals form part of the regular pattern of life. They are looked forward to by everyone and, in a life which may lack many other satisfactions, they can provide comfort and even highlights, as well as necessary nourishment for growth, keeping well, and creative energy. The atmosphere of meal times is important. Even delicious food can be 'poisoned' by tension, anger, spiteful criticism, or a climate of fear and apprehension. Digestion can be adversely affected; there can be feelings of bitter disappointment and resentment; important relationships can be damaged and developing feelings of security set back. Every effort needs to be made to see that food is not only healthy, nutritious, tasty and well presented, but that it can be eaten in an atmosphere of good will and as much calm as possible. Children's eating patterns need to be treated with patience and understanding. Their habits mature over time and a child who initially will eat little more than cornflakes and cucumber, providing the quantities are adequate, will survive until a more balanced diet is attractive to him or her. Children should be offered a choice of food but not compelled to eat what they do not want. On the other hand, if a child does not enjoy any food, this must be a cause for concern, particularly since eating disorders are on the increase. The converse is the child who eats a great deal and still seems to want more. This may be related to emotional difficulties and many deprived children need to eat and eat and should be allowed to do so. Food, including fruit, should always be available, as it is in most children's own homes. These simple freedoms need sometimes to be insisted on!

Departmental Guidance:
'There should be fruit freely available in the children's homes'.

Comment overheard at staff meeting:
'But the children would only eat it!'

[Names and place available to the Editor]

It is vital that food is not 'institutional' and, as far as possible, there should be choices. This will be easier to achieve in large establishments than in small, but even small homes can overcome this by involving children and young people in making decisions about menus. Variety is important, and menus should be changed as often as possible. They should never become a standard pattern which is predictable according to the days of the week. Older children might sometimes be involved in preparing some meals, as another part of their preparations for living independently.

'There should be a choice of food in which children themselves engage; children should be involved in buying the food .... bulk buying is not a satisfactory means of getting food; food....... should not be locked away'

(Welsh NAYPIC)

Dietary differences for individual children, whether they relate to religious or cultural needs (for example, *halal* meat for children from Islamic cultures), or because of medical requirements, should be catered for and provided. In doing so the children should not feel vulnerable or that they are being singled out for special treatment. This can be achieved by menus which sometimes incorporate dietary differences into the general diet. Indeed, the great variety of food available today is a consequence of the culinary differences between cultures and religions in our multi-ethnic society. It is also important to use meals to mark special occasions and celebrations, birthdays, achievements, festivals, and surprises. Children, like all of us, are likely to store up happy memories of 'feasts' and 'special meals', carrying them forward as highlights of their childhood and adolescence. We all need happy memories and children away from home are no exception.

5.3 Grounds and gardens

Grounds and gardens are areas where the size of an establishment has to be taken into account. Most schools, and some larger children's homes, have grounds which accommodate sports facilities. Access to outdoor space provides that combination of geographical and emotional space that all children and young people need to let off steam, or just to put distance between themselves and other people. In addition, younger children in particular, both girls and boys, need areas where they can build 'dens', small territories which 'belong' to them as individuals or small groups. Since they may not always be under supervision, it is important that grounds and gardens are free from hazards and that garden implements, machinery, equipment and chemical substances are kept properly locked up when not actually in use by an adult.

In a small establishment, for example a children's home in a converted house, there may be a garden. The children should be encouraged to see this as part of their own space which they are able to use as and when they wish, and in a variety of ways, whilst respecting it as a facility which is also used by adults. Some, or all, of the residents may want to take responsibility for the upkeep of part of the garden and, where practicable, this should be encouraged. Children and young people are likely to benefit from being able to take pride in the garden, as they should with all areas of their home. Sometimes there is a difficult balance in achieving this. Managers and staff will wish to discourage the parent organisation from seeing the upkeep of the garden as a centralised responsibility (eg. of a local authority's recreation or parks department). On the other hand, it is not reasonable to expect busy child care staff to maintain gardens to save money. Outside help is likely to be necessary and, in some cases, a part-time gardener might work closely with the children and young people in maintaining and developing the garden. Where gardening can be incorporated into the normal caring activity of the home, and staff are willing to work with children and young people in the garden, this need not be a contentious issue. However, it should not be allowed to become a burden on heavily committed staff who have more important responsibilities. In considering properties for use by teenagers, a sensible approach would be to minimise external garden maintenance as far as possible. Most teenagers have a limited interest in gardens other than somewhere to sit in the sun when it appears!

5.4 The environment as a whole: The feel of the place

Suitable and well-maintained buildings and grounds are only the first step in creating a high standard of physical care. Staff and residents need to ensure that the living environment is one of which they can all be proud, and which they will want to look after and help maintain. There are two elements to this. Firstly, all furnishings and fixtures and fittings should be of a high standard; secondly, children and young people should be able to personalise their own spaces and be involved in making decisions on common areas such as living and common rooms. The aim should be to give children and young people a sense of investment in and responsibility for their home.

The quality of the furniture in a home or school is extremely important. In many establishments (including some local authority children's homes and some house units in boarding schools), the furniture looks as if it has been bought in a second-hand shop, or 'handed down' from somewhere else. Chairs and tables first bought many years ago and, in spite of heavy use, never repaired, renovated or replaced, are found too frequently. There is often, too, a dreary uniformity in curtains, soft furnishings and other equipment. This produces an institutional image even in a small building. Some inquiry reports have declared such low standards to be totally unacceptable. If the message children receive is that where they live does not matter to anyone, they are more likely to treat it without care themselves. It is an important part of their development that they should learn to understand and appreciate the importance of quality in their daily environment, and take responsibility for environmental matters. Furniture should be attractive, comfortable, 'homely' and every effort should be made to neutralise the institutional effects of things like fire extinguishers, etc.

Devolving budgets to the level of the individual establishment is fundamental to achieving a pleasant environment. Central purchasing of standardised items of furniture and other fittings does not produce a home of which residents can feel proud. All too often choices are made by staff elsewhere who have no interest in the home and little understanding of the task it performs.

When children or young people anticipate an extended period of residence, involving them in decisions about how to spend the money provided for obtaining their own furniture and fittings will increase their respect and investment in their living environment. The appropriate forum for such discussions may be an item on the agenda at regular weekly or monthly meetings, or it may be considered on a more ad hoc basis as and when the need arises. Whichever it is, it is an important educative process and staff can use it beneficially. Where decisions are made with young people, the process may be most successful if they have a range of options clearly related to the practical limits of available resources, rather than entirely open ended choice.

Where a young person's own personal space is concerned, usually a bedroom or study area, as far as possible, they should have some choice of furnishing and decoration and, within appropriate budgetary constraints, be left to make the final choice. Having to work to a limited budget; choosing wall paper, curtain material, duvets, chairs, wardrobes, beds and desks; dealing with other practical requirements will help their own development in taking responsibility for aspects of their own lives, and educate them in budgeting and other elements of independence.

5.5 Legislation

Underlying all discussion of the physical environment must be an awareness of relevant legislation which affects all buildings where children are looked after in groups. In particular this includes fire prevention requirements; health and safety at work legislation; building regulations and food hygiene regulations. It is also important that each establishment has a careful health and safety policy. There should be at least one member of staff on site who is trained in first aid and there is no reason why some young people should not also be trained in first aid techniques. Apart from the obvious benefits of having more than one 'first aider' on site, this too will help build up their sense of responsibility and self-reliance. The manager and others responsible for a home or school must ensure that all appropriate legislation is properly observed. They should therefore develop links with local fire prevention, building safety and food safety authorities in order to be sure their premises satisfy all legal requirements.

The Children's Homes Regulations 1991 and *DES Building Bulletin No. 7*, govern the standards which apply to fire safety precautions in children's homes and boarding schools respectively. All staff must understand these requirements, and ensure that they are also understood by the children and young people. Specific requirements include the need for fire alarms, extinguishers, fire escapes and fire stop doors; regular fire drills by day and night; testing of the equipment; and reporting to the local fire authority. We recognise that, particularly in smaller establishments, this may detract from the 'homely' feel of the establishment, but careful planning of such matters as where to place fire extinguishers could help to reduce this effect.

6   The Common Core

6.1 Introduction

This chapter looks at what we have called the 'common core' of good practice in residential settings. We ask what should be good practice and try to define what we mean by good care which can be applied wherever children and young people live away from home in groups. Issues particularly appropriate to individual settings are addressed in later chapters. Common factors are addressed here. These include involvement of children and young people in decisions about their daily lives and futures; their right to privacy; their need for stability in daily life; questions of control and discipline; relationships between children and young people; sexuality in young people; cultural issues which may affect any child; and the problems of misuse of tobacco, alcohol and drugs.

6.2 Care

6.2.1 Caring for Children and Young People

> *View of a residential worker:*
>
> 'Caring is about ... negotiation and compromise. It is about sharing parental responsibility ... It is about discussing the issues ... with parents and foster parents ... with field workers and discussing things with the youngsters themselves ... sometimes choosing the time when they are in a better mood.'

What is Care? What do we mean by 'care'? In the most basic terms it is the provision of physical and emotional comfort by another person. Care staff are not substitute parents, although their task inevitably involves some aspects of 'parenting', ie, taking on some of the roles, attitudes and day to day responsibilities which 'natural' parents exercise in caring for their children.

The caring task involves some essential ingredients in all residential settings. In 1979 Henry Maier, an American University child care teacher, discussed these ingredients[1] and suggested that they included the following, which we discuss briefly:

Bodily comfort. Providing bodily comfort, making sure that the physical needs of a child are met, and that the environment s/he lives in provides security, is the first task of staff. Maier commented

> *'as a child's bodily comforts are met, so does he or she feel actually treated with care'.*

A lack of physical comfort can make a child feel uncared for. Having needs for physical sustenance and comfort met will help children and young people be more receptive, and interested in experiences beyond immediate bodily demands. The more individualised or difficult elements of caring will then become easier to carry out. Bodily comfort is especially important when newcomers are being welcomed to a residential setting.

Differentiating between individuals. All children and young people are different. The world will not fall apart if children are treated as individuals and uniformity lost, nor is it necessarily fair to treat every child alike. Recognition of their individual needs (for example, for prolonged periods of personal attention, or to be left to themselves) is essential to their care. Staff need to differentiate the way in which they respond to children and young people, even if they appear in general to behave in the same way. Maier thought responsiveness to the individual more important than trying to achieve 'consistency across the group'. Caring is thus, in Maier's words, a

> *'reciprocal interactive process of mutual adaptation which requires time and experience'.*

Predictability. Knowing what is likely to happen in the immediate future, whether it be the next few minutes or the next few weeks, lends order and sanity to life. This is no less true for children and young people than it is for adults. It is essential therefore that care offers to them a sense of order in their life, enabling them to give meaning to their activities. If there is no sense of predictability and permanence children and young people are unlikely to be able to value and learn from their experiences, and their development will be affected. Feedback from adults is a vital element of that predictability. Maier noted that the use of approval by carers towards children is crucial in their upbringing, and should change with the age of the children. With younger children

---

[1] Henry W Maier 'The Core of Care: Essential Ingredients for the Development of Children Away from Home' Child Care Quarterly 8(3) Fall 1979

approval is easily used, and is essentially non-judgemental; with older children carers tend to evaluate and regulate activities. As Maier says:–

> *'Children require feedback on their competence rather than another check-off on adults' list of approved conduct'.*

He also stressed the importance of rhythm in childhood development, citing a baby's enjoyment of a rattle and a teenager's passion for music. The rhythm of relative predictability in day to day living provides a sense of security which is reassuring and enables young people to accept change when it is inevitable.

Dependability. As children and young people come to know and predict the way others in their lives will interact with them, they will be more able to develop a sense of dependence upon these people. The feeling of dependence creates attachment, and having attachments is essential to the well-being and sense of security of any child. Maier argued that in order to become independent it is first necessary to have experienced secure dependence on another person. It has been common practice in recent years, especially with older children, to discourage any dependency for fear that they may not be able to achieve independence and move on. Studies of attachment development, however, have concluded that a

> *'lack of dependent experience creates greater havoc in a child's development than prolonged dependence',*

and that dependency is natural, desirable and basic to child care. Recognition of this factor should encourage those responsible for placing children and young people not to move them on as soon as they appear to have settled down in a home or school, before they have had time to benefit from the experience of being able to be safely dependent. Staff in residential settings need to be allowed and encouraged to feel good about children who become dependent on them. The fear expressed by some professional social workers that, by allowing this to happen, the expectations of children will be raised unnecessarily, has too often prevented dependent relationships forming between residential staff and children. In recognising the need for dependence, residential staff may justifiably be advocates for stability, when others are proposing that a child be subjected to yet another move in the search for an 'ideal' placement. Some children have a deep need for time in which they can form a safe, dependent relationship before they should have to face further change.

Training in Personal Behaviour. As part of the caring task, staff have a duty to try to ensure that the children and young people in their care acquire acceptable standards of behaviour, both at home and in society at large. Maier believed this goes hand-in-hand with a close relationship between children and adults, and is therefore contingent on the effectiveness of the components of care already outlined above. He also considered that

> *'in child care settings, the children's continuous involvement with their larger community and with their own family or future foster or group home setting is of utmost importance'.*

Thus part of the role of residential staff is to foster and develop 'self-management', enriching the children's range of acceptable behaviour and involving the world outside the school or home in this task. By 'self-management' we mean children's capacity to set their own boundaries, make sensible decisions and generally behave appropriately.

Care for the care givers. This last component is vital. Maier urged that

> *'care can only be received to the extent that the care givers are personally prepared and ready to engage in these interactions'.*

To ensure that this is the case, carers need to be supported, assured of their own physical comfort and personal space, and given the proper resources for carrying out their task. Managers must ensure that staff have the resources and support necessary for them to do their job properly, and staff must feel able to tell their managers where this is not being provided. This element in Maier's 'ingredients' is one which has been highlighted again and again in inquiry reports in the UK, as Chapter 3 has shown.

PARENTING

'At the time that most of the group were in care official attitudes, training, and child care policy generally were discouraging residential social workers from attempting to be substitute parents and encouraging what was believed to be a more professional approach to the task. The group members were unaware of this trend and thus uninhibited by it in the emphasis which they gave to their own priorities.

Buildings, equipment, opportunities to play and the general physical atmosphere of homes were important, but to them the attitudes of staff and the atmosphere they created were the essence of any establishment as they saw it.

The staff who had twenty four hour a day responsibility for children, especially when those children were either without an effective parent or saw their parents relatively infrequently, had to respond to the child's basic human need for parenting or he remained deprived'.

'Growing up in Care – Ten People Talking' – Barbara Kahan 1979

Care staff, including house staff in boarding schools, as we have said, have to assume a number of roles in providing care for children and young people. Perhaps the most important involves many of the tasks a parent would carry out if the child were living at home. The term 'parenting' is important because although staff are not parents, they inevitably substitute for them in many ways.

The extent to which staff should assume the task of parenting depends on a number of different factors. The age of the child is one. Young children living away from home for the first time will feel the absence of parents keenly. They may need continual reassurance that their parents still care for them, and will be in regular contact. They may feel they have been rejected. Their parents may have tried to explain to them why they are being sent to live away from home but the children may still feel homesick or abandoned when they are first away from the love and affection they have known all their lives. Young children have an even greater need for comfort, affection and sympathy, than older children who may have learned to be more self-sufficient and come to rely more on their peers. Comfort and sympathy are usually provided by parents, but staff will need to provide them when children live in a group.

Children also differ in their rate of development and staff will have to judge how 'parental' their caring should be, according to the characteristics of each individual. Emotional age does not necessarily synchronise with chronological age, and emotional immaturity can occur where natural parenting has been inadequate. Older children living in groups may not require much 'parenting', particularly in later adolescence. They may feel more independent going on to university, work or training – and, as in the family setting, may to a large extent have taken control over most of their own life. Even so some, particularly those whose lives have been disrupted may have more need for parenting than they are willing to reveal. Even young people in loving and stable homes fluctuate in their need for dependency during adolescence and, although they may claim to be independent, they continue to make many of the demands of dependents.

Another factor to be considered in providing substitute parenting is the family background. Many children and young people enter group care, especially social services care, because they come from a background of family tensions, and often breakdown. Residential staff are entitled to know a child's background and family history, so that they can understand the extent of parental care and nurture. This will help them to decide how much of the parental role they should assume. A child may have no natural parents, or the parents may not have provided any of the parental love and support which most of us expect in childhood. In such cases staff may have to provide as much of the missing love and support as they can. In other cases, children and young people may feel their experience of family life has been so painful that they do not wish to have anyone acting 'parentally' towards them though often those who reject relationships which involve an element of parenting, when they have learned to trust their carers actually require more 'parental' care as though they were making up for lost time.

The feelings of parents always need to be taken into account. Parents, particularly the parents of children in care, will rightly feel aggrieved if they believe their position is being usurped by relative strangers. These reactions may be increased by feelings of guilt and residential staff will need to be sensitive to parents' reactions, particularly when they themselves have formed strong bonds with individual children. Discussions between staff and parents in some instances will help to determine the amount of 'parenting' which children require. In most cases, and especially with younger children, parents will understand better than anyone the needs, desires, character and idiosyncrasies of their child, and, if encouraged, may be a valuable source of information and advice. Staff can then develop a form of 'verbal contract' with the parents, agreeing what their child needs, and who will carry out various tasks.

The key is flexibility. Staff, in whatever setting, will need to consider how much of a parental role they should play. As a general rule the younger the child the more they are likely to need the affection and support which natural parents would normally provide. As children and young people grow older the need for parental support tends to attenuate (in a similar manner to the way in which parental rights over a child attenuate). In every case, though, judgements should be based on assessing the needs and views of both children and parents.

The task of residential care staff in relation to parenting will depend to a degree on whether a child is simply separated from parents, or is being looked after because, for the time being, there are no functioning parents. For the latter group, staff have to find ways of compensating children for loss of family life, whereas in the former situation it may be more a task of supplementing it. The residential staff's task can be seen as setting conditions and providing opportunities for children to take developmental steps appropriate to their age. In *'Looking After Children – Assessing Outcomes in Child Care'* (HMSO 1991), Parker et al have suggested there is a good consensus that satisfactory development is achieved along seven dimensions and have systematised the monitoring of good practice in a very practical way. They propose records should be used to assess children's progress from birth to adulthood, ie 18 years. Age ranges of varying length are used and the scheme as a whole is

'built upon what reasonable parents would do in order to achieve the best for their children.'

Each record form is divided into sections which, taken together, relate to the whole spectrum of development: health, education, identity, family and social relationships, social presentation, emotional and behavioural development, and self-care skills. The latter is omitted for children under one year old.

Each section begins by outlining what should be aimed at for a child of that age, and ends by asking how far these aims are being met. The records are intended not merely to measure performance, but also to identify how it might be improved. The aims assessed are closely linked to a number of practical tasks which both research and commonsense suggest are necessary to their achievement. The questions about these necessary practical tasks are intended to break down the task of bringing up children into a series of steps which can then be undertaken in order to improve their chances of achieving long term well-being in adulthood. When taken, these steps combine to provide a high standard of care.

Children away from home often experience homesickness. It is a healthy reaction and, in comforting a child, staff should acknowledge this and allow time to soften it. The distress which may be shown should not be seen as abnormal nor should a child be discouraged from telephoning home. In *'School Life – Pupils Views on Boarding'* – Roger Morgan found that:–

'Some pupils questioned the assumption that being distressed after phoning home was necessarily a bad thing, or made you more homesick if you took the whole day or week on average – 'it makes you cry just afterwards, but later on you feel better knowing you can phone again another time''.

Comfort may also be needed to relieve distress related to day to day incidents which would usually have been taken to parents. Staff need not try to emulate parents but should comfort children in a way which is appropriate to their own relationship with them. Sometimes distress is engendered by parents who are themselves over anxious and seem unable to let their child settle. In these circumstances staff may need to spend time reassuring the parents and even dealing with their distress in order to prevent their undermining the child's adjustment.

All that we have said about 'parenting' in this section is relevant to children and staff in boarding schools as well as children's homes. Boarding staff will need to offer comfort, counselling, support of many kinds just as care staff elsewhere do. For some, this will be part of their main task; for others it will be an addition to their teaching task. As such, it may not only be additional demanding work, but may at times present a conflict of roles which is not always easy to resolve. They should have their school's explicit support and recognition and not be left to do as much, or as little, as they can without the establishment taking corporate responsibility.

6.2.2 Ethnicity and Culture

In a multi-cultural society, schools and homes are likely to be microcosms of the differences arising from cultural, ethnic and religious groups. These differences can be seen as a positive feature of group life, emphasising a positive approach to being part of a society where individuals are valued for themselves and in which any attempt to stereotype groups or individuals on the grounds of ethnicity, religion, gender, culture, social background or sexual orientation are outlawed. Racist or sexist remarks, harassment or teasing should not be tolerated from anyone, staff or children, or in any circumstances. Instances which may arise need to be discussed both with the people concerned, and more generally in group discussions, so that staff and children understand clearly that everyone is valued for his or her own uniqueness.

RACIAL DISCRIMINATION

It may be helpful in considering racial discrimination to refer briefly to what the law requires, particularly the *Race Relations Act 1976*. What role can race relations legislation play in the lives of children and young people and their carers? Can it be used to promote equality of opportunities and esteem? Racism has many facets, one of which is racial discrimination. Under the *Race Relations Act* this is defined in four ways: direct and indirect discrimination, segregation and victimisation. [A note on the law as it relates to racial discrimination is contained in APPENDIX 5].

ETHNICITY AND CULTURE IN DAILY LIFE

Any children and young people arriving in a new home or school want to feel welcomed and valued. They need to see positive images of people like themselves around and, where possible, hear their language spoken and see books and papers written in it. Parents also need to know that staff will deal sensitively, caringly and positively with any racial incidents and that their child's racial and cultural needs will be met. Since every child is unique, their needs will not necessarily be met in the same way. Staff can prepare themselves in practical ways, by learning about the past experiences of each child and finding out, for example, something about the nature of their religious worship, festivals and other cultural events which are of importance to them. This may be especially important for refugee children and should be part of the caring task.

Cultural and religious festivals can become part of a home's or school's annual events and thus be valued and recognised. Space and privacy are needed and arrangements should be made for children of a particular religion to worship in their own way, and to engage in religious activities. Religion often plays a central role in their lives, and may be part of their 'duty' in honouring their family and life elsewhere. Allocation of part of a room, or a suitable quiet place in the house can provide for a shrine at which young people can offer their homage to the deity of their culture with security and without embarrassment.

Particular attention should be given to children and young people for whom English is not their first language, both in providing adequate opportunities for them to learn English quickly so that they can benefit fully from education and group living, but also in providing adequate interpretation wherever necessary.

For black and other ethnic minority children, daily routines and activities can create self-worth and confidence, and should emphasise the credibility and importance of their cultural norms and lifestyles. In many establishments, most routines and activities are based entirely on white European cultural experiences. This is not good practice. Access to black and other communities, links with other cultures, and a positive spirit which welcomes a variety of cultures in the school or home should be actively encouraged. Black children in homes and schools have special needs stemming from their ethnic background, colour, culture and position in British society. Different cultural groups have different views of the family and for children from ethnic minorities who have spent their early life within their own family and then come to live in a group for the first time, what are considered appropriate British behaviour and responses to staff in the school or home may vary from what the young person is used to. The strength of family life is very rarely replicated for any child in a residential establishment, but it may be much less so for children from black or Asian families. Gaining their advice on appropriate pictures, individual items of furnishings and choices of food can help to create a mutually acceptable climate for daily living which is the essence of good cross cultural relationships.

Residential care provides a real opportunity to introduce children and young people to new ideas. Why should a home not, for example, equip itself with a small collection of recipe books demonstrating food preparation in different countries. Even if they do not all find their way on to the meal table, some could and would, in any case, be a colourful and interesting conversation starter. Similarly, vegetarian cook books demonstrate how tasty meals can be made without meat.

What we are saying is that staff must not be 'colour blind'. Attempting to 'treat everybody the same' is not good practice. It is likely to result in some groups being treated less favourably than others where there are different cultural groups in a home or school. In a similar vein, it should not be assumed that black staff are the only ones who can care for black children and be responsible for everything concerned with ethnicity. They may find themselves in the role of trying to provide all the answers to the establishment's ethnic minority issues, and also being expected to provide support for white staff members. This is unfair and amounts, in itself, to a form of discrimination. In dealing with the prejudices which underlie racism we also need to recognise differences in life experiences between generations and the additional stress this can bring about. For example older black staff may be holding on to the past rather than embracing the present and future with which a young person is grappling. Acceptance of ethnic and cultural differences needs to be embedded in everyday living with choice about staff to whom to relate. This must include recognising that a young person may not want to relate to a particular ethnic member of staff, because although they may be black they may have generational or cultural differences which need to be discussed and worked through. Young people need sufficient detailed knowledge of their culture to understand it fully, and it is important for their identity to see black people in positions of authority. For some young people who are particularly confused about their origins, carefully planned visits to their parents' home country could be helpful.

Finally, and this is especially true in social services settings, there can be problems about placements of black children being made in inner city areas primarily on the basis that they will then be amongst black people in the community around them. This is not a straightforward issue and should not be over simplified. To make such choices there need to be ongoing contacts in and out of the home and young people's horizons and options should not be limited by rigid adherence to location primarily or mainly on the basis of skin colour.

6.2.3 Privacy Issues

Privacy and the opportunity to be alone is as important to children and young people as it is to adults. In settings where children and young people are required to share bedrooms, they need space elsewhere to enable them to have time to themselves in private. In general, the need for privacy increases as children get older. Young children often prefer to share a bedroom with others; it can give a feeling of security, and may help to prevent them from feeling frightened at being left alone at night. Older children often prefer their own room. Although some establishments will not have sufficient accommodation to provide for every child who needs or wants a single room, wherever possible this should be the objective.

Children and young people should be asked about their preferences, and these preferences should be acted on, as far as possible, when allocating rooms. There are no hard and fast rules about how many people should occupy a bedroom. In boarding schools many children share bedrooms with several other pupils for much of their school careers. For those up to about the age of 14 groups are probably better kept to not more than four to six, a size which seems generally successful in that context. Those aged 14–16 generally prefer twin or single rooms, and those over sixteen are likely to want single rooms. This is particularly important for older children who need sufficient room for private study. The gradual growth of independence is also an important factor in provision of private space.

The situation may not be as straightforward with children and young people looked after by social services departments. The survey commissioned for the Warner Inquiry found that up to one-third of residents in children's homes were likely to have been sexually abused before they were admitted. This means that great care has to be taken in considering backgrounds and past behaviour before children and young people are asked to share rooms. Children who have been sexually abused may, through no fault of their own, have responded by showing high levels of sexuality even at a young age and it cannot be assumed that, for example, because a child is only ten or eleven, he or she will not act in a sexual manner towards other children. Following the publication 'Another Kind of Home' the Scottish Office Social Work Services Group has published guidance about 'Children and HIV' and also on working with children and adolescents who sexually abuse other children.

> 'Placing a youngster who has abused another youngster in residential accommodation should be prefaced by careful planning. The vulnerability of the other children in the unit will need to be considered alongside the ratio of staff to children. The ethos of the unit and the attitudes of staff will also need to be taken account of. Residential staff and carers will require to be clear about their task and have worked out safeguards to ensure that opportunities to abuse are not created'.

100 *Growing up in Groups*

(*'Working with Children and Young People who Sexually Abuse other Children'*, Chapter 4, *Child Protection: Practice Guidance for Social Workers*, Social Work Services Inspectorate (Scotland) (Draft) 1994)

The need for privacy includes privacy while changing, showering or bathing. Although some variation is likely according to age and sex, once children reach about 11 they require such privacy, and many would prefer it at younger ages. They should never be obliged to shower or bathe in the presence of others if they do not wish to and even if there are communal showers and bathrooms, some choice of privacy should be available. They should also not have to appear naked in front of staff who need to be sensitive to children's modesty and embarrassment.

Pupils' Specifications for Boarding (from School Life) – The Pupil's 'Best Buy':–

3.2.20. 'bathrooms and toilets distributed through the house and near dormitories, rather than centralised in one area or block; individually curtained or partitioned showers (with the option of a bath in privacy) for personal washing (communal showers being acceptable for after games or swimming, but not generally for personal washing)';

3.2.21. 'toilets in individual cubicles with lockable doors and 'full height' doors and partitions, regularly cleaned, well ventilated, not smelly, in working order, and with a constant supply of toilet paper';

Privacy for children is particularly important in relation to the presence of men where girls live, and the presence of women where boys live, in bedroom areas in the evening, or when children are likely to be undressed. Staff need to be aware both of the sensitivities of children and young people to visits from adults and peers of the opposite sex, and the need for those who share common-rooms, bedrooms or dormitories to have their privacy safeguarded. This equally applies to staff visiting bedrooms. Although there cannot be 'no-go areas', privacy should be safeguarded by a preliminary knock and a polite request 'May I come in?' Politeness of this kind does not undermine staff authority – it is more likely to enhance mutual respect.

'There is no quiet room at X ... If you want to be quiet you have to go to the toilet'

(*'Answering Back' – The Dolphin Project*)

It is essential for children to have and be secure about space that is private to them, and into which others cannot come without being invited. Such space should include bedrooms or parts of bedrooms.

Where rooms are shared, this may mean having spaces between desks or wardrobes and beds in a shared bedroom, and the space around a desk. Children and young people should also have space in a lockable cupboard where they can keep personal possessions. Sometimes curtains or screening attached to furniture can increase privacy where sharing is unavoidable. Children should not be asked to change bedrooms either frequently or as a matter of routine. This can, and often does, happen for reasons of administrative convenience, and every effort should be made to avoid it. It undermines any sense of permanence and security, and often creates strong feelings of resentment not only because of the disruption but towards the hapless child who may be seen as the cause of it. Where there is weekly boarding in boarding schools, ie. four or five nights per week, staff need to be especially careful to create a secure base for each child otherwise weekly boarding can prove unsettling.

6.2.4 The Daily Routine

Life in a residential group is likely to benefit from rather more organisation of time and activity than ordinary family life and staff need to encourage participation in activity although it should not become a cause for confrontation. Instead staff should make as many opportunities as possible for young people to enjoy life and broaden their experience, whilst keeping necessary routines and rules to a minimum. This is especially important in children's homes in which care and control have to go hand in hand. Young people frequently describe life in children's homes as intolerably boring and control problems often increase as a result. Research identifies acquisition of useful skills as a factor in the success of a residential setting, and activities will be a main factor influencing this.

THE USE OF TIME

Time can hang heavily for children and young people in groups, especially at weekends. During the week normally everyone will be involved in some form of education or training. Unhappily, experience demonstrates that nowadays this is not always the case in children's homes. Places in schools may be difficult to find; some children will have been excluded from school; places often cannot be found on training schemes for those beyond school-leaving age. This can make the job of residential staff far more difficult than is reasonable. Children and young people with a low boredom threshold need to have constant opportunities for activities, play or purposeful occupation. If a residential home has such an accumulation of difficulties, senior management may need to provide additional help; for example, extra staff or teaching help from outside.

Time spent on 'routines' is best kept to a minimum, although some structured use of time gives order to the day. Children and young people benefit from being free to decide for themselves what to do in their spare time, as long as it does not harm themselves or others or infringe on similar rights of other children and young people. An imposed structure of 'uplifting' activities is unlikely to be as helpful to children and young people as encouragement to use their time constructively. Adolescents especially like to spend time with their friends and should not be obliged to undertake structured activities in what they see as their leisure time.

During each day, however, a certain amount of time needs to be structured closely and spoken for eg. meal times, school or lesson times, and bedtime. There will also be times when activities are organised, as already described. Then time is needed when children can do something on their own or in cooperation with others, or just do nothing. As they grow older they should be able to take more responsibility for themselves and have more opportunities to make choices about the organisation of their lives, including spending some of their own time in a place which they can call their own, where they can do what they wish without having to ask others for permission.

TIME SHARED WITH STAFF

'My ideal person is honest, open, not frightened to let you know what's going on and able to fight for the things you need.'

(Birmingham Youth Forum – comment on residential staff)

Children and young people need time with staff in a similar way to 'prime time' in many families. Prime time will occur, for example, during meal times, which should be important social events, and evenings or the quiet times before lights-out. It is important that these 'family times' are allowed for in planning daily routines and working patterns because they can easily be squeezed out and lost.

Staff routines in home or school, where practicable, may usefully allow older children to take a degree of responsibility for younger ones. This may not always be possible, and staff will have to judge carefully the ability and readiness of older children to take on this responsibility. In any event, routines should never be so fixed and inflexible that older or more dominant children have opportunities to hold sway over younger or more vulnerable individuals, otherwise harassment and bullying can and are likely to occur.

Young people themselves welcome being more involved in decision-making in their home or school. They can contribute to the care, upkeep and running of the establishment if encouraged to do so. The planning of activities can also usefully be discussed between staff and young people, on a regular basis. This may be particularly useful during holiday times when time can hang heavy and the supportive structure – especially of a children's home can begin to fall apart. Schools also should not forget pupils who board termly or for 52 weeks per year and may be there when the majority of pupils have gone home either at weekends or for the school holidays. As well as the children being able to participate with staff, schools need to be sure that there are sufficient staff on duty to provide the proper level of care at such times, not just a 'skeleton' staff. The children's inability to go home may be underlined for them if they see that the arrangements made for them are makeshift. By engaging both individuals and groups of children in planning and looking ahead, staff can provide good role models, a supportive structure for them and the ground work needed to ensure good control without having to resort to sanctions. Not every aspect of daily living, however, can be negotiated and some routines may be necessary to simplify certain aspects of community life particularly if groups are large and the children themselves bring little stability. Where rules and routines are necessary, as some undoubtedly are, involving young people in discussion and contributing to what the rules should be, as we have said earlier, is likely to be a constructive method. Getting up, bedtimes, homework arrangements and planning chores are especially likely to need certain routines and rules. If kept to a minimum, and agreed as reasonable, they will enable and encourage good order, and be seen to be necessary.

Talking seriously and constructively with children and young people is also important in the staff's general care of them. All too often staff and young people, without intending to, can fall into an exchange of banter and good-natured abuse which, whilst having its place, can lead to communication never rising above the banal. Adult style conversations and exchanges outside an educational setting help young people to feel they are being taken seriously and enable them to test out their own verbal and reasoning skills. Talking together in this way will also develop staff/children relationships and add interest and stimulus to daily life in the home. Staff themselves may also see new perspectives of the children and gain opportunities for better individual communication. A frequent task is sorting out petty rows between children, very important to them, but difficult to deal with sensitively unless the adults know the children well.

ACTIVITIES

Many residential establishments, particularly boarding schools, place a great deal of emphasis on the activities they provide for their pupils. In schools it is especially important for both boarders and day pupils to share in the range of activities, even to some extent over a weekend. Children of all ages have a right to play. Good practice will mean that a wide range is provided to suit all ages and abilities. Activities may usefully include some which involve the children and young people in the life of the local community, perhaps by contributing to the welfare of other groups in the community, eg, helping out in a local youth club or doing some voluntary work.

The range of activities in any establishment is likely to depend on its size and resources. Boarding schools are generally better equipped than children's homes, although contact with community groups may compensate to some extent for this. We recognise that staff in children's homes, looking after some disaffected young people, may feel that organised activities are 'pie in the sky' and doomed to failure. This can be seen as a difficult 'chicken and egg' situation in which young people become disaffected, partly because they are so bored and partly because disaffected staff are sceptical of the value of creative occupations which challenge habits of despondency and depression.

It may take a lot of persistence and optimism in these circumstances to initiate and develop interesting activities, but they are important, particularly when education may not be providing satisfying experiences and opportunities to learn and develop. Volunteers may be of help in this context, particularly if they have skills, hobbies or interests which may engage the children's interest. The television is likely to be in great demand, but it is not good practice to rely on it as a time filler or to allow it to take the place of adequate staffing when young people are not in school or further education. It is not good practice to assume that, providing staff 'cover' is available, 'parental' responsibilities are honoured. Senior managers need to recognise the importance of adequate staff time, particularly in evenings and at weekends when activities can provide many opportunities for building helpful relationships with young people less directly and often more effectively than in face to face discussions.

6.2.5   Continuity and Change

In this section we argue that stability and continuity are not only essential for good care but they are the necessary conditions for a child to grow up well. If a child is uncertain of where s/he will be living, and more importantly, who with, in a few weeks or a few months time, s/he is unlikely to be able to develop the network of friendships and relationships so essential to security and care. It is traditional in boarding schools for pupils to board from the age of 8 or 11–13 and remain there until the age of 18. A few pupils may be moved from school to school throughout their childhood. Where this happens, there is likely to be an adverse effect on both their care and their education. Even so, it is uncommon for more than a small minority of pupils to change schools within an academic year.

'The friends I have made in boarding school are friends for life because I have shared a large and important stage of my life with them and intend to continue to do so.'

(Girl in boarding school – Response to Wagner Group Inquiry)

The picture is often very different in social services care. We have already seen how children and young people being looked after by a local authority may have to endure many changes in placement throughout their care experience, and local authorities need to consider ways of avoiding this as much as possible. There is little benefit to be gained by constantly moving from one setting to another in an attempt to find the 'right' placement, while the child or young person becomes increasingly damaged and unable to trust adults.

'I was moved so often I gave up trying to make friends'

(Boy in care)

'The reading of several hundred voluminous files on secure unit children is a sobering experience. They are an indictment of the child care system. Children are shuffled from one short term placement to another in the vague hope that they will stick somewhere. Some boys have had eight placements in a year ..... They return occasionally to assessment centres for additional uncomplimentary labels and then they are on their way again. They find the experience disintegrating ....

'Locking up Children' – Spencer Millham, Roger Bullock, Kenneth Hosie – 1978 Saxon House

The first factor in ensuring continuity is the family. For example, when children are being looked after by a local authority, acknowledged positives in a family which may, in other respects, have been unable to support the child, should be built on and participation between them and the children's home encouraged. In boarding schools, parents also need to be involved as much as possible. Some will be based overseas, but increasingly schools with boarding serve a regional rather than a national or international market. Parents are likely to be encouraged to attend matches, social events, parents' evenings and to take their children out. The growth of weekly boarding sustains close parental contacts with school and more flexible approaches to overnight home leave enable parents of termly boarders to gather their families together for weekends at more frequent intervals.

Children's homes may be able to learn much from these kinds of
activity, especially where contact with a child's family is infrequent, or
there are other difficulties such as those caused by long distances.
Holding small events or social occasions, providing facilities for
occasional overnight stay for parents, provision of fares or arrangements
for transport may make it much more possible and enjoyable for some
parents to visit. Sharing parental responsibility means carers and parents
taking a positive part in the daily lives of children and young people in
order to ensure that continuity is sustained. Parents who often feel
defeated by their lives, need encouragement to be more involved. Where
a child in a children's home has little or no contact with family, building
a relationship with the child's independent visitor may go a little way to
fill the gap.

Everyone who has responsibility for a child, whether a parent or
voluntary, private or public authority, must regularly ask themselves
'how well is this child growing up?' and then go on to ask what is
needed to best enhance the child's development. Residential staff have a
key role to play in supporting children and young people through
changes. This means 'sticking with the child through the good times and
the bad times', putting up with difficult behaviour, and where necessary
demonstrating disapproval of the behaviour, but not the person. In
boarding schools house tutors may be a child's advocate when there are
discipline problems and although not every home or school has 'non
exclusion' policies, the professional value that children stay with you
and that difficult behaviour does not automatically mean moving on,
should be the rule wherever possible rather than the exception.
Residential care may not be able to provide totally unconditional love,
but a very real kind of loving can be conveyed through the expression of
genuine concern for how well a child is growing up coupled with a
willingness to hang on when 'the going gets tough'.

Some children and young people live away from home in a group
setting for as much as 60 or 70 percent of their childhood years,
especially if they attend boarding school from seven or eight years old,
or are looked after by a local authority from an early age. Each one
arrives in the system as a pre-adolescent child and leaves – if they stay
the course – as a young adult with most of the rights and responsibilities
of adulthood. Staff who care for them need to be aware of the
implications of this and homes' and schools' guidelines for care staff and
day to day practices should reflect this major responsibility. Good
practice will involve planning for a child's growth and development
through the care that is provided and in the way responsibility is
progressively encouraged, first for self, then for others, and then with a
growing awareness and concern for their environment.

A child has a right to learn to exercise responsibilities in these areas.
Opportunities to do so exist in all areas of residential group life: through

work in the classroom; in a school; taking responsibility for peers and younger children in home or school; participating in organising activities; as well as the way in which attitudes towards and appreciation of the community and the environment develop. These targets can be embodied in the aims of a home or school so that they are explicit and shared by staff and children.

> 'Boarding Experience has helped me to learn to compromise socially .... try to give and take while getting what you want. Learn to respect other people's rights, privacy, thinking , way of life etc'
>
> *Response to Wagner Group's questionnaire from young person in boarding school*

6.3 Behaviour

6.3.1 Control Issues

> 'I don't think they should use pocket money to get back at us'
> 'I think they should ground us for short periods but we should still be able to see our families'
> 'They shouldn't hit us or stop our pocket money'
>
> *'Answering Back' – Report by Young People Being Looked After on the Children Act 1989, The Dolphin Project 1993*

There can be no doubt that where children are cared for in establishments which have a clear purpose; where staff are clear about what is expected of them; and which are well managed, control is less likely to be a problem. If control is a constant preoccupation of residential staff then this is a matter to be addressed by senior staff and external managers. It is likely that adequate support and clear enough objectives are lacking.

Evidence from SSI inspection reports suggest that, where there are serious control problems in a children's home, they are likely to be associated with ineffective and ill informed external management, poor leadership in the home, lacking in clarity of purpose, and inadequate training. General problems of control are not the result of paucity of sanctions or specific techniques of control. The DoH guidance on permissible means of control clarifies when physical intervention or restriction of liberty is appropriate but this guidance alone will not bring good order to a home where staff are poorly managed, poorly trained and poorly led.

It would be unrealistic, however, to think that children being looked after in residential settings will not present problems of control or discipline if they are simply cared for well. But care and control are interrelated and part of the staff task is to engage with children to discuss the circumstances in which they may need to be controlled or disciplined. A process of negotiation between the staff and the children can mean that, as far as possible, the children 'own' the control measures. By 'own' we mean that the children are aware they have participated and agreed in the decisions reached. As we have said elsewhere, as children get older they need to be able to take more responsibility for their own actions. This also means that staff have to take some risks by 'letting go' of them, allowing them to take their own risks so that they gradually learn to manage their own lives. Staff also have to make judgements about the level of risk involved in 'letting go' and be prepared to defend their decisions if things go wrong. (There is discussion of degrees of risk-taking in Guidance issued by the Department of Health, extracts of which are attached in APPENDIX 6). This means too that senior managers must recognise that staff who have to carry out these negotiations, and make such difficult decisions, are entitled to guidance and support in doing so.

Interventions and consequences, and the impact of one child's behaviour upon another, need to be a discussed between children and young people and staff during the quieter times when there is no crisis. The group can then understand and 'own' what will ensue in the event of unacceptable behaviour. New children too, will need to be inducted into this process. Discussions can be stimulated by 'what if' games – proposing situations, and asking children and young people to discuss how they should be dealt with. An anticipatory approach to control is essential if children are to develop self-control through making choices as they grow up. They will make better choices if they have been able to rehearse them beforehand.

When controls are necessary, good practice will stress the importance of rewards rather than sanctions. Rewards may be good conduct marks, additional privileges or some other measure, but the most successful rewards in any school or home are those provided by staff who recognise effort and provide genuine praise and support for what a child is doing. Sanctions may be necessary, but in a good home or school they will not cause lasting resentment. They will be seen to be fair by all concerned, and administered promptly and recorded. Where children have behaviour problems it is not helpful to 'tot up' their transgressions until they are so overburdened they cannot cope with the result. It is likely to be better to deal with each event as seems most appropriate at the time, seeing each day as far as possible as a new start. A sanction, when deemed necessary, should be reasonable in the sense that the child can understand the connection between the 'offence' and the sanction.

Sanctions in the form of withdrawal of privileges are likely to be the most effective. Often privilege and responsibility are linked in the ethos of the home or school and privileges have to be earned through effective fulfilment of responsibility.

> 'Frustration with rules and discipline of communal school life featured consistently as a perceived negative aspect of being a boarder in all types of schools, being reported as being 'a worst thing' by approximately a third of pupils in preparatory, secondary and special schools. Pupils expressed their view of this aspect of boarding life in terms such as being organised by bells and timetables, seen generally as a necessary negative. One pupil said' life is set"
>
> *(School Life: Pupils Views on Boarding – Roger Morgan)*

Corporal punishment is illegal in children's homes, in maintained schools and, for certain categories of pupils, in independent schools. Most independent schools now no longer use it. Research[1] indicates that corporal punishment, apart from considerations of child abuse, is rarely, if ever, an effective sanction and in most cases will be contrary to effective control and discipline.

The Department of Health guidance on control for staff working in children's homes, referred to earlier, although not appropriate for all settings, contains valuable advice for group living situations generally and could, with benefit, be used as an in-service development document. Meanwhile, we turn to discussion of an issue which has deeply concerned many staff and which, in essence, led to the publication of the Guidance. Staff in some residential settings had felt themselves disempowered by provisions of the *Children Act 1989* and by the severe public criticism engendered by inquiries such as *Pindown* and the Frank Beck affair. We believed that in attempting to assist staff by publishing a book on good practice in group life for children and young people, we should not evade such issues which inevitably arise in the care of very difficult children.

6.3.2 Looking After Very Difficult Children

This is a problem which primarily concerns children's homes but is also experienced by a number of special boarding schools, particularly those for emotional and behaviourally disturbed children and young people. Some children in residential care at times can present behaviour which is bewildering, unpleasant, frighteningly hostile, self destructive and undermining of all attempts at control. The confusion which gives rise to

1 See "Issues of Control in Residential Child Care", Dartington Social Research Unit, HMSO 1981.

it is particularly evident in young people who, through their childhood and adolescence, have experienced periods in foster homes, children's homes, in-patient psychiatric units and secure accommodation. At times there is uncertainty about whether the *Children Act* or the *Mental Health Act* is the right framework to use to keep them safe and try to meet their needs. There may be a problem of diagnosis, but more often there is reasonable understanding of the broad causes of their behaviour but very little specific treatment available other than good consistent care. It so often falls to residential staff to provide just that when a child or young person appears to be doing everything possible to frustrate their attempts to do so.

It is easy to deride the prescription for 'good consistent care' in treating children whose behaviour is extreme and bewildering. Some staff need to feel they are achieving something more specific. We suggest, however, that it is an important professional discipline in homes or schools to establish 'good consistent care' as the prevailing method. Whatever specific treatments are provided in a residential facility, they should always take place within this context. Volumes 4 and 5 of the *Children Act Guidance* series make this clear and set out in broad terms the constituents of good care. Part of good consistent care is recognising that difficult behaviour can be very difficult to 'manage'. Knowing how to 'manage' it is important not only for the individual concerned but also for other residents and staff as well. It is also important to recognise that managing the behaviour does not preclude understanding it or, at least, seeking to understand it. The question 'why?' should always be asked and continue to be asked as long as necessary. An example we were offered demonstrates this. A young person was found on the roof of a children's home slashing his body with broken glass. He had been increasingly aggressive for a few days before and efforts had been made to 'manage' him safely. However, the staff group had forgotten the fact that he was due to go to court in a few days for a serious offence which had also involved the accidental death of a close friend. No one had asked the young person about what he was feeling. In addition, no one had spent time helping him to prepare for the court appearance. No wonder he had resorted to extreme behaviour to let people know he was distressed.

Specific approaches or treatments can sometimes concentrate on a particular aspect of a child, for example an undesirable behavioural trait such as spitting, or losing one's temper. Where they are indicated they should of course be provided, but if the entire care regime is made up of a series of treatments directed at aspects of a child's behaviour, there is a danger that the 'whole child' will be lost in a range of fragmented treatment encounters.

The message is that no matter how difficult a child is, it is the care staff's job to find ways of integrating children into a milieu of good care;

to get them to enjoy a meal in a sociable group; to help them take pride in their appearance; to encourage education in whatever form is possible at the time; to understand the significance of their right to be consulted and to work out plans for the future. These are not unrealistic expectations. They are the fundamentals the care worker must address, even in the face of unrelenting 'testing out'; 'detached indifference' in an affectionless child; or 'confused despair' in a child who has suffered prolonged abuse.

The extremes which staff have to face include young people who have committed serious crimes eg rape, or young people on remand who are preoccupied with a delinquent crisis of offending. They may also be expected to care for children who experience complex self destructive urges; butane sniffers, those who take overdoses, and slash their wrists, and some with disturbing behaviour which has not been properly diagnosed, and may be on the brink of psychiatric illness.

This seems like a 'tall order' and it is. The care of difficult children requires skills and understanding at a number of levels. We are not saying that because good and consistent care is basic, it is therefore straightforward, easily provided or a relatively low status and low skill task. We are saying that the delivery of basic care to difficult children is a difficult and specialised task requiring basic skilled practice, professionally authoritative oversight and strong internal and external management as well as considerable commitment in the individual staff concerned. The staff also need help in holding on and coping with failure which, from time to time, is inevitable.

What are the key pointers to providing good and consistent care for the difficult child?

(i) *Care and assessment as repeating and linked activities*

It is too simple to expect assessment, diagnosis and treatment to form a simple sequence. The way a child is cared for may change behaviour and therefore require reassessment. This may change perceptions of the child's needs and consequently how the child might best be cared for and treated. We should not be surprised at this, since growing up itself is a process of change and a child whose life experiences cause his route to maturity to be unusually difficult will make frequent changes of direction. The care worker contributes to understanding an individual's growing up process by noting how they respond to the prevailing care conditions. Is the child responsive to firm direction, or is this rejected out of hand? Does the child seek affection and what happens if it is offered? Outbursts of dangerous or destructive behaviour need to be brought under control, but they also need to be understood in the context of their happening. What sparked it off? The worker may have his or her observations, but this is also something that needs to be talked through with the child:–

> *'Lets try and find out what made you lose your rag this evening. If there is something wrong we may be able to put things right or we might be able to find ways to help you keep control a bit better.'*

In the course of caring for a child the care worker will engage them in a way which discovers more about background, needs and motivations. This should not and need not be intrusive: children should not be put under pressure to divulge more than they want to. But good care of difficult children needs to keep the door constantly open so that a child can offer insight into the way past experience has shaped current response to the world. This expectation could be part of the 'deal' struck between a child and his carers at the time admission is negotiated:–

> *'We will try to care for you as best we can and put up with how awful you can be at times, but in return we hope you will help us understand you better by telling us about your life as far as you can'.*

Residential child care workers need to keep good written records. Writing skills are important for the professional task. As part of recording events, care staff may record observations on how a child responds to changes and conditions in the home. It is one of the tasks of the key worker to review the records of their child with a view to discovering what trends the cumulative information reveals. These observations can then be usefully recorded in a periodic commentary. Quarterly summaries may be appropriate in long term placements whilst weekly summaries would be necessary in short term transition placements. Whatever the circumstances, the purpose is to use record keeping, necessary in any case for reasons of accountability, as a tool to gain a better understanding of individual children through the pursuit of good consistent care.

(ii) *To the extent that a child will allow, work needs to be done on the problems which led to admission to the home or school*

An approach to behaviour which is confined to the here and now can become mechanistic and irritate a child, unless s/he can see a sensible purpose in relation to making progress through life. If children from generally supportive families are in residential care because of learned delinquent behaviour, then systematic achievement levels and rewards for good behaviour to help them get back on course may make sense, at least while they are there. Children who have suffered intra familial abuse, distorted or dysfunctional family relationships, however, are unlikely to benefit solely from systematic sanctions and rewards. They will need opportunities to talk and try to understand the origins of their distress and behavioural difficulties. This may require both receptive and sympathetic care from home or school and psychotherapeutic counselling provided by an outside professional. Many complicated and difficult children between these two extremes will be in residential care for a 'cocktail' of reasons. These may involve parental ambivalence or partial rejection, low educational achievement and fear of learning,diversionary crime and substance abuse. Residential care staff will need to engage each child individually in planning to tackle their problems. This may mean finding an educational input which a child can face; establishing an acceptable means of communication with the family; examining the circumstances in which offenses occur and, trying to work out legitimate diversions or 'escape routes' to avoid further offending. Good care planning and the ideas and schedules advocated in *'Looking After Children'* (described later in this chapter) will help the care worker in this task.

(iii) *Consistency does not mean the same for everyone*

Children with difficulties are likely to find it harder to conform to uniform expectations than most able and privileged children. They will inevitably have to make some concessions to group living and the way respect for others is observed will be a regular feature of group and individual discussion. However a child will not experience consistency if his needs are always subordinated to the needs of the group as a whole. That will feel like regimentation and alienation. Consistency for the child means being able to rely on an appropriate response to his or her demands whether these are expressed maturely or acted out through dysfunctional behaviour. Appropriate responses may differ from child to child, and consistency has to be tailored to individuals. This is particularly true for example with children who have learning disabilities or are autistic. How individual consistency of response is achieved will be a matter for care planning and behaviour management meetings which should be recorded in the child's case notes. Experience demonstrates that consistency can easily disappear if a young person does not respond immediately to a demand or sanction. It needs to be maintained for some time for a young person to learn. Simply increasing the expectations or the sanctions will, in the face of 'no changes' be unlikely to be productive and may worsen the problem.

(iv) *Do not gloss over the evident concerns in the hope that they will go away when the child has settled in*

Sadly there are research studies (*Child Care Research, Policy and Practice,* ed. Barbara Kahan 1989, Hodder and Stoughton) on children in care which demonstrate that problems often get overlooked. Young people looking back on a period of living in children's homes often complain that 'nobody took any notice'. This may have been about a specific health problem, a desire to make contact with a person significant to the child, or a learning problem. These concerns may not be obviously or directly related to immediate difficult behaviour but if they are important to the child, the fact that they appear to be ignored contributes to his/her overall sense of despondency and frustration, as the same situation would in an adult.

Glossing over anxieties can sometimes take the form of jollying the child along, or making light of a worry in the hope that it will help the child 'to get it into proportion'. But there is a limit to how far a child can make light of, for example, a minor disfigurement which s/he is struggling to live with. Good natural humour, may have its place in helping 'fragile egos' become more robust, but if these responses seem to the child to deny his pain or anxiety, then they are destructive and will provoke bad behaviour. There are important professional judgments by care staff to be made here. Good humour, even gently making fun of children, can sometimes help them strengthen their ability to cope with adversity, but this can only occur if the problem has been acknowledged and worked with and more importantly that the staff member concerned is trusted by the child because they have shared the experience of tackling the problem.

(v) *Keep other professionals right up to date and require their support, advice and direct intervention*

Residential staff looking after children with bewildering and difficult behaviour need support from other professionals. This was recognised in the Utting and Warner reports, particularly with respect to psychiatric and psychological support. The availability of this support is a matter for senior managers in health, education and social services to achieve but residential staff can help by making intelligent, apposite referrals or requests for support. By keeping other professionals informed, there is less likelihood of a referral being seen as off-loading the problem. Too many difficult young people get passed around from agency to agency, placement to placement. There is a better chance of stabilising a difficult child through good consistent care in a home or school supplemented with continuing additional professional support. It is most important that this support is both forthcoming from other professionals and nurtured by care staff if we are to avoid situations where children are moved yet again because the current placement does not meet all their needs. Some placements in in-patient adolescent psychiatric units might have been avoided if a psychiatrist were supporting a child and the work of the care staff in a children's home. On the other hand, if there were more adolescent psychiatric beds, some young people who are inappropriately cared for in children's homes could be given the right treatment in the right place.

Essential to working alongside other professionals is the need to sort out who does what, and who is responsible for what. Residential care staff will be closest to and in touch with the whole child and his world and, in consequence, will be key figures in coordinating the work of other professionals even if this is often still mediated through field social workers. Residential workers should not hesitate to put these understandings in writing. Although the natural medium for care staff may be the telephone, confirmation in writing both avoids misunderstandings and concentrates the mind. It is important that child care staff should not allow themselves to become isolated with serious problems which impinge on the proper concern of other professionals eg. doctors, teachers, police and probation officers. Written communication adds significance and professional formality to the message and will help care staff to be afforded proper regard by other professionals.

(vi) *Residential child care is teamwork within a competent workplace*

Residential staff must be constantly working at enhancing their own collective competence. Staff meetings are an essential component of good, consistent child care; they are not an unavoidable requirement of management disturbing the routine. As much as time will allow they should be child centred. Significant events for particular children need to be made known and the implications for care discussed. Strategies for working with difficult behaviour need to be worked out. The expertise of experienced staff can be 'cascaded down' to junior staff. Routines for dealing with actual or threatened crises can be rehearsed.

THEORIES AND APPROACHES TO BEHAVIOUR

In this section we review the main approaches used in work with children whose behaviour, for various reasons is troubled. At the beginning of it we acknowledge that whichever methods are used staff encounter major stresses. We also offer an explanation of the role which therapy plays so that the various approaches may be considered in context. Four main points may be helpful.

- Psychotherapy for children with uncertain or unclear care plans may often not be appropriate. Fundamental decisions about placement and other important life decisions are the first priority. Some stability is necessary before therapy can become useful in treatment of the child.
- Children with complex, long standing problems need a total therapeutic environment and help. Therapy once a week from a

clinic is no substitute for properly planned care and will not solve uncertainty in decision making.

- Children who present very challenging behaviour, whose moods fluctuate wildly and who are difficult to contain and control need the therapeutic endeavour to be absorbed into and become part of day-to-day care ie. therapy becomes the care offered on a day-to-day basis.

- All children's homes can be therapeutic. The difference between a therapeutic community and a children's home does not need to be great. The primary difference is that a therapeutic community is likely to give more planned time to children, to have staff with a mixed range of skills and usually has a 'model' to work with, which helps understanding and assists staff to survive through difficult times.

There are many theories on which residential child care practices are built, and three broad schools of thought.

(i) *Approaches based on behavioural psychology*

One set of theories looks at the here and now behaviour of individuals and tries to set conditions which will change it. These include social learning theory which finds practical expression in approaches to care described broadly as behaviour modification. Behaviour modification approaches construct a care regime in which a child experiences rewards for improved behaviour but experiences no reinforcement for unacceptable behaviour. This may be achieved by a token economy in which good behaviour is (immediately) rewarded by receiving a token which can be exchanged for a privilege of some sort. Alternatively a regime may be stratified into 'levels' which have associated privileges such as home leave, or later bed times, or more physical comfort. A child who demonstrates a record of improved behaviour progresses to a higher level.

The theory stresses positive reinforcement through reward. Care regimes vary in their approach to negative reinforcement which, in every day terms means punishment for unacceptable behaviour. This may find expression in the removal of tokens or being required to drop back a level. Such sanctions are important to demonstrate the limits of unacceptable behaviour. However some children have such low self esteem, and possibly an inner belief that all they deserve is punishment, that they will not be able to respond to a system of rewards. If a child is constantly being relegated then it is likely that such a system of care is not working for that child and alternative approaches will need to be explored.

Behavioural regimes run the risk of becoming little more than systems in which children are not differentiated other than by where they are within the system of rewards and sanctions. This is likely to occur when junior staff have no understanding in depth of the theory of behaviour modification, but simply apply by rote a system devised by senior, and possibly remote, staff. Programmes of behaviour modification need to be devised individually for each child with personal achievable targets identified. These individual programmes have to be reviewed regularly and the child fully engaged with his or her own progress on a personal basis. It should be the child who experiences a personal sense of 'winning' over their own dysfunctional behaviour. It is they who should themselves be sensing their achievement, rather than being told by the system.

Behavioural regimes lend themselves to being explicit and straightforward. Children should know where they stand. There should be a transparency of purpose which managers, care staff, children and families, and indeed the general public are able to understand and support. The 'absence of mystery' about this approach to care can be exploited to enhance the credibility of the home or school.

(ii) *Approaches based on cognitive psychology*

Behaviourist ideas, at least in their most radical form, do not dwell on the processes of the mind – but rather on relating external stimuli upon people to their behaviour, as a response to the stimuli. Approaches to influencing people's behaviour therefore concentrate on carefully organising the stimuli they experience.

Approaches based on cognitive psychology look a little way into the workings of the mind and try to influence the way people think about or 'process' their perceptions. Therapies based on cognitive psychology try to adjust the way people process their perceptions so that they react in a different, more satisfactory, way. To quote Martin Herbert[2]:–

> *'What, essentially is being claimed is that people can be taught to eliminate some of their maladaptive behaviours by challenging their irrational beliefs and faulty logic or by getting them to instruct themselves in certain ways, or to associate wanted behaviour with positive self statements, and unwanted ones with negative self statements.'*

A cognitive theory of depression, for example, would postulate that a depressed person interprets perceptions in a way which has negative consequences for the individual. A person not suffering from depression having the same perception would interpret it in such a way as to have neutral or positive consequences. A cognitive approach to treating depression would be to find ways of suggesting or demonstrating to the

---

[2] Clinical Child Psychology: Social Learning, Development and Behaviour published by Wiley, 1991

'patient' that there are alternative ways of interpreting perceptions which have more positive consequences.

In child care this approach to achieving positive behavioural changes may take the form of carefully exploring, in discussion, why a child makes certain assumptions or has acquired certain beliefs. It may take the form of more robust challenges or exercises designed to demonstrate in given circumstances that there are alternative interpretations or choices which can be made.

This is not a complex idea, and it is just this simplicity which offers a powerful basis for working with children. It finds particular application in working with children who are delinquent. Some children have poor ability at appreciating others' points of view or reasoning through moral issues. Some believe that their behaviour is determined much more by external influences, eg. peer groups or the occurrence of opportunity, than by their own personal control. Some feel that they get themselves trapped into social situations which will lead inevitably to delinquent behaviour but from which they do not know how to escape.

Constructive work with such children may entail role playing in which children are obliged to 'perform' a role with which they have little affinity, for example the victim of one of their crimes. Discussion groups about moral dilemmas of suitable complexity, where the objective is to arrive at a consensus, are intended to enhance moral reasoning power and empathy with other viewpoints. Individual or group work in which the children 're-live' problematic social situations, such as peer group pressure to commit an offence, can be used to train the ability to recognise the problem and devise solutions which avoid trouble. These techniques can be made more real and enlivened by cartooning, drama or role playing. Care must be taken in the use of role play or work with drama. It can be a very powerful medium and can touch very painful and personal issues unless used carefully by a person trained to understand the pitfalls as well as the value. Techniques such as these should be carefully thought through and supervised.

More sophisticated cognitive approaches involve getting in touch with what children 'say to themselves' at the time they are dealing with problematic moments in their lives. These reveal that some children's thinking is maladaptive and likely to route their behaviour in a destructive direction. Techniques have been devised which teach children to consciously make statements to themselves (out loud during their treatment) which are designed to enhance their understanding of a situation and to reinforce an appropriate behavioral response. Approaches of this kind have been found to have particular application in helping children and young people control their anger.

Cognitive psychology provides a theoretical basis for a number of established child care methods including life story book work in preparing children for transitions; the 'correctional curriculum' for intermediate treatment; and the 'what if' games suggested as an anticipatory approach to 'control' in children's homes referred to elsewhere in this chapter. However some of the therapeutic techniques are sophisticated and some are still being developed and need to be practised or closely overseen by qualified psychologists. There can be considerable danger in inexperienced or unqualified staff professing to employ psychological techniques without professional oversight, as has been demonstrated in the *Pindown and Leicestershire Reports*.

(iii) *Approaches based on analytical psychology*

The third broad category of theories are those which see behaviour as having meaning in itself and an underlying explanation which needs to be understood in terms of the child's life experiences. Behaviour, whether acceptable or otherwise, is part of a process which can be resolved.

Many people feel they have been helped to cope better with life by psychotherapists or counsellors who practice according to psychoanalytic ideas derived from the theories of Freud and his numerous followers. Psychotherapy and counselling are specialised activities which require qualifying training. However some basic ideas, such as the mechanisms by which people defend themselves against anxiety, for example displacement and projection, and ideas of transference and counter transference, are taught in social work training and can, with care be usefully applied in residential child care. They are valuable in helping residential care staff to understand that behaviour may not be directed at them personally, but rather because of who or what they represent for the child. Once a residential staff member is freed by this understanding to interpret a child's behaviour in the context of the child's life experiences and significant relationships, he or she can engage **professionally** with the child's feelings. Without such understanding, working with difficult children can be intolerably confusing and emotionally exhausting both for the worker and the children.

Some psychoanalytical ideas can seem abstruse and even improbable, and there is a danger of real events in a child's life, for example sexual abuse, being dismissed as fantasy. Nevertheless, the simple idea of trying to relate a child's behaviour and feelings to what has gone before can provide a basic approach to care which staff trained for residential work can use. Furthermore for some children who have experienced chronically dysfunctional family relations, emotional neglect, or chronic abuse, this approach to care may be the only way their needs can be met adequately to enable them to be held and helped within substitute care.

Some children's very early experiences have not allowed them to put the building blocks of their personality together. As they grow up their behaviour reflects this lack of integration of their personalities. Feeling and behaviour are poorly differentiated. Some theorists believe that the only way ahead for such children is to allow them to relive their earliest childhood and return to infantile experiences such as primitive rage and the warmth of maternal comfort.

The emotions and needs of small babies are self evident. They cry uncontrollably when they are hungry or uncomfortable. They are comforted by food and warmth from a mother who, understandably, becomes intensely important to the child. If an infant is denied these experiences, by being punished for crying, and left alone instead of comforted, then it is understandable that they may grow up unable to control their behaviour or relate confidently and affectionately to others. This may be profound damage, and residential staff may be called upon to look after the child when his family breaks down and he becomes physically unmanageable.

A child damaged in this way is likely to regress when sympathetic and comforting care is offered. Regression is not something done to a child; it is not a therapy applied by a therapist. Children are cared for in such a way that allows them to regress. Ways are found to tolerate infantile behaviour in a manner which does not risk abusing or humiliating the child.

For example, a recurrence of bed wetting will be dealt with routinely and without fuss. **The child will not be put in nappies!**

A child's need to be fed like a baby can be achieved symbolically by a member of staff who has a significant relationship sitting close together with the child whilst he eats his meal. **The child will not be spoon fed or given a bottle**.

A child can be offered a hot water bottle in a soft cover to take to bed for comfort. **An older child will not be obliged to take a cuddly toy to bed, although he or she may well choose to**.

A child will be held or hugged in preference to verbal injunctions as a means of bringing him under control when he is fizzing about or disturbing other children. If the child is behaving dangerously, full physical restraint may be necessary.

The place of regression in the care of difficult children became greatly misunderstood as a result of Frank Beck misappropriating and perverting Barbara Docker-Drysdale's valued insight and ideas about the care of children with psychological damage sustained in infancy. Beck provoked children to lose their tempers and sexualised their responses for his own abusive ends under the guise of what he termed 'regression therapy', a phrase which has no meaning in either psychology or psychiatry. Regression is something which can happen to any of us in certain circumstances, for example when we are ill or acutely distressed and our need for physical comfort is enhanced. Another person cannot impose regression on another. Regression is a phenomenon which is accepted or allowed in certain circumstances, for example in hospital wards, or in children's residential care.

Psychoanalytical approaches to care have the advantage of engaging the whole child both in terms of their current personality and their life experience. They do however run the risk of being used with too little knowledge and being 'mysterious' and esoteric. Staff who engage with the 'inner selves' of children work very intensively and rely heavily on their working environment for the understanding and emotional support they need. There is a danger that they come to see themselves as inhabiting special worlds which outsiders cannot be expected to understand. This can take the form of insularity and rigidity and can in consequence lead to opportunities for various types of abuse, as also can behaviour modification if wrongly used. Senior staff in such establishments need to invest a proportion of their energies in achieving openness and flexible engagement with the wider world of child care.

The need for children to be safely controlled is common to all these broad approaches to care although this may be manifested rather differently. In the behavioural and cognitive psychology approaches there is generally a strong expectation of conforming to the rules of the regime. Good behaviour is tangibly rewarded and progress is made explicit by means of levels or tokens.

In the analytical psychology approach there is often a strong expectation that failure to conform will be accounted for and explained both to staff and the peer group in the home or school. Progress is acknowledged within the individual or group relationships, rather than through anything more explicit.

(iv) *'Eclecticism'*

We have discussed some theoretical ideas underpinning the care and therapy of children. Specific treatments occupying a small part of a child's life may well be appropriately based on a single theoretical model. The processes of growing up and the mystery of human personality, however, are too complex to be understood by any one 'model' or theoretical explanation. An approach to looking after the whole child, which adheres exclusively to one theoretical orientation will be a depriving rather than a nurturing experience. It is not surprising therefore that many residential establishments for children profess to maintain an 'eclectic' approach.

An eclectic approach to care, that is, using more than one source for its theoretical orientation, must, however, incorporate the different components to make a valid professional whole. This must be clear to the outside world and be able to be understood by children, parents and other professionals. It should be written down in the establishment's statement of purpose and function. If the approach cannot be easily and clearly written down, it is probably not a safe child care proposition.

The cumulative writings of the Dartington Research Unit suggest that homes which claim to be eclectic, but cannot be specific about their theoretical underpinning, may be conducting child care which is tantamount to chaos. (The importance of theory is discussed in *'Residential Child Care: A Review of the Research'* prepared by the Dartington Research Unit and published by HMSO). Better outcomes tend to be associated with homes where there is clarity of intent and method directed at the primary needs of children. Homes and schools which propose to care for difficult children should consult fully with qualified psychological practitioners when designing their approach to the task and, thereafter, either employ psychologically qualified staff or build in regular external consultancy.

(v) *Approaches based on 'good parenting'*

We began this section by invoking the essential value of 'good consistent care', a phrase closely allied to the concept of 'good parenting'. To what extent can there be a theoretical basis for ideas such as these? To what extent can there be a theory of child care which is distinct from a theory of child development or a theoretical basis for therapy or treatment?

The book *'Assessing Outcomes in Child Care'* (Parker et al) comes close to a theoretical approach to caring for children by regarding parenting as a sequence of activities which promote a child's growing up along seven dimensions of development. These dimensions, based on an assessment of the consensus of reasonable parents' expectations for their children are health, education, emotional and behavioural development, family and peer relationships, self-care and competence, identity, and social presentation. There are too many extraneous influences affecting how a child will develop to make it feasible to associate specific positive outcomes with specific 'inputs' at crucial stages of the child's life. The process of parenting can however be seen as one in which those responsible set the conditions or put opportunities in place which allow the child to achieve 'intermediate outcomes'. These are developmental achievements in their own right but also essential building blocks for the next stage.

This idea is important for those caring for children with many problems and very difficult behaviour because it helps to cut down to size what otherwise might all too easily be an overwhelmingly daunting task. It provides a framework for deciding, in consultation with the children and their families, just what issues, at a particular time, need to be tackled and what short term goals should be set. Practical assessment schedules are available and being further developed which assist in the planning of child care objectives and recording developmental progress.

Children whose paths to adulthood are proving hazardous often experience disruptions and changes of carers. All child care effort must be directed at reducing these changes to a level consistent with good parenting, but in the real world there may still be many more forced moves than anyone desires or than are in a child's interest. Good parenting then becomes, at best, fragmented but if a systematic approach to assessing development can be preserved throughout these changes it will, at least, allow current carers to build upon the work of others. This facility is surely a minimum requirement for looking after troubled children in the public care.

THE 'CHILDREN ACT CLIMATE'

The approaches we have just outlined are all having to adjust to children's rights as set out in the *Children Act* (or *'Scotland's Children' – Proposals for Child Care Policy and Law*). The requirement to consult with children has sometimes been interpreted as children being able to do just as they wish thereby undermining rules of home or school and the authority of staff. Similarly, complaints procedures have been seen by some as a licence for children to attack staff through false allegations. Critics of the Act claim these provisions distort relationships between children and members of staff, removing boundaries between acceptable and non-acceptable behaviour, destroying concepts of right and wrong, and leaving staff powerless. It is clear that an approach to care which conceives of children as being entirely beholden to staff for the determining factors in their lives will have difficulty with the provisions of the Act. Similarly an approach in which expectations of children's behaviour is systematically codified so that there is no room for negotiation would have difficulties. In both instances it may be the residential establishment which needs to review its theoretical basis of care so as to adjust to the *Children Act* changes.

If a residential child care establishment cannot tolerate a child having the right to complain or the right to be consulted, then such a regime is unlikely to perceive children as individuals. Complaints imply that a child may be being treated in a way which calls into question the universal probity of the care regime. Consulting a child implies that the care regime does not have all the answers and, what is more, that responses to children should not be uniform but tailored to one child to another.

If residential child care is to provide for children who present difficult behaviour, the complexity underlying and explaining their behaviour requires individualised responses. These will be different from responses to children whose developed self-management enables them to forgo or postpone personal gratification and conform to the fairly uniform behavioural expectation of ordinary day or boarding schools. To allow for individualisation, it is necessary to consult a child's preferences before making decisions. Accepting that children may complain is a necessary check that treatment of individuals is not abusive or unfair. Rather than being perceived as detracting from parental authority, children's rights to be consulted and to complain should be regarded as positive legislative cornerstones in child individuation.

If consultation and complaint are regarded as additional burdens laid on an established regime then they will be seen as extraordinary and threatening. If on the other hand they are accepted as part of a home's whole approach to care they can be regarded as part of the range of 'tools' of child care intervention. We have tried to pictorialise the difficult balance described above. The following diagram presents a matrix which contains a number of the concepts and attitudes which need to be balanced. In doing so, we assume that the prevailing approach of staff to children will be the 'good parenting' which is the core of care.

The Interplay of Rights and Responsibilities
(A Matrix)

ADULT

| Rights | Responsibilities |

CHILD

Rights

An accommodation of interests will characterise the exchanges between children and staff, otherwise competition or conflict.

'Parental' authority relationship with child in 'neutral.'

Emphasis on rules and negotiation, balancing two sets of rights. Complaints, staff discipline and grievance procedures matters of high importance.

Staff assume a responsibility for addressing the rights of the child. The child receives responsible adult care (parenting).

Staff will exercise an authority based upon their responsibility to safeguard the rights of children.

Children's rights which denied that authority would prohibit an exchange in this sector and undermine parenting.

Responsibilities

Child accedes to the reasonable rights of the staff member to exercise authority.

The child behaves 'well' in response to properly exercised staff rights.

BUT if staff rights are not grounded in legal, professional or moral authority, the child's reciprocal responsibility (obedience) becomes perverse and child is oppressed or abused.

Mature exchange between child and staff with each reciprocating the perceived responsibilities of the other.

This exchange resembles a dialogue between mature altruistic adults. That is, they are both concerned to exercise responsibility for the other irrespective of the others rights in the situation.

An analysis of the relationship between staff and children which confined itself to consideration of the rights of the parties involved would provide a very limited description and would be very likely to lead to conflict. Our matrix does not represent mutually exclusive alternative ways in which adult and child may relate to each other, but components of a complex relationship. Features of each quarter of the matrix will be found in relationships between staff and children but the weighting given to each will depend upon the age and maturity of children and staff, and the prevailing circumstances.

Staff caring for young adults may need to accept that the top left hand box, with its negotiation of an accommodation of interests and its potential for conflict will be a prominent dynamic, tempered at times with welcome mature exchanges more typical of the bottom right hand box. At other times, the young people's vulnerability will invite, even demand, that the adult should act with parental responsibility, as in the top right hand box. A young or developmentally immature child will need to be cared for within a staff relationship heavily weighted towards the top right hand box.

Reciprocally, staff must be able to appeal to the responsibility that can appropriately be expected of children, as indicated in the bottom left hand box. It is reasonable to expect a child to be as obedient as s/he can be, provided the adult exercises rights which are proper and respects the child's rights.

We recognise that any attempt to convey the complexities of these relationships will be incomplete. However, we hope that the matrix may be useful in triggering discussion and further thinking.

CONTROL IN THE ANTICIPATORY MODE

If behaviour and control are issues for the staff and children in a residential establishment then they are far better tackled positively and prospectively. If control is only seen as a reaction to unacceptable behaviour, then staff will tend to feel they are always defending good order from the ravages of unruly children rather than using good order to help these same children. Staff should take the initiative where good order and control are at stake, and capitalise on the quiet times when children can be positively engaged.

Children who lose control need to be afforded opportunities to reflect on their behaviour once they are again in control. We suggest that staff should make a point of talking with children about what is unacceptable behaviour, how it comes about, and what reactions and consequences might be expected. Children might benefit from receiving feedback about how their behaviour was perceived by their peers and strategies for avoiding the circumstances which trigger loss of control might be devised.

These discussions will serve to train children to anticipate consequences and to change their patterns of response. This will mean that staff, and other children in the group, will challenge the interpretations or train of assumptions which lead a young person to react inappropriately. Assertions such as 'I had no choice' or 'what else do you expect me to do' can be examined and alternative views and responses demonstrated. To examine past trouble, by agreement with the children concerned, may be constructive particularly if children can see that there were 'escape routes' which might have led them out of the trouble or avoided their losing control. They may be able to identify patterns which trap them into situations they cannot deal with without losing control or infringing the rules.

As suggested earlier, helping children to anticipate and make choices might take the form of playing 'what if' games in which they are invited to imagine situations in which they can reflect on how they should behave or what should be done. Imaginary situations may be more acceptable for some children than raking over old misdemeanours.

SITUATIONS NEEDING INTERVENTION TO ENSURE CONTROL

Certain combinations of circumstances may predict the need for intervention in order to maintain control. These include times of heightened anxiety and tension, boredom and opportunity. In its handbook for residential child care staff Southwark Social Services Department identified potential "hot spots' and ways of dealing with them. The following draws heavily on this material.

'Hot spots' include:–
- forthcoming court appearances and casework meetings;
- discharge from the establishment;
- meal times;
- going to and getting up from bed;
- returning from a visit home;
- staff handover times;
- group trips;
- lengthy unstructured periods of time.

These are all circumstances which can be anticipated and are therefore amenable to preparation and management. Good deployment of staff to ensure adequate supervision and sensitive handling of transitions will clearly help set the conditions for good order.

More immediate threats of disorder and violence can be discerned which will allow for on the spot corrective action by alert and active staff.

Immediate signs that 'trouble is brewing' include:–
- restless behaviour involving pushing and jostling;

- deliberately provocative conduct;
- unusually withdrawn behaviour;
- alternatively quiet and boisterous behaviour;
- over-sensitive reactions to reasonable corrections or instructions;
- a feeling of tension in the care unit;
- actual threats of violence;
- drug or alcohol abuse;
- peer group pressure or bullying;
- personal frustration arising out of serious illness or disability;
- reactions to events unknown to staff;
- testing out of staff.

How can disorder or violence be averted or ameliorated? Some suggestions include:–

- be present, be seen, do not hide in the office;
- be calm, reasonable and reassuring;
- move at a normal, relaxed pace;
- speak using normal speed, volume and tone;
- avoid aggressive gestures and presenting a threat to a child who is threatening others;
- avoid aggressive eye contact or staring into the eyes of a young person;
- avoid getting too physically close to a child unless he or she appears amenable to being calmed by touching or holding, or when physical restraint is necessary to prevent injury or damage;
- do not get drawn into a dispute and avoid taking sides when tensions are high. Seek to resolve an argument at the time only if this can be done immediately by making a commitment which can certainly be honoured;
- talk about the behaviour and where it is taking people in preference to the rights and wrongs of an argument;
- suggest the argument itself be deferred, but only until such time as it can be dealt with in a less tense climate;
- remember that it is easier for members of staff to risk losing face by backing off and deferring the confrontation than it is for young people. Use this to find ways out for a young person in a confrontation which will maintain his or her self esteem and dignity;
- suggest 'onlookers' move away if their presence contributes to the tension;
- try to separate antagonists in an argument;
- try to keep people seated;

- take a dispute out of the arena where others can egg it on – 'Lets go into my room to talk about this shall we?';
- ascertain where other staff are in the unit and alert them to the need to be at hand should trouble escalate;
- be watchful of colleagues present to check that they are remaining calm and not contributing to the tension. If necessary suggest that they are needed elsewhere. Be receptive to signals from colleagues that you are adding to the tension and withdraw if necessary.

THE AFTERMATH OF BAD BEHAVIOUR

Although there has to be some price to pay for bad behaviour, children should be relieved of the burden of past transgression as early as possible so that they are freed to take a more positive view of their prospects. Children who are never without the consequences of transgression hanging over their heads will be pushed into some form of depression which may take the appearance of complete indifference to the expectations of care staff. Such children may behave as if they have nothing to lose because that is exactly how they perceive the situation. Some children who become persistent offenders find themselves with a string of outstanding court cases constantly pending which serve to reinforce their habit. It is good child care for the consequences of individual acts of bad behaviour to follow promptly and to be resolved quickly.

The price a child needs to pay may well carry some pain but it can be a positive price. Sanctions should avoid being pointless punishment if at all possible. If the circumstances permit, reparation or making amends for a transgression can be seen very positively. If it is the way the home or school works, having to explain and account for unacceptable behaviour to the group is seldom a painless business but can be a positive opportunity for learning and insight. Less positive sanctions whose purpose is simply to signal disapproval will have their place and are generally preferable to no action being taken and the children feeling that they 'got away with it'. However, purely retributive punishment does not serve children who are struggling to gain control of their behaviour. It serves mainly those who exercise the retribution.

THE NEED TO PHYSICALLY RESTRAIN CHILDREN

The circumstances in which it is appropriate to use physical restraint to control a child have been set out in the *Department of Health Guidance on Permissible Means of Control in Residential Child Care.*

> '*The guidance expects staff to intervene in a number of ways to help children remain within control. It stresses the importance of positive care practices aimed*

at creating an environment conducive to good care and control and in particular verbally engaging children pro-actively on issues of behaviour, responsibility and good order. It makes the point that, inherent in the caring role of staff, is the expectation that they are there to supervise children and that the authority members of staff carry through their physical presence is a contributor to control. This was stressed because there have been instances of staff remaining passive in the face of incipient disorder. The guidance suggests that in certain situations holding children may be an effective and caring way to maintain or secure their control'.

This guidance reserves the term physical restraint to using physical force to overpower a child. This is justified when immediate action is required to avoid injury or serious damage to property. Although the guidance spells out in some detail the circumstances in which physical restraint is necessary, it cannot cover all eventualities or eliminate the need for residential child care staff to make difficult judgments in times of great stress or even danger.

The use of physical restraint itself carries risk of injury to all those involved. For this reason alone confrontations which provoke the need for such action should be avoided as far as possible by means of the anticipatory practices described above. When faced with the threat of injury or serious damage, staff will need to judge whether the risks associated with physical restraint outweigh the risks of not intervening in this way. Crucial to this judgement will be whether the passage of time is likely to be a calming or an escalating factor. Knowledge of the history and behaviour patterns of the child may be significant in deciding this. Staff in a home or school which has sound record keeping and information exchange at staff meetings should be familiar with this information.

The purpose of physical restraint is to overpower the child in order to restore safety. This form of intervention must be positive and likely to succeed. Anything less than this may simply result in a fight. Three staff may be needed to bring an adult size child swiftly under control. Certainly one adult alone cannot be expected to bring another adult size person under control.

At the time of writing there are no techniques officially approved for restraining children. Some trainers have adapted methods used for restraining adults for use with children. Because of the obvious abhorrence of inflicting pain on children, techniques which rely on holding limbs in such a way that the person experiences pain if they struggle are thought by many to be inappropriate. There have been publicized instances where children's limbs have been broken and it must never be forgotten that even a large child is still more at risk of fractures or damage to joints, spine and neck than adults. It may be, however, that for adult size young people selected specialized holds may be the safest.

Approaches which involve forcing people to the ground by means of body weight run the risk of broken limbs if the bodies overbalance and fall together. Heavy pressure on the bodies of people held to the floor can lead to collapsed lungs. However the controlled weight and strength of an adult may safely restrain the significantly smaller body of a child by means of pinioning the child's arms to his or her sides with another adult preventing the legs from flailing.

As the Guidance indicates, when such methods are used staff should be constantly watchful to relax them as soon as the child becomes less excited. This discussion cannot hope to describe in words physical techniques which need training through demonstration and practice. It can however, serve to stress that in homes which look after children who are so disturbed as, on occasion, to provoke the need for physical restraint, it is necessary to include methods of restraint as part of a training programme which addresses the control aspects of good care. It has been reported to us that, once trained, staff feel much more confident about their controlling role generally and instances of physical intervention tend to decline. Nevertheless, we would wish it to be clear that for reasons of both safety and good child care, physical restraint of recalcitrant young people should always be a last resort. The 'general principles governing interventions to maintain control' drawn from the Department of health guidance form APPENDIX 6.

6.4 The Contemporary Hazards of Growing Up

In this section we consider several issues which are relevant to children and young people being looked after in all residential settings. These issues, smoking, drugs, alcohol and sexually transmitted diseases, and the problems associated with them are not unique to residential settings and group living. They can arise in any family, and it cannot be assumed that, for example, because a young person is in a children's home, he or she is more susceptible to problems such as drugs or alcohol. Experimenting is part of growing up. The role of staff is to advise and explain potential problems and dangers, and try to ensure that natural curiosity and experimentation does not develop into something more serious and long term. We believe that all these issues should form part of a comprehensive commitment to health and health education, and that staff have an important role in promoting an awareness of health issues and a healthy lifestyle. It is also essential that staff in children's homes develop full cooperation and consultation with any local schools which children attend.

Wherever they are working with children and young people, staff need to be alert to potential dangers, know how to detect when there might be a problem, know where the resources and agencies which can provide advice and support are, and take action when necessary. They will also need to try to instil, as far as possible, a responsible attitude towards smoking, alcohol, drugs and sexual behaviour. Setting a good example themselves will be part of this. Links with schools and other organisations such as churches and youth clubs need to be made. When people work together in dealing with difficult issues such as these, there is always a temptation to assume that someone else will deal with it, although this may often be a false assumption. Thus, for example, staff in boarding schools need to let parents know their approach to smoking, drugs, alcohol and sexual activities. Then, when they feel a young person has transgressed the boundaries of what is acceptable they should seek to understand the background to their behaviour, and not simply punish them.

6.4.1 Smoking

Smoking in residential settings for children and young people is always likely to cause problems. It is unlikely ever to be possible to convince them all of the dangers, and dissuade them from experimenting with it. Despite the general move in society towards reducing smoking, young people, and increasingly young girls, are beginning to smoke, often at a very early age. Sadly, the proportion of young people in children's homes and some schools who are already confirmed, even addicted, smokers is surprisingly high.

What can staff do? First and foremost staff can lead by example. A policy needs to be formed and accepted. We suggest it should be that staff should **never** smoke in front of children and young people in any setting, nor in any areas which they use regularly. Given that many children and young people are habituated to smoking, it may not always be feasible to declare a home or school an absolute 'no-smoking' environment; this might simply drive smoking underground, and create more problems than it solves. However, staff can work towards establishing a non-smoking culture, developing the rules in partnership with the residents. In some settings it might be acceptable to designate certain areas or rooms as smoking areas. No one who does not smoke should have to endure others' smoking unless they specifically state that they have no objections. The question of smoking in individual rooms should also be discussed but, because there are obvious safety as well as health hazards, smoking in bedrooms should never be allowed. The Department of Health issued *Guidance on Smoking and Alcohol Consumption in Children's Residential Care*, (LAC(94)4) published 18 January 1994. This circular requires responsible authorities to devise policies which are designed to firmly discourage smoking habits.

In most boarding schools, smoking is not allowed in any circumstances. However, where smoking has been tolerated in the past, to impose limits on smoking, especially age limits, will be difficult. It is illegal to sell cigarettes to children under the age of sixteen, but many are able to buy cigarettes and smoke regularly. For a home or school to try to prevent fifteen year olds from smoking when sixteen year olds are able to do so, is likely to create tension and ill-feeling, and lead to discipline problems. In children's homes staff will have to accept, as a fact of life, that some children and young people are already smokers when they first come into their care. Their efforts should be directed towards helping them to give it up, under medical direction if necessary, rather than trying to establish immediate and ineffectual bans which may lead to a spiral of confrontations and punishments.

Staff need to see their role as preventive and educational. In boarding schools smoking should feature in any personal, social and health education (PSHE) programmes; in other settings staff can ensure that, where group discussions are taking place, smoking is on the agenda. Where children and young people do not already smoke, it will be important to try to avoid them taking up the habit, whilst helping the smokers to give up, or at least to cut down. This will involve discussion of the dangers (and cost) of smoking, and of any help available. A member of staff who smokes might consider attempting to give up at the same time as a young person, since a role model can be stronger than exhortations. Children and young people will experience a great deal of pressure from their peer group to begin or continue smoking, while school, family and adults may urge them not to begin or to give up. The issue will need to be handled tactfully and patiently, rather than in a moralising way and it would be over-optimistic to expect quick or universally good results.

6.4.2 Drugs and Solvents

Drugs and solvents are a problem for young people throughout society. Controlled drugs are illegal, and involvement with them can often lead to criminalisation of young people. They have greater access to illicit drugs today than in earlier times, and it is difficult for adults to be vigilant enough to prevent all experimentation. Staff may be aware of previous problems with drugs and solvents when a young person enters a home or school, and when this is so they need to know about the patterns of drug use and the young person's medical history, to help them detect any subsequent use of drugs.

In this, as in other issues, the emphasis needs to be on education. Staff themselves will need information about prevention of drug and solvent abuse; recognition of the symptoms of abuse; counselling skills available for support and guidance; and how to recognise signs of abuse. This is likely to require in-service training and agencies should expect to provide it. Children and young people themselves should be encouraged to discuss drug-related issues in groups and in PSHE lessons, the emphasis being on preventing experimentation with drugs and solvents, rather than dealing with the results afterwards. Heavy-handedness will alienate and antagonise children and young people, and staff will need to discuss the issues with sensitivity and humour. As national propaganda has shown, grim and dire warnings of the ill-effects of drugs and solvents have little effect, and can actually help to glamorise them. Links with local authority drug prevention units and local police-schools liaison units, can help provide experienced workers to assist staff in getting the messages across. In addition managers and senior staff need to give thought in advance to what action they would take if young people in their establishment became involved in using or possessing drugs, or being in contact with drug pushers. The dilemma for staff, whether in schools or homes, is that they must be seen to be upholding the law on the one hand, but on the other they have to take into consideration the best interests of the young people for whom they are responsible. Parents of boarding school children may not welcome knee jerk reactions without consultation and staff in children's homes trying to rehabilitate children who have perhaps already been in trouble with the law, may lose opportunities to gain their confidence if their first reaction is automatically to call in the police. Planning in advance which, considering the wide use of drugs, would be a wise policy, should include the police and seek a mutual understanding of the dilemma outlined above. Staff in charge of children and young people who face these difficulties need to understand that to tolerate is not necessarily to condone. Schools and homes need to cultivate an anti-drugs culture which will provide opportunities for open discussion and health education in this context.

Possession of controlled substances is a criminal offence, and staff should be careful to ensure that where a crime has been committed, the police are told and given every assistance if they decide to undertake an investigation. Whatever action the police take, which could range from no action at all to an arrest in more serious cases involving dealing in drugs, staff have a duty to counsel those involved **and** other children and young people about the consequences of what has happened. A drug incident involving the police will be traumatic and disturbing for any group, and staff need to discuss the issues raised with the young people. This is important not only to allay fears and doubts, but also as part of overall education about drug-related issues. Young people directly involved will need particular attention. Immediate discipline should not take place automatically: staff should attempt, with the involvement, if necessary, of others such as drug counselling services and social workers, to determine the root of the problem, and to consider the extent to which the behaviour is likely to be repeated. It is probably unnecessary to add that, as with other addictive substances, and particularly because of legal constraints, staff need to provide good role models.

6.4.3 Alcohol

In his report *Another Kind of Home*[1], Angus Skinner said:–

> 'In respect of alcohol it is important that young people should see models of sensible limited drinking rather than perceive there to be a choice between abstention and drunkenness'.

We support this view. It would be foolish for staff to attempt to persuade all young people to abstain completely; likewise staff should be attentive to the possibility that some young people might abuse alcohol from a very early age. Once more, they need to set an example. There may be special occasions where it may be appropriate for small quantities of alcohol to be consumed in the school or home, but if this is the case staff should always discuss with young people their approach to alcohol consumption and as with smoking, provide a good example. As young people mature they will have more opportunities to drink and, if they work, they will have more resources. When these opportunities arise it is the duty of staff to try to ensure that they are responsible in their consumption. The Department of Health issued guidance on the consumption of alcohol in children's residential care in circular LAC(94)4 already referred to above.

Staff should engage young people in discussions on the issues involved with alcohol and alcoholism. There may be opportunities for experts from outside the home or school to come in to talk about the issues and to lead discussions. Where a young person has a problem with excessive drinking or alcoholism, staff will need to call upon other experts from the community to assist them. For this reason homes and schools should develop links with agencies dealing with alcohol abuse and its associated problems.

6.4.4 Sexually Transmitted Diseases

We discuss sex and sexuality in a different section of this chapter because we wish to emphasize that it is a normal part of growing up and should not be seen as a problem in itself. Sexually transmitted diseases, however, are a risk for growing young people and adults everywhere and staff in residential settings need to be knowledgeable about them. In recent years the publicity given to sexually transmitted diseases has been

---

[1] Skinner A (1992) 'Another Kind of Home – A Review of Residential Child Care' HMSO, Edinburgh

overshadowed by the world wide alarm over HIV and Aids. This should not mean that other less life threatening conditions are ignored. For the most part, those looking after children in homes or schools can deal with these matters by means of straightforward, open guidance and information dealing with prevention, identification and the importance of seeking prompt medical attention. The Scottish Office Social Work Services Group has published valuable guidance on *'Children and HIV'* (1993) for local authorities and voluntary organisations. It deals extensively with a wide range of issues, including a chapter on residential care. In addition *'Another Kind of Home'* – already mentioned above, contains a chapter on health issues, including sexuality.

6.4.5 Personal Relationships

FRIENDSHIP AND SUPPORT

Confidence in and good rapport with particular adults is a fundamental element in good care practice. Children and young people want to be treated as people and not patronised. They may have many positive and enjoyable experiences while living away from home, but there are likely to be some crises to face while they are in the care of residential staff. Problems may arise with family, friends or staff, and there may be illness, accidents or bereavement to cope with. At times of stress or crisis every child needs an adult to turn to. Peer group support at such times should not be overestimated, and it is important for staff to be able to respond adequately.

Nowadays it is recognised that staff need training in how they can best give this kind of personal support. Warmth and understanding are essential, but everyone needs to know and understand when a relationship may become too intimate. The fine line between what is 'proper' warmth and understanding and what is regarded as 'improper' is likely to vary from one home or school to another depending on the particular ethos of the establishment. What is important though is that staff need to be aware of their own sexual inclinations and interests, putting children's interests first and always considering what is appropriate in any given situation with a particular child. Staff relationships also need to be sufficiently open and confident to allow discussion with one another and to provide opportunities for joint consideration of each other's actions.

At least three factors may be relevant when considering how to interact with an individual child on a personal basis. The first and most important is the needs of the child. Staff must have knowledge and understanding of the child and his or her background, and be able to recognise and respect any emotional 'barriers' the child has erected. Secondly, staff need to be aware of their own feelings. They may believe they are the best person to provide care for a particular child in a confidential, one-to-one situation but they should discuss this with senior staff. They must also be sufficiently aware of their own sexual feelings, so that if they see any danger of a relationship with a child becoming sexualised, they would stop to consider what they were doing. Finally, other people's feelings and views, both adults and children, need to be taken into account. If there is a possibility that staff or other children view a relationship as inappropriate, the staff member concerned should discuss the matter with other staff in order to understand their concerns and to explain their own perspective. In general, if they feel in any doubt about their own or other people's feelings, staff should step back, consider what they are doing and discuss the issues with their colleagues. It is not a matter of staff **never** becoming involved in a close, caring relationship with a child; this is a vital part of the caring task. It is rather that they should be conscious of the dangers, justified or unjustified, which these relationships can bring with them and be clear where boundaries in such relationships lie. What seems to those in child care an inappropriate way of dealing with the issue is described by Isobel Menzies Lyth in a study of nursing.

'The care of the anxiety situation for the nurse lies in her relationship with the patient. The closer and more concentrated the relationship, the more the nurse is likely to experience the impact of anxiety. The nursing service attempts to protect her from the anxiety by splitting up her contacts with patients .... The implicit rationale appears to be that a student nurse will learn to be detached psychologically if she has sufficient experience of being detached literally and physically .... The pain and distress of breaking relationships and the importance of stable and continuing relationships are implicitly denied by the system, although they are often stressed personally – that is, non professionally – by people in the system'

Containing Anxiety in Institutions, Vol 1, by Isobel Menzies Lyth – Free Association Books 1988

This method is not appropriate in child care. Instead, easing problems by sharing them and looking for appropriate ways to handle them, can prevent particular relationships between children and adults getting out of hand. It can also mean that children benefit from the shared wisdom and experience of a group of caring staff. Secrecy, deception and intimidation of staff cannot flourish if there are honest, open and committed relationships in a staff team.

Research in boarding schools[2] suggests that the really important relationships for pupils are with other pupils and that relationships with

---

[2] Morgan R (1993) 'School Life: Pupil's Views on Boarding' HMSO, London

staff are, surprisingly, of lesser significance. This is unlikely to be the case in children's homes, except where siblings live together in the same home. Children in homes are less likely to make strong investments in relationships with other children whose stability and continuity cannot be guaranteed in the same way. Peer group relationships between children in children's homes are often tentative, conditional and transitory, although some children and young people, given the opportunity, form strong friendships which should be acknowledged and taken into account in making plans for their future. Despite relatively high staff turnover, children and young people are likely to look towards staff with greater expectation than in boarding schools. Regrettably, there is evidence that in children's homes the children frequently feel let down by breaks in their relationships with staff because of the turnover and movement within the service. Nevertheless, the residential care staff's job is to work with the child in maximising opportunities for forming and benefitting from such relationships with adults.

Continuity of staffing and reducing turnover as much as possible are therefore vital. In boarding schools, there is also often a high turnover of care staff, especially those without teaching qualifications. Teachers have a clearer role for which they are respected by their professional colleagues, and perhaps because of consequently higher job satisfaction, the problem of turnover may not be so serious. We hope that the situation in children's homes will improve following acceptance of the recommendations in the *Howe and Utting Reports* in relation to training, conditions of work, remuneration and status, all of which would increase acceptance of staff as a professional group undertaking one of the most difficult tasks in social services.

PEER GROUPS, ISOLATION AND BULLYING

'I've had a really hard time ... I've been picked on and bullied ... If you tell the social workers you are known as a grasser and get even more'

(Young person in care – Dolphin Project)

'Bullying, like illness will inevitably occur in a community but it should nevertheless be identified and minimised and all pupil groups endorsed this need .... pupils differed in how much they could stand of verbal teasing, physical confrontations, theft or destruction of their property or being 'sent to Coventry'. A few saw bullying as an inevitable part of school life; 'We don't have it except at a natural level'...'It does toughen you up a bit'. Others needed to escape; 'I need to go and cry it out'

(School Life – Pupils views on Boarding – Roger Morgan)

Peer group relationships are an important element in any group living situation. Both boys and girls rely heavily on the support of peers throughout their childhood. Peer group bonds will become strong and enduring as a result of shared experiences, good or bad. When young people are subjected to poor or oppressive care the bonding may take the form of a covert, distrustful sub-culture in which bullying and intimidation can flourish and, ironically, children may then be less ready to turn to an adult when in distress. A new child or young person who is recognisably 'different', or particularly vulnerable, may find him or herself isolated or excluded from the 'group'. This often leads to bullying, subsequent deterioration in standards of behaviour and further marginalising. In some cases it can lead to self harm, suicide, attempted or actual. In January 1993 a 16 year old pupil at a well known public school in Berkshire committed suicide. The inquest said bullying might have been a factor in his death. An independent report subsequently called for pupils to have agreed means of contact with the Social Services Department's inspection unit and for a survey to be commissioned about bullying.

Good practice is related to staff understanding that a cycle of rejection can exist (even in the best run establishment), recognising the symptoms at an early stage and being able to intervene sensitively. They will also recognise that, although the welfare of the victim is of first importance, the perpetrator may also require their understanding, and that his or her claims on their time and sympathy should not be dismissed. A bully's unacceptable behaviour may derive from personal unhappiness or feelings of inadequacy, and staff should be prepared to try to understand the cause of this. Staff also need to be alert to the possibility of racial harassment and victimisation, and should take action to deal with it immediately it occurs.

> 'When the other kids used to call me Paki, the staff never took any notice, or just told you to ignore them. I know Mr X hated anyone who wasn't White by the way he treated us. It's no good complaining though, because no one really cares'.
>
> *(Young Asian in Care)*

In schools, peer groups, for much of the time, are single-gender, and may remain so but staff will need to be aware of changing dynamics in peer friendships, especially at about the age of 15 to 17 when single-sex bonds can come under stress as many boys and girls pair off and separate from the group. For example, where a school admits girls only to the sixth-form, tutors and staff generally need to be particularly aware of potential problems, as well as recognising the benefits for boys and girls of living in a mixed-sex establishment.

Staff in children's homes, and to some extent also those in boarding schools, need to be realistic about the nature of the relationships a child has with a peer group. Anecdotal evidence from young people who have grown up in children's homes point to the existence of a life between children 'hidden' from the staff. This life may, at times, be characterised by bullying and intimidation. We know that sometimes children entering children's homes are fearful of the existing peer group and construct coping mechanisms which are not conducive to establishing positive relationships with either staff or other children.

Residential staff need to try to understand the children's network by acknowledging it exists, being prepared to talk about it with the children and, most importantly, not being afraid of the existence of something of a 'secret life' in the home which they cannot know about. This is after all normal adolescent behaviour; adolescents in a family have secrets from their parents. Good parents can take responsibility for the whole life of their adolescent children without necessarily knowing the details of every aspect of it. A similar principle can be applied by staff working in a school or home. By being prepared to talk with the young people about it, staff can signal that they consider themselves responsible for the consequences of what is happening within the children's sub-culture without having to know every detail of it. Such an approach should clearly indicate to the young people that abusive behaviour is an acknowledged danger and that, whilst respecting their growing maturity and independence, any hint of it will lead to direct staff intervention.

Good practice will recognise the problem of bullying and staff working in an open and trusting community will provide support for all children and young people when they feel vulnerable. They need to be prepared to be constantly vigilant, without being over-bearing and intrusive. In schools, trained prefects, monitors or other senior boarders may also accept some responsibility for younger boarders, realising that they have a pastoral role. Older boarders should not, however, have completely unsupervised access to younger ones nor should their duties be unmonitored.

It will also be important to discuss bullying in any meetings between staff and children and young people. In schools bullying needs to be addressed in the personal, social and health education (PSHE) programme on the curriculum. In children's homes staff need to know the approach to bullying and the extent of the problem in any local schools attended by children from their home. They should also take the opportunity to raise the topic from time to time with small groups of children and young people, or with individuals when necessary. Above all there should be an unmistakeable atmosphere of tolerance and respect for every individual and a clear expectation that bullying will not be overlooked, no matter whether it is just children the others find odd, or girls, if they are in a minority, or whoever they may be. Adults will be open with children and young people and willing to talk frankly with them and listen sympathetically to their views. If this is so, it is likely that the children will, in their turn, be open and frank, both among themselves and with staff.

Finally, the question of what we might think of as 'institutional bullying' particularly in some boarding schools, needs to be addressed. Although this form of intimidation is less common than it was, regrettably, practices appear to continue in some schools, often as initiation rites for new boarders. They are usually of a ritualistic nature and, because they may be seen as a 'tradition' of the school, they may be ignored (even sometimes condoned) by staff. Such rituals, apart from any inherent physical danger, are often abusive and undesirable. Efforts should be made to root them out and put a stop to them, no matter how long they may have formed part of the life of the school. Autobiographical literature gives ample evidence of the serious fear, pain and humiliation which can be suffered, often by young and very vulnerable children, in such 'institutional bullying'.

'Bullying is .... a very serious matter for pupils who are being bullied even if relatively few are seriously affected. This is all the more so since there were wide variations between schools in the number of pupils reporting bullying as a 'worst aspect' of boarding, suggesting that attention needs to be paid to the issue (as the vast majority of pupils themselves propose should happen) where it is prevalent even for a minority.'

(School Life: Pupil's views on Boarding – Roger Morgan)

COMMUNICATION

'What I need is a good listening to.'
(Acknowledgments to The Children's Society)

'Shut up, don't ask so many questions, can't you see I'm busy'.
(Overheard parent)

'I remember in those first exchanges how calm we were with one another. Perhaps the presence of an absolute stranger, but one who listened and understood what I said was comforting in a very real and physical way. My whole body seemed relaxed, and the anxiety and tension melted away quickly and painlessly'

Brian Keenan describing his first meeting with John McCarthy as hostages in 'An Evil Cradling' Vintage Books 1992

Photographed by Clive Arrowsmith.

"What I need is a good listening to."

Registered Charity Number: 221124.

The Children's Society
Making lives worth living

WE GIVE YOUNG PEOPLE A VOICE IN SOCIETY. TO FIND OUT MORE, PHONE 081-812 0822.

'One of the very young children who experienced Pindown, (isolation with no communication) a ten year old .... was described in the log book: 'He's just a little boy (Emergency Duty Team) delivered him at 12.40 ...... still crying at 2.30am'. The next day this child was so distressed another member of staff recorded that he was trying everything to get out. He had attempted to abscond three times 'then tried to bite himself to death, made himself sick and finally tried to open his tummy up with his finger nails .... He cannot understand why he can't

(a) see mum

(b) watch television

(c) go outside and play'

'The Pindown Experience and the Protection of Children'

A Levy and B Kahan, 1991

Communication is the main tool the residential care worker has. This, of course, is about talking, non-verbal communication, appropriate touch, but most importantly about listening. Without listening and communicating, children's needs can pass unnoticed, even when they are quite serious needs. Communication , being listened to, being understood, are universal human needs as the above quotations suggest.

The most important function of staff in residential care is to be with children and young people, but they must learn to listen patiently to them. When a distressed child or one with a problem approaches a member of staff their opening remarks may cover something of much greater importance and concern than appears at first sight. Staff need sensitive antennae for this kind of thing and management should ensure that there are training opportunities for them to learn how to listen and communicate with children. Doing so is not a skill which comes naturally to many people but it is an essential skill in communicating with children.

'The key to successful communication is having a common ground with the child. Some interviewers interpret this as meaning that they should be childish and should pretend to have interests and an outlook they do not have. This is ruinous – children are quick to spot such a phoney approach It is not so much interests and preferences that are important as an attitude to life. If a child says that he loves milk chocolate and the interviewer says that he personally prefers olives, they are still on common ground because the interviewer can get as enthusiastic about olives as the child can about chocolate – we can have interesting conversations with children even though our likes and dislikes may be very different. A child might not be able to understand how we can spend a whole evening playing bridge, but he could easily understand our spending a whole evening doing **something** we like because that is just what he does himself. He may not recognise the common ground unless it is pointed out to him, but it is the interviewer's job to do this.

Adults often do not recognise common ground because of their assumption of moral superiority. One of the pervasive qualities of our adult outlook is that we have built up a hypocritical self-image that successfully fools, not only our friends, but ourselves. It is surprising how often an adult will give a self righteous lecture to a child about lying when he himself has just refused an unwanted invitation by untruthfully pleading a previous engagement. He will tell a child how wicked it is to steal when he himself has been padding his income tax return for years. He will give the child a lecture on the immorality of trespassing and then drive home at ten miles an hour over the speed limit. The adult attitude might be more impressive if the child were as convinced of our superior morality as we are ourselves. The chances are that a child will see through our hypocrisy, and teenagers are especially good at doing this'.

'Interviewing Children and Adolescents' – Dr John Rich MD (MacMillan)

The writer quoted above, although talking mainly of arranged interviews, highlights many issues which are important in communicating with children and young people in other circumstances, including:–

- age and culture related vocabulary;
- body language;
- putting children at ease;
- the pros and cons of physical comforting gestures;
- intelligence levels;

- special difficulties like shyness, aggressiveness, manipulativeness, the 'desperate need' of deprived children 'to be accepted and understood';
- children's views of adults' roles, dress, authority and power;
- aides to communication like furniture, setting, refreshment, pets, etc.

He wrote the book because he had observed that:–

'many people (including a large proportion of interviewers who are experienced and competent in adult work) find it hard to communicate with children'.

Confidentiality is of great importance to children. They need to be able to trust that what they say will not become the subject of gossip among staff or be mentioned to other pupils without their permission. However, they also need to be helped to realise that not everything they disclose can be kept confidential. What is vital is that children should be confident that they know what is likely to happen and understand why it will happen. Staff must explain the possible consequences of what they say and reassure them that, if it is impossible to keep the information confidential, the child will know what is likely to take place subsequently, and need not be frightened of the consequences. Staff can help each other in this very difficult and sensitive matter, drawing on each others' experience.

Sometimes it is necessary for staff to initiate communication with a child about painful or difficult matters. It is probably best for the member of staff, having secured the attention of the child within appropriate privacy, to state the information simply and directly. It will not be helpful to soften or understate the position in an attempt to preserve the child's equanimity. Being direct at the outset will relieve the child of the burden of trying to uncover the true position if he senses that the full picture is being withheld. The member of staff will then need to listen to the child's response, helping him or her to find the right word and cope with the stress or anger but not at this stage to offer solutions or other suggestions. Given time, the child will indicate when s/he is ready to try to resolve the situation facing them. At this stage the member of staff might offer suggestions for the child to consider but these should be tentative and aimed at enabling the child to formulate his/her own proposals. It may be necessary to return to the subject again with the child after a period of reflection.

FAIRNESS AND JUSTICE

One of the issues about which children and young people feel strongly is injustice and unfairness. Homes and schools can harbour injustice, often in only small matters, which are nevertheless important as far as the children are concerned. Even the best run of them may have occasions of injustice on a daily basis. These can readily go unnoticed and are often accepted on the part of both staff and children and young people as just being a part of everyday life. But it is important that children and young people have the opportunity to challenge perceived injustices and to talk through grumbles, grievances and other problems either in an open forum or with someone of their choice when there is a need. It is also important that, when life appears to be falling about them or the dead hand of discipline threatens, the child is able to have someone of his or her choosing, an adult, an older girl or boy, or a friend, to act as an advocate. In all cases good practice will decree that where the trouble has occurred outside the home or school a member of staff will take an advocate's role and support them.

PHYSICAL REASSURANCE AND TOUCHING

Care has to extend to the provision of real comfort and solace when these are needed.

> 'Say the welfare officer (social worker) has to come and criticise the child in some way, then its got to have somebody to turn to .... even if they just fling their arms around them and sob like hell, its just to know that there is somebody there' (*concerning a boy who had expected probation to be recommended but was told it would be custody*)
>
> 'The poor kid's just split into a thousand fragments. At this point he desperately needs the help of someone on the residential staff of the establishment' (*recollection of an adult formerly in care*)
>
> *'Growing up in Care': Ten People Talking – Barbara Kahan*

An important aspect of communication in everyday life is touch and touching. Touch is also an important component of staff skills in communicating with children. This was recognised in the Department of Health guidance on 'Permissible Forms of Control' where it is clearly stated that staff may demonstrate 'parental' type affection by touch. However, because of certain abuses in children's establishments which have become the subject of enquiries, many staff have become nervous of physical contact with children and some organisations have even imposed restrictive rules on them. We cannot explore this important subject in depth, but we would urge that it should be the subject of training and discussion as an integral part of care. Children need, as all human beings do, to be touched and to deprive them of touch completely is not good practice.

'Two men came, ... walked me out (blindfolded) and helped me into some kind of van .... I sensed as I clambered in that other people were there, other prisoners. They were too silent to be guards .... The guards made ready to drive us off. Waiting there, waiting to go to where I didn't know, I felt a hand touch my foot. This was not the hand of a guard. Some other prisoner had reached out and touched my foot. I took some reassurance from it and I am sure that the man who touched me was reassuring himself. I fumblingly put my hand upon his and patted it gently. It was a strange first human touch conveying such warmth and companionship in such desperate circumstances. I remember it still, that first mutual reaching out of concern.'

An Evil Cradling – Brian Keenan. 1992

The key principle in the Department of Health guidance is the need for staff to discover the significance of touch for each child preferably before or certainly at the time of admission to the home. All staff have the responsibility and the right to understand the significance of touch for each child if they are going to make good judgments in this sensitive aspect of care. They also need to understand and accept that children, like all of us make instinctive and informed choices in relation to those we wish to be physically close to, and it is no criticism of an individual staff member if a child does not like to be touched by them. We suggest that staff who have particular relationships with children (not necessarily just key workers or house staff) should in quiet moments sit down together with a child and discuss how they would feel about the particular staff member showing comfort by touching them in times of distress. This would give child and worker a chance to reflect on the matter and gain greater understanding by discussion .

When a child is acutely distressed a member of staff has to make a sensitive judgement about whether the best thing is to talk to the child, or whether to put an arm around them without asking. It may be wise to be cautious and gently ask whether they would like to be touched or hugged just at that moment. On occasions when it is necessary to restrain a child physically, it may be important to keep talking while checking simultaneously with the child whether they are feeling more in control so that restraint can be loosened. Some children may wish to avoid any verbal communication, but these decisions inevitably relate to sensitive judgements and detailed knowledge of children and their individual personalities. It is not possible to set down precise rules of conduct in such matters. What is possible is to broaden understanding and deepen sensibility by discussion, training, reading and by communicating with children themselves.

We advocate that on, each occasion, before touching a child in distress or physically restraining a child out of control, a member of staff should endeavour to talk with them. For example, in the case of a distressed child, a staff member may say,

> *'You're really upset, I feel I would like to give you a hug to help make you feel better – is that okay?'*

In the case of a child nearing the limits of control a staff member may say,

> *'If you don't calm down, we are going to have to restrain you physically – you do realise that don't you?'*

Both approaches invite the child to reply. When incidents require recording it is a good safeguard to the member of staff to be able to record the verbal conversation which took place, including how the child responded, before touch or restraint was applied.

6.4.6 Sexuality and Sexual Relationships

'The Consumers Association recently asked 150 children where they found out about sex. Most learned from friends. Magazines came next, then in order, teachers, parents, television, brothers and sisters. This has predictable consequences. Each year in the UK more than 8,000 girls under sixteen become pregnant, the highest rate in Europe ... 'We tend to assume that teenagers nowadays know it all' said Ruth Grigg of the Family Planning Association. 'But they don't. You still get people writing to teen magazines agony columns to ask whether they will get pregnant if they use the same bath water as their boyfriend''

(Sunday Times 9 May 1993)

'Parents will have to bring their fireside chats about the birds and the bees forward several years if they want to influence their children's sexual behaviour. According to Mildred Blaxter, who coordinated the ESRC's programme on Behavioral Research into HIV and AIDS, many children are already sexually active by the age of 13 or 14.'

(Taken from a research programme 1987–1991 reported in Social Sciences – News from the Economic and Social Research Council March 1993 Issue 18.)

'Rosetta Smith had tried everything to stop the teenage mothers at her school from becoming pregnant a second time. Then she let them have a contraceptive implant and suddenly found herself at the forefront of an American struggle over reproductive rights. Accused of undermining their morals, risking their health and – because most of the recipients were black – of fostering 'racial genocide' – to all these charges Dr. Smith has a caustic answer: 'Morality is fine for an ideal world. But I'm dealing with the real world. We know these kids are having kids. We know they're sexually active. How are we going to deal with that? With whatever it takes. That's all."

(Ian Brodie, The Times 5 May 1993)

The growth of awareness of sexuality in themselves and others is essential to the development of all children and young people. Good care is needed to ensure that they grow into thoughtful adults with responsible and mature attitudes to sex. The subjects of sexuality and sexual relationships are almost always fraught with difficulty. Adults often have problems talking about the issues, they feel embarrassed or unsure of themselves, and young people are often unwilling, or feel it unnecessary, to discuss their feelings and problems with adults. The quotes above demonstrate that when dealing with issues concerning sex and sexuality staff are working in an area in which there is a wide range of values. The moral climate surrounding sexuality has changed rapidly in recent years, and is continuing to change; and the values which different people hold cover a constantly changing spectrum. This means that whatever staff do they are likely to be criticised. It is important therefore that they make their approach to the issues clear and be prepared to defend decisions against what might sometimes appear to be unwarranted attacks from others further away from the situation. It is also important to remember that sexual behaviour in residential settings is relatively public compared with elsewhere, and ensure that undue fuss is not made because of that. This means being clear what is normal (though public) and what is harmful or dangerous.

A number of principles should apply in discussing issues of sexuality:–

- Young people have a need for information and education on issues concerning sexuality; (*Sex Education in Schools: Proposed Revision of Circular 11/87* indicates a national approach to this issue).
- Staff have a duty to discuss these issues when a young person asks for advice or help.
- Staff should discuss and agree with parents and/or schools who will take responsibility for a young person's sex education.

- Young people should be encouraged to feel positive and responsible about their sexuality and their sexual identity.
- There should be clear and understood ground rules about sexuality within homes and schools.

Young people need to grow up with accurate knowledge and awareness of sexual issues. This is not to say that staff should encourage sexual activity, but that they should foster a responsible attitude to all issues of sexuality. It is important that both house staff in schools and staff in children's homes know the arrangements for sex education in the respective schools. Where appropriate, schools need to be aware of the role of care staff in this area and, above all, there should be a close working relationship between house or home and school. Consideration must also be given to the needs of children and young people with learning or physical disabilities, which can present staff with particular difficulties; for example, making it possible for a physically disabled adolescent boy or girl to masturbate, or helping them to discuss sex and sexuality without embarrassment. Staff should only attempt to address these issues when they are confident that they really understand the children's needs. This is a very specialised area of child care which we cannot address in this book. Staff who work with disabled children and would like more help than we can offer can approach the Council for Disabled Children at the National Children's Bureau. We suggest that any establishment, school or home, which cares for disabled children and young people should seek to establish some form of training which will help staff to understand and deal with the inevitable human problems.

It is well known that parents have great difficulty in discussing sexual matters with their children. In fact it provides a regular source of material for comedy writers. For care staff working in residential settings the difficulties are at least as great as for parents, but in many cases, particularly with children who have been sexually abused, the difficulties can be much greater. This area of work is an important subject for training initiatives. However, all staff can derive confidence in addressing children on sexual matters by using staff discussions which will increase their capacity to articulate the subject; in particular to be verbally direct without embarrassment or coarseness. Managers can best provide support by recognising the central importance of issues of sexuality for residential staff responsible for the proper upbringing of adolescent young people. External managers and officers in charge should ensure that training programmes are available and that sensible discussion of sexuality is a regular feature of staff meetings.

SEXUALITY

Adolescent sexuality, although it is an essential part of being a teenager, can be a cause of much distress and worry for the young people themselves and for the adults who care for them during some difficult times. Openness between them is vital. Young people need to know that there is an adult to whom they can turn in confidence for advice and comfort. This adult need not be a member of the care staff in a home or school; it may be a teacher, a parent or even an older brother or sister but staff should see their task as helping young people to decide who they feel they can rely on in these circumstances.

Young people should not be put under pressure to talk about their sexuality and their sexual development if they do not wish to and, if they are not willing, this should not be interpreted as a problem in itself. Openness means that if a young person wants to talk to someone they should feel able to do so quite freely, but without pressure.

One of the first steps in ensuring that there is an open atmosphere in which issues of sexuality can be discussed, including individual orientation, is for residential staff themselves to be aware of their own sexuality and their attitude to other people's. If necessary discussion in supervision sessions with line managers, or group discussions should be used to enable staff to reach the understanding and approach needed. This is especially important if there are issues of gay and lesbian sexuality either with staff or young people within the home or school. There is no place for homophobia in any setting and some individuals may need support in reaching the adjustment of attitude that may be required. Young people will be discovering their own sexual orientation for the first time, and must feel that they will be accepted and supported by staff, whatever their orientation. A sense of value and self-worth are essential for children and young people. If gay or lesbian young people face prejudice from staff who should be caring for them, then it must be understood that those staff are not doing their job properly. The environment in which young people determine their sexuality must be free from prejudice. Many adolescents pass through a period of confusion, during which they may feel sexually attracted to people of both sexes at different times. There must be no pressure from staff to accept or reject either orientation; the role of staff should be to help them to come to terms with their feelings, not to decide what those feelings might be, and to understand that the human process of maturation brings questioning and uncertainty for most people.

Lack of conformity to a perceived group sex identity can lead to teasing, harassment and bullying and some young people may need support at such a time. Intolerance can be a reflection of poor relationships or an unhappy ethos in a home or school. The sexual behaviour of young people may reflect their own poor self-image and their craving for closeness, tenderness and a sense of belonging. They may mistake sexual activity for love and, after initial sexual experiences, end up feeling cheated and abused. Adolescent girls may be particularly at risk, and staff must make special efforts to ensure that the girls do not allow themselves to be exploited by others. A great deal of time will be needed in discussing these and related issues and establishing a set of values with the young people.

SEXUAL RELATIONSHIPS

It is natural for young people to experiment with sex. The role of staff in 'managing' this aspect of behaviour of young people in their care needs to be seen as similar to that of a good parent. Ground rules which have been discussed and agreed to by young people and acceptable standards of behaviour have to be established. One fundamental rule in residential establishments may differ from some private households ie. that young people cannot be allowed to sleep with one another in a children's home or school. Although this is prescriptive, it is common sense that staff should neither openly nor tacitly encourage young people into sexual activity. The legal aspects of sexuality must inevitably form the basis of any rules although these will not be sufficient guidance on their own. Adequate factual information should be available to enable staff and young people to be quite clear about the legal restraints on sexual behaviour, as well as being informed about other important aspects of it.

If staff find that young people have transgressed the rules on sexual behaviour on the premises, it is unlikely to be helpful to react in a 'knee-jerk' way. Current practice in some establishments is often to expel or move the young person from the school or home immediately, with little thought for the long-term consequences. This is usually because it is considered that any other action might be interpreted as condoning the behaviour. We would suggest that such a reaction may not be appropriate. Two factors need to be considered. The first is the balance between the needs of the individual and the needs of the group. Would it put the stability of the larger group at risk if the young person were to remain? The second factor is the need to consider the possibility of further risk to the young person if they are not allowed to remain. For example, if a young woman in care becomes pregnant, it is not uncommon for her to be moved from the home to bed and breakfast accommodation. This will invariably put her welfare in even greater danger, and may have long term consequences for her and her baby. Although specialist accommodation for young pregnant girls is often not readily available, the alternative is not to act like 'a Victorian father' and 'push her out in the cold'. In a well run home where children and young people participate in decision making, in planning daily life and discussing problems openly with staff, in some cases at least it should be possible for a pregnant young woman to remain in residence.

The first step in dealing with transgression of rules on sexual behaviour must be to ensure that all young people are aware of what the rules are. This will mean discussion with them at the school or home. If they are involved in drawing up the rules, and have a sense of 'ownership', they are more likely to respect them. If the home or school has an open and warm atmosphere and young people actually enjoy living there they are much less likely to want to break the rules, and thereby jeopardise an enjoyable and pleasant environment. They are also likely to put pressure on their peers to abide by the rules, rather than 'rock the boat'. Rules on sexual behaviour should be discussed with newcomers when they join the group so that they too understand the importance of keeping them. Where individuals choose to ignore them, staff must make a judgement in each case on the appropriate action to take. Occasionally, expulsion from school may be appropriate. Often it will not be, and other less severe sanctions may be used. Even if a young person is expelled or moved on elsewhere it is important that staff do not act as though they no longer have any responsibility for that young person's welfare. Appropriate support, guidance and counselling needs to be arranged and they should liaise with the new home or school to ensure the transition is a smooth as possible, and does not worsen an already difficult situation.

As with other aspects of child care, the model of behaviour offered by staff plays a significant part in the setting of standards and attitudes. Inevitably personal relationships, sometimes sexually focused, will develop between staff members. The existence of warm, non-exploitative, open and caring relationships between adults as well as between adults and children can add to the positive environment of the home or school. Staff must, however, recognise the potentially damaging effects of relationships which others in the establishment, staff or children see as inappropriate. Additionally, staff behaviour on duty or in the vicinity of the establishment must take these sensitivities into account. Children and young people are acutely aware of the behaviour of adults who are responsible for them, and it is reasonable to expect staff behaviour to conform to the overall standards expected of young people living in the establishment.

Problems can arise when the difference in age between staff and young people in their care is not very great. There can be advantages in having some quite young staff because of their understanding of the feelings of young people and how they set their priorities as a generation. Young staff, however, must be able to identify with and be sure of the support of older staff. Otherwise their position can become very difficult and major problems of control and general management may arise as a result of the narrow boundary between them and the young people they care for. Staff in any establishment whose primary purpose is to provide for the needs of others have to be able, as part of their professional development, to consider the impact of their work on their own emotions and feelings. Supervision and support systems need to be adequate to assist staff of all ages to understand and deal with these aspects of their work.

Sometimes staff may become aware of a sexual component in their relationship with a young person. Professional relationships between staff and young people will **always** preclude sexual relationships, but the possibility of sexual feelings, which might in other circumstances be quite legitimate, needs to be acknowledged, and managers also need to be aware that these possibilities exist. Rather than automatically taking a punitive attitude, towards either staff or young people, managers need, wherever appropriate, to try to understand problems which a member of staff may be experiencing and help him or her to deal with it. Changing a staff member's shift or duties may be ways of reducing tension or strain. In the absence of professional codes of conduct, such as those for doctors and staff working in higher education, local policies and procedures should make it clear that sexual relationships between staff and young people constitute disciplinary offenses. This would create a simple rule for staff to follow in their relationships with young people in their care, and would also provide a clear basis for handling breaches of the rules when they occur.

Supervisors need to be aware of staff, sometimes young or inexperienced but not always, who confuse sexual attraction towards a young person with what they believe to be professional concern. Such staff may insist that they have a 'special', even 'therapeutic' relationship with a particular child and that they should be allowed to pay special attention to them, both within and outside the home or school. They may be resistant to any suggestion that their intense involvement with the child is anything other than in the child's best interests. Considerable firmness on the part of supervisors may be needed and they may need to take disciplinary action as well as offering counselling and support.

Depending on local circumstances it may be that staff, while off duty and away from their place of work may come across young people in various social environments, for example in a cafe, club or pub. In such circumstances, even though they are off duty, staff need to recognise they have continuing responsibilities to the young people,including ensuring that they are not, for example, drinking under age. Although it may be a demanding situation for both the member of staff and the young people, the kind of relationship which should exist is not one which can be switched on and off according to hours of shift working. Nor is it reasonable or fair to expect young people themselves to make the relatively sophisticated distinction between a working relationship with a member of staff and a private one.

SEX EDUCATION

Many schools provide at least some form of sex education, but not all. Some young people, including some in children's homes, may be excluded from education. It may therefore fall to residential staff to educate and inform young people about sex and sexuality and they therefore need to be able to discuss these issues with young people in their care, both on an individual and group basis.

In recent years twenty six organisations, educational, health, family planning and religious groups, voluntary organisations and marriage guidance, set up a sex education forum. This promotes the best means for parents, schools and others with responsibilities for young people to provide them with suitable and adequate sex education. The Sex Education Forum stresses that the three fundamental dimensions of sex education are knowledge, social skills, and attitudes and values. (*A Framework for School Sex Education* produced at the National Children's Bureau 1992). Although baseline knowledge of the facts of human reproduction is undoubtedly an important part of any sex education programme, education about sex should stress the importance of strong and loving relationships, whatever the sexual orientation of the young person. It is also essential that young people are given information about the possible dangers to health of sexual activity, including the potential threat to life of unprotected sex. This means that they must be given full and sound information about safe practices, and in particular where to obtain confidential advice about contraception and family planning issues. The role of staff in this will depend on the individual young person concerned, but they all need to be able to give information and advice. Leaflets and written information can be useful and contacts should be made with local agencies such as family planning clinics, and voluntary organisations such as Brook Advisory Clinics, Relate and Care for the Family. They may be able not only to provide information, but also a member of staff who can advise young people and perhaps help to train staff. Contact addresses for these organisations are provided in APPENDIX 4.

In June to September 1991, the Sex Education Forum carried out a survey into local education authority support and monitoring of school sex education. This showed that there was inconsistency in policies and monitoring of sex education; confusion concerning the roles and responsibilities of teachers and parents in providing sex education; and widespread anxiety concerning the teaching of sex education.

> 'The overall impression gained from the survey suggested that the anxieties of those significant adults involved in the provision of sex education are overriding responses to the needs of the young people receiving the education.'

It concluded, amongst other findings, that teachers should be provided with adequate support and training if they are to be expected to give sex education in the classroom, and that *'the views and needs of young people should be fully considered during consultation for, and planning of any sex education programme.'*

Children's homes and residential schools are as much a part of this national scene as ordinary families. Residential staff in children's homes have an even more difficult task than teachers. They carry some parental type responsibilities and many of the children and young people they care for have had very unhappy experiences in relation to sex. They need as much help as possible in overcoming these and preparing for future relationships.

In 1991 it was estimated that 84,000 15 year old girls in England had sexual intercourse but only 18,000 had visited family planning clinics. The rate of conception among 15–19 year olds for England and Wales was one of the highest in Europe, 69 per 1,000, seven times the corresponding figure in Holland. The teenage abortion rate was six times that of Holland. The 'great silence' of British reluctance to talk about sex, was blamed in a ministerial speech in 1993 for these regrettable trends.

'More than 8,000 under 16s become pregnant each year – the equivalent of an average of two per secondary school in England and Wales.'

Research suggests that the Netherlands' acceptance of teenage sexuality, their widespread sex education and easy access to confidential services are key factors responsible for their much lower pregnancy rate. These approaches do not, however, appear to lead to earlier sexual activity. The median age of 17 years at first intercourse is the same as in Britain. The difference in pregnancy rates appears to be due to more effective use of contraception by Dutch teenagers.

Homes and schools should, as indicated earlier, make it clear that sexual activity on the premises is not permitted, and staff must try to educate young people to ensure that they have a healthy and responsible attitude to sex. Such a stance is not necessarily incompatible with making condoms available to them. Young people are sexual beings and may well be sexually active; this has to be accepted by staff. In recognising the threat to life of unprotected sex through AIDS in particular, and the problems associated with unwanted pregnancy, including the quality of life for babies of very young mothers, it cannot be right to deny access to condoms for those young people who are sexually active. *'Child Facts'* published by the National Children's Bureau show that one in seven young women who leave care are pregnant. Public opinion is changing and has recently indicated that such a practice ie. provision of condoms, would not be totally unacceptable. Calls by politicians advocating the free provision of condoms in schools to those over the age of sixteen have evoked support, as well as dissent, from all sides of the political spectrum. Staff will need to consider whether condoms should be available on the premises and, in doing so, seek the views of parents, senior managers, elected members of local authorities, and managers and governors in the voluntary and private sectors. The dilemma is national and not one they face alone. Responsible agencies and parents must be encouraged to address it. Young people cannot be expected to ask staff for condoms – this would be self-defeating. It might, however, be possible in a well run establishment with the right ethos and atmosphere, for condoms to be kept in bathroom cabinets used only by older adolescents. In carefully controlled circumstances, it might also be appropriate for some establishments to consider installing a condom machine, inaccessible to anyone other than those for whom it is intended.

A further issue which has gained recognition in the context of sexuality is that of cross dressing. Although relatively uncommon, it is possible that staff in a home or school may be caring for a child or young person who enjoys dressing in clothes of the opposite sex. This trend is partly reflected in contemporary fashion, but for some children may represent a specific psychological need. It is important that residential staff do not confuse this inappropriately with homosexuality or an attitude to sex which might be a risk to others. Clearly, as with other unusual behaviour, it may need to be explored with the child on a personal basis and the primary aim is likely to be how to manage it in a group care setting without engendering ridicule and bullying.

The problem of HIV/Aids presents many delicate issues for residential staff. As noted earlier, Scotland has developed guidance on the subject which will be of value to services elsewhere. A number of children in Scotland have been orphaned by Aids and residential staff and foster parents have had to prepare themselves for helping them as much as possible. Staff who have to confront the loss that children may suffer, or care for children who have become infected themselves, should be assisted by adequate information, in-service training and counselling, if necessary. This work, and the issue discussed in the following section, presents staff with very difficult tasks for which they should not be expected to carry sole responsibility.

SEXUAL ABUSE

The question of the abuse of children and young people by staff is considered in Chapter 8. In this chapter we are concerned with staff who are likely to find themselves having to deal with children and young people who have been sexually abused in the past. This is a problem in children's homes in particular. The survey commissioned by the Warner Committee found that heads of children's homes believed that up to 30% of children and young people in their care had suffered sexual abuse before admission to care. In most focused treatment centres the proportion could well be higher. This demonstrates the scale of the challenge of child sexual abuse.

A potential danger for staff is that young people who have suffered such abuse may act towards staff with inappropriate sexualised behaviour. Staff need to be aware of these possibilities. One of the skills of managers in charge of a residential home will be to balance staff members's 'need to know' about a child's background against a child's understandable reticence that his or her troubled history should not be 'common knowledge ' to anyone who works in the home. At the same time they need to avoid making the child feel s/he is seen as a risk to other children and also to gain the trust of children who may well be distrustful of adults and suffer low self esteem. Residential staff need to understand the issue in some depth and to be able, for example, to respond without displaying shock to sexualised behaviour or children making disclosures, whilst staying with the child's pain and accommodating his or her ambivalence towards adults in spite of the adults' manifest good will. The complex issues of confidentiality ie. not telling other children, but also protecting them against risk, have to be worked out between a staff group and considerable help may be needed in doing this. External consultancy, psychiatric or sex counselling, may be required to give the staff the support required, or specialised child protection staff trained in disclosure work.

When sexual abuse has distorted a child's expectations of caring adults, staff do need to know in order to respond sensitively and safely to the child. This also protects individual adults and allows staff generally to provide the kind of climate in which the child can re-establish confidence in adults.

One further aspect of sexual abuse which staff can find difficult to deal with, is taunting remarks by young people. They may use verbal abuse, make sexually explicit remarks or ask embarrassing questions about a staff member's sex life and sexual orientation. Probably the best way to deal with this is to ignore it as far as possible, and recognise it as an aspect of a particular child's behaviour which should be discussed at a later and quieter moment. Dealing with the problem in this way, by quietly discussing it after the outburst has finished, is likely to make the young person less ready to repeat their taunting. Reacting angrily at the time of the incident may simply inflame the situation though it may be difficult to avoid because of the pain and humiliation which any adult will feel in these circumstances. This is one of the occasions when staff support to each other is very important.

SUPPORT FOR STAFF

We acknowledge that the problems outlined above are some of the most difficult which staff have to face. Society as a whole has been changing rapidly in its attitudes to morality, sexual behaviour, the relationships between males and females and between younger and older people. Many young people in children's homes, and some in boarding schools, have had premature sexual experiences of various kinds and most face acute adolescent anxieties. Their role models, parents or other guardians, have not always provided a clear and secure pattern for their growing up and they may also be resentful about being away from home, even if they were not happy when they were there. All of these factors mean that residential staff have a great deal to contend with and may frequently suffer doubts and uncertainties themselves.

If staff have met with sexual advances by young people they should feel able to discuss it in meetings with colleagues. Practical arrangements to be made for the young people concerned should include ensuring that they have a bedroom to themselves and that in their day-to-day life they are not given any opportunity to abuse other children and young people. It is likely that if, as we suggest, staff create a warm and caring environment, some young people may react in a sexual manner because of their previous experiences. Staff need to be prepared for this too and learn to deal with the problem in as professional a manner as possible, avoiding over-reaction, if they can.

Openness within a staff group enables individuals to raise and discuss issues with each other without fear of retribution or ridicule. Discussions can take place either in group meetings or in individual supervision sessions. Those responsible for managing staff should ensure that they feel confident in talking about the many aspects of sexuality, and there might well be a role for counselling and support from psychologists and counsellors from outside the home or school in dealing with these problems. Where it is known that a young person is likely to behave in a sexual manner towards staff, particular rules may need to be drawn up by staff. They may include the need to avoid staff being alone with the young person, by always having a third person present.

7   Arrival and Settling In: Leaving

7.1 Welcoming

> *'There is no word in Greek for stranger; the word is guest'*
>
> A favourite saying of the late Dr Sheppard, classical scholar and Provost of King's College Cambridge

Children and young people may feel bewildered and frightened when they first arrive at a new home or school. They may well have felt anxious ever since they knew where they were going to live. These natural fears and anxieties cannot be eradicated entirely, but the ideas and suggestions in this chapter could help make the few weeks prior to arrival, and the first few weeks there, a little less traumatic. We have divided the process of arrival into three distinct stages:–

- the period before arrival;
- the time of arrival;
- the first few weeks after arrival.

In boarding schools, newcomers tend to arrive as a group at the start of each academic year. Some schools develop a comprehensive induction process which enables new children to work together to overcome some of the problems of arriving to live in a new setting. Thus this chapter will be particularly relevant to boarding schools which a child or young person enters at a time other than the start of the academic year; and to children's homes, where a newcomer may be required, at any time, to join a group of residents who know each other and have been living together before his or her arrival.

Some boarding schools plan admissions well in advance. This overcomes the problem of facing both residential and academic challenges at the same time and contrasts markedly with the contemporary experience of staff working in most children's homes where the norm appears to be that admissions are nearly always emergencies. This need not be the case. Research shows that many placements in children's homes are made in an emergency because social workers do not accept that residential care may be the right place for a child and delay making a decision until proper planning is no longer possible.

'There is a sense in which a defensive 'last resort' stance – much the most common reaction, in our experience .... actually contrives to reinforce these failings (obvious faults in the child care system itself) ensuring that public care is .... something to be avoided. Some of the precipitate entrances into care, with their distressing lack of preparation, hastily arranged placements, and all the attendant risks of breakdown and further disruptions to follow, seemed to be directly attributable to such negative attitudes. A 'rule of pessimism' operated about the care system, which meant that admission was sometimes almost unthinkable, until it became too late to think at all. 'Last resorts' are, after all, seldom desirable or constructive places to be'.

Who Needs Care – Social Work Decisions About Children – Jean Packman with John Randall and Nicola Jacques, 1986

This practice characterised a period when residential care was a last resort, undervalued, abused and neglected. The failure to allow children's homes to get off to a decent start in their work with individual children has made their task much more difficult and made life unnecessarily traumatic for the children. Contrast this with the degree of preparation which goes into some foster placements.

7.1.1 Before Arrival

There is a common core of good practice which applies across all types of setting. Specific factors to take into account before children and young people first enter a children's home are considered later in this chapter.

In the days before arrival staff should do their best to see that new children experience as little trauma as possible. This means, for example, staff finding out about the children, providing them with information about the home or school, and arranging visits prior to arrival. A child needs to know what to expect and should not arrive on the first day without any idea of what the home or school looks like; where his or her bedroom is and where meals will be eaten and leisure time spent. Evidence from children themselves shows that they want to be involved in seeing and talking about their placement in a children's home or boarding school and it will help them accept and gain the maximum benefit from their stay if staff extend a welcome towards them, and their families, prior to arrival. Primary sources of information that staff need will include records of academic progress and achievement, social history, social work case notes, and medical or psychiatric records.

Wherever practicable, it would be valuable for the new key worker or house tutor to visit the child or young person at home, or foster home, school or health unit. They can then see how the child lives, find out about personal preferences, such as food, sleeping arrangements, and other important likes and dislikes. The new staff member/key worker should be able to talk to the child's parents or other carers and get some impressions of how the child is likely to react to the change of circumstances. In addition, the member of staff can introduce him/herself to the child and start to get to know them. This will help to reassure the child because there will then be at least one friendly face when s/he arrives. Change is bound to cause anxiety when a child moves from one place to another but the kind of measures outlined above could reduce it significantly. For schools, wherever possible, staff should be encouraged to visit 'feeder' schools to meet prospective pupils.

Boarding schools, wherever possible, arrange visits for parents and new boarders in advance of entry. This would be good practice in every type of setting. If a new resident can be given the 'feel' of an establishment by meeting some of the people they will be sharing their lives with, and can see some of the activities, the settling-in process will be greatly helped. Many schools arrange for a long weekend in the term prior to entry. If admissions to other settings such as children's homes or hospitals are properly planned, similar introductions could happen in those settings also. Even if a children's home placement does not finally happen, the visit may be helpful in clarifying what is best for a child, and allow him/her and their parents to voice their wishes and feelings about placements.

Introductory visits include showing newcomers around, introducing them to staff who will be caring for them, showing them their bedroom and facilities such as dining and common rooms. Daily routines can be explained to them, and the times when they will have freedom of choice, for example, when they will be able to go out of the home or school, and arrangements for receiving visitors. They should also, if possible meet other residents, especially those with whom they may spend a lot of time, and be allowed to talk privately with them so that they can know from them what life will really be like. If practicable, visits should take place at a time when social activities are taking place, such as meal times, so that children can experience the everyday atmosphere and perhaps be invited to join in.

As part of the preparation for admission, it would be helpful if staff and existing residents collaborated in producing a simple guide to the school or home, attractively presented and illustrated. Such a publication could remove some doubts and fears by giving very specific information on the workings of the home or school, including details of the people or organisations to whom a new child might go with a problem. An 'unofficial' guide prepared by children and young people who arrived recently, for example the previous year's entry to a boarding school, could also be a useful document for newcomers. Where unplanned emergency admissions to children's homes are unavoidable, a brochure could be a good way of providing at least a minimum of information for a child prior to arrival, and would help to answer some inevitable fears and doubts. It would also provide an opportunity for discussion which might fill in some of the background of the establishment. Reassurance needs to be given that parents, or other responsible adults, are being informed of the child's whereabouts, telephone number and how to get there. In addition, it may be important to help a child construct a 'cover story' to discourage probing questions from other children. Plans to fetch clothing and belongings will also need to be made as part of reconstructing the child's immediate personal world. If at all possible, for the first night or two the child should be able to have privacy in a single room so that information such as a tendency to bed wetting or any potentially embarrassing physical traits can emerge without other children being involved.

Homes or schools should always receive records or other documents about newcomers from previous homes or schools. This may involve pursuing close collaboration with each child's previous establishment. The head teacher or head of home will have to decide who,other than the child, needs to see a child's records. In general, a child should have access to his or her own file (see Chapter 4), although information that needs to be confidential to staff should be kept in a separate section.

Discussions prior to placement, wherever practicable, should involve both parents and child, and residential staff must feel able to talk with the parents from an early stage. In children's homes staff need not assume that this is solely the job of the field worker. If information is lacking, residential staff need to be able to research this information themselves in order to help create a full picture of the child and make proper preparation for his or her arrival. Black staff may have a particular role here in making contact with black families. *Home from Home*, published under the auspices of the Wagner Development Group, suggests that ethnic minority staff, because of their understanding of the dynamics of family life in their culture, which may be different from that of white families, are especially well positioned to deal with the families of children of the same culture.

Staff should make it a priority before a child or young person arrives, to ensure that their bed and living space are ready for them. If other children and young people can be involved in this process, so much the better. As far as possible, the whole home or, in a boarding school, the house or year group, should help prepare for a new child. Their presence will inevitably change the dynamics of a small group, and their arrival is important to everybody.

Proper planning for newcomers results in ensuring that staff are informed about physical or medical problems, such as bed wetting or conditions such as asthma or epilepsy. This information ought to be passed on to them from the child's home or previous placement. It is neither necessary nor desirable for children to have to provide this information themselves. These things should be accepted without fuss so that the child does not have to suffer embarrassing and difficult questions which may make them feel they will have difficulty in being accepted by other people. They must not be made to feel 'different', nor that they are causing extra work for staff. They need also to be reassured that things which make them feel at ease, like an extra pillow or blanket, will be forthcoming without difficulty.

Most people, including children, settle into somewhere new if, when they arrive, they can have some familiar possessions around them which are recognisable and provide tangible links with home or family. It is common good practice in boarding schools for children to bring some personal possessions with them and most children's homes also encourage this.

Planning for arrival takes the needs of each individual child into account and particular attention has to be given to those with specific needs. For example, it would be disastrous for a young person who has to use a wheelchair to arrive at school only to find that he or she cannot attend lessons because there are no ramps to give access to classrooms! Similarly, children and young people who need certain types of medication, for example, inhalers for asthmatics, must know that their medicine is readily available or have it in their own keeping. Careful planning will be helped by consulting parents and children or the previous school or home to determine exactly what is required.

For children and young people of different cultures and from different countries, for example, refugees, as we have already discussed (in Chapter 6) both staff and residents need to understand the importance of each child being treated as an individual, with respect for different faiths and religious practices, different diets, clothes and languages. It cannot be emphasised too strongly that the range of cultures from which children who are not white come, is extremely varied and rich and that the differences between them as individuals are very important eg. a Muslim child is no more related to Afro-Caribbean culture than to a white child, and vice versa. Particularly for those who have come from other countries, recognition of the problems they may have faced, is important; long and perhaps hazardous journeys, immigration control, language difficulties, culture shock and even loss of loved ones. In the case of refugees, from a management point of view, it is also important that financial support has been clearly decided so that a child's education and settling down are not disrupted by disputes between agencies.

7.1.2 Settling In

If care has been taken in making preparations for the arrival of newcomers, the immediate shock of having to live with a large number of strangers can be lessened. However, initial experiences can still be intimidating or frightening, and it is important that staff are able to offer support, guidance, comfort and reassurance wherever necessary. Administrative tasks, as far as possible, should be held over until later. It is important that new children do not feel they are being 'processed' as part of a standardised induction procedure. Over-emphasis on bureaucratic procedures can be very diminishing, and make newcomers feel that their needs are secondary to those of the organisation. Instead, children should be made to feel as comfortable as possible on first arriving at a home or school. A drink and a biscuit, and some discussion, early in their arrival, about what they like to eat can be an important indication that staff are concerned about their physical comfort and general care. Children can be upset and 'turned off' by quite tiny problems, particularly when they are in a very sensitive state eg. when having to leave home.

When appropriate, other children may be involved in receiving a new child but the newcomer should not be handed over to a group of children to be shown around, without careful planning. It will not add to the child's sense of security to feel that, as soon as they have set foot through the door, they are committed to the children's own sub-culture, whatever that may be!

There may be merit in considering whether an older child could take special responsibility to 'look after' a new arrival, in the way that a welcome guest would be received. The older child would gain responsibility in caring for another person whilst the newcomer could gain some comfort from having a 'friend' at the outset. Staff need to provide some training for this task, and be on hand to deal with any problems that might arise. Other older children, for example house prefects in schools, may also play an important part. We feel, however, that at the very early stages the staff member who will have primary responsibility for a child should also take responsibility for introducing him or her to other children and for keeping a very careful watch on the settling-in process.

The introduction of children to a home or school will be greatly assisted if they feel that they have somewhere safe to put their private possessions and treasures. Fear that they may be broken, lost or stolen could be very great indeed.

> 'Each child should have his own room with his own key; theft and 'borrowing' does go on . . . .'
>
> *Welsh NAYPIC*

This means, as we have suggested in Chapter 5, that all children and young people ought to have a lockable cupboard, locker or chest of drawers in which personal possessions can be kept safely. If necessary, they need also to be able to entrust them temporarily to a 'safe' adult.

Unless there are important reasons why contact with parents, family, friends or anyone else significant in the child's life should not be made, arrival in a new home or school will need to be followed very closely by helping the child to contact the people from whom they have been parted, and who are important in their life. They should be encouraged and, if necessary, helped to telephone whoever is important to them so as to make early contact and confirm that they are settling in. If the trauma from which the child has come makes this difficult, staff could discuss with them whether they (the staff) should telephone instead. The importance of contact with parents and others can be demonstrated by providing a child who does not have any money with a Phonecard or 10 pence pieces for the pay phone, or with stamps, postcards or paper and envelopes, so that they may write if they do not telephone. It goes without saying that they require privacy for writing a letter as well as making a telephone call.

In order to help the settling-in process, and to provide continuity with home and family in the first few days, a few younger children might benefit from the presence of a parent or other member of their family overnight. This would normally only be appropriate in schools if a child arrives mid-term but, in some children's homes or hospital units, a very distressed child may need this. Schools, homes and hospitals should provide some facilities for overnight visitors, which may also be needed in emergencies or to help those who have very long journeys. Some parents of children in special schools may need this kind of help in visiting.

7.1.3 The First Few Weeks

In the first few weeks, newcomers will be settling in to new routines, making friends, and beginning to find their way around the home or school. Most will suffer from spells of home-sickness, and some anger or even despair. They will need staff and older children to whom they can turn for advice and sympathy. It is also important that they have plenty of activities to occupy them, either within or outside the establishment. These are critical weeks, and care and teaching staff need to be particularly alert to changes in mood generally, and attitudes to school work. Such monitoring needs to continue at least through the first few months. We understand that a number of boarding schools ban any contact with home for a period of some weeks at the outset of a child's boarding life. This policy, where it still exists, runs contrary to all current thinking and professional good practice and reconsidering it would be wise.

The first few weeks and months may be particularly difficult for some newcomers. Staff may need to work hard to provide a caring and supportive environment to enable new arrivals to cope with the stresses which will arise. Although a child may have one particular person in whom he or she confides, successful handling of problems usually results from team work between the adults, and discreet sharing of concerns and solutions between staff should be encouraged.

The good supportive arrangements already discussed need to be accompanied by well-developed good practice in the induction of new arrivals. Apart from obvious physical considerations such as sleeping and eating arrangements, a number of other aspects of life have to be addressed in the first few weeks. These include:-

- Details of arrangements for keeping in touch with parents, family and friends, information about receiving incoming phone calls, use of pay phones, arrangements for having visitors and time away from the school or home.

- Information on where to go for help with problems, in particular arrangements for dealing with health problems. For older children this will include advising them of their right to choose a General Practitioner. For younger children it will mean advice on who they should see when they feel unwell, and for those who need medication or special help, making sure they are happy and clear about the arrangements for their health and well-being.

- A thorough and formal introduction to the complaints procedure, including what to do if a child wants to raise problems with someone independent of the school (see Chapter 4).

- A carefully thought out programme of leisure activities to engage the interest and energies of new arrivals. This will also have long term importance, as children and young people develop interests which may last beyond when they leave.

- An introduction to facilities available in the local community. These include leisure centres, youth clubs, shopping facilities, parks and sports facilities;

- Taking newcomers through the fire drill and walking them through the designated escape routes in the establishment.

As part of the induction process, the newcomer needs a written version of all he or she has been told. It is not always possible to absorb information at a time of change and upheaval, so having details of complaints procedures, local facilities, domestic arrangements etc in the form of a handbook will help children and young people to assimilate the information, because it will be all together and accurate. The induction period is intended to integrate newcomers into the life of the school or home as quickly as possible to ensure that any feeling of being an 'outsider' is removed. Knowledge of how the formal and informal systems work is important in making a good start in life at a new place. It is also an important element in gaining acceptance into peer groups. The longer a child remains on the 'outside' the more difficult full assimilation into the group will be. This can then lead to rejection by other children and young people, and to problems of loneliness, isolation and perhaps bullying. These, in their turn, may then adversely affect learning, achievement and behaviour.

7.1.4 Short Term 'Guests'

Many child care residential placements are short. Sometimes this is unsatisfactory; on other occasions they represent an interlude which makes sense in the overall context of the plans for a child. Either way, staff should view placements of even a few days as a positive opportunity to contribute to the child's overall well-being. The Dartington Social Research Unit in their book 'Issues of Control in Residential Child Care', suggested there were five conditions for ensuring good standards. We have taken these and suggest that each item can be important even in short term placements, as follows:–

1. *'Young people feel enriched by their residential experience in which they should perceive some caring role'.*

    eg. providing some new experiences such as an interesting meal which they have not previously experienced, or a new game to learn.

2. *'The young people see themselves as acquiring clear instrumental skills during their stay'.*

    Perhaps the easiest example is an opportunity to learn to cook something, use the telephone or video recorder.

3. *'The pursuit by the institution of a set of goals which are matched to the primary rather than the secondary needs of children; that is to the needs which necessitated absence from home rather than those brought about by living away. These aims should be reiterated in a wide variety of ways and permeate the whole control process'.*

    Much energy is often spent on problems created by being away from home care – for example, distress, behaviour and control – which could instead be directed to working with the children on the problems which led to their needing to be admitted to the children's home, like using the resources of the home to facilitate a positive meeting between child and parent. This would need collaboration with the field worker but could be very valuable in the long term.

4.   *'Effective institutions demonstrate some consensus amongst staff, children and parents about what the goals should be and how they should be achieved. To maintain this consensus, leadership should be clear and consistent. Staff should be reminded of the strengths of residential care as well as warned against its weaknesses'.*

Staff who expect to meet and welcome a child need to be conversant with the purpose of the placement and a likely positive outcome. They can use this brief encounter to help bring the child, the staff and the family to a common agreement about what everybody is trying to achieve. This clarity is itself useful even if the expected length of stay is very short.

5.   *'The institutions should make efforts to fragment the informal world of the children by a variety of structural features. This may be by creating small group situations, by giving children responsibility or by encouraging close staff/child relationships'.*

For short term placements, the balance of relationships between child and staff will outweigh relationships between the child and other children and should convey sympathetic interest and concern. The child should not find himself unduly caught up in the unwanted machinations of the children's informal world.

7.2 Moving on

In this section we discuss good practice when children and young people leave residential settings. Whatever their circumstances, and wherever they are going, a common core of good practice can be applied. This includes planning and preparation; continuing care and support after departure in many cases; and the importance of maintaining links between schools and homes and their ex-pupils or residents.

The reasons for children and young people leaving schools and homes are as varied as the settings where they then go to live. They include transition from preparatory schools to senior schools; returns to families from children's homes; transfers between similar establishments, for example one school to another, or a children's home to a foster home. They also include young people moving out of residential establishments to further or higher education, work, training or, regrettably, unemployment and occasionally into the penal system.

Leaving any group is a significant transition for a child or young person, but for reasons of loss and change, it may be particularly traumatic for young people leaving local authority residential child care. Staff need to make the transition as positive as possible; planning to minimise the trauma of sudden change; and ensuring that changes which have to be made, benefit the children and young people as far as possible and do not jeopardise their welfare further. The after care and planning provisions of the *Children Act 1989* are only applicable within social services but the principles of the legislation are likely to be good practice in any setting. Planning the future care of children and young people, and providing after care when needed, are likely to be constructive ways of helping children who are leaving any type of establishment.

In this context, although there are similarities, we acknowledge some major differences in current practice between boarding schools and children's homes. In a boarding school the leaving date will usually have been predictable and agreed between parents, young person and school. Everybody has known what the next stage was going to be and what was likely to be most beneficial. In this respect boarding school children are privileged compared with many in children's homes whose lives have often been punctuated by one move after another and who have constantly had to live with uncertainty and anxiety about the future. As we have suggested earlier, better planning, less prejudiced attitudes towards the value of residential care, and more acceptance of young people's own views on their placements, could mean that the advantages of the greater predictability of boarding school life could also characterise social services child care.

Other features of boarding schools which we would like to see emulated in social services care are the positive associations which young people carry away from school when they leave and the feeling that they can return if they wish to, and be welcomed. Hard though it might be currently to achieve this, we believe it could be of great value if both child care staff and the young people they care for were able to have similarly positive feelings and associations.

Some of the major national child care voluntary organisations try to provide for the understandable human desire to retain contacts with people and places which are part of one's childhood. In the National Children's Home, Action for Children for example, there is an annual event at headquarters to which 'old boys and girls' can come and meet each other and people who worked with them or were responsible for their welfare when they were children and adolescents. In addition the organisations' 'branches' (geographically based divisions) hold local events regularly. Letters and accounts of reunions published regularly in newsletters describe the meetings between 'old boys and girls' spanning many years; groups setting up special arrangements to hold annual events together, and the pleasure expressed in the progress made by people who had been brought up 'in care'. The newsletters also provide opportunities for former 'consumers' to comment critically on what they see as the less personal methods of 'modern' child care services. Many boarding schools, even some university colleges, have similar functions and run old students' magazines. It must remain a matter of some concern that local authorities have not only done little to meet this common human need, but that for many years contacts between young people and the residential homes where they had spent part of their childhood were actively discouraged. They were even described as 'unprofessional' by some social workers, thus discouraging members of the most needy groups from gaining comfort and reassurance from harmless links with the past. It is superficial thinking to assume that people benefit from 'cut-offs' in their lives and that children cannot cope with loyalties to more than one set of carers at a time. It can also be seen as a further unnecessary deprivation of relationships which were significant to children and might have lasted for many years. Such 'cut-offs' often, in our experience, have more to do with the needs of the organisation and the staff than of the young people themselves. They are a sad reflection of failure to understand the emotional impact of changes as experienced by the children and young people.

7.2.1 Planning

In this section we look at the need to plan for the next stages of care for children and young people, whether they are moving to a substitute family, another residential setting or to independence. We have already discussed the need for stability and continuity as part of good care practice in all settings. The importance of planning for the next important stage in their life, whilst maintaining stability and continuity **after** they have moved on, needs to be recognised.

Under the *Children Act 1989*, planning is required wherever children and young people are looked after by a local authority. Although plans look ahead to adulthood, the essential priority for planning is the next stage of care. Plans, and the method of planning, will vary from setting to setting. The length of time a pupil remains in a boarding school may be determined in advance because the school accommodates a particular age group. Some pupils go on to full-time higher education and planning for this can only begin when academic potential has been assessed and choices made about possible career intentions. Residence in children's homes, on the other hand, may be followed by a variety of later placements, and the planning process required by legislation should take the next move into account, as well as issues affecting the current placement.

Planning does not mean that as soon as a child enters a residential setting, staff should be able to predict the date s/he will leave. Plans for leaving need to evolve flexibly enough to take account of developments and changing circumstances of individual children. The *Children Act* requires that, where children are looked after by a local authority, their plans should be reviewed at least every six months (more often at the start of a placement) the reviews allowing both for assessment of present plans and planning of future work. Is there any reason why a process which is essentially coordinating past and future in the child's interests should not also happen in other settings? Boarding schools are likely, in any case, to review the children's academic and social progress regularly. Involvement of the school's care staff would make for a fuller and more rounded picture of each individual child; identifying their needs and helping staff in education and pastoral care to work together in safeguarding and promoting the welfare of the child.

Any child anticipating leaving care must be central to and have an essential role in constructing future plans. (*The Arrangements for Placement Regulations 1991*). Others with an interest in the child's welfare should also be involved; the child's parents and, when appropriate, grandparents and other close relatives, or health care providers and representatives of education.

This may sometimes be a difficult and protracted process as circumstances and views change. However, at the stage of preparing to move on, engagement in the planning process is of great importance. To try to construct a 'perfect' plan may not be realistic and there should always be scope for revision if necessary. It may also be necessary for a young person to return and start again. If this happens, it should not be greeted with dismay but seen as the natural, sometimes faltering process of gaining independence which is replicated in families everywhere. At the same time, whilst recognising the fact that some 'false starts' and 'blind alleys' are likely, it will not be helpful to assume that because young people have been in care they cannot have the determination and ability to follow a career line and succeed in it.

7.2.2 Preparation for Leaving

Throughout their time in any home or school, children and young people need to be able to maintain links with the outside world and to be in close touch with it. In boarding schools, the curriculum needs to include aspects of health education, careers and further and higher education (FHE) counselling, how to deal with living away from home, coping with money, form-filling and benefits and all that comes under the heading of life-skills appropriate for the age-range of the school. In children's homes, where education takes place in the local community, and is not geared to the needs of residential life, many of these elements may have to be provided by the staff as part of essential preparation for young people leaving and entering the adult world. In addition, much of what children and young people do in the daily life and activities of school or home, and in the community, should be planned as essential training for independence and developing responsibility for self and others.

Whilst trying to keep the child's current life closely connected with future plans, staff will need to take a number of practical steps aimed at the transition causing minimal disruption. There are close links here with preparations for the arrival of newcomers. Just as schools and home prepare to welcome new arrivals by visiting them in advance, when children and young people are moving to another setting they should try to ensure that satisfactory arrangements have been made for them in the new settings. Contact should be made between the two places some weeks before the move to ensure that essential information has been passed on about the child's particular needs, likes and dislikes, and to assist, where practicable, in preparing the new setting for his or her arrival. The school or home where the child has been living should make sure that preparations have been made. Their responsibility for the child or young person does not end as soon as the next placement is known. They should try to ensure that the care s/he receives in future is sufficient to safeguard and provide for their welfare.

Introductory visits to the next school or home should be regarded as essential. Two visits would be ideal; one when the child can talk to staff and see the home or school eg. during a weekday, and another perhaps in the evening or at a weekend to enable the newcomer to see the home or school in its social context. If only one visit is possible, it may be best at a time when everyday normal life is going on. There should also be contact with future care staff and, in the case of schools, the tutor and any mentor. Relevant information on the new placement, such as guides or brochures, should be obtained for the child. It would also be immensely useful for the child and the staff of the receiving school or home if they visited the current setting reciprocally. Appropriate and detailed records need to be passed on to the next school or home and, in boarding schools, these may include a portfolio of original work.

Where young people are moving out to live independently, their homes or schools have a responsibility to help them prepare for their new life. Some young people leaving school go on to university or other further education institute. Others may be moving on to employment or training, and living independently. Unfortunately too many may face unemployment. The level of preparation needed for independence will depend on the individual young person and where they are moving to. If they are going to university they may find many of their needs are provided for while, at the same time, they have considerable independence. Preparation for life in a university will not need to be as thorough as for other destinations, although this may depend on a young person's overall family resources. A young refugee, for example, might need a good deal of family-type support and help for a protracted period.

Where young people are moving on to independence in the community, it is important that preparation for it should begin in plenty of time. As we have said earlier, some part of daily living should be geared towards learning skills for adult life but, in addition, specific preparation should be made nearer the time of departure. Some children's homes have accommodation on the premises which allows for a 'semi-independent' life for young people. This may be a bedsit with cooking facilities, attached to the home, or a programme designed to address the problems young people will encounter. It is important that this 'training for independence' is understood from the young person's point of view. It can, unless sensitively handled, become a relatively mechanistic process which ignores the major life change which is taking place.

'The dominant 'independence' message of 'managing on your own' and 'coping by yourself' subtly negates the significance of **interdependence**, that is, young people giving as well as taking, getting on with other people and negotiating reality with the support of agencies, neighbours, friends and partners; the very important interpersonal and relationship skills that our young people needed all the time, and which they found so difficult'.

Leaving Care: Policy and Practice – Mike Stein and Kate Carey, p.158, Blackwell 1986

In boarding schools older pupils generally have studies of their own and assume progressively more and more responsibility for their own lives. Whatever the setting, young people need information and training in skills required for living an independent lifestyle, and should not have to leave a residential setting without them. Some of the areas which are particularly important include welfare services – especially social security, employment, housing and health, and how and in what circumstances they are entitled to them. They also need careers guidance and knowledge of available training opportunities; entitlement to assistance with housing, including housing benefits, and any special housing bodies such as Housing Associations which may be able to help them. Health know-how includes how to register with a general practitioner and dentist; where to go for advice on contraception; and how to obtain free prescriptions. This will be an opportunity for staff to develop or build on existing links with agencies in the community, who can provide information, advice and assistance on all these issues.

Volume 4 of the Children Act Regulations and Guidance provides a useful checklist of practical and financial skills which all young people moving to independence should have. We reproduce the list here:–

- Applying for social security benefits;
- Applying for housing, and locating and maintaining it;
- Contacting the social services department and other caring agencies;
- Contacting organisations and groups set up to help young people who are, or who have been, in care;
- Knowledge of the emergency services (fire, police and ambulance);
- Household budgeting, including the matching of expenditure to income, the cost of living, the regular payment of bills and avoidance of the excessive use of credit;
- Safety in the home and first aid;
- Applying for, and being interviewed for, a job, and the rights and responsibilities of being an employee;
- Health education, including personal hygiene; and sex education, including contraception, preparation for parenthood, and information and advice on HIV/Aids;
- Applying for a course of education or training;
- Registering with a doctor and dentist;
- Finding and using community services and resources;
- The role of agencies such as the Citizens Advice Bureau, local councillors and MPs, and how to write letters to complain or to obtain advice and information;
- How to carry out basic household jobs such as mending fuses (which will involve basic electrical and other knowledge), and safety in the home and first aid;
- Laundry, sewing and other mending and household skills;
- How to use a washing machine and iron
- How to shop for, prepare and cook food;
- Eating a balanced diet.

Of course this list is not comprehensive, nor will it apply to all young people in all settings. It does, however, provide a useful basis of preparation for independence and needs to be part of the day-to-day development of young people.

Staff also need to know about young people's particular problems and needs and their specific strengths and weaknesses so that they can offer adequate help to prepare for the next stages of life. They also have a responsibility to continue to offer support after young people have left a home or school. In the following section we suggest how this support can be provided but we also want to draw attention to the needs of young people leaving the care of local authorities, in particular. Currently, expectations of them are alarmingly unrealistic compared with the general population.

'It is agreed that we must train and prepare young people to be able to manage on their own from the age of sixteen onwards .... Our research .... question(s) this emphasis on the young people's independence, as only 0.5 per cent of all sixteen to nineteen-year-olds in England and Wales live alone. The vast majority, 99.5 per cent live with other people, mainly families, until their early twenties when many then move to live with friends or sexual partners. The independence approach and the expectation of complete independence is, in effect, requiring young people who have experienced difficulties in past relationships and whose current family relationships may be stressful, broken or non-existent, to achieve a particular level of skills and maturity before their peers from non-care backgrounds. Put another way, a group of young people regarded as being in need of care and control up to the age of sixteen, seventeen or eighteen are catapulted into a position of greater vulnerability than that of other people their age'.

Leaving Care, Policy and Practice – Mike Stein and Kate Carey, p.156, Blackwell 1986

7.2.3 Support

Section 24 of the *Children Act 1989* requires a local authority to 'advise, assist and befriend' anyone who has been looked after by the local authority once they leave their care. There is also a duty on local authorities to *'advise and befriend'* other young people under the age of 21 in their area who they consider to be in need of their assistance. Comprehensive guidance on the aftercare provisions of the Children Act is provided in Volume 4 of the series of *Guidance and Regulations on the Act*. The Scottish White Paper *'Scotland's Children'* also emphasises the importance of after care and preparation for adulthood

Although the legislation applies only to local authorities, and in particular to young people leaving their care, we suggest that the principle embodied in this section of the *Children Act* ie. that responsibility for a particular young person does not end when they leave a home or school, is applicable much more widely. The extent to which it may apply depends, of course, on the setting. Many young people leaving boarding schools have families able to provide all the support they need, financial and emotional, to move to independence, and contact with school will be based on social identity and tradition, rather than financial or emotional need. Nevertheless, this is not always so. Attention should be paid, for example, to the needs of pupils from overseas, who may not be returning to their home country, and for whom school may provide the only solid base in their adopted country.

In these situations staff need to know where and to whom these young people can apply for help and what they can expect to be provided for them.

Homes and schools do not have to provide services which are the responsibility of a local authority as a whole. What they can provide, however, is continuing emotional support, in the same way that a family would do when a young person first leaves home. This may mean a bed for the night when a young person feels lonely or homesick; a visit to their new home to see how they are coping, or maintaining contact with their previous home; helping to arrange meetings with friends from home or school; in other words, doing what any good parent would do for their own children in the circumstances. There should, of course, be liaison with the local authority social workers who may themselves be providing aftercare services, and staff will need to sort out what role they can play in providing those services. Their first task will be to tell the young person what aftercare services are available, and who to approach about them, in the local authority. In helping a young person through aftercare, liaison is important to ensure that it is neither overlooked, because it is assumed the local authority has taken responsibility, nor that effort is duplicated. 'Befriending' may not be necessary if a young person already has adequate friends and support from their previous home or school.

7.2.4 *Maintaining Links*

In this section we discuss the need to maintain continuing links between children and young people and the home or school in which they have previously lived. We see this as separate from support, because we are looking at how it can benefit the establishment, rather than the young person, though continuing contact with a previous home or school should also benefit ex-residents and, as we said earlier, we believe former residents should be entitled, and encouraged, to return if they wish.

The concept of the term 'alma mater', which means 'benign mother' is common in boarding schools. Ex-pupils are proud to be associated with an institution they have enjoyed attending. Even if they did not enjoy it, it may have provided them with a good grounding for success in later life and school reunions and networks of ex-pupils are common. Boarding schools recognise the benefits of inviting ex-pupils back to talk to current residents. If they are seen as successful in their lives this can be a source of pride for the school as a whole and for individual pupils, as well as providing good role models for children and young people.

Unfortunately, it is comparatively rare that the same can be said for other settings, especially children's homes. This is largely due to the public and professional stigma which has become attached to children's homes. We have discussed elsewhere how they have too often been seen as places of last resort, even 'dumping grounds' for hard-to-place children and young people. We have argued that this is now an out of date attitude which does not accord either with reality or with the law and national policy. Instead children's homes should provide 'real' care in which children and young people are not made to feel they are 'second class citizens', and can enable them to enjoy and be proud of the home in which they live. This will need a radical change in attitudes, not least among external managers and field social workers, but a start can be made by homes being encouraged to express pride in their achievements and to maintain contacts with their former 'boys and girls'.

Local authorities and voluntary organisations not infrequently decide to close children's homes. Some of these decisions are taken on sensible, but nonetheless cold grounds of economics and political expediency. Do authorities ever pause to consider the significance of these closures for children who have, in the past, spent part of their childhood in them? Should they perhaps endeavour to contact these children, who may now have become adults, or perhaps put together a memento of the home with photographs and documents which could be made available should some of them seek information about their past? These considerations would go a small way to acknowledging the permanent significance of homes for their residents, rather than simply regarding them as 'transit camps' easily dispensed with and forgotten. Earlier in this chapter we referred to the reunions of 'old boys and girls' who lived together in the National Children's Home 'branches'. Barnardo's has also sustained its Barnardo's Guild for a hundred years or more. While local authorities are unlikely to offer parallels, they might nevertheless emulate some of the practices of current boarding schools. Regular contact might be maintained with ex-residents; this would not be difficult to contemplate if a young person had lived in the home for a significant period of time, and if the home had provided the support discussed above. Homes should not be afraid to invite 'ordinary' ex-residents to make return visits. They need not be a spectacular success or have had a dazzling career to provide good role models for current residents. They may provide surprising support for the staff in telling current residents some of the realities of life as they see them from an adult perspective.

To wish to return to it, children in a children's home must feel that they lived in a stable and caring environment and have experienced 'real care'. This is unlikely to be the case if they have been moved repeatedly from children's homes to foster homes and back again. Nevertheless, for former residents to be invited back to the home where they spent a significant proportion of their childhood is likely to be welcomed. It may be that, as part of telling their own children their family history, they may wish to show them where they spent some of their childhood, and perhaps be able to meet some of the staff they knew.

8 Protecting the Welfare of Children and Young People

8.1 Introduction

In this chapter we consider the welfare of children and young people who are looked after in residential settings; in particular the role of staff and management in protecting their welfare, the role of child protection procedures and the roles of other people and services outside the home or school. By welfare we mean both the safety of children and young people, protection from abuse of all kinds, their physical safety, and their proper growth through good caring practices and opportunities for education and development. Thus, while protection from sexual and physical abuse is of prime importance, it is also important for staff to be vigilant throughout the time children are in their care to ensure they live in conditions and an atmosphere which are happy, pleasant and conducive to their achieving the best they can in social terms and education. The many factors which can affect a child's well-being include health and social matters within the home or school, family background, and effective liaison with teachers, educational psychologists and others concerning the child's educational development. Senior staff have a responsibility to ensure effective management structures, comprehensive written guidance on procedures, and careful monitoring of how staff carry out the guidance in practice.

We have already discussed a number of ways in which the welfare of children and young people can be adversely affected. Lack of continuity and constant change in their lives can mean that they never have time to grow up in a stable environment and to fulfil their true potential. Evidence from the Bridge Child Care Consultancy, which advises on 'hard to place' children referred by social services departments shows that some children have frightening numbers of placements.

'Our experience at the Bridge, in helping local authority social service departments and voluntary organisations assess the needs of individual young people, is that initially very often limited information is available about their history. People may think they know the history but what they in fact know is the contents of the last case summary and/or review report. It is the attention to detail in .... assessing need which holds the key ....
Taken overall the young people with whom we have had an involvement will experience changes as follows by the age of 13:−

- average number of changes   136.6
- average number of changes of
  sets of carers   33.5
- average number of new sets
  of carers   22.5

...... Many of the changes occurred before admission to care and life in care seemed to mirror the earlier experiences. A profile of this kind indicates considerable emotional needs which has implications for the ultimate plan'.

John Fitzgerald, Director of the Bridge Child Care Consultancy Service − extract from a paper given to a BAAF conference in 1987, Adoption and Fostering Vol. 11 number 4, 1987

Coupled with the need for continuity is the need for children and young people to feel able to trust those who care for them: to build proper relationships with adults and to learn to become independent and self-confident. Stability is the key. Assuming that staff are capable of providing the care needed, and are trained and supported to do so, it will be the responsibility of those deciding where a child should be brought up − families, teachers, social workers, residential care staff, managers, courts, to ensure that the stability necessary to build trusting and beneficial relationships is achieved. Although this book is focused on residential living experiences, continuity for any child depends on a range of adults. In the case of children looked after by local authorities and voluntary organisations, it is frequently damaged by changes of field social workers who, from a child's perspective, move jobs far too frequently (not always because of turnover of staff). It is tragic that a peripherally involved consultant child psychiatrist may, as we know happens, provide more continuity of understanding of a child than a more actively involved social worker, because of such changes.

8.2 The role of staff

'One of the most poignant contributions made by a member of the group underlined the need children have for someone in whom they can safely confide, someone who is prepared to give them special attention and comfort in distress. It also illustrated how children often need residential social workers to play a substitute parenting role whether those staff wish to or not, whether it is considered professional or not. Anne and her brother and sister had been deserted by their mother and were initially placed together in a small children's home. Anne got very upset at nights.

I used to cry for hours. I used to be heartbroken sometimes. It was my mother really, being aware that she wasn't going to come back and I couldn't take it . . . . . It was the only outlet for me, I did not try to be aggressive or anything, though sometimes I was . . . . I would cry louder and louder until somebody did come in. I suppose it was really my mother's arms I wanted, you know, more than anything. It was nearly always Auntie Betty (who came in) . . . . . . I adored her for when she used to come at nights'

'Growing up in Care: Ten People Talking – Barbara Kahan

Proper care cannot be provided for children and young people without ensuring that their welfare is protected and promoted. This is the factor on which all the other elements of caring we discussed in Chapter 6 stand or fall. Staff need to see this as their overarching task and, in carrying it out, they need to consider what a good parent would do to protect the welfare of a child. This will mean, for example, that although they will not normally be prevented from going out and about, children and young people should expect to tell staff where they are going, who they are going with and what time they are likely to return. It will also mean arrangements will be made, if necessary, to collect them after an evening out with family or friends. This is not unnecessary interference in their lives. It is what good parents would do in similar circumstances. Children and young people often say that they appreciate such 'interference'; it gives them a feeling of safety and of being cared for. Although they may grumble, as young people in their own homes do, they are likely to feel more valued and reassured than if nobody appears to mind where they go, who with or for how long.

Reciprocally, staff should not underestimate their own significance to children by neglecting to tell them when they are going out and where they are going. For example, *'I am going off duty now, but I shall be back on Sunday morning at 7.00am in time to wake you up and get your breakfast'*, does not infringe their privacy but gives the children a feeling of security and knowledge of what is going to happen. Children who have suffered many unexpected losses in adult relationships are likely to be constantly fearful of being abandoned again. In these days of non-residential staff and shift work which some children may find bewildering, staff can help a lot by explaining their own movements and making sure the children know who will be with them and when.

In the task of protecting the welfare of children and young people staff are particularly likely to find themselves taking on the parental role we discussed earlier.

'What would I do if it were my child?' is a touchstone question which needs to be asked again and again. It means, for example, that staff in a children's home will be ready to go to a child's school to discuss their education, or to help them attend youth clubs by arranging for them to be dropped off and collected later. It will also mean that careful attention is given to small health problems, and signs of sadness or depression.

Staff need to be aware of their own limits. Some children they look after have been extremely damaged, or sexually abused and present very difficult behaviour. It may not always be possible for one person to provide everything an individual child needs. Staff must be able to say to their colleagues and managers *'I am having difficulty with this child'* and be able to ask for help. They will only feel able to do so if they are confident that help and support will be provided. They will gain this confidence through a mutually supportive and understanding relationship with colleagues, and through effective management.

Mutually supportive relationships between staff tend to spring from openness about day-to-day practice within the staff group. It is good practice for individual staff to make sure that colleagues are aware of progress made with particular children for whom they are especially responsible; the children's needs and current work with them – anything which can help colleagues to support the member of staff in his or her work. The process of sharing problems and solutions may take place in staff meetings, group supervision or personal supervision. Communications between staff which are centred on the children and their relationships with staff are likely to safeguard the staff group from malpractice or negligence more effectively than communications which focus directly on staff needs or 'institutional' issues. Colleagues should be a source of help, advice and support to each other without embarrassment or fear of negative responses. In schools it is important that similar openness allows care staff and their teaching colleagues to co-operate in achieving mutual growth and development.

Staff need to know about their colleagues' work in order to provide advice and support, but also to be able to spot when something is going wrong. We are not proposing that they should constantly be looking over each others' shoulders. That would create an atmosphere of mistrust and recrimination, the antithesis of good child care. However, they should, in effect, be taking some responsibility for each other in carrying out what is essentially a very difficult task. The first step will be ground rules and principles agreed by all staff and, wherever practicable, by children and young people as well. These ground rules should cover doubts raised by staff actions, possible residents' accusations against staff, and situations in which more than one member of staff might be needed. Ground rules and principles will help to protect children and young people and reduce the possibility of unjustified accusations against individual members of staff. Staff need to have the confidence to say to each other, for example, *'I think you are getting too involved with X;'* or *'I find Y very hard to like. Is it just me?'*. Being honest about such feelings is a good way of helping to avoid abuse.

Particular issues of practice which staff might agree include being alone with young people and when to go into their bedrooms. In some establishments, especially children's homes, staff are unwilling to go into bedrooms alone in case accusations are made against them. They therefore have a rule that no member of staff may enter a resident's bedroom unaccompanied, in any circumstances. This is not the only, or even a good, solution to the problem and staff working in groups should work out rules and procedures based on their knowledge of children and their needs, and knowledge of their colleagues. Similarly, rules will be needed about numbers of staff required on night duty, taking children on outside trips, and staff of both genders being on duty at any time in mixed homes or schools. Procedures on measures of control and discipline also need to be discussed and agreed. Involving children and young people in discussing these issues will help to prevent misunderstandings and also mean that staff meet with less opposition and difficulty than they would otherwise.

If, in the course of their work, staff think that something is going wrong, they should think very carefully about the nature of the problem. At the simplest level they may have learned something about a particular young person which a responsible colleague such as a key worker does not know; for example that the young person is involved with drugs or has previously been sexually abused. If this happens the colleague needs to be told in order for him/her to deal with the situation as necessary. If a member of staff suspects that a colleague's practice is deteriorating and in consequence residents may be at risk they have a duty to act, difficult though this may be. The action taken will depend on the circumstances of the case and the professional 'atmosphere' in the establishment. It might be possible simply to have a private word with the colleague so that the concerned staff member can express the anxiety. In a well run home or school there should be sufficient openness for fairly minor issues of this kind to be discussed in staff meetings without recrimination or personalisation of the issues. If this is not possible, or the issue is a serious one, then managers should be told of the individual problem and, more importantly, acknowledge that there may be a problem within the establishment itself. If staff cannot constructively criticise each others' professional work, the ethos of the home or school is not 'open' enough for good practice to flourish. In these circumstances problems may continue, to the detriment of both children and the work of the establishment.

Where a problem is of a serious nature, for example that professional negligence is suspected or evident, there is again a duty to act. Professional negligence, even when it does not constitute abuse, may be a disciplinary matter. A member of staff who suspects that a colleague's practice could be described as professionally negligent should inform the line manager or head teacher. If the suspicions are about the line manager, then the member of staff should go to a higher level of management. Professional loyalties are never easy to override, and an individual member of staff is likely to find it difficult to take action which might lead to disciplining of a colleague. However, failure to act may mean that children suffer, and staff who are aware of professional negligence and do not report it, could find themselves accused of collusion. Staff should, whenever possible or appropriate, discuss their concern with colleagues before talking to a line manager. Although having to 'tell tales' on a colleague might feel like an act of betrayal, the first responsibility must always be to the children in their care and, in the longer term this is the best way to safeguard the staff group as a whole.

Recent inquiries, notably the *Leicestershire Inquiry*, have graphically described the forces at work which intimidate or discourage staff from 'blowing the whistle' on bad practice or abuse by colleagues or senior staff. These are particularly evident in working environments which become politicised or where personal and professional lives of senior staff overlap. Staff working in such situations are undoubtedly in a very difficult situation if they have evidence of abusive conduct by a colleague and will need courage to take action.

A member of staff who suspects a colleague, a manager or member of the public of abusing a child or young person in the establishment, has no ethical or professional alternative but to report it without delay. Management must then take immediate action. Child protection procedures which exist independent of the establishment will have to be brought into action. These are discussed in a later section in this chapter.

The duty to protect the welfare of children and young people does not lie only with care staff. Line managers and staff who have responsibility for junior staff, in particular, have a vital role to play, and we discuss this in the next section. We suggest there are a number of general principles which both staff and managers should act on at all times. They are as follows:–

- The welfare of children and young people takes precedence over loyalties to staff colleagues.

- Openness and honesty amongst staff are conducive to an open and caring regime. This will help protect the welfare of children and young people, and safeguard staff.

- Problems should be anticipated as far as possible, and ways of dealing with them should be discussed within staff groups.

- Where a problem arises it should be acted on without delay.

- Staff must never be afraid to tell managers of their concerns. Managers should ensure that staff feel able to discuss problems with them, and should never discourage proper concerns from being expressed.

8.3 The role of external management: support and security

We discuss management issues in greater depth in Chapter 12. However, managers or governors have an important part to play in the protection and promotion of children's welfare in the homes and schools for which they are responsible. It is their responsibility to ensure that working conditions allow staff to carry out their work in a professional and open way. They are required to monitor arrangements to ensure that all is well. Proper and regular supervision ensures that staff carry out their duties to the best of their professional ability, and allows staff to discuss problems as they arise with their immediate line managers. Most schools and many homes, especially smaller ones, have relatively simple and informal management structures. If this is so, it is important that parents, placing agencies and others with an interest in the children have regular access to the home or school to help ensure the children's welfare is properly safeguarded and promoted. However, this in itself is not enough. Regulation 22 of the *Children's Homes Regulations* requires that the directors (council members) of voluntary or private organisations or establishments, or members of local authorities, must receive monthly written reports on the conduct of homes for which they are ultimately responsible. The visits on which these reports are based can be undertaken by senior officers on behalf of directors or members, but there is clearly merit in their undertaking some visits to enable them to see at first hand the living circumstances, and the children for whom they are responsible. *Department of Health Guidance (Volume 4 Residential Care)* stresses the importance, wherever feasible, of these monthly visits being undertaken by organisational representatives who are independent of line management so that reports of visits are not compromised by those who write them having direct responsibility for the home and its work. Although not required by statute, the principle of this arrangement could, with benefit, be applied to schools, hospital units and other establishments which do not fall under the *Children Act 1989*. Governors, directors and managers can have an important influence on the overall service provided, both by carrying out their responsibilities sensitively and carefully, or by neglecting them and thus depriving the children of an important safeguard.

Everyone involved with a school or home has a part to play in protecting and promoting the welfare of children and young people. A wide range of people go in and out of homes and schools. Some have statutory duties, local authority inspection units, schools inspectors, local authority councillors. Others have statutory duties towards individual children, social workers, independent advocates, health workers, teachers, independent visitors, local authority members. A third group visit individual children on an informal basis; family, friends and relatives. A difficult balance has to be achieved between the need for children and young people to feel that where they live is **their home**, and not open to visitors passing though at all hours; and the need for external scrutiny of day-to-day functioning in the home or school. In the main this latter task is one that should fall to managers of homes or schools, but experience shows that external attention is also necessary.

What we advocate is that everyone who visits a home or school in an official capacity should be aware of their responsibility to play a part in safeguarding the welfare of children and young people in it. To do so they need to be informed of its purpose and aims and realise the importance of reporting any doubts or concerns to someone outside the home or school, the board of governors, board of trustees or local council. Before they call the first time, they should have guidance on the proper conduct of visits, and training in how to carry them out so that they can achieve their objective in a sensitive way. The children and young people need to know who visits the establishment, what their role is, where they come from and how often they visit so that if they wish they can approach them. This information should be provided when they arrive at the home or school, perhaps in the form of a leaflet, or as part of a pamphlet or brochure. Anyone who regularly visits a home or school should be subject to the same background checks which apply when a new member of staff is appointed, ie. reference to the Department of Health Consultancy Service and/or List 99 held by the Department for Education and local education authorities and, wherever possible, background checks for a criminal record. Experience has demonstrated the importance of these precautions.

Parents and informal visitors should also be told how to make their concerns known, where to find out about complaints procedures and how to make use of them. Complaints procedures established under the *Children Act 1989* and the *NHS and Community Care Act 1990* are required to be open for use by parents and others with a legitimate interest in the upbringing of a child. We would suggest that complaints procedures in establishments other than children's homes again might, with benefit, adopt this principle. Department of Health Guidance on the welfare of children in independent boarding schools expects the provision of suitable complaints procedures. (*Children Act 1989 Guidance Volume 5*). Parents may need to be reminded that in placing their children in a boarding school they have entered into partnership with those who will care for them. They may well need reassurance that complaints will be properly investigated and discussed and that they will in no circumstances rebound on the children.

Managers also need to make sure that their staff have sufficient support from outside agencies, in providing suitable and adequate education and health services. This will not always simply mean providing a child with a place in a local school, or making sure that primary health care services are available. It may mean arranging for individual tuition within a children's home; making sure that an educational psychologist is available to help a child; arranging for psychological and psychiatric support for a home or school; or organising the provision of regular health and dental checks. This role is particularly important. If a children's home has difficulty in finding a place for a particular child in a local school, it is the manager's task to take this up with the local education authority, and to insist that children and young people for whom s/he has responsibility receive the service to which they have a right, like other children. There are powers under Section 13 of the *Education Act 1993* for appropriate authorities to direct that a child who has been excluded or refused admission, be admitted to a school. This can occur only after consultation with the parent, the governing body of the school to be specified in the direction and the authority maintaining the school. This provides a statutory framework for resolving situations in which schools are unwilling to admit children resident in children's homes. Of course there will need to be very constructive collaboration between homes and schools obliged to receive children under such directions. Similarly with health services, managers must make sure that children receive the health care they need. As we have said earlier, the health of children living away from home can suffer greatly from lack of the vigilance that good parents exercise daily.

Managers should encourage a climate of openness and trust between children and themselves. Staff need to feel that line managers can be approached with problems at any time, and that they will be dealt with sympathetically and in confidence. Line managers in particular need to ensure that staff, as well as children, have confidence in complaints procedures, and that independent and confidential counselling services are available for staff suffering from stress, if they need them.

A system of effective monitoring of arrangements and activities in a home or school is part of a manager's job. This will include regular review meetings of staff, regular written reports by staff (in schools this might be at the end of each term), reviewing the work and development of the home or school, and other matters such as children and young people's behaviour. Feedback from children and young people should be part of the review, as well as others associated with a home, in particular local authority inspection units. Supervision and appraisal systems will involve regular monitoring of individual staff members' work and development. New staff in particular need careful supervision and monitoring during induction and probationary periods. It may also be valuable to carry out a spot check on case notes to see whether drift and delays are happening, or whether action is being taken appropriately. (These issues are discussed in more detail in Chapter 12).

8.4 Child protection

In this section we look at the arrangements needed to protect children and young people from abuse within a home or school. Abuse may be sexual, physical or emotional; it can take place in families, schools, homes, youth clubs, or anywhere where children and young people live or frequent. It can be perpetrated by relatives, strangers, staff in schools or homes, teachers, police officers, doctors, anyone. Most importantly for our purposes, it can come about as a result of systems which fail to provide proper forms of care. The 'Pindown' regime in Staffordshire and the use of 'regression therapy' in Leicestershire are well known examples of this form of abuse.

It is the duty of all staff, wherever they work, to be aware of the possibility that children they care for may be abused, within or outside a home or school. Possible evidence of abuse may arise through a child's direct complaint or through distress and attempts to communicate. It may also relate to a child's physical condition or behaviour, eg. bed wetting, bleeding, a sore anus or emotional withdrawal. An important principle which should always be applied is that a child making a direct complaint should always be listened to and the complaint taken seriously. Staff should *never* assume that a complaint of abuse is not being made seriously, and should never allow knowledge of a child's previous behaviour to cloud their judgement in this. The Police Complaints Authority investigation into handling of accusations of abuse in Leicestershire found that police, in many cases, had simply not believed young people who complained that they had been abused. They assumed that, because the majority had previously committed offenses, they could not be trusted to tell the truth. This demonstrates the danger of making assumptions based on prejudice and the importance of keeping an open mind about even the most troublesome child. Staff have a duty to take as neutral a stance as possible to allow objective examination of the facts of a case. Children who have been abused are often not able, for various reasons, to formulate a clear complaint. Instead, perhaps all they can convey is distress, shame and feelings of guilt which may affect their behaviour. For some, the way they have been abused may serve to make them feel guilty even though it is not their fault. Even some of the language used by adults may reinforce this. Staff will need to reassure them that they are not to blame for any abuse they have suffered and reassure them, as far as possible, of the confidentiality of their personal background. It may, however, take some time before they feel confident enough to disclose what has happened.

The third way in which evidence may occur, that is through a child's condition or behaviour, requires painstaking observation and sensitive, discreet investigation. - *'A child is a person and not simply an object of concern'. (Report of the Inquiry into Child Abuse in Cleveland 1987).* It is therefore important not to overreact on the basis of inconclusive evidence. Patient and careful work with the child is needed until the situation becomes clearer and overreaction to inconclusive evidence should be avoided. As soon as staff are sure they have evidence of abuse, they have no choice but to institute the established child protection procedures. Clearly they will need to discuss the issues with colleagues, but discussion should not be the cause of delay. The *'Working Together'* (*A Guide to Arrangements for Inter-agency Cooperation for the Protection of Children From Abuse, HMSO 1991)* procedures apply in residential settings as well as outside.

Homes and schools, as we have said before, need an open and trusting environment in which the children's needs and their care and development have clear priority. Such an establishment is less likely to harbour abusive staff, systems or relationships that are closed and secretive, although it cannot be guaranteed that abuse will never occur. A staff member or visitor, bent on abusing children, may not always be deterred whatever the atmosphere in a home or school. However, such people are more likely to be attracted to, or survive in, a 'closed' institution, where there is little outside scrutiny or safeguards, and where there may be a climate of repression or fear. The *Pindown, Leicestershire and Castle Hill* inquiries identified certain common factors in the establishments investigated. These were that either those responsible for oversight and scrutiny from outside were denied access to the children they 'cared' for because the regimes were secretive and repressive, or that those responsible for oversight did not exercise the vigilance they should have done. Successful protection of children from abuse requires the encouragement of environments in which abusive systems and regimes cannot take root. This is the responsibility of everyone from the board of governors, social services committee or board of trustees to the staff working in the home or school.

To deal with complaints and incidents of abuse, it is essential that every home or school has a properly worked out and agreed child protection procedure. At least one copy of 'Working Together: A Guide to Arrangements for inter-agency co-operation for the protection of children from abuse' should be kept in every establishment. If a school, home or hospital unit does not already have at least one copy they should obtain one and give a senior member of staff the task of coordinating child protection procedures in the establishment, ensuring they are compatible with the requirements of the local Area Child Protection Committee. Copies of local guidance should also be available to residential staff. Staff in children's homes should also use Volume 4 of the *Children Act Guidance and Regulations,* and staff in schools, Volume 5.

Allegations of abuse against staff can have a powerfully destructive impact upon the whole staff group, indeed the entire life of the home or school. Careful planning of the necessary investigation can reduce this however, and heads of establishments should seek to be included in strategy discussions required in accordance with Working Together.[1] In this way the head can assist and so help to speed up the investigation, and the interests of home or school can be taken into account in the way it is conducted.

In other settings where neither legislation nor guidance require the establishment of child protection procedures, it is wise practice to establish them. For example, hospitals and adolescent psychiatric units would do well, if they have not already done so, to approach their local social services department with a view to establishing links with the local Area Child Protection Committee, obtaining advice on appropriate procedures, and involving staff in training in child protection issues.

Staff in every setting need to be trained in child protection procedures, as part of their induction or continuing training. The training should ensure that staff are able to recognise the signs of abuse in children and young people, are aware of the appropriate action to take, and have a thorough understanding of the procedures in their home or school. *Working with Child Sexual Abuse, Guidelines for Trainers and Managers in Social Services Departments, Department of Health 1991* is useful in this context, and also provides information about other training materials. Once a basic framework of knowledge and experience has been established, staff will then benefit from longer term training opportunities to enable them to develop a deeper knowledge of the subject and greater skill in working with it. They also need outside stimulus, books, conferences, regular staff meetings at which outsiders are invited to speak. In-service development is valuable, but without outside stimulus as well, can become inward-looking.

---

[1] *"Working together Under the Children Act 1989" - A Guide to Arrangements for Inter-agency Cooperation for the Protection of Children from Abuse, HMSO 1991*

9   Boarding Schools and Therapeutic Communities

9.1 Introduction: The Commonality of Care

The basis theme of this book is the 'commonality of care'. There are significant differences in various group settings in which children and young people grow up, but we argue that they are less than the similarities. Topics such as arriving and settling; departing; parental involvement; premises and accommodation; activities; relationships; children rights; and bullying have been discussed elsewhere, notably in Chapters 4, 5, 6 and 7. Some of them, however, are of sufficient importance in the context of boarding schools, residential special schools and therapeutic communities, to merit some further discussion here. Although therapeutic communities, in particular, have much in common with children's homes, they also have major differences.

In opening this chapter we wish to acknowledge that a number of the ideas in it have also been discussed in a recently published book '*Applying the Children Act in Boarding and Residential Environments*' (Anderson E W and Davison A J (eds) 1993). The membership of our steering group included one of the editors and a number of the contributors to that book. We also want to explain that we are describing three groups of establishments which are all different but which have many common factors. In consequence the chapter has, in effect, three parts; Boarding Schools (Maintained and Independent), Boarding Special Schools and Therapeutic Communities.

9.2 Boarding Schools (Maintained and Independent)

9.2.1 The Relationship Between Boarding School and the Family

Most children in boarding schools are there as a result of carefully considered decisions by parents or, increasingly frequently, by the whole family. It cannot, however, be assumed that all have stable and united home backgrounds. A growing number have experienced disruption and been exposed to potentially damaging and stressful experiences. Belonging to a community that patently cares for its members can provide a much needed element of stability and, where the majority of pupils come from stable backgrounds, it is undoubtedly easier to create and sustain an ethos which promotes stability. While some boarders may claim *'I like boarding school because the holidays are long'*, requests to remain at school during the holidays in order to avoid the pressures of home life are not unknown.

The advantages of boarding do not rest only with frequently catalogued academic success and enhanced career opportunities. It is now common for both parents to work. Such parents may choose boarding school education because it enables them to avoid the dangers of 'latchkey children'. Instead, they are able to regulate their lives in such a way that they can give full attention to the children during holiday periods and at weekends, when all the family can spend uninterrupted time together. As a consequence, family relationships may even be enhanced rather than diminished. Boarding education, in spite of many critics, can provide a positive way of promoting a steady growth towards maturity, assisting personal and social development without necessarily diminishing the strengths of home life. It can complement a sound family life and school and home should, and usually do, work in close partnership.

9.2.2 Events in School Life

Arrival and Settling in

Older children who may have helped to introduce a newcomer to the school (see Chapter 7) may be able to act as guides and mentors for the first two or three weeks of a new term. They will benefit from some training to help them fulfil this task of overseeing and being available to a new pupil should problems arise. Senior pupils eg. house prefects, can play an important part, working alongside house staff and tutors to give extra support to the mentors and their charges.

The school also needs to have a well developed practice for induction of new boarders. Homesickness, unhappiness and even depression can strike once the excitement of new experiences wears off. Staff need to be alert to the signs of these and might, from the start, help children in the use of their time. Balancing hectic and energetic activity with quieter pursuits, is vital in settling down.

The first term or two may be particularly difficult for pupils new to boarding, especially 'first generation' boarders. Staff must be ready to help in a warm and supportive manner with the stresses which can arise. Although a boarder may have a particular person in whom he or she confides, successful handling of problems is likely to be achieved as a result of team effort and the school system should allow for discreet sharing of concerns and solutions.

Staff may require special training to meet the needs of those who have distinctive and 'different' needs and who, in consequence, may find the settling in process much harder. The particular needs may arise because they are black, have a different religion, come from a different cultural background, have a poor grasp of English, or some form of disability. The school should provide clear guidelines about settling in late comers. All potential problems can be exacerbated when a boarder arrives well after the beginning of term, when friendship groups have already been established.

Early information about fire drills which, like other matters of safety, is always important in group life. Fire drills should become an automatic part of life for all boarders. It is good practice to give clear instruction and a walk-through practice on the first day or evening and thereafter have full fire practices at regular intervals and at different times of day and night, starting at different locations.

(i)   Transfer of records and preliminary contact with school

A visit, or visits, to the new school by parents and boarder are likely to have been arranged before residence begins. If new boarders can get the 'feel' of the school, meet some of the children, and see something of the current activities, their settling in process is likely to be much easier. Some schools achieve this by arranging for new children to spend a weekend at the school prior to entry.

The transfer of records may, in some instances, be the only link established by a new school with a prospective boarder's previous school. The new head teacher will need to determine who sees this record although, in general, a boarder should be able to have access to his or her own file, even if certain limited information is kept separately and confidential to staff only.

Getting on With Life at School

(i)   The Basics

Accommodation: We discussed in Chapter 5 the importance of buildings and the environment generally; all accommodation needs to be attractive, practical and free from health and safety hazards. Individual boarders need privacy but also adequate facilities to allow for as wide a range of leisure activities as possible, including quiet pursuits, and space for personal belongings, photographs, posters etc.

For those up to the age of 14, groupings of four to six in sleeping arrangements seem to be acceptable if individual rooms are not available. Those aged 14–16 are likely to want twin or single rooms. Sixth formers, 16–18, require single study bedroom accommodation. Mascots and teddies in dormitories and bedrooms can be welcomed whatever the age of the children. Although there may be a need to limit the number of garments possessed by each boarder, there should be adequate storage for all clothing and other personal belongings.

Bathrooms and lavatories need to be reasonably warm, well-ventilated and comfortable; and lockable showers should be privately curtained.

Common and living rooms can be varied to suit the age range and gender mix of boarders. allowing for quiet activities, such as reading, talking to a friend, playing board games, model making, etc, as well as boisterous activities, such as table tennis and pool. Boys and girls need to be able to mix socially, but also to be able to withdraw from each other when they so wish.

Health Care: Monitoring and safeguarding boarders' health is of paramount importance. Good provision includes warm and non-intimidating accommodation for boarders who are ill and have to spend time in the sick-bay or sanatorium. The friendliness and approachability of medical and nursing staff is a vital element in providing good confidential counselling and an advisory service for boarders.

It is important that boarders are well prepared for leading a healthy life-style. This includes nutrition and healthy eating, sex education and the misuse of drugs and alcohol. Those responsible for delivering elements of health education in a personal, social and health education course and in subjects such as science, should cooperate with those who have direct care and welfare responsibilities for boarders, the house staff, matrons and medical staff. There is a very real need for academic and house staff to work together to increase knowledge and understanding of these issues. Close involvement of some house staff in the school programme can be of mutual assistance to house and school staff. Equally important is the need for all house staff to be involved with the school staff in any in-service training programme in this area.

(ii)   Pupils' Feelings and Views about Boarding School

'School Life – Pupils' Views on Boarding' The views and feelings of children and young people about what they hope to find in their boarding schools and what they most dislike or deplore have been vividly portrayed in this publication[1] from which we have quoted in earlier chapters. It was based on work carried out with twenty two boarding schools in Oxfordshire in 1991, in which there was extensive consultation with 2,600 individual pupils about welfare issues. The schools included preparatory and senior schools, independent, maintained and special schools. Twenty consultation meetings took place with groups of pupils and similar meetings with groups of staff. In addition, six exchange visits were made between boarding schools in which pupils observed and reported on the boarding standards and practices of each others' schools. The author commented on two striking factors in the consultation.

> *'Firstly, pupils themselves have been impressively sensible, logical and practical in their views. What they have said made sense, was rarely extreme or lacking in appreciation of practicalities such as cost or*

---

1 "School Life: Pupils' Views on Boarding" — Dr. Roger Morgan HMSO 1993

competing viewpoints, and was always as valid as the views expressed by adult professionals. There were no more silly comments than one receives when consulting adult professionals. Secondly, pupil's views show a remarkable consistency, despite great differences in their ages, backgrounds, and between the schools they live in . . . . this consistency of view suggests that the findings may be relevant to the welfare of pupils in special education settings where, because of handicap or communication difficulties, pupils cannot easily be consulted directly themselves'.

Some schools also practice an 'openness of society' which can be beneficial to pupils and staff, and which can help to establish and maintain the setting as a safe place to be without undermining school or staff discipline. Roger Morgan's work has conclusively shown, supported in a different context by consumer studies of young people in care such as *Not Just a Name – the Views of Young People in Foster and Residential Care* (a survey by the Who Cares? Trust and the National Consumer Council) that if you ask children sensible questions you are likely to get sensible answers.

'The Class of '91' – The Eton Experience: The concern which is increasingly being shown by schools for the well being and happiness of pupils from the start of their boarding life was well shown in a television film about Eton College entitled 'Class of '91'. Apprehensive young boys accompanied by parents, and almost in tears in some cases, were seen putting up a few personal possessions in their own sleeping space. They admitted to being *'a bit scared'* and realising that *'you have to make your own way now'*. However, it was seen that a careful tour of the school, explanations of the timetable, help with understanding how to manage their collars and shirts, photographs of themselves in their new uniforms and general recognition of their 'need to know' were likely to help, at least to some extent.

The new entrants, black and white, were met by staff, black and white. One boy who had won a scholarship said *'my accent wasn't what they were used to'*. Some boys said it *'took . . . . . . .about a month to feel at home'* but they were able to talk to certain older boys and for those who experienced more than usual difficulties a school psychiatrist, who specialised in child and adolescent psychiatry, was available. Some boys did not want to be at the school and felt very daunted by the experience. They needed opportunity for the confidential discussion afforded by the psychiatrist.

Powerful indications of the acceptance of individuals as individuals were a black student with left wing politics who set up a discussion forum; and pupils' own recognition of the different 'types' in the school, the 'macho' parade drilling ones, and the 'arty types' who *'wouldn't be seen dead on a playing field'*. Complaints were aired. For example, the Arts Review Magazine was *'not allowed to mention condoms and sex'*. The school *'hinders our sexuality'*, it was said, and there were *'hang-ups about nudity'*. Boys from Stowe school were understood to use communal showers while the *'Etonians are inhibited'*. Some boys complained they had to work very hard and were *'still treated like twelve year olds, locked up in the house every night'*.

There was a long standing tradition of a time each day when staff were available for personal discussion and a signal, tugging the staff member's gown, indicated a boy's wish to have time to talk.

It is very easy to find critics of long established and privileged schools like Eton who question whether there is anything to be learned from them, either by less prestigious group living centres, or by group situations in which the dice of life have been loaded against the children in them from the start. A more open minded approach acknowledges that cross fertilisation through experience, knowledge and research not only can, but is taking place and this example is one indication of it. One of the lessons of 'Class of '91' was that confidence engendered by being identified with a valued tradition is a great strength to individual children, regardless of their personal backgrounds, not all of which are helpful. We have commented elsewhere that if children in less privileged settings were enabled and allowed to feel identified with and proud of their own particular group life, they would be more positively assisted than by being forced to feel stigmatised by it.

(iii)   Peer Groups and Their Problems

Peer group bonds in boarding schools are stronger than in children's homes, as *"School Life"* also demonstrates, even though in children's homes 40% of residents are there with one or more siblings (D Berridge). These bonds may be very strong and problems being experienced by an individual may be brought to the attention of staff by a friend who is a member of the group. Where there are underlying or deep seated problems in a school house, the strength of the peer group bonds can result in children being less ready to turn to an adult in distress. If this is so, the newcomer, or someone who is recognisably different or is vulnerable in some way, could find him/herself isolated or excluded from peer groups. This may lead to bullying behaviour, and further marginalisation. Good practice means that staff understand that this cycle of rejection can exist even in the best run house and recognise the symptoms at an early stage, thus being able to intervene sensitively. They must intervene but in doing so recognise that, while the victim's welfare has priority, the perpetrator(s) also requires attention, and staff should not be dismissive of their claims on time and sympathy. Their own unacceptable behaviour may well spring from personal unhappiness or feelings of inadequacy.

Bullying is endemic but nonetheless cannot be condoned. Good practice recognises this, and in an open and trusting community staff will provide support for any boarder who feels vulnerable. They need to be about the school and house at all times, without being overbearing and intrusive. Trained prefects, monitors or other senior boarders may accept some responsibility for younger boarders, realising that they also have a pastoral role to do so, but older boarders should never have completely unsupervised access to younger ones; nor should their duties be unmonitored.

In Chapter 6, the subject of bullying is dealt with in more detail and reference is made to a recent inquiry in a boarding school in which bullying was thought to have contributed to a pupil's suicide. Bullying is also a hazard in children's homes although it seems to receive less professional attention. It is equally damaging in its impact, however.

Senior Pupils, Prefects and Monitors: The existence, or otherwise, of prefects or monitors is not significantly related to how well a house functions. In most schools older boarders are given some form of responsibility. Good practice provides all boarders with increasing levels of responsibility and authority as they grow older, and it is right that this should be so. Whether or not they actually hold office senior boarders should be encouraged to recognise that a contribution to the welfare and pastoral care of the school is part of their role as they grow older. Training for taking responsibility for others and having such experience can be important elements in a boarder's personal development.

(iv) Equal Opportunities

Schools and houses can benefit by celebration of differences amongst cultures, ethnic and religious groups. Differences can be seen as positive features and not as threats. The school, in its curriculum, and both school and house through their joint pastoral activity, need to emphasise a positive approach to living in a society where individuals are valued for themselves. Attempts to stereotype or oppress individuals or groups on the grounds of ethnicity, religion, gender, culture or sexual orientation must be decried. Racist or sexist remarks, harassment or teasing have no place in the classroom, houses and elsewhere. Any instances of racism should be discussed with the boarders concerned and more generally. Posters in bedrooms and study areas which are in bad taste in this context, are perhaps best used by staff to discuss boys' or girls' attitudes to the subject and what it is that constitutes bad taste or unacceptable behaviour.

(v) Pupils from Abroad

Increasing numbers of pupils whose first language is not English are nowadays attending boarding schools. Many of them come from Hong Kong, Japan and Malaysia. Good practice necessitates that they can attain a working grasp of English as quickly as possible and that continuing language and social support are available for a long time thereafter. It is of vital importance that the school system enables pupils' who have little grasp of English to have real access both to the curriculum and learning and to the care and support system. In addition, a good school will tactfully integrate foreign boarders with English speakers without detracting from the expression of their own cultural heritage.

Other foreign pupils, mainly from Africa, the USA and, increasingly, from the EC, will need to have their welfare sensitively monitored by their tutors in order to make them secure and confident in a friendly community. Even though their parents, in many instances, want them to benefit from a British education, their own culture remains of great importance to them.

Parents or those responsible for students from other countries should be asked to appoint a family friend or relative resident in the UK to act as a 'guardian' or 'holiday-time carer'. If this is impossible, the school may undertake to find a suitable family to act in this capacity, although the requirement to check on the background of anyone who will have substantial access to children should be noted. They have a duty to ensure that the welfare of the child is secured by this arrangement, and to check with the police that nothing is known which would make potential carers unsuitable. If the school makes these arrangements rather than the parents, the school bears the responsibility for safeguarding the pupil's welfare. Recent changes to the law require certain independent boarding schools which look after children during holidays as well as term time to register with local authorities as children's homes. Schools will have to decide for themselves how suited they are to provide adequate care during holiday times. Some may not be well placed to do so and may choose instead to assist parents to make their own arrangements for their children during holidays.

(vi)   Worries and complaints

A house or school where there is good practice will have an ethos that is open, trusting and supportive of all boarders. In this atmosphere grumbles and grievances will normally be readily sorted out long before any complaints procedure needs to be invoked. House staff or older boarders will be prepared to support and act as advocate for those who transgress or who feel unfairly treated in some way. The existence of some form of written complaints procedure or procedure for airing worries will not cause problems for staff. It is unlikely to be abused by boarders and will be very much accepted as a normal part of the democratic working of the house and discipline system at large.

Access to independent advocates and to others outside the school organisation including, perhaps, a social worker from the local authority's social services department, will provide a further means of safeguarding the welfare of the boarders.

(vii)   Rebellious Behaviour

It is the task of staff to promote good practice by actively contributing to the school ethos; and by recognising, reviewing and changing practices which may not be in the pupil's best interests, or where practice falls short of the school's professed objectives. At the centre of the task is the need to nurture and care for each individual child. As children and young people strive to express their individuality and to demonstrate their ability to make their own decisions, it is not surprising to find them kicking against the establishment and flouting rules which are intended to contribute to the comfort and well being of all. Most of the time such behaviour can be contained. Sometimes those who rebel have a legitimate cause in which case, although the method employed to make the point might not be condoned, an offending rule or directive should be reconsidered and perhaps changed. In some cases, where the action of pupils threatens the safety and well being of others, it could be that the pupils must cease to be members of the community, a decision which can never be taken lightly. Should this prove necessary, the school ought not to stop caring for individuals, and every effort should be made to help them to transfer elsewhere as painlessly as possible.

(viii)   Sanctions and Rewards

Good practice, as we have said elsewhere, will stress the importance of rewards rather than sanctions. Rewards may be good conduct or work marks, additional privileges or other positive symbols, but the most successful rewards in any school are given by staff who recognise effort, offer genuine praise, and support what a pupil is doing. Sanctions may be necessary, but in a good house or school they will not cause lasting resentment and will be seen to be fair by all concerned. Sanctions in the form of the withdrawal of privilege are usually the most effective. A note should be made of occasions when sanctions are used. Often the link between privilege and responsibility is built into the school ethos; privileges are earned by the effective fulfilment of responsibility.

Corporal punishment is statutorily forbidden in maintained schools and for certain categories of pupils in independent schools. Most independent schools themselves no longer allow its use. It is rarely, if ever, an effective sanction.[2]

Conversely, symbolic acknowledgement of good behaviour and good results helps to create a climate which is based on rewards rather than sanctions. Praise and recognition are important to all of us, adults, as well as children. The Honours system in the UK, any official occasion at which medals, awards, etc are worn or given, bears ample witness to the powerful influence of praise and recognition.

---

2 "Issues of Control in Residential Child Care," Darlington Social Research Unit HMSO 1981

Once upon a time the Sun and the North Wind were having an argument about which of them was the most powerful. Their eyes fell on a lonely traveller making his way across open country, wearing a heavy top coat.

'Let us see which of us can make him take his coat off' said the Sun to the North Wind. *'That is no problem'* said the North Wind – *'watch me!'* And he blew and he blew and the more he blew the more the poor traveller pulled his collar up and his coat tightly around him as he staggered along in the cold.

'Now you've had your turn, let me try' said the Sun. The North Wind reluctantly stopped blowing and the Sun directed his shining rays on the traveller. Very soon he was turning his collar down, unbuttoning his coat, and in no time at all, had taken it off and was carrying it while he enjoyed the warmth of the Sun.

'There you are' said the Sun to the North Wind, *'what did I tell you?'*.

An Old Fable

A more modern example, applicable both to schools or children's homes comes from the experience of a residential child care worker who found that a lighthearted weekly competition for 'Resident of the Week' with a small token prize at the end did more for good behaviour and discipline than any amount of rules and sanctions. Such a device need not be 'institutional'; it can be fun and is not dissimilar to what parents do in ordinary families.

A 'cracking down' approach in most organisations, adults' as well as children's is likely to be a sign of bankruptcy, not confident success. Ironically, sanctions are more likely to be successful in settings in which children and young people are mainly stable and 'all together' than in settings in which children's personalities have been buffeted at home, at school and in welfare systems. Children in boarding schools are likely to bring some stability with them to add to the stability of others, whilst children's homes have to try to counteract a deficit factor by every means they can muster.

(ix) Links with the Outside World

Throughout their school career, members of the boarding community must maintain links with the outside world. Good practice will enable boarders to take part in normal activities such as shopping, visits to the theatre, cinema, amusement parks, ice rinks, etc. The school will make every effort to forge links with the local community through arranging community activities such as visits to elderly people's homes. Many schools also find it is possible and worthwhile for boarders to make use of local clubs and societies and even adult education facilities.

Whatever the outside activity, the school is responsible for safeguarding boarders' welfare and requires a clearly stated policy about the way arrangements are made. This policy should clearly indicate how it applies to boarders of different ages and, where necessary, how adults who have significant contact with boarders are vetted. The advice of the local social services' department will be valuable in this context.

What boarders are allowed to do will clearly relate to their age and maturity, and schools will safeguard their welfare while allowing them an appropriate degree of freedom to manage their own affairs and take part in activities in the local community. Good practice will clarify for boarders matters such as 'bounds' and 'out of bounds', signing out, and the need to be in pairs or threes when visiting the local shopping area. It will also reflect the particular local circumstances of the school.

Preparations for Departure

(i)   Moving Schools

Where a pupil is leaving to attend another school, the current school should cooperate as fully as possible, and release the pupil to enable visits to be made to the new school. Records, particularly Records of Achievement, are of great value when transferring between schools. When fully adopted, they will document views of relevant teachers, tutors and house staff,and will include pupils' own views and their self-assessment of progress. The contribution made by all concerned with a particular student, and the availability of records to all who need to know will be of immense value.

(ii)   Moving to Life Beyond School

In all that it does the school will affect boarders' outlook on and preparation for the next stage in their lives. It is important, therefore, that the school is fully aware of this and plans its pastoral arrangements as well as its timetabled curriculum with this in mind. Staff should take a broad view of all aspects of school and boarding life, and relate what they do, and plan to do, to the level of intellectual, emotional and social growth that each boarder has reached.

This means that the school will not only want to plan their curriculum to suit the pupils' needs, but will also seek to provide a range of experiences and responsibilities that promote growth and development. Pupils' awareness of the society in which they are a part, must continually be enhanced.

The school's curriculum should include health education, careers and further and higher education (FHE) counselling, how to deal with living away from home, how to cope with finances, form-filling and benefits and all that comes under the heading of life-skills appropriate for the age-range of the school. A detailed careers programme will be necessary for those who are leaving school at 16-plus, either for work or for further or higher education. This naturally includes provision of information, individual counselling and planning of career strategies designed to assist the individual pupil in making sensible and informed decisions about his/her future.

The house or care staff will wish to be fully aware of what is happening in the curriculum in all these areas, and should be trained to complement curricular provision as mentors, tutors and friends. In addition, much of what boarders have to do in the house and in activities outside it can be seen as essential training in growth and maturity, and in preparation for responsibility for self and others.

9.3 Boarding Special Schools

This group of schools is the second largest category of residential establishments for children and young people. Some are provided by local authorities (maintained), some by the voluntary sector (non-maintained) and some by the private sector (independent). The schools provide boarding education for children and young people deemed, within the meaning of the Education Act 1993, to have emotional and behavioural difficulties, and for those with learning difficulties or physical disabilities needing specialised care as well as specialised teaching. Many schools looking after children with emotional and behavioral difficulties in particular, face problems and challenges similar to those faced in children's homes. It is therefore important that staff in schools accept the need for a similarly high standard of caring practice. Material in this book which is relevant to good practice in children's homes is equally relevant to boarding special schools. The boarding special schools also have similarities with other boarding schools and good practice in them is equally desirable.

Residential special schools, although classified as schools, can be seen as something of a hybrid, combining care of children and young people similar to those in children's homes with the educational environment of other boarding schools. Although this presents many challenges, there are also benefits: children and young people usually remain in residential special schools for relatively long periods of time, and there are fewer problems with disruption and discontinuity than in children's homes. This allows staff to look to longer term outcomes rather than feeling that their work may be undone by the child moving on after a brief period. It also allows for a greater sense of community, similar to that in other boarding schools, but not always experienced in children's homes because of the many changes taking place as children come and go. There is a danger, however, that through absence away at school, a child's place in the family becomes insecure and that return to live permanently at home either for reintegration into day school or at the end of their schooling may be very difficult for all concerned. Because residential special schooling is chosen as a response to family circumstances having seriously hampered children's ability to learn, it is incumbent upon these schools to engage very positively with pupils' families. If this is neglected, pupils will be ill served. Progress in education and personal adjustment may be to no avail if, at the end of the day, pupils' overwhelming experience is detachment from their own family. Some pupils referred to residential schools have not received adequate educational supports in the community. In some instances the question has to be asked whether they should have been separated from home. Once in the schools it may be argued that if they are doing well their education should not be interrupted by returning home. On the other hand, if they are not doing well it may be argued that they need to stay longer.

9.3.1 Who is Looked After in Special Boarding Schools?

Precise statistics are not collected and, as Chapter 2 demonstrates, estimates vary considerably, from 20,000 to 33,000 at the time of writing. About 8,000 children and young people are placed in boarding schools because of emotional or behavioural difficulties. This was almost the same number as the children and young people estimated to be in local authority children's homes in March 1992 when the *Warner Committee* carried out its survey. The remainder have either physical, including sensory, disabilities or learning difficulties, or a combination of needs. The *Fish Report: 'Educational Opportunities for All?'*[3] identified eight categories of need which indicated that children require special educational provision. These were as follows:–

- emotional and behavioural difficulties;

- moderate learning difficulties;

- severe learning difficulties;

- delicate;

- visually impaired;

- physically disabled (including motor impaired);

- autistic;

- communication difficulties (including hearing impaired).

There was provision for other identified needs to be included.

All these categories of need can be represented in residential special schools (day and boarding), although children receiving full-time boarding education and care are likely to include those with the most

---

3 REPORT OF THE COMMITTEE REVIEWING PROVISION TO MEET SPECIAL EDUCATIONAL NEEDS (1985). Educational Opportunities for All? (Fish Report), London, Inner London Education Authority.

severe needs. The *Warnock Report*[4] recommended that, wherever possible, children with special educational needs should be provided for within the community, by integrating their education with that of other children. To a certain extent this has occurred, but even so many children and young people with special educational needs are educated and cared for in schools which only look after children with a particular kind of need.

Children in residential special schools cover the whole age-range although, as in the 'mainstream' sector, very young children are rare. Some of the youngest children are in schools for those who are visually impaired or have communication difficulties. As in most other settings, boys outnumber girls by 72% to 28%. There is little data available on the ethnic composition of residential special schools.

Children who attend residential special schools are usually placed by a local education authority or social services department, or jointly. It is rare for a child to be placed by parents. Those placed by a local education authority should have a statement of Special Education Needs; those placed by a social services department need not have a statement. A local authority social services department which places a child in a residential special school must carry out its duties under the *Children Act 1989*, including the regulations in respect of child care plans and reviews of children's cases.

9.3.2 Care

The spectrum of provision within the residential special school sector is extremely wide; some are essentially boarding schools catering for pupils with mild learning difficulties and able to progress within an environment offering structure and protection only slightly greater than for children in an unspecialised school. Other schools are for children and young people with severe physical disabilities and/or learning difficulties which require a specialised and highly intensive level of care. Whatever their particular disability, the children are children first and foremost, and it is important that the principles and good practice we have described in Chapter 6, *The Common Core*, should set standards for residential special schools as well as for other settings. The main caring task for staff is the same as in other settings. What is different are the additional specific needs of the children and young people because of their disabilities.

Physical environment
The physical environment is of great importance particularly in enabling children and young people to have the special help they need to

---

4 COMMITTEE ON THE EDUCATION OF HANDICAPPED CHILDREN AND YOUNG PEOPLE (1978) Special Educational Needs (Warnock Report), Cmnd 7212, London, HMSO

achieve their full potential. Those with physical disabilities and sensory impairment may need a range of special facilities both for their education and their life out of the classroom. Computerised communication and control systems sometimes seem to envelop the living space and children with multiple disabilities. For them, however, these sophisticated aids make the world work better and bring 'normality' closer to their experience. Children with emotional and behavioural difficulties need as 'normal' an environment as possible, but are likely to benefit from plenty of space, with outdoor facilities in which they can be free to play and experiment without encountering too many neighbourhood constraints. Those who are responsible for the schools, we hope, will find Chapter 5, *The Physical Environment*, helpful.

Privacy

Privacy is as important for children with special needs as it is for other children. It must not be assumed, for example, that because some children have such severe learning difficulties that they cannot carry out basic functions such as going to the toilet, washing or dressing without assistance from staff, that their right to privacy is any the less. These functions should not take place in the presence of other children or staff who do not need to be there. A disabled child may often come to depend on and trust a particular member of staff and, where this is the case, that member of staff, whenever possible, should undertake personal care like helping the child to dress, undress and wash. Communal washing, bathing and dressing are not good practice. Privacy is particularly important for children with learning difficulties. They may have little else to hold on to other than the care and love they receive from staff which, for them, can take on a very personal dimension. For very dependent children, whether very young, disabled, or with learning difficulties, staff are the custodians of the children's dignity.

Daily life

In the children's daily life, all the issues of good practice discussed in Chapter 6 are relevant, subject to any particular practices relating to their specific or special needs. This means, for example, that wherever possible, children and young people should be consulted and involved in making decisions, and in the routines and activities planned to meet their needs, whether as individuals or as a group. They need a feeling of stability and continuity as much as other children. Control issues also need to be carefully thought out and planned. This may be particularly important in residential special schools because children may respond very differently to methods of control which might be appropriate in other settings. For example, staff may promote the behavioural development of children with severe learning disabilities by anticipating the need to physically hold a child in certain known situations, whereas for other children recourse to physical intervention would be essentially more reactive. Staff also need to listen to and talk to children, and linguistic, cultural and religious needs have to be met. Where children have particular emotional or psychological problems, it is particularly necessary in planning for them to ensure that individual approaches to care and control have been discussed and recorded. For example, a particular child may become uncontrollably excited if he remains in a group for an extended period. Care plans may need to indicate that s/he will require regular periods of brief separation from the group in a calming environment.

An issue sometimes overlooked in the care of children with especially severe needs is the requirement to keep them in touch with parents, family and friends. For example, when a child has a sensory impairment, communication difficulties or severe learning problems, staff will have to take initiatives to help them stay in contact. The use of a telephone is vital, but staff may also need to help them write to their families and read them the letters their families send.

Links with children's families are particularly important since some of them stay in residential special schools for most of their childhood; from the age of seven (or even younger) until sixteen or eighteen. Many have disabilities which make it is difficult to be looked after at home without a great deal of support. In their time away, unless the school has forged close links with their family, the family may have become accustomed to their absence, and have built their lives around the fact that one or more of their children lives away from home for a great part of each year. All too often in the past children have left residential special schools without adequate support for their family. Their return home may then, instead of being welcomed, be a cause of disruption and trauma. This situation should be prevented from arising as far as possible. This will mean involving the family at every stage of the child's life. Visits should be encouraged, if necessary by helping parents with the cost of travel and providing facilities for overnight stays. The school will not care for the young person beyond late adolescence and parents will have to provide stability and continuity for many years.

Parents' visits can provide a great deal of comfort while children are in school. When a child arrives, staff should agree what responsibilities parents will continue to carry out; for example, buying clothes or taking the child on holiday. Regrettably, residential special schools are often at a great distance from children's own homes. Failure to take positive steps to maintain family ties can and does lead to their breakdown. When the impact of having a child at home is very disruptive it may sometimes be valuable to provide a respite period during a long school holiday. A respite foster home relating closely to the child's family might be the best way to manage holidays, rather than the child returning to the school. Such respite care is best anticipated and planned rather than provided in an emergency when life becomes intolerable for the family.

Similarly, it is important that residential special schools build links with their local community. This is important to ensure that schools do not become isolated, as has happened in the past. Good practice will flourish best in an environment which is open, and which welcomes external influences. There should be good liaison with local health and social services or social work authorities, and the school should make efforts to create similar links with local schools and youth organisations, in order to integrate pupils into the life of the community. Some schools have developed local volunteer groups, who provide assistance in caring for children, and help to create relationships with community organisations which may be of great benefit and stimulus to individual children and the school itself. If such schemes are developed, all volunteers who help with the care of children must be asked to agree to police and other checks for staff similar to those for full time staff.

Planning for children

Written plans for a child's care should be produced when he or she arrives at a residential special school. Again, this is a statutory requirement if a child is placed by a local authority social services department, but planning for an individual child's care is good practice and, whatever the route by which children arrive in a residential special school, they should have a plan setting aims, detailing care and development, and considering outcomes. Plans should be produced in partnership between the school, parents or other carers, health professionals, for example, the child's General Practitioner, psychiatrist or physiotherapist, and any other professional who will play a significant part in the child's care, development and education. However, the participation of parents is perhaps the most crucial component of planning, particularly for those children placed by LEAs with parental agreement, and not looked after by local authorities.

Plans detail the type of care to be delivered, including behaviour management, arrangements for education and activities outside the school. Agreement on who should take which role, how outcomes will be monitored, arrangements for regular reviews of progress, and who should be involved in these reviews is essential. Plans for children's return to their families are best considered from the start even if this is several years in the future. The plan will also consider at what stage the children might be ready to leave, that is, by identifying the nature and degree of progress necessary to permit them to be integrated into the community, if this is possible and desirable. Finally, the plan should address what will happen when the children leave school. What preparations should be made for learning to live independently and what continuing support will be provided for those who are to look after them? What other agencies should be involved, for example, the local authority social services or social work department, social security and housing departments. As soon as these agencies have been identified they should be included in the planning and review process.

9.4 Therapeutic Communities

9.4.1　*What are Therapeutic Communities*

Therapeutic communities are sometimes defined as integrated, residential and educational environments which provide psycho-therapeutic treatment for exceptionally emotionally damaged children. They are not all of the same model but they aim to have some if not all of the following characteristics:–

- A physical environment emphasising care and self-worth, actively maintained to a good level, and open to children in all respects to enable them to make good use of the experience of life in the therapeutic community.

- Staff and children share the experience of living in the environment to forge a 'therapeutic alliance' between them and thereby assist the children to achieve the changes needed to help them with their problems.

- Staff share and are strongly identified with the ethos of the community and some are specially trained in group work and personal therapies.

- High levels of staff support and of psychiatric and other outside consultancy, focused on particular treatments and therapies offered, are available to staff.

Such communities may be legally classified as children's homes, schools, nursing homes or health care establishments, and children and young people might be referred by a local authority social services department under the *Children Act*, by a social work department in Scotland, by a local education authority, or by a health authority. We have included them in this chapter because they have many similarities to residential special schools: they often look after children with similar needs, and they provide full-time care and education on the premises. They also have some similarities with children's homes.

9.4.2　*Two Studies Which Took a Closer Look*

Apart from the writings of individuals involved in the therapeutic communities and limited circulation publications such as *The International Journal of Therapeutic Communities* and the former *Journal of the Association of Workers for Children with Emotional and Behavioural Difficulties*, little general information is available about therapeutic communities. Responding to this, and their own wish to explore areas of common interest, the heads of ten therapeutic communities, nine in England and one in Scotland, formed a body known as 'The Charterhouse Group' and, subsequently, commissioned and paid for a small study of the ten establishments. This was carried out by John Fitzgerald, Principal of The Bridge, an organisation for assisting agencies with the placement of 'difficult to place' children and young people. The report entitled *'The Hurt and the Healing'* was published in September 1990. It was the first time that therapeutic communities had been scrutinised in this way. At the time, most of the communities were charitable trusts; one was part of a social services department. It is unusual for a group of 'like minded' child care establishments to examine itself in this way, and we therefore address some of the detail of the report of their initiative.

Under the heading *'Information about Therapeutic Communities'*, Fitzgerald reported that:–

- there were 322 children in residence at the time of the study;

- the total number of places in 10 communities was 366;

- the smallest had 14 places, the largest 80;

- 8 were for boys and girls, 2 for boys only;

- all communities provided education on the premises;

- 5 provided full time care, 4 operated on a school term basis, 1 offered 44 week a year care, 1 offered 52 week care as well as school term care, another had 6 short terms, and another had flexible arrangements to suit each resident;

- total number of professional staff was 236;

- 5 had a staff/child ratio of 1 to 1, 3 had a 1 to 2 ratio, and 2 had 2 staff members for every 3 children or young persons;

- in addition to professional staff 121 domestic and ancillary staff were employed;

- professional qualifications of staff included teaching, social work, youth work, nursing and community work;

- ethnic backgrounds of 336 out of 357 professional and domestic staff were:–
  White   331
  Caribbean   5
  African   0
  Asian   0

(A similar pattern characterised advisors and consultants);

•• ethnic backgrounds of children and young people in residence at the time of the study were:–

African	7	– 2.2%
Caribbean	28	– 8.7%
Asian	4	– 1.2%
White	275	– 85.4%
Other	8	– 2.5%
Total	322	

•• a sample of 95 children and young people at admission stage showed:–

numbers and ages at admission

Boys	11–15	43
Girls	11–15	22
Boys	5–10	26
Girls	5–10	4
		95

•• the children's legal status was:–

Care orders	56	58.0%
Voluntary admission ('looked after' since 1989 Act)	32	34.0%
Parental rights assumption (no longer available)	3	3.5%
Wardship	1	1.0%
Other	3	3.5%
	95	

From other information in the study it was clear that there were major differences between the communities, at the time of the study, in size, style of regime, qualifications of staff and type of care offered. Some were much closer to boarding schools in their pattern and others closer to children's homes.

Subsequently, a further study on behalf of the Charterhouse Group was carried out on nine therapeutic communities by Christopher Beedell, formerly tutor in charge of a senior residential work training course at Bristol University. It was published in 1993 with the title *'Poor Starts, Lost Opportunities, Hopeful Outcomes'*.

The study states that its members gave common support to certain principles, summarised as follows:–

- An approach to the problems of children in their care which is informed by a psychodynamic understanding of individuals.

- A belief in the value of education. . . . . individually delivered in small classes and directed to the whole child.

- A commitment to some form of shared responsibility between and among staff and children.

- A commitment to what is often termed a 'non-punitive' approach.

- A commitment to staff training and development – carried out in various ways . . . . in particular by the employment of independent external consultants of high professional skill who are not part of the general management

The children studied were:–

10 or under	42
11 to 15	110
Over 16	34

'They were nearly all in Care in one way or another' Two thirds were the subject of Special needs Statements. They were all referred by local authority social services or education departments, or jointly, and similarly funded. Problems reported at referral put in rank order of total mentions were:–

School problems – behavioural	88%
Physical aggression	73%
School problem – learning	70%
Withdrawal	44%
School problem – attendance	41%
Persistent fears	41%
Enuresis	25%
Suicide threats	24%
Self-maiming/mutilation	22%
Anorexia/eating disorder	12%
Sexual abuse of other/s	15%
Cruelty to animals	13%
Encopresis	13%
Suicide attempt	9%

The study was exploratory and makes no claims to clear findings. It gives more detailed information than had formerly been available about the task that therapeutic communities were undertaking in the early 1990s. It was not known whether the histories of children admitted were better or worse than those of many other children.

'Similarly we do not know how many children with comparable experiences .... are living in ordinary LA children's homes. We can be fairly sure that there are a sizeable number because over two thirds of our children have come through regular residential facilities and it is unlikely that the source is drying up .... We do not know either how many children with comparable histories have already taken, or been taken, a step further into youth custody or secure accommodation across the country'.

In conclusion the author says

'The results display a cumulation of adverse experience which must demonstrate the pain, bewilderment and lack of trust and hope which these children have. **They show too the emotional load which those dealing with them have to be ready to share and survive with realism and determination'.**

A common characteristic of the therapeutic communities has been that they have operated as a separate system of residential establishments, separate from boarding schools, separate, with one exception, from local authorities. Staff training received post appointment has often been provided on site or in therapeutic community groupings, rather than through the national training system used by local authorities and voluntary child care organisations. Within the group of communities practice has shown marked differences, not the least in terms of staff selection and support. Some have used a rigorous system of staff selection and provided regular, outside, high level professional support for staff. Some have been less rigorous, and sometimes have not included police and other available checks. However skilled people may consider they are in staff selection, children are entitled to the maximum protection available, and experience demonstrates that many bad mistakes have been made with destructive consequences for children.

The following sections are based on the best therapeutic community practice. The study commissioned by the Therapeutic Communities in 1990 if carried out in any range of residential establishments for children and young people, would reveal major differences of standards amongst establishments purporting to be very similar. Part of the purpose of this book is to help practitioners and managers to reduce these differences and raise all standards to the level of the best. The provisions of the Children Act 1989, under which local authorities are required to inspect therapeutic communities, will also bring about changes in them as in other establishments.

9.4.3   Admissions

Therapeutic communities take particular care to ensure that admission is the correct decision for the child.

The admission process typically includes the following elements:–

- A detailed paper assessment to establish whether the community is able to offer what the child needs. Staff should ask, 'Is this child likely to benefit from treatment?' If after careful consultation the answer is likely to be negative, it is unwise to raise false expectations in the child's carers. Clarity about objectives is essential.

- A visit by the young person with their carer, for example parents or social worker, is always important, but should not be offered unless a place is likely to be available.

- The admission process should be controlled by the head of the therapeutic community, not by managers or governors external to the establishment.

- Young people already in the community should share in the admission process. How this will be achieved will depend on each establishment, but the capacity of the community to cope with the new member will always be an important factor affecting admission.

9.4.4 Treatment and Good Practice

Children and young people who enter a therapeutic community are there specifically to receive treatment. They and their families should, therefore, wherever possible, give their consent to admission. Where this has not happened staff should be very cautious in making decisions for and on behalf of young people. Gaining consent to treatment and therapy should be a major objective. Staff should be aware of the laws governing consent to treatment, and the limitations on their powers to work with children and young people who express doubt about a particular treatment or therapy. 'Treatment' does not only refer to medical and clinical treatment, but also to psychological and psychotherapeutic treatment.

The nature of therapeutic communities is such that all elements of a resident's life can be considered to be part of continuing treatment, and this can raise difficult issues for staff. What, for example, should staff do when a child refuses to take part in a group activity such as play which, although 'normal' in the sense that it is a part of every child's life, is considered to be an element of the treatment of a child in a therapeutic community. Each community must develop its own set of procedures and rules to address these issues, which should be discussed and agreed by all staff and residents.

There are a number of elements of good practice in therapeutic communities which are distinct from other settings, or which are given greater importance because of the nature of the work of these establishments. The first rule is that drugs should not be used in treatment programmes. Residents may in fact be following a course of medication which has been prescribed by a general practitioner or clinician and this may need to continue, but drugs have no place in the treatments or therapies provided by the community.

The home should provide a variety of spaces for young people; for the routines of daily living; for private and communal leisure; and for study and privacy. There should also be a good level of comfort and equipment to promote feelings of self-worth among residents. Clearly this has to be supported by rapid refurbishment of damage and wear and tear whenever it occurs.

Consulting with children and young people and identifying their views is not normally a separate issue for therapeutic communities. Within the community, recognising and responding to the needs of residents is integral to good practice, and is a key component in the treatment.

To a large extent, the children and young people in therapeutic environments are those who are exceptionally damaged, often from very early in life. Their needs are such that they are often unable to behave well and care for themselves, and are unable to let others do so for them. Hence therapeutic communities seek to fulfil a number of basic needs:

- to manage and contain chaotic, dangerous or self-destructive behaviour;

- to provide nurturing experiences to make up for what may have been missed earlier in their lives;

- to help children and young people assume control of their own present and future development, and to feel less trapped by past traumas, disturbance or deprivation.

Programmes of treatment will normally incorporate psychological, emotional, social and educational elements, and take place in a residential environment which has relationships at its heart, and an emotional climate which encourages openness.

To meet and treat the needs of these highly disturbed children and young people requires careful attention to a host of details about the physical environment, routines and activities; and to overall continuity in day-to-day living. Given the individual family, social or educational traumas which many children and young people have suffered, they are in need of an environment that is reassuring in all its physical and non-physical elements; that welcomes them; and that provides consistency and containment with sensitivity, sincerity and tolerance. To develop, children and young people must be helped to trust in the staff and the physical setting. When a visitor to one such community tried to pinpoint exactly what it was that impressed her, it turned out not to be the building, the grounds, the food or even a particular adult, child or group. Instead she observed that *'the children had the confidence of taking things for granted'*. The contrast with prior experiences was profound and central for them.

An essential ingredient in the environment of a therapeutic community is commitment to and an emphasis on relationship-building. Children need to experience trust from others so that they may develop the sense of trust in themselves and in other people that is the basis for healthy development and living. Staff must learn to accept behaviour which at times will be inappropriate, unacceptable and even intolerable; not in order to excuse, but to understand. Staff must seek to intervene and interrupt, yet to understand the source of the behaviour and feelings, and what sustains them so that they can help the child understand and change for the better.

Much of the work in therapeutic communities is in 'living alongside' the children, focusing on helping individuals and groups to learn to live with themselves and with one another. This is what is most distinctive about such communities, even those for the very young. Each resident should learn that individual responsibility extends towards accepting responsibility for others as well as oneself. Continuity of staff with children is of considerable significance, and some therapeutic communities seek staff who are prepared to commit themselves to substantial periods of service to provide this for individual children and young people.

To sustain the emotional climate in therapeutic communities staff must offer themselves as intermediaries between a child and the events and routines of the day. In this way, the children will not feel a sense of being left to fend for themselves. Sometimes, this will be a physical act, such as helping or accompanying a child through daily activities such as bathing, eating, playing, activities or education. Staff should work both with the group and the individuals in it to enhance positive features of group living and minimise negative ones. In doing so, staff and children need to think and talk about events and feelings, hopes and fears about what has happened. This will help to give meaning to events, even those which may initially have appeared inexplicable or meaningless. With the many positive features of care and treatment in therapeutic communities, there are inevitably negative aspects which were raised in discussion of our text. One of these was a suggestion that children who repeatedly break the therapeutic community's rules are likely to be expelled and since they may have had many previous rejections this can be a very serious matter. The closeness of the previous relationship will reinforce the trauma. The departure, if it has to take place, will require very sensitive handling, but is likely to remain a very damaging experience. A further point made to us, which is relevant to outcomes, was that families are not always encouraged to be as close a part of the whole experience for the child as they need to be. Distance plays a part in this, since the therapeutic communities are few in number and scattered thinly. A third point referred to 'care' cases in therapeutic communities and boarding special schools where their status may be 'voluntary'. It was suggested that they are frequently a low priority for field social workers and thus little is done to build up and develop better family/child relationships and, sadly, once more, the divide between residential services and field social work is reinforced.

9.4.5 Staff

Staff are likely to live 'on campus'; this is necessary in order to develop the sense of community and continuity which is essential to the care and treatment provided by these establishments. They should not, however, take on a key worker role with children and young people until they have completed a settling-in and probationary period, usually of around 6 – 12 months. This time should be the formal induction period, in which training programmes and comprehensive supervision should be provided. In addition, all staff should receive individual casework supervision on a continuing basis.

An element of staff support in the therapeutic communities should be 'sensitivity meetings', which will help them to cope with the great pressures and stresses which working in such an intensive way can bring about. Such meetings will usually be best organised as group supervision sessions, or non-agenda meetings supported by a trained, external consultant.

9.4.6 Training

Some therapeutic communities provide in-house training of various kinds. The need, however, to keep in close touch with the mainstream of residential care and education and the content of Chapter 11 is relevant to them as well as to other residential settings.

Training to enable staff to meet the particular needs of the children and young people is essential. Whilst taking into account the aims and functions of an establishment, it should not simply focus on the specific needs of the children but be child centred and address the requirements of good care common to all children. Special needs are best understood in this context. Chapter 11, on training, is relevant to the needs of staff in special boarding schools and therapeutic communities.

10   Medical and Health Service Settings

10.1 Introduction

In this chapter we look at the fourth group of residential settings. In these, children and young people live for various periods of time while they receive treatment for physical, emotional or mental health needs and conditions. Unlike the other settings we have discussed there are no legal requirements relating to the care of children in the health services, unless they are admitted under the *Mental Health Act*. The children's needs may range from acute physical illness at any age from birth to adolescence, to long periods of time for protracted illness, severe disability or mental health disturbance in later childhood and adolescence. Also, unlike the other settings we have discussed, because of physical or mental health needs, there are overriding clinical and practical constraints conditioning the type of setting, the care of patients, their ability to interact with their environment and other people, and their freedom of movement and action. Nevertheless, we argue that, as in disability, it is important to give priority to the essential core of care, rights and needs of children and young people in health care as well as in educational and child care settings. Even with the best endeavour and intentions it is very easy for long stay patients to become marginalised in society and to miss many educational opportunities, for example, long stay chemotherapy patients, and children with orthopaedic conditions who have to be hospitalised regularly. The Dartington Social Research Unit's 'Return' study showed their social and educational needs to be very important in this context.

10.2 Children in hospital

10.2.1 The Platt Report

Considerable changes in attitudes to the care of children in health service settings have been achieved. Dr John Bowlby, James Robertson, Dr James Spence and Dr Donald Winnicott pioneered these changes, particularly in the care and treatment of young children in hospital in the late 1940s and 1950s. In 1959 the publication of the Platt Report, named after the surgeon who headed the inquiry, 'The Welfare of Children in Hospital' provided a detailed series of recommendations about the 'non-medical' aspects of the care of child patients from birth to sixteen years. The three which drew most attention at the time were:

(1) that visiting to all children should be unrestricted;

(2) that provision should be made to enable mothers of children under five years of age to stay with them in hospital (at least for the first few days) in order to help in their care and prevent the distress and risks to mental health associated with separation;

(3) that the training of medical and nursing students should be improved to give them greater understanding of the emotional needs of children.

Change, however, does not happen overnight. Films made by Robertson such as 'A Two Year Old Goes to Hospital' and 'Going to Hospital with Mother' were shown widely and helped to change both public and professional opinion. The foundation of NAWCH (*National Association for the Welfare of Children in Hospital*, now known as Action for Sick Children,) was originally founded by parents and still works on behalf of children's interests. It was tirelessly supported by certain consultant paediatricians and by some other doctors, nurses and administrators, as well as by social workers, parents and others. A 1969 survey by NAWCH showed that ten years after the Platt Report, only 57% of children's hospitals in the South West Metropolitan Region allowed unrestricted visiting, defined for the survey as a modest 45 hours per week. Of 65 hospitals surveyed 36 still had no arrangements for mothers to stay with their children. The following year, in a second edition of *'Young Children in Hospital'* by James Robertson, published in 1970, attention was drawn to the *Platt Committee's* failure to recognise the problems of long stay child patients in hospital for whom it was argued that there was a high probability of severe emotional deprivation because of prolonged separation and lack of stable motherly care in consequence of shifts and changes of ward staff. Robertson quoted in support of what he called *'a sobering picture for anyone hopeful of quick solutions to the plight of young patients'*, the following:

'Whereas the child, by reason of his physical and mental immaturity, needs special safeguards and care, the child of tender years shall not, save in exceptional circumstances, be separated from his mother'

United Nations Declaration of Rights of the Child, 1959

and

'In 1966, the last year for which statistics are available there were in England and Wales 374,000 admissions to hospital of children under five years of age'.

Report on Hospital In-Patient Inquiry for the Year 1966

The Royal College of Nursing and National Council of Nurses in the United Kingdom published, in 1974, a study of nursing care of children by Pamela J Hawthorn entitled *'Nurse – I Want my Mummy'*. At the end, one very important recommendation based on the findings of the study was:

> *'The very urgent need for senior nursing staff in paediatric units to be given the opportunity of learning the current child care theories and their application to modern nursing care. Until there is understanding of these theories, the need for changes in the ward organisation is not apparent and they will not occur. It is now fourteen years since the Platt Report was published and the recommendations made. This survey only serves to underline the need for full acceptance of these recommendations'.*

10.2.2 Long Stay Hospital Care

Research carried out by Maureen Oswin (*Spastics International Medical Publications*) based at the *Thomas Coram Foundation* and directed by Professor Jack Tizard, drew attention in 1978 to the needs of *'Children Living in Long-stay Hospitals'*. The 223 children and young people in the study lived in 'special care' wards, a term used to describe wards which accommodated only children with multiple physical, mental and sensory handicaps. The great majority were permanent long stay patients who had been living in hospital for between one and 27 years. Some went home for occasional weekends or holidays, and a very few spent most weekends at home and were referred to by staff as 'boarders'.

The children's needs were divided into four categories and described as follows:

'1   **Medical Needs**

(a)   Diagnosis of disability.

(b)   Special treatment (for some children): drugs (for epilepsy); orthopaedic correction of deformities; surgical correction for eye defects; cosmetic correction (ie. plastic surgery for grave facial deformities); and psychiatric help for emotional disturbances.

(c)   Supervision of general health care (as for ordinary children); treatment of common childhood illnesses, accidents, dietary problems, skin diseases; dental care; glasses and hearing-aids if necessary; and referral to other specialists as required.

2   **Paramedical and educational needs**

Physiotherapy for supervision of movement, position, aids, furniture, wheelchairs, callipers, boots, and for assisting to become more independent.

Speech therapy, especially when there are early feeding problems. The grave handicaps of these children make it necessary to explore various means of communication, by all disciplines of staff, and then some experimentation to find the best method for each individual child.

Occupational therapy to assist independence, for example in learning to hold a cup, spoon or flannel and sponge, to put on shoes or pull on socks, to lift arms to help with dressing. Occupational therapists can advise on how to make use of any ability, however meagre.

Psychological advice on helping the children to become more independent, for example through carefully worked-out programmes of individual teaching, and for the correction or prevention of behaviour disorders.

Education covers the needs to play and to communicate; special educational help for children who are blind, deaf, partially sighted or who have physical disabilities (eg. equipment, aids, teaching methods). Referral to other special educational centres (perhaps schools outside the hospital) if necessary.

3 Nursing needs
These will be required for some, but not all, of the children: drugs; medicines; occasional enemas; special diets; care during and after major epileptic attacks; prevention of sores when children are emaciated or very physically deformed; attending to children with colostomies; caring for children with severe handicaps resulting from spina bifida; and care of children after operations or during illnesses.

4 Residential care needs
Routine physical care: supervision of clothes; food; cleanliness; attention in the lavatory; safety; care during minor illnesses; general health care, as for ordinary children living away from home.

Mothering[1] essential for all children in residential care, whether disabled or not.

Family contact: important for all children in residential care, whether disabled or not.

Personal possessions: essential for all children in residential care, whether disabled or not.

Play: essential for all children in residential care, whether disabled or not.

Outings: essential for all children in residential care, whether disabled or not.

---

[1] 'Mothering' as used in this study does not imply care which can only be given by a woman; it is used in the sense of affectionate individual care being given by a man or woman. The word parenting was considered but discarded in favour of the more meaningful word 'mothering'

As the study pointed out:

> '..... *the majority of the needs listed above are not different from those of ordinary children in residential care or in the family home. In order to meet these needs of multiple handicapped children in residential care, there must be adequate numbers of care staff, who need to be supported in a practical way by specialist staff; there has to be inter-disciplinary cooperation'.*

The findings of the study were very negative about existing services and, with other work done since, have led to major changes in the care of disabled children in hospital. Some of the recommendations made at the time serve to underline quite powerfully the commonalities which this book seeks to identify in the care of children away from home in groups – and to support the multi-disciplinary nature of the tasks and the learning experiences which services can contribute to each other. A few examples have been chosen from the many recommendations the study made; they illustrate how basic some required improvements were.

'Hospital Management

(1) The hospital should have a Families' Association, which would be involved not only in fund raising and social activities, but also in influencing hospital management in so far as it affects the children (eg. there should be a parent representative on the hospital's management team).

(2) Parents should be invited to attend ward staff meetings.

(3) Parents should be given full information about any changes in hospital administration which might affect their children, for example the possible closure of the physiotherapy department because of lack of staff, or a reduction in ward staff, difficulties in transporting their children to the hospital school, or the lack of speech therapists.

(4) Parents should be informed of any student or post-graduate research taking place in the hospital which might involve their children (eg. in sociology, psychology, medicine, education), and be given some idea of the aims of the research.

Helping families to maintain contact

(5) A member of staff (not necessarily at senior level) who knows the child should be responsible for writing personal letters to parents to give news of their child. The aim would be to keep the parents informed about details such as any outings the child has been on, his reactions, any new clothes he may have been bought recently, any slight progress he might have made, and his general health. These letters would be non-medical, of the kind that would be written by house parents for a child in residential care who cannot write for himself.

(6) The parents should be invited to join any hospital outings their child goes on: even if they cannot go, they should be given the choice.

(7)   If family problems make it likely that the child is at risk of losing contact with his family, the possibility of taking him for short visits to his family should be considered. Perhaps these visits could be organised by student nurses or volunteers if regular ward staff could not be spared.

(8)   If families find it difficult to get transport to and from the hospital, a system of voluntary transport could be organised.

Parents' visits

(9)   Parents should be made to feel physically and emotionally comfortable when they visit.

(10)   They should be given a chair to sit down on, beside their child's wheelchair.

(11)   If staff are having a tea-break, they should offer a cup of tea to the parents.

(12)   If parents like to be alone with their child when they visit, they should be able to go into a bedroom or some other small room which is not in use.

(13)   Any progress made by the child, however meagre, should be mentioned to the parents when they visit. It may only be some small achievement, such as the child's lifting his arm unaided when he was being undressed, but the parents should be told about it because it may help them to feel that their child is not a complete write-off.

(14)   New ward staff should always be introduced to parents by name, and it should be explained if they are students, temporary staff or new permanent staff.

(15)   Parents should be told the names of other children who are near their own child.

(16)   Parents should be introduced to other visiting parents in the ward.

(17)   Parents should be given the opportunity to help with dressing, feeding and putting their child to bed. If the child is difficult to feed, parents should not be left to struggle with him on their own so that they feel foolish in the presence of staff who may be more experienced in the techniques of feeding difficult children; they should be helped tactfully. If they wish to help with putting their child to bed, they should be shown where all the materials are (clothes, flannels, soap and suchlike) so that they feel at ease in the ward.

Helping children who are unvisited

(18)   There should be some special help available to ensure that outside links are maintained for those children who have little or no family contact. Volunteer visitors could become regular 'hospital foster parents', not necessarily with the idea of taking the children to live at home with them, but in order to take an active part in the unvisited child's life so as to improve his outside contacts. They might take him on outings and holidays, and they could join the Parents' Association as his 'foster

parents'. At present, children may only be officially fostered through being taken into the care of local authorities, but for children in long-stay hospitals who are not officially in care and whose parents would not agree to them being so, there should be some half-way scheme whereby they might have an adult assigned to them who would take a long-term personal interest in them if their families cannot do so. These 'hospital foster parents' would have their expenses paid when they visit the child and if they take them out. Such a scheme would enable the child to make a relationship with somebody outside the hospital, in an attempt to improve his lifestyle.

(19) Unvisited children who are already officially in care, but who have no foster parents because they have lived for many years in hospital, should be included in the above scheme'.

Some of the recommendations for good practice within the nursing care itself also demonstrated the importance of the *'Common Core'* elements of care which form the material of Chapter 6. The examples which follow were proposed as the basis of guidelines to ease the children's deprivation;

'(1) There should be continuity of staff, ie. a definite ruling against constant changes of staff in children's wards.

(2) If some members of ward staff make a relationship with a child it should be respected and encouraged, and not derided as 'spoiling' the child.

(3) If a child has a special member of staff who is off duty, other staff should be aware of any small personal routine which the child and that member of staff have developed, and it should be maintained in order to give the child some security.

(4) Staff should be aware that certain groups of children are especially vulnerable to lack of attention; for example, being non-ambulant children.

(5) Staff meetings on the *development and maintenance of good child care practices* should be regularly held. (The production of the report necessitated spending 18 months in hospitals, but never during that time was there any evidence of hospital staff meeting to discuss principles of child care in relation to the residential care of handicapped children).

(6) All staff working with children in long-stay hospitals should be given some insight into child development, the effects of institutional care, and the children's play and mothering needs. This could be done through lectures, discussion groups, films, visits to other centres for handicapped and non-handicapped children (day centres, playgroups, residential homes and schools), recommended reading, and demonstrations of good practice'.

10.2.3 Adolescents in Hospital

The Court Report – 'Fit for the Future' (Report of the Committee on Child Health Services chaired by Professor S D M Court, 1976) had drawn attention to the special health needs of adolescents.

> *'In recent years it has become increasingly evident that adolescents have needs and problems sufficiently distinguishable from those on the one hand of children and the other of adults to warrant consideration as a distinct group for health care provision'.*

A working party set up by the British Paediatric Association to look at 'The Needs and Care of Adolescents' published its report in International Youth Year 1985. Concerning the in-patient provision for adolescents, the report urged, amongst other recommendations that:-

(1) Adolescents requiring hospital in-patient care should be in wards specifically for them and this consideration is usually of greater importance than the needs of system specialities.

(2) Patients in this age group have a special need for privacy.

(3) Accommodation should be provided for recreation and for educational purposes.

(4) Overnight accommodation for parents should be provided.

(5) Adolescents with a physical illness are at risk of emotional disturbance and a child and adolescent psychiatrist should have close links with the ward.

(6) The personality of the sister or charge nurse is of prime importance and should be a critical factor in his or her appointment.

(7) Educational provision is essential and should be continued throughout the year.

(8) When adolescent patients cannot be accommodated in an adolescent ward, special provision should be made for them in the departments to which they are admitted and they should, if possible, be able to participate in the educational and recreational activities of the adolescent ward.

The report contained other recommendations close to the main themes of this book. They included self referral community clinics offering advice about growth and development, sexual problems and emotional difficulties; health education for adolescents, with particular attention to smoking, abuse of alcohol and drugs; education for parenthood and family life; care for pregnant school girls; sex education as part of health education; user-friendly contraceptive advice and help for young people;

expansion of adolescent psychiatric services; long stay psychiatric units for very disturbed adolescents; and supra-regional secure units for aggressive, disturbed young people.

'BRIDGES OVER TROUBLED WATERS'

The following year, 1986, the NHS Health Advisory Service published their report, *'Bridges Over Troubled Waters'* on the subject of services for disturbed adolescents. In its preface the author said:-

> *'In recent years HAS teams have repeatedly found serious shortcomings in the way services are provided to adolescents and particularly those manifesting abnormal behaviour'.*

The young people who were the subject of the report were described as 'disturbed' – but the report explained that this covered

> *'not only those who are **disturbed within themselves** but also those perceived as **disturbing** by others'.*

In general they were between 12 and 19 years of age, a period which the HAS considered

> *'represents a unique phase of life deserving special and separate consideration .... It has become clear that services for adolescents are not the province in isolation of health authorities nor of education departments nor of social services departments .... More than for any other client group, services for adolescents overlap many agencies, statutory and voluntary .... housing, employment, probation, the courts and the prison services'.*

'Adolescence represents a time of great developmental significance. For the vast majority, the 'bridge' between dependent childhood and independent adulthood is negotiated more or less smoothly. For a few, the transition period is stormy and help is needed to prevent long term personal damage'.

Peter Horrocks, Director NHS Health Advisory Service

We shall return to adolescence and psychiatric services later but before doing so we add a little more to the bird's eye view of the development of health care practice for children and young people in groups which has been attempted in this chapter.

10.2.4 Action for Sick Children (formerly National Association for the Welfare of Children in Hospital)

During 1988 NAWCH drew together a collection of policy papers concerning children in hospital, including the emotional needs of those undergoing surgery, in accident and emergency wards, neo-natal care surgery, nursing care and leave for family reasons, a wide range of topics, and published them accompanied by a **NAWCH Charter for Children in Hospital.** Once more the common ground in good practice related to children away from home and living in groups can be clearly seen.

---

(1)
Children shall be admitted to hospital only if the care they require cannot be equally well provided at home or on a day basis.

(2)
Children in hospital shall have the right to have their parents with them at all times provided this is in the best interest of the child. Accommodation should therefore be offered to all parents, and they should be helped and encouraged to stay. In order to share in the care of their child, parents should be fully informed about ward routine and their active participation encouraged.

(3)
Children and/or their parents shall have the right to information appropriate to age and understanding.

(4)
Children and/or their parents shall have the right to informed participation in all decisions involving their health care. Every child shall be protected from unnecessary medical treatment and steps taken to mitigate physical or emotional distress.

(5)
Children shall be treated with tact and understanding and at all times their privacy shall be respected.

(6)
Children shall enjoy the care of appropriately trained staff, fully aware of the physical and emotional needs of each age group.

(7)
Children shall be able to wear their own clothes and have their own personal possessions.

(8)
Children shall be cared for with other children of the same age group.

(9)
Children shall be in an environment furnished and equipped to meet their requirements, and which conforms to recognised standards of safety and supervision.

(10)
Children shall have full opportunity for play, recreation and education suited to their age and condition.

In 1989 and 1990 NAWCH contributed further to the development of standards which would achieve the Charter by the publication of training materials in a Quality Review series on setting standards for children in health care and for adolescents in hospital.

10.2.5 *Research*

The Department of Health (formerly DHSS) commissioned overviews of research on child health care for several years after 1984. The first overview of the care of children in hospital was commissioned in 1986 and published (Roche and Stacey) in 1989. An update was published in 1990. The key question which was seen to remain was:-

> *'How may therapy be delivered to children in hospital without doing other unintended damage to the future life of the child, and his/her family, of a potentially serious kind?*

In an analysis of the 96 research studies available, only three papers on adolescence were found and 6 studies dealing with provision of residential care for handicapped children. Several studies were focused on nurse/client interactions and ward organisation. Perhaps understandably, in the context of clinical concerns, the great majority of studies were not concerned with care issues.

'Over the past three decades in Britain the care of children in hospital has been transformed. Thirty years ago children used to face long, lonely admissions to hospital. They were passed over like a parcel, usually to a nurse at a reception desk. They would be visited infrequently or not at all and collected days or even weeks later, physically recovered but sometimes emotionally harmed. Today most children's wards are welcoming, caring and family centred. Many parents have been enabled to participate fully in their children's care, to sleep beside them, to be with them when they go to the operating theatre, to be there to comfort and support them when they 'come round' again, to make them feel secure and safe in this strange place'.

Peg Belson, Vice Chair, Action for Sick Children (formerly NAWCH) – 'Children in Hospital' in 'Children and Society – Thirty Years of Change for Children' -National Children's Bureau Vol. 7, No. 2 1993

10.2.6 *Department of Health Guidance 'Welfare of Children and Young People in Hospital' 1991, and Volume 6: 'Children with Disabilities' (Children Act 1989 Guidance)*

'Welfare of Children and Young People in Hospital' was described as a guide. Its main aim was

'to bring together in a single document relevant good practice guidance on the care of children in hospital in a form appropriate to the new role of district health authorities and their provider units'.

It identified links with the *Children Act* and other child centred legislative requirements. These included the need for local authorities to be informed when a child has spent three months in hospital; collaboration with local education authorities to provide education for children in hospital; collaboration with social services departments in the identifying, assessing and protecting children at risk; contributing to assessment of children's health, educational and social care needs; and recognition of the duties, training and experience required of medical staff in care and treatment of children. One major section, *'Meeting Children's Special Needs'*, brings together current good practice: involvement of parents; play; education; special educational needs; children with disabilities; 'children from ethnic, religious or cultural communities'; arrangements for adolescents (in which NAWCH guidance referred to earlier is incorporated); life threatening illness; protection from abuse; security; diet; and oral health care. It clearly builds, in many respects, on the campaigning, research and multi-disciplinary work carried out over more than forty years.

In contracting for hospital services, district health authorities need to have in mind the Guide's **Cardinal Principles** (which have much in common with the NAWCH Charter quoted earlier):

'•   Children are admitted to hospital only if the care they require cannot be as well provided at home, in a day clinic or on a day basis in hospital.

•   Children requiring admission to hospital are provided with a high standard of medical, nursing and therapeutic care to facilitate a speedy recovery and minimise complications and mortality.

•   Families with children have easy access to hospital facilities for children without needing to travel significantly further than to other similar amenities.

•   Children are discharged from hospital as soon as socially and clinically appropriate and full support provided for subsequent home or day care.

•   Good child health care is shared with parents/carers and they are closely involved in the care of their children at all times unless, exceptionally, this is not in the best interests of the child. Accommodation is provided for them to remain with their children overnight.

•   Accommodation, facilities and staffing are appropriate to the needs of children and adolescents and separate from those provided for adults. Where possible separate accommodation is provided for adolescents.

- Like all other patients,children have a right for their privacy to be respected and to be treated with tact and understanding. They have an equal right to information appropriate to their age, understanding and specific circumstances'.

Readers may agree that if the context of these principles were changed from hospitals to children's homes or boarding schools, they would fit well with those discussed earlier in Chapter 6 and elsewhere.

THE CHILD'S POINT OF VIEW

Children's own points of view, the right to be involved in decision making about their life and to information and understanding, are increasingly influencing policy, service providers and professional staff. Lothian Region's *Family Charter*, the Charter of the Association for Children with Life Threatening or Terminal Conditions and their Families (Institute of Child Health, Bristol) and a forthcoming book *'Children's Consent to Surgery'* by Priscilla Alderson are examples. This latter book contains the following passage which is part of its last chapter 'Respecting Children's Consent'.

'Children's competence to consent is continually changing in several ways: within each maturing child; in society's growing acceptance that a vital way to protect children is to help them to defend themselves and the adults they will become; in generally rising expectations and growing respect for children's rights and abilities. A surgeon, said approvingly:

'Today's teenagers are very competent, particularly girls. An 11 year old girl will have very strong views on what she wants, what she'll tolerate, and what she won't. Attitudes have changed and children are given more freedom, and encouraged much more, not just to listen and do as they're told, but to have strong views'.

Professionals mentioned teenagers who were more informed and sensible than their parents, or who spoke English much more fluently.

.... here is an example of how having surgery can help children to mature. Before his operation, 13 year old Nigel agreed with his mother that he would not be able to decide about proposed surgery until he was 18. A week after his operation, lying uncomfortably in a broomstick plaster, he said spontaneously.

'I think I'm changing from that idea that I have to be 18, for big things as well as little things. I've made sensible grown-up decisions before, and I can take care of myself. I see others in here going through so much, so bravely. I think I can make difficult decisions and understand them now'.'

In spite of the fact that children and young people can behave in an unexpectedly mature and often courageous way, there is no reason why they should have to suffer more anxiety or fear than is absolutely unavoidable in medical processes. Even when inherently unpleasant and nasty procedures have to be carried out they can often be done in such a way as to minimise the trauma. A children's psychiatrist developed the issue as follows:

'I remember watching an anaesthetist work 'magic' on children to achieve their cooperation to be anaesthetised. Equally I watched others have to fight and struggle to get children to accept a face mask. Points such as not telling untruths (eg. 'this won't hurt'), describing machines in advance (eg. brain scanners) and telling children what they may notice when they wake up from an operation are important. Equally, a child's capacity to cope with the trauma may be very dependent upon their carer's confidence and acceptance of what is going on. Careful explanation to parents with plenty of opportunities for questions may help them care for their children more effectively.

In addition we have found that many problems arise because different members of the medical/nursing team say different things to parents and children. Careful recording of what has been said to whom and how, can pay dividends. Platitudes are offered instead of facts. Reassurance can often be false and misleading. For example – to a diabetic teenager – 'Once you have got the hang of the injections and diet you can have a normal life!' Taking injections twice a day, managing a special diet for the rest of your life and being careful about exercise, drinking, etc, is NOT normal. This does not mean that you have to be pessimistic but a little honesty helps.

Many adolescent patients with chronic illnesses become uncompliant with their medication. The reasons why this occurs need to be understood and dealt with without blaming or being punitive'.

The child's point of view should also not be totally restricted to the patient. The same psychiatrist points out:-

'When a parent stays with a child in hospital, who is looking after the siblings? Is there a spouse or are there other relatives having to care for the other children? When facilities are available for parents to stay in hospital, the guilt they may feel at neglecting other members of the family can easily be forgotten. Child psychiatrists often have to pick up the pieces from other family members at a later point. Help and advice has to be given which is not just focused around the needs of the sick child'.

10.3 Psychiatric hospitals and units

10.3.1 *'Bridges Over Troubled Waters'*

Early in the chapter we promised to return to this special area of health care for children and young people. It is not only important in its own right in a book on *'Growing Up in Groups'* but it is also an important area in which close links exist with other services, particularly for adolescents with problems, in specialised children's homes, secure units, youth treatment centres, therapeutic communities, young offenders institutions, and even prisons which are still used for the custody of boys and girls in their adolescent years.

As *'Bridges Over Troubled Waters'* commented:

'Psychological, social, educational and psychiatric interest in adolescence is relatively new; having begun in a recognisable way only at the end of the last century .... Historically it is evident that relatively little interest was taken in adolescence as a concept until the period of economic dependence on parents became prolonged'.

They urged that the principles on which a good service for disturbed adolescents should be based would include:

- Special separate consideration and provision.

- Interventions should be designed to restore normal progress to adulthood with minimum delay.

- As far as possible, care and treatment in ordinary surroundings as close as possible to home.

- Individualised planning of care and treatment.

- Coordinated and interrelated services, shared expertise and mutually recognised skills.

- Specialist support, education and assessment to non-specialised staff and organisations.

- Clear understanding by staff of the legal framework and ethical implications of the work.

- A broad range of treatment options in local services for adolescents.

Specific recommendations concerning psychiatry included skill and advice being widely available to other professional staff and agencies; more uniform admission policies; and patients under 16 not being treated in adult psychiatric wards. The Report counselled against restricting the liberty of disturbed adolescents unless they were an immediate danger to themselves or others. It was also against any use of solitary confinement unless approved by the Secretary of State and combined with stringent limitations and safeguards (as in the child care system). Handbooks for young people were advocated. These should set out in *'clear and digestible form'* their rights, any specific rules of the institution, how to make a complaint, and the need for greater attention to the needs of young ethnic minority patients.

We turn now to current legal provisions concerning admissions, principles of good practice in psychiatric hospitals and units, and certain practice issues.

10.3.2 Admissions

Children and young people may be admitted to a psychiatric hospital or young people's psychiatric unit under a section of the *Mental Health Act 1983* or, as is more usual, on a voluntary and 'informal' basis. In certain special circumstances there may be a need for an order for assessment and treatment to be designated by a court in the context of *Children Act* or *Wardship* legislation.

Great care needs to be given to consideration of the appropriate legislation required if treatment is considered to be necessary but also when the child and/or parent or guardian either are against such an admission or are unable to ensure that it takes place. The circumstances under which admission can take place in a compulsory fashion do not differ for children and young people from adult patients except where issues of effective control or dispute with the responsible adults are pertinent. As with adult patients, if compulsory admission is being considered, care must be taken to ensure that assessment and treatment are both necessary and clearly in the best interests of the child and also that it can not be provided in another context in which it can be undertaken by mutual agreement.

- When children, whether under the age of 16 or not, are detained under the *Mental Health Act* the conditions for such detention do not vary from those applicable to adult patients.

- When children are admitted informally and are under the age of 16, parents should give consent to such an admission. However, where it is decided that the child has the capacity to make such a decision for him or herself, the parents have no right to compel their child to be admitted or to keep their child in hospital on an informal basis against his or her will. Equally, if a child wishes to receive treatment and is of sufficient maturity and capable of understanding the implications of such treatment then a parent can not deny them that treatment. When in doubt, it is clearly desirable to seek legislative support to any treatment programme under the *Mental Health Act* or *Children Act* legislation to ensure that both the interests of the child are met and the rights of both children and parents are respected.

For young people aged 16 or over, admission and treatment can only take place informally with their consent. However, a recent judgement in relation to treating a patient over the age of 16 with anorexia nervosa has raised the possibility of compulsory treatment without recourse to the *Mental Health Act* but with the backing of the High Court [Re W(1992) 3.WLR.758].

SOURCES OF GUIDANCE FOR PATIENTS AND STAFF

All staff working in psychiatric hospitals or units should have access to the Code of Practice issued under the *Mental Health Act 1983*, and should receive training in the provisions of the *1983 Act*. *The Children's Legal Centre* have also produced a *Mental Health Handbook*, which provides a guide to the relevant legislation, as well as discussing what should be done when things go wrong. This handbook could also be used by staff as a source of information and advice when addressing questions of the rights of children and young people living in psychiatric hospitals and units.

THE REASONS FOR ADMISSION

The reasons for psychiatric admissions are various. While a young person presenting either with highly disturbed behaviour as a result of schizophrenia or with severe depression and associated suicidal intent may leave little room for doubt that admission is both necessary and desirable there are other circumstances in which the need for hospitalisation as opposed to some other course of action is less clear, eg. for children with severe behaviour disorders, non life threatening eating disorders or school refusal as a result of severe anxiety. Research by Malek[2] suggests that where a particular child or young person is accommodated often depends as much on which of the major service providers – health, education, welfare, juvenile justice – was the first to become involved with them. This results in young people being treated in a number of different environments for what appear to be similar types of behaviour. Malek estimated that 46% of the young people looked at in her study could have been prevented from coming into residential psychiatric care if some or all of the following resources had been available:

- residential special school for children and young people with emotional and behavioral difficulties;

- social services residential child care;

- support in the community from community psychiatric nurses;

- support for parents to enable them to cope with difficult behaviour;

- earlier identification and referral;

- social services support with psychiatric input on an outpatient basis.

The research shows that many children and young people in psychiatric hospitals and units are often similar to and face the same problems as those in other settings. The reality is that while there will be overlap between the types of problems leading to young people residing in different settings there will be other young people with specific types of difficulty or situation where a particular course of action, such as hospital admission, is the best and only appropriate course of action. There is some evidence from recent statistics to suggest that there has been a significant increase in the admission rates for children and young people to NHS psychiatric hospitals. Whether this relates to a genuine increase in psychiatric disorder or simply reflects a change in the balance of resources between agencies is not entirely clear.

---

2 'Psychiatric Admissions' — A Report on Young People Entering Residential Psychiatric Care — Mhemooda Malek, Children's Society 1991

'Mental health charity MIND has described as 'worrying' the rise in the number of children admitted to psychiatric hospitals.

The latest health department figures show a 65 per cent rise over five years in the number of children aged between 10 and 14 admitted to psychiatric wards.

In 1985, 38 out of every 100,000 in this age range were admitted, but by 1990 this figure had risen to 63 – a total of 1,700 children.

Child psychiatrists point to spending cuts that have closed children's homes and special schools, run down child guidance clinics and reduced money for specialised therapy'.

Care Weekly, 15 April 1993

'The ADSS is to raise concerns with the government about a dramatic rise in the numbers of children placed in psychiatric wards over the past five years.

DoH figures reveal a 65 per cent increase in the number of children between 10 and 14 years old admitted to psychiatric hospital.

In 1985, 38 children per 100,000 were admitted, while in 1990 the number had risen to 63 children per 100,000. The figure for 15–19 year olds has also risen by 21 per cent.

The ADSS wants to examine whether the rise in hospital admissions is the result of cuts in local authority children's services.

Tom Foster, secretary of the mental health sub committee, said:

'There is evidence the increase in numbers is due to the closure of special children's units. The picture around the country for local authorities is one of reduction in children's services'.

The fear is that stretched resources have led to a reduction in places specifically for the most troubled children.

The ADSS warns that placing children with psychiatric problems on adult hospital wards may not be the most constructive way to help them.

'Their problems may be acute, and there is a risk of being swallowed up in the mass of an adult ward. Often on these wards there are not the resources to deal with the specific needs of children'

said Foster. But more ominous is the risk that children without mental health problems are being 'dumped' on the NHS, the ADSS said.

Mike Jarman, director of child care at Barnardo's warned:

'There are few options left to social workers when they seek help with troubled children. We have to look at what has dropped out of the system'

(*Health and Personal Social Services Statistics 1992*, HMSO)
Community Care, 15 April 1993

Some people will view as regrettable the possible inappropriate 'medicalisation' of problems which could be dealt with in alternative ways. However, the degree to which the problems are medicalised by admission to a psychiatric unit will in fact depend upon the situational context of that unit, the mix of young people cared for and the range of assessment and treatment approaches available. Operational policies for adolescent units vary and some offer a more specifically 'medical' approach than others. Careful matching of the young person's needs with the right resource is always essential. Staff in these units should always consider alternatives to hospitalisation where these exist.

Children and young people with similar behaviour, needs and behaviour are looked after in different settings. If they are to receive the highest standard of care the core of good practice discussed throughout this book should be followed. The skill is to provide opportunities for a child or family to feel that they really have a voice in any treatment plan. We recognise that this is not always possible. However, where it **is** possible to assert control over process, decision making and environment, these opportunities should be provided. Little things can be extremely important. Pamphlets about standard procedures geared to the age of the child can be helpful. An 'identity parade' board in the ward with pictures and names of the staff is quite commonplace now.

All staff should know how to obtain interpreters.

The welcome, if it is a planned admission, should preferably be from someone that the child has already met ie. a member of the out-patient staff or a person from the ward if they have already visited. Alternatively, it should be from a person that is likely to have a key role in the care of the child while in hospital. Much of this is easier said than done, needless to say.

It is also important that the physical environment should be one which allows families, if at all possible, to play a continuing role eg. suitable rooms to relax in, and suitable rooms to meet with medical staff to receive 'bad news' ie. not the sluice or the corridor or the nurses' changing rooms. Although space is at a premium, such rooms need not, as they sometimes are, be seen as inefficient use of space or a luxury. There are many occasions in any hospital when such a space is needed to provide a proper opportunity for human emotions to be faced with dignity and in privacy.

THE CARE AND TREATMENT OF YOUNG PEOPLE IN PSYCHIATRIC SETTINGS

(i)   Principles

Staff and managers of psychiatric hospitals and units which care for children and young people under the age of 18 can be guided by the following principles:

- Children and young people should be kept as fully informed as possible about their care and treatment and their wishes and feelings should be taken into account when decisions are being made. For this to be effectively implemented explanations should be geared to the level of understanding of the child. Some information (eg. about medication) may be offered in the form of a pamphlet backed up by discussion with a trusted member of staff. Involvement, where appropriate, of parents or the whole family in decision making may facilitate the acceptance of treatment. If parents are confused or suspicious of the intentions of staff they cannot be expected to act as a support or be reassuring to their child. Time spent in open, informative discussion in this way will not be wasted.

- Apparent lack of cooperation should be sensitively dealt with. It may not be as ill-intentioned as it is often perceived to be. Fear of the strange surroundings of a ward environment, of the treatment itself or of other disturbed patients may make a young person's lack of cooperation only too understandable. In addition, particularly during adolescence, the young person's determination to exercise some age-appropriate autonomy, while not necessarily seen as advantageous to that young person, should be respected even if the adults hold different views. Equally, parental lack of cooperation may lie within the understandable wish not to believe in their child's 'illness'. The acceptance of a diagnosis such as schizophrenia, with all its ramifications, may involve quite a lengthy process of adaptation which may be akin to a process of mourning. Appreciation of the young person's perspective or the family perspective can only arise if time is set aside to listen to the views of all concerned.

- Unless legislation (for example, the *Mental Health Act 1983, Part IV*) specifically provides otherwise, young people of sufficient understanding should have the right to make their own decisions, in particular treatment decisions. Recent court decisions have created some uncertainty in people's minds about the legal issues involved in both the consent to treatment and also the withholding of consent by young people. This particularly applies to young people within the age range of 15 and 18 who may appear to be competent enough to make decisions but who may be denying themselves potentially life saving treatment. Who, if anyone (eg. parents or the Courts) has the right to overrule the young person? How liable would a doctor be to litigation if he or she carried out treatment on a young person against their wishes but with the authority of a parent? A critical and informative view of the current legal position is provided in *'Removing Rights from Adolescents'* by Michael Freeman. (*Adoption and Fostering, 1993* Volume 17, No.1, pp. 14-20). In addition, in 1991 the *NHS Management Executive* issued a document entitled *'A Guide to Consent for Examination and Treatment'*. This was followed by a leaflet on *'Informed Consent'* published by the *British Paediatric Association* in October 1992.

- Any intervention in the lives of children and young people considered necessary by reasons of mental disorder should be the **least restrictive possible**; and should result in the least possible segregation from family, friends, community and school. If the nature of the disorder creates fear in others or leads to bullying of the young person, for instance, then everything possible must be done to ensure that appropriate people are kept informed so that such negative effects can be avoided by their understanding the nature of the problem. Needless to say the rights of all people to confidentiality must be respected when seeking permission to talk to other relevant people in a young person's life.

- The rights of children and young people to confidentiality should be strictly observed. Problems may arise, however, if confidentiality is necessarily broken in situations where it is believed that a young person may be at risk of serious harm, (for example, when there is the real threat of suicide but the person does not wish his or her parents to be informed). There is a serious risk that trust may be lost if this eventuality is not handled well. Much can be gained by discussing the extent and limits of confidentiality during the first contact with a young person and his or her carers and if confidentiality is necessarily broken then the young person must be fully informed about what is said to whom and why. Ideally, the young person is present at the time such information is handed on and it will have been discussed with them beforehand. Problems may also arise if parents have unrealistic expectations about being informed of the confidential contents of their child's private sessions with a mental health professional. Sometimes the rights of children may appear to be in conflict with the rights of parents. Once again, an early discussion about these boundaries, before problems arise, may prevent misunderstandings arising during treatment.

- Children and young people admitted to a psychiatric hospital should ideally not be placed in an adult ward, and younger children should not be placed in an adolescent unit, unless no alternative is available. The ease with which it is possible to admit a child to a unit geared for their needs and age will vary around the country and will also depend upon the capacity of a particular service to deal with the problem leading to admission.

Where it looks likely that the only facility available is not one that is age-appropriate it may well be preferable to seek an alternative solution. For example, by providing close and regular contact with the family on an 'out reach' basis at the child's home. If, for reasons of safety for instance, such a solution is not possible then all necessary steps must be taken to ensure that the ward environment and care is adapted to the needs of the young person and that a more appropriate resource, if needed, is found as soon as possible.

- All children and young people in hospital should have ready access to complaints procedures, as should their family or other carer. These procedures should be drawn to the attention of children and young people and their carers on admission. Many complaints relate to lack of information, conflicting information or poor communication. A regular dialogue between staff and the child and/or family gives opportunity for misunderstanding to be nipped in the bud. A full discussion about such issues as the circumstances in which physical restraint may be used or medication given, creates the opportunity for the views and attitudes of all concerned to be acknowledged, differences of opinion sorted out and alternative strategies devised if necessary. When problems arise (for example when a young person runs away from a ward) prompt communication with the appropriate parent or guardian may not only lead to a an early solution but will more easily lead to cooperation in the future. Group meetings for young people on a regular basis also allow more minor complaints to be ventilated at an early stage and the opportunity for views of the peer group, in addition to those of the staff, to be heard. They allow for the sensible resolution of most problems and the maintenance of a balanced perspective without things getting out of hand. Care must be taken to ensure that the 'adult or professional view' is not based upon misguided dogma or professional arrogance. Phrases such as 'it is in the best interests of the child' or 'it is my professional/clinical opinion' can sometimes cloud a lack of critical thinking and can not be guaranteed to withstand more detailed analysis.

- All children and young people in hospital for any length of time should receive appropriate education. Those who are **informal** patients have a right to full time education from the ages of 5 to 19. There has been some reduction in the availability of education within the hospital environment over recent years. It is up to health managers to ensure that there is an appropriate forum to meet with the local Education Authority to ensure that, as far as possible, there is continuity between courses initiated at school and teaching in hospital and the child's home. In addition, there should be the appropriate facilities and skills available to encourage participation of young people in constructive leisure activities. The need for exercise is very important in general health and can too readily be overlooked in an institutional setting. (While this book was in preparation the Department for Education issued a circular of guidance on the subject of the education of sick children[3].)

(ii)   Practice issues – Measures of Control and Restraint

Section 18 of the *Mental Health Act Code of Practice ('Patients Presenting Particular Management Problems')*, sets out the principles underlying the methods and procedures which are aimed at 'reducing or eliminating unwanted behaviour'. This details clearly what may or may not be done by staff to restrain behaviour physically, to control behaviour by medication or to place a patient in seclusion. *The Code of Practice* stresses the need to create an atmosphere in which incidents are less likely to occur, and as such is consistent with the good practice which this book advocates in 'The Common Core'.

However, we recognise that there are likely to be particular problems in psychiatric hospitals and units caused by the nature of the problems from which children and young people suffer. It is important therefore that all staff and managers follow the guidance in the *Mental Health Act Code of Practice* and ensure that their unit or hospital has a written policy on control and restraint which is understood by all staff and, where possible, by the children and young people themselves.

In addition, Section 19 of the *Code of Practice ('Psychological Treatments')* draws attention to the permitted scope and limits of particular treatment techniques, and emphasises the safeguards that must be observed in the application of behaviour modification programmes and the use of 'time out' (ie. removing a child or young person from a group or environment for a period of not more than fifteen minutes) as a means of managing unacceptable behaviour.

3 The Education of Sick Children — Department for Education, Department of Health and NHS Executive Circular No. 12/94 DH LAC(94)10, NHSE HSG(94)24

'*Bridges Over Troubled Waters*', as we have quoted earlier, urged in 1986 that restriction of liberty and 'solitary confinement' in psychiatric care should be subject to the same constraints as child care secure accommodation. In 1992 the Children's Legal Centre sent a questionnaire to the 60 units in England and Wales on their measures of control. Responses were received from 22 units. The Centre found, amongst other measures used, that

> '*restricting access to parents (forbidden under The Children Act) was routinely used in some units to deal with 'separation anxiety*';

'*Suspension and exclusion from the unit*' was used by a number. It had not occurred to the compilers of the questionnaire that this would be likely since psychiatric units are widely seen as places of last resort and raised the question illustrated by Malek's research (see earlier in this chapter) as to how mentally ill are some young people in adolescent psychiatric units and how different are they from 'difficult' adolescents in other placements.

Some responses showed pleasant methods being used as positive incentives to better behaviour. Some units, but only half of those who responded, gave young people written information about expected behaviour and complaints procedures. Those who did define expected behaviour ranged from '*no violence, sex or drugs*' to twenty six rules including '*chewing gum and bubble gum is not permitted in the unit*' and '*residents not allowed out on unit trips with love bites or evidence of self harm*'.

Some units gave staff guidelines on physical restraint and measures of control, but they were not available to young people. Only four units said they kept log books in which the measures would be recorded, although nursing notes and daily unit reports may have meant the same.

Physical punishment was not used in the responding units, although the Centre states it has been told of units which use pain and deprivation of food as measures of control. Although unethical, these measures are not unlawful in the NHS or private units. Peer group disapproval and meetings were the most commonly used measures. Fines were the next most common sanction, some only for reparation. Deprivation of 'ordinary pleasures' and 'special treats' was commonly used. Behaviourist regimes used points systems to earn outings and activities during holidays and confiscation of personal radios and tape machines took place.

Restriction of liberty '*by placing the young person in a room or unit from which they are not allowed to leave*' was used by ten units.

> '*One unit used restriction of liberty 'often' for 'any persistent disregard of rules': the young person could be confined for 'up to 24 hours*''.

The Children's Legal Centre found that some of the answers indicated the units were unaware of the legal constraints on restriction of liberty. In addition to the legal requirements for detention under the Mental Health Act 1983, under *The Children (Secure Accommodation) Regulations 1991,* children accommodated in health units can be placed in *'accommodation provided for the purpose of restricting liberty'* only if criteria under Section 25 of the *Children Act 1989* are satisfied (that is, essentially, risk of harm to self, others or because of persistent dangerous absconding). It is not necessary for the room to be locked. The *Pindown* case demonstrated that liberty can be restricted if young people are intimidated by staff presence and prevented from leaving, although no locks are used.

A few units used removal of clothing and shoes to deter threatened absconding. Early bed times were used, although not more than two hours before normal time.

The Children's Legal Centre found evidence in the questionnaire results that *'even the most difficult young people can be managed without punishment'* but the survey highlighted the absence of regulations to prohibit unacceptable sanctions or to restrict use of extreme measures of control. Looking after highly disturbed and often aggressive or manipulative young people can be a very stressful experience for staff. The report argued that without such limits, there has been ample evidence in a variety of contexts that they can be tempted to abuse their power.

Privacy

All children, but older children and teenagers in particular, have a need for privacy and freedom from other people. The environment should be arranged to cater for this need as far as possible. Where children and young people are accommodated in wards rather than bedrooms or dormitories, there should be ample bed space with moveable partitions around beds, or pairs of beds. Privacy in toilet and washing areas, room for the storage of personal belongings and access to telephones and kitchen facilities, are of utmost importance. Creative attention to ward design allows for the development of quiet and secluded areas for young people to go when needing to be alone (especially when depressed or distressed) which nonetheless allow staff to maintain necessary supervision if the nature of a psychiatric disorder demands it. Close observation, which may be required if a young person is at serious risk of harming themselves or others, can be carried out without denying a young person the respect they deserve. Careful monitoring of the impact of such observation may be required to ensure that the sense of humiliation or 'crowding' that may be engendered is not counter-productive. The art of judging when a young person needs personal space and to be quiet, and when they need to be with a member of staff, is not easily acquired. It is easy to get it wrong! Sensitivity to both possibilities, is, however, necessary. The right to privacy does not only apply in the physical sense. It is easy in a group living environment unwittingly to break confidentiality or embarrass a young person by ill-considered public discussion.

Visiting

A young person's relationship with his or her family may be, to a greater or lesser degree, part of the problem. Relationships may have become fraught and destructive. Alternatively, they may be seen as too close and over protective. At their worst, either parents or child may not want to have any contact with each other but may not be able to separate without massive distress. These situations are a great challenge for staff to negotiate the frequency of useful contact and visits. Some institutions create 'rules' which are applicable to all but can become quite restrictive. Indeed, a culture may develop in which wishes and feelings of the young person and their family and friends are lost sight of, and the real reasons for the visiting 'rules' lie more in staff convenience or, more dangerously, are justified by some obscure and unsubstantiated belief in what is good for the child concerned. This is not to say that some procedure for managing visits and contacts is not required. In fact the nature of the relationships might make it an essential part of a treatment programme. Care therefore needs to be taken to create sensible 'rules'. These should be written down and copies given to young people and their families at the time of admission. There may need to be formal contacts, perhaps in the context of family therapy or feedback after a period of weekend leave and informal contact where privacy can be respected. If changes in the frequency of visits seems necessary then adequate explanation must be given. When contact between the young people and their families is fraught and seen to be damaging, or when rejection exists, then it is usually best handled by each 'side' being allocated a separate worker, that is, a member of staff to work with the young person and another to work with the parent(s) or family. Even if young people have rejected contact with parents, they are usually quietly reassured that someone is looking after them and maintaining the link. Support for families (parents, siblings and close relations) can often best be provided by a 'family care worker' who is not directly involved in the medical care of the child. They can sometimes also act as a mediator when mis-communications arise.

Loss of Personal Autonomy in Hospital Care

It must be remembered that a great deal of control and personal autonomy is given up when a patient enters any hospital. Communications between staff and patients should recognise this, particularly when the patient appears to be hostile. Greater sensitivity towards these issues can often prevent misunderstanding. Mistakes rarely occur by giving too much information. Equally, it must be respected that some decisions depend on difficult judgements and, while some participation is helpful, sometimes children or families need to feel that staff will take responsibility when they feel that they cannot. This may particularly occur during treatment of seriously ill or dying children. There is no excuse, however, for not keeping people informed.

Age-appropriate Care

Ward environments should be age-appropriate. While there may not be a call for a purpose-built adolescent ward, a six-bedded cubicle, which does not have bunny rabbits on the walls could be possible. Equally, if a fifteen year old finds themselves on an adult ward similar consideration should be given. Ideally, each service will have doctors and nurses who take a particular interest in looking after the medical care of adolescents.

The Impact of Medical Routines on Children and Families

Ward rounds can be frightening events. Medical teaching has to take place but professional discussions which may be exploring issues of peripheral relevance to the immediate care of the child should probably take place separately. This is not about secrecy but about ensuring that some degree of sensitivity exists concerning direct contacts with child and family. If they are present then most medical discussions should reflect their needs rather than staff needs.

It is extremely easy to ignore the fact that some children might not wish to be 'exposed' inappropriately in front of others. The need for privacy in medical and nursing care is no less relevant for children than adults. Equally, families might wish to talk to doctors, etc. in private and should be asked if they wish to do so. Open discussions on the ward, at the doctors' convenience, is another way of disempowering patients and parents.

Key nurses need to be identified for each ward shift because they are important to the patients to whom hospital can seem like Paddington station.

Adolescents admitted to adult wards should also have their educational needs considered. If a hospital school still exists then adult services should know how to contact a teacher when appropriate. If not, active steps should be taken to involve education services in providing appropriately for patients in hospital.

Tensions Arising from a Child's Need to be in Hospital

Distressed parents can be hostile, critical and may appear destructive. Meeting like with like will not make the care of the child easier. People cope with stress very differently and such displays may not be representative of their behaviour at other times. Listening before telling usually pays dividends.

Support for nursing and medical staff, perhaps from members of the local child mental health service can be very valuable for staff who find themselves coping with the stresses of intensive care, cardiothoracic surgery, etc. Equally, early referral to or advice from such services for children or families that are having difficulty with coping is important. There are other situations where a psychological component to a physical presentation exists. Careful discussion about how best to take this up and some planning before introducing a mental health specialist can save a great deal of misunderstanding.

Outreach services should be considered to facilitate any transfer from specialist to local services. Relationships established with a specialist team may be more precious to the child and family than is realised by the professionals and care needs to be taken at the handover. Equally, transfer from child to adult services should be considered in the same light. Sometimes the establishment of young adult clinics can be helpful.

Where children are on statutory orders it is incumbent upon all staff to know who to liaise with and who has powers of decision making and giving consent.

When child abuse is suspected or when child sexual abuse is disclosed staff must be clear about the child protection procedures and who to call for specialist advice. Careful handling at this stage saves the occurrence of problems later.

(iii)   Child Psychiatry and Social Services

(The material in this section draws from *'Seminars in Child and Adolescent Psychiatry'* published by the Royal College of Psychiatrists 1993, Chapter 13 pp. 268–273. Editors Dora Black and David Cottrell, reprinted by permission of the Royal College of Psychiatrists).

Changes in legislation and clarification of the statutory roles of different agencies, together with more knowledge about factors affecting child development and the escalating demands of work with children who have been sexually abused (Royal College of Psychiatrists, 1988) have all contributed to the increasing liaison between child psychiatric services and social services departments. However, the pace of change has tended to enhance the confusion about the roles and responsibilities of all the contributors to children's services. The knowledge base, the clinical skills and the responsibilities of all professionals working with children overlap. It is therefore incumbent upon child psychiatrists to delineate their role when working in conjunction with social workers and to have a clear understanding of both the extent and the limits of their expertise (Department of Health, 1991). A child psychiatric opinion, however valid, may be easily discarded by a social services department if it is presented insensitively or if it betrays a lack of awareness of the framework and context in which social workers operate. Unhelpful psychiatric reports may be avoided if the referral makes clear what is being requested and, where possible, what options are available as far as the referring agent is concerned.

Assessment, Planning and Treatment

The reasons for referral from social workers vary considerably from case to case and from service to service. For example, an opinion may be sought as to whether a child in the interim care of the local authority following episodes of non-accidental injury, should be rehabilitated with their family and whether the family is likely to change sufficiently to prevent recurrence of physical abuse. Another common reason for referral arises from severe and aggressive behavioural disturbance of a young person within residential care. Can this young person be helped by psychiatric intervention? There may be several possible clinical interventions and any single intervention will depend upon many factors.

In the first example above, it may be that a family centre is involved in working with the family, and consultation will clarify the issues. Equally a full and detailed assessment of the family may be required in order to contribute to the evidence in care proceedings when there is uncertainty as to the best course of action. In the second example, consultation may also play a role, as the young person's disturbance may be as much related to the dynamics of the residential setting as it is to psychopathology. Alternatively, a combination of factors in the young person's life eg. specific learning difficulties leading to educational failure, bereavement or sexual abuse, may lead to a recommendation for specific types of child psychiatric treatment.

As indicated above, a preliminary analysis of the referral is the first step. The reason for the referral needs to be clarified, as it may not be immediately evident. This can usefully be done by defining the question(s) being asked (Dare, et al 1990). A request for a 'full assessment' that does not define what or who is being assessed, let alone why the assessment is taking place, can lead the clinician into trouble. The response to a referral may vary according to whether the request is from the court for an evaluation of a person's parenting capacity or whether the request is for individual therapy for a 16 year old in residential care. Time spent on an analysis of the referral followed by careful planning of the intervention will not be wasted. This may involve a preliminary face-to-face consultation with the referrer. At this stage issues such as the legal status of the child, the role of all professionals involved, the requirements for confidentiality, and so on, should be sorted out (Royal College of Psychiatrists 1988).

The child psychiatrist must consider the long term needs of a child; in the case of young children particularly, everything should be done to ensure 'permanency'. The concept of permanency has arisen over the last 30 years in recognition of the damaging consequences of leaving children in long term care without the benefit of a clear plan to achieve stability and consistency of care, preferably within the child's own family or adoptive family (Shaw 1988), Familiarity with the advantages and disadvantages of long term fostering or adoption or residential care is essential (Hersov 1990). There is a great variation in the usage of all types of child care provision and knowledge based upon local circumstances is insufficient. Applications for secure accommodation orders, in which children can be detained in 'secure' premises for periods defined by a court and for certain legally prescribed reasons, show enormous geographical variation (Millham et al 1978) and factors other than the 'needs' of the young person (Lawson and Lockhard 1985) play their part in many other child care decisions.

Requests for 'treatment' need to be considered equally carefully. Not infrequently such requests may be inappropriate; for example, the provision of individual therapy when care proceedings have yet to take place may not be desirable if the confidentiality of therapy is compromised by the need to produce evidence. Equally, the uncertainty of the child's future placement and his or her current instability may make the psychotherapeutic task impossible until the child's future is secured. A clear view about the range of treatments available, but also the limits of both the effectiveness and appropriateness of treatment, and its best timing, is helpful information for a social worker. The child and adolescent psychiatrist is most helpful to social workers and residential child care staff if they recognise that these staff are frequently engaged with looking after young people whose behaviour is bewildering and frightening. No clinical diagnosis of a psychiatric condition may be obvious, but this should not be a signal for psychiatric professionals to withdraw. It is sometimes crucial that they remain involved to help unravel the causes of seemingly abnormal behaviour and to advise on its management.

Consultation

Since Caplan (1964) first described mental health consultation, a wealth of experience has developed about ways in which this can take place. However, there has been little evaluation of its effectiveness for social services. The objectives of consultation may relate to enhancing the general skills, confidence or morale of the consulter, or may be directed at specific child related issues. Consideration should be given to who is seen eg. a field social worker or a group of residential care staff; the setting in which it takes place eg. a child psychiatric clinic or a children's home; and whether it is to be a series of contracted sessions or a single consultation. Once again, time will not be wasted if the terms of consultation are negotiated, for example by taking into account the managerial structure of the consulter's organisation and negotiating with an appropriate senior manager, ensuring the purposes and aims of the consultation are defined clearly (Steinberg 1989).

It is essential to understand the different responsibilities of the consultant and the consulter and to differentiate the consultative process from supervision or other types of interprofessional work. There is much to be learned in this regard from the report on *'Pindown'* in Staffordshire children's homes (Levy and Kahan 1991). Between 1983 and 1989, a 'system' of control for children resident in four Staffordshire children's homes was in operation. Some of the children were highly disturbed. The control mechanisms used were repressive, humiliating and dehumanising and the report described the practice of 'pindown' as falling *'decisively outside anything that could be considered as good child care practice. It was in all its manifestations intrinsically unethical, unprofessional and unacceptable'*.

One of the many worrying features of Pindown was the fact that it was a structured and institutionalised system of controls which contravened established regulations and yet was allowed to continue in operation. The authors of the report believed that it was *'likely to have stemmed initially from an ill-digested understanding of behavioural psychology'*. However, *'the regime had no theoretical framework and no safeguards'*.

No advice was sought with regard to the practice of Pindown from psychiatric, psychological or educational professionals, but nevertheless a great many professionals working within the child care services of Staffordshire allowed the practice to continue and even participated in its operation. There were deficiencies from management down and, despite some concerns being voiced within the organisation, it continued for six years. This collusion with such unethical practice by so many people within an organisation for so long illustrates not only the potential hazards for an outside consultant, but also the extraordinary responsibility that such a person might have.

While a consultant may not be directly accountable for the work of another agency, the duty to act if unethical or unsatisfactory practice is discovered is clear. Contributions from more than one agency or professional group can help minimise the chances of bad practice becoming institutionalised.

Many of the most troubled children and young people that a child psychiatrist is likely to meet are primarily the responsibility of social services. A good child mental health service will play its part, whether by direct work, consultation or training, in helping social services to undertake their task as effectively and benevolently as possible. Mutual understanding of the agencies who are 'working together' is essential.

The child mental health specialist can only be effective in a residential setting if the child care residence is efficiently managed with continuity of staff and a clear, accepted policy for joint work.

(iv) Concluding note

This chapter demonstrates that great changes have taken place in the care of children in medical and health service settings. We believe the chapter further illustrates the overall need for acceptance of a common core of good practice in relation to children and young people living in groups, whatever the reasons for their placement in them, whatever their age, sex, and ethnic or cultural identity. In the 'CONCLUSIONS' (Chapter 13) we attempt to draw together what we believe this book has contributed to the better understanding of this important principle by practitioners, managers, service providers and policy makers.

We wish too to acknowledge, as we have tried to do elsewhere, the needs of staff. The capacity of busy nursing and medical staff to remain sensitive and caring when faced with the enormous pressure of looking after very sick children may often be severely stretched. Health service managers and senior professional staff need to consider whether support services should be available to staff involved in daily patient care, as well as to the children and their families.

PART THREE

SETTING THE CONDITIONS
AND MAKING IT WORK

11   Training

11.1 Introduction

The task of looking after children and young people living away from home in groups, as we have said earlier, has traditionally been underestimated and undervalued. People assume it is a 'natural' role like parenting in a child's own home. This ignores both the differences between the two tasks and the complexities and skills of so called ordinary parenting. The training of staff for residential child care in particular has, for nearly fifty years, been the Cinderella to field social work training. In boarding schools, similarly, while most teaching staff nowadays have received vocational training as well as higher education, pastoral care staff are usually unqualified and any training they receive has, at best, been piecemeal, in-house and unstructured. In the health service where clinical needs are the prime cause for children and young people being in hospital, care needs can easily be seen as secondary to nursing and medical needs and training for care remain undervalued or ignored.

Successive reports in recent years have addressed the issue of training in residential child care. Utting's *'Children in the Public Care'* recommended that all heads of children's homes and estimated that one-third of the staff should be professionally qualified. In response, funding was provided for training of heads of homes and senior staff. This has enabled numbers of places on Diploma in Social Work courses to be significantly increased since 1992. *'Choosing with Care'* (*Warner Committee Report 1992*) whilst building on most of Utting's findings, recommended a separate qualification for staff working with children in residential settings. The opinion of interested bodies, however, has not generally supported this proposal for separate development. Concern that residential care should not leave 'mainstream' training with possible negative consequences for its status appears to have been one factor in this. Lack of certainty of the advantages of European models may be another. Awareness of the urgent need for training in residential settings has, however, been heightened and initiatives in government support for Open Learning is one indication of this. Open Learning, as previously developed in the child care field, notably by the Open University, has the advantages that it is multi-disciplinary; it addresses staff in health and education as well as social services; it is flexible to the student's personal situation and able to be workplace based. It is also convenient for staff who cannot be mobile and has positive advantages for the student and work place.

11.2   The competent work place

When we use the term 'competent work place' we mean a work setting in which the whole staff team is committed to achieving good quality care and in which the structure of working practices is directed to this goal.

The development of competent work places is essential to the development of good residential care and to the growth and development of good practice by individual staff. Looking after children and young people in groups is inevitably a continuous learning process and should be recognised as such. Natural parents learn many of their skills, to some extent, as their children grow up. Staff are not parents. They do not share the early experiences of infancy with the children they look after which is necessary both to understand the developing individuals and to encourage the mutual regard between children and parents. Staff, even in the less problematic boarding school settings, or the relatively short term health settings where special clinical needs predominate, face formed personalities, some of whom have been severely damaged and whose efforts to preserve themselves in adversity have produced behaviours which would, and often have, exhausted the experience and skill resources of ordinary parenting. Yet it is disturbing to see how new, inexperienced, untrained members of staff are often expected to respond effectively as soon as they start work. Even when support is available, the job, whether in a children's home, boarding school house or hospital unit, must be a learning process. What staff learn depends on existing practice in their work place and their opportunities for organised and systematic training.

The general pattern of training should make provision at a range of levels. Induction; vocational training directed at NVQ; open learning; in-house training; sometimes full time college based training; and learning by doing are all part of the pattern. It is the responsibility of senior staff to make sure that all staff have continuing training opportunities. They themselves should be included in these opportunities and work processes, like staff meetings and personal supervision sessions (as described in Chapter 12), should be used as learning processes too.

The whole climate of the work place needs to be one of mutually developing knowledge, skill and understanding through every means available. Questioning, discussion and debate should be encouraged. The openness which we have urged in other chapters in relation to caring for children and young people is also important in development and training of staff. New and inexperienced staff do not easily know whether they should question practice which is new to them and which they may not understand. They may feel that staff who seem more experienced, and knowledgeable, and who may be professionally qualified 'know best' and that they should not question their guidance. The *Pindown and Leicestershire Inquiries* clearly indicate that some staff felt uneasy about the methods of care being used but had insufficient confidence or courage to question them. Questioning, debate and day-to-day discussion are essential whether practice is good or bad. Staff need to understand why they are being advised to act in one way rather than another, what alternatives there might be, and what experience and research have shown to be undesirable or effective. Only in this way can they develop their own self criticism and learn good practice in an intelligent and thoughtful way, rather then merely copying what they see others do.

11.3 Work place structures which support training

11.3.1 Staff Meetings

Staff meetings as part of management are discussed elsewhere. They are also a vehicle for staff training. Well run staff meetings keep everyone informed; they help staff to latch in and pick up connecting links, absorbing the general approach of the work being carried out. Through a mixture of formality and informality they communicate rapidly and give opportunities for explanation, guidance, participation and setting day-to-day priorities. They also demonstrate underlying attitudes to the task, the agency, other professionals and to children and their parents. Training should be a regular item on the agenda so that each member of staff can see the overall design for staff training, senior staff commitment to its importance and timescales for achieving different aspects of it. Feedback on training should also be discussed so that opportunities are used to improve the next round of training in everyone's interests. Staff meetings may also provide specific training opportunities by, for example, the addition of a visiting speaker at the end, or feedback from attendance at a conference.

11.3.2 Group Supervision

The distinctive feature of residential life – whatever the setting – is working and living together. Most of what happens in the daily life of the home or school is seen by staff and children: the successes, routine work and failures are all the result of the interactions of groups of people rather than of individuals acting alone. The groups of children and staff are powerful forces influencing what is possible and the standards of practice in the home or school. They are a rich resource to promote the greatest opportunities for the children and young people who are being cared for. Group supervision recognises the importance of the team and staff can expect at least the following:

- Feedback from colleagues which can reinforce what has been discussed in individual sessions.

- Space to learn about each others' skills and abilities, strengths and weaknesses.

- A means of checking that children and young people are properly involved and consulted about what is happening to them as individuals and as a group.

- Time to examine how difficult incidents have been handled and to plan how to respond in the future.

- An opportunity to involve children and colleagues outside the home or school in reviewing and planning care practice.

- Time to review the objectives and policies of the home. assess how far they are being met, and what changes in practice are needed.

- A chance to review and plan staff development for the group aimed at improving the way the establishment as a whole meets its objectives.

Group supervision requires experience and skill to conduct and may not always be possible, but when it is it can be a valuable resource for increasing awareness of children's needs and the responses which adults can provide. It can also help individual members of staff to understand the variety of abilities within the staff group and the way in which these different capacities and skills can be harnessed together in effective team work. Skilfully led group supervision can also help individuals to develop the readiness for openness, self criticism without fear of ridicule, and willingness to seek help. This is discussed elsewhere, particularly in Chapter 12. Individuals should gain insight into their own functioning in group settings and develop skills at giving feedback to others which will be directly applicable to working with children on their problems. Group supervision, though not a substitute for individual supervision, is a tool of training and staff development.

11.3.3   Individual Supervision

The importance of regular, uninterrupted and structured supervision is also described in Chapter 12. It is a key element in staff development and, along with staff appraisal, forms a continuum of training on each occasion with an overall analysis of longer term needs which can be integrated into a staff training programme. By discussing an individual's work, including relationships with children, positive achievements and weaknesses, a supervisor can link them with the overall concept of training as an integral part of every day's work. This will make it a constructive learning experience which continues as long as the job itself.

Individual supervision focuses on the evaluation of interactions of the care worker with children and their families, colleagues, people from other professions, and of the member of staff's own development of support needs. Good supervision provides positive feedback and reinforces ability for self-assessment. If supervision is recorded, these notes can become a sound basis for staff assessment at annual or other regular intervals. The approach used may vary so as to be appropriate for the individual member of staff but should promote the atmosphere needed by all staff, including managers, to develop and maintain high standards of care.

11.3.4 Individual and Group Study

A work place can link itself into open learning programmes such as the Open University courses Caring for Children and Young People and Working with Children and Young People. These materials can be used and reused as new staff join and develop skills and knowledge. The head of the home, assisted where possible by specialised trainers, can integrate attention to studying one of these courses into the working structures of the home.

Staff who have chosen to work in child care should expect to augment their knowledge and understanding by undertaking some individual study. This may intrude to some extent in to their own time, but this is the nature of working in a way which aspires to be professional. For residential workers this is a particularly tough expectation. When they return home 'shattered' after an exhausting and stressful shift they understandably just want to 'switch off' from work completely. Managers might be able to help in the way that the timetable of shifts is constructed by building in some study time or identifying some light shifts for staff in the course of studying. Study packages are best designed to be tackled in short bursts as and when the energy and motivation is there.

Individual study can be irksome without opportunities to share experience with others similarly engaged. The workplace can be made the context for this mutual support in a way that is entirely consonant with the objectives of the home. Discussion of some of the themes in the courses can legitimately be part of the business of a staff meeting. Staff who are further along or have completed a course of training can draw on this material when working alongside less experienced staff in ways that directly relate theory to practice in the work place. This is analogous to what happens in the more conventional and long established professions such as medicine and law.

11.3.5   Composition of Shifts and Team Work

A further essential part of the competent work place structures is the composition of shifts and related team work. Careful thought needs to be given to pairing junior staff with senior, more experienced colleagues who are prepared to act as mentors in a planned and reliable way. A clear statement of the establishment's aims and purpose, an open management style, staff meetings incorporating training opportunities, and individual performance supervision, all enable detailed learning to take place in day-to-day working. Experienced staff can thus help young, and/or less experienced colleagues, to apply the principles and detail of good practice in their daily work with individual children and the group. This form of apprenticeship, provided the other structures are in place, and opportunities for systematic training available too, can be a most valuable form of training at the earlier stages of a career.

11.3.6   A Structure Which Values a Range of Qualifications and Experience

Our view is that all staff looking after children should receive training appropriate to their task and to the competence of the work place generally. In any group there is likely to be need for a range of qualifications, not all of which would necessarily be professional qualifications. For example, not all staff working in a children's home need the Diploma in Social Work, nor do all the staff in a boarding school need to be qualified teachers. What is required is training appropriate to the caring task, which provides the necessary knowledge base and skills for the job and which is nationally recognised, accredited and therefore portable.

Any approach to training should recognise and value the fact that staff are adults who already have some experience and skills. This is particularly important in work in which relationships are an essential element in the job. Differences in gender, race, culture and religion are a rich resource in promoting young people's development and preparing them for adulthood. Similarities in the caring task in different settings, which we have noted in earlier chapters, mean that there will be some broadly similar training needs. In the next section we discuss the common core of knowledge and skills which are likely to be needed by all staff working with children and young people in groups away from home, whatever the setting in which they work.

11.4   The common core of skills

There is a common core of knowledge and skills which applies in all settings in which children and young people are looked after in groups.

It is part of the common core of caring and is additional to the particular knowledge and skills which are essential to boarding education, health care or residential child care. Care staff may have professional qualifications in nursing or teaching, for example, but, while these will certainly contribute to the caring task, they will not necessarily be adequate to meet the social and developmental needs of the children and young people they are looking after. In addition, these trainings do not normally cover care or counselling, working with groups and group living, sex education, child protection and a range of other specific areas of child care knowledge and skills.

During 1991, in response to recommendations in the Utting Report, the Central Council for Education and Training in Social Work set up an Expert Group to examine the appropriate context of residential child care training. We have drawn on the findings of the Council's Report, *Setting Quality Standards for Residential Child Care – A Practical Way Forward*, CCETSW 1993. The following requirements appear as knowledge and skills needed to work with children and demonstrate very clearly the importance of systematic and planned training:

- Child and adolescent development and psychology;

- Child care theories, values and attitudes;

- Group living, including working with groups and promoting young people's ability to contribute and their ability to learn from group living;

- Creating a stable, safe and stimulating environment for children;

- Sex education;

- Discipline and control;

- Working with social care, education and health care staff to promote young people's development and safety, eg. from physical, sexual and emotional abuse;

- Listening and communication skills with children and young people;

- Understanding of and skills in maintaining links with families, friends and communities;

- Promoting a positive identity with and a sense of belonging in the young person's culture, history and religion; awareness of the particular needs of black and disabled young people;

- The law relating to children: the *Children Act* and other national legislation; rights and responsibilities; complaints procedures;

- Knowledge of and skills in adult/child relationships maintaining appropriate boundaries whilst providing appropriate care;

- Child protection issues: local authority and police involvement; non-statutory guidance; abuse at home, outside home, at school;

- Dealing with sexual and other forms of abuse; the resources available for coping with them;

- The role of management and supervision; group management; time management; lines of communication; lines of management; supervision and appraisal; resources; administration and record keeping;

- Primary care; health; HIV and AIDS awareness; smoking and alcohol; drug abuse prevention; safety aspects;

- Structuring time for its constructive use;

- Teaching instrumental skills;

- Creating developmental opportunities;

- Working with families and parents to enable them to contribute effectively to their children's development.

A number of these areas of knowledge and skills concern contact with families, with whom residential staff are increasingly likely to be asked to 'work'. Few have yet had the opportunity to acquire the skills or experience for this task although it is clearly a positive development and they should undertake at least part of it. Family work which aims to increase understanding between family members and also change parental as well as children's behaviour, requires skills which need to be taught. Not all field social workers have them either as a result of generic social work training in the past.

A basic understanding of how families function and how changes can be achieved without undermining individual family members, needs to be acquired. There are many missed opportunities in residential child care because of the emphasis which naturally falls on work with children rather than with parents and the associated system. The importance of systemic work of this kind should be recognised in any training package. It is also important to emphasise that much of the child care process involves the enhancement of opportunities for development as a result of changes on the part of parents or carers. Too much burden is often placed upon the child to change without acknowledgement of the need for adults to make equal or greater changes.

These common core skills also need to be accompanied by **Residential Child Care Skills** – which are of additional and particular relevance in the settings we have discussed. Again we draw on the *Expert Committee's* report in presenting these:

- Handling dependent relationships, and the use of relationships in the context of 'living alongside' as well as in structured interviews;

- Undertaking the broadly educative functions of parenting, for example helping children to learn about their social world, about themselves in relation to others, etc; helping children to understand 'the system', so that they know how it works and how to negotiate with it;

- Understanding and responding appropriately to children's communications, especially about their distress or concerns, but also about their minor everyday concerns and interests, and listening to children and taking seriously what they say;

- Helping children to feel valued and important both individually and as a group, and helping them to develop a sense of identity and of belonging;

- Helping children to feel loved and genuinely cared for;

- Handling issues of sexuality, intimacy and physical contact in child care;

- Participating in and promoting children's enjoyment of everyday events such as meal times and leisure activities;

- Being prepared to be a positive role-model for children, and being able to deal with the negative responses which such modelling may evoke in some children;

- Developing children's enthusiasms and interests, and providing appropriate cultural opportunities;

- Providing for the special needs of children with disabilities;

- Learning details of family-support and other 'out-reach' work, of helping children to manage family and friendship relationships and, where necessary, to cope with the denial or loss of contact;

- Handling appropriately the range of personal and ethical responsibilities involved in looking after other people's children;

- Handling the specifics of control-issues and dependency-issues in residential child care;

- Providing appropriate day-to-day responses and participating in longer-term treatment programmes for children who have been abused, and for children who have abused others;

- Coping with ambiguity, differences, uncertainty;

- Learning about therapeutic residential care; the specifics of using the opportunities in residential care to 'reach' children who are distressed and confused;

- Setting limits and boundaries, establishing structure and flexibility, and acquiring tolerance.

It is important in considering these important areas of skills to be aware that they can, and need to be, learned from a basic level of understanding to an advanced standard as experience and knowledge develop and increase. As already indicated, they can also be taught by staff development through working processes, work based open learning, college based training, National Vocational Qualifications (NVQs), the Diploma in Social Work and other relevant qualifications.

11.5 Qualifications and accreditation

11.5.1 Vocational

The term qualification here relates not simply to the acquisition of a professional qualification such as the Diploma in Social Work, Diploma in Management Studies, Post Qualifying Qualifications, and degrees such as MBA, but more widely to encompass vocational qualifications envisaged within the Scheme of National Vocational Qualifications (NVQ) or Scottish Vocational Qualifications (SVQ). By vocational qualifications we mean the accreditation of a person's skill and knowledge which have been demonstrated in the work place, to the required level. The training and development which enable people to demonstrate their competence can take place flexibly over a period of time and to a pattern of learning which suits the individual. It is not a requirement of vocational qualifications that a candidate undertake or pass a course of studies. The concept of professional qualifications implies a course of learning through an officially accredited academic institution which encompasses, in addition to any practical training, knowledge, skills and understanding regarded as essential by a statutorily defined body and taught to agreed academic standards.

Qualifications and accreditation are important for many reasons, not least to the member of staff who is building a career and requires tangible evidence of the training undertaken to equip him/herself for the task. Thus one of the aims of a scheme of qualifications should be to ensure that staff who have attained the required standard of skill and knowledge receive recognition, so that they can use their qualifications to make progress in a career or to acquire further qualifications and training. It is important for the motivation of junior staff to feel that qualifications and accreditation are accessible and offer real opportunities rather than remote prospects. Qualifications allow managers to judge the level of skill and experience of staff by widely accepted standards. They also assist those responsible for inspecting homes and schools to determine the level of expertise in a home or school as a whole.

In the personal social services the pattern of training since the early 1970s has been to see the basic social work qualifications as **generic**, that is, covering the whole of the broad areas of social work, both in client groups and methods. However, the currently accepted need for vocational qualifications and associated training now means that staff in particular settings, including residential child care, will learn knowledge and skills in some detail around the specialism of the work in which they are actively engaged. This represents a significant conceptual shift from the thinking behind the current structure of social work training in which the primary qualification is generic and in which specialist training remains a relatively small part.

Unpublished research by the National Children's Bureau concerned with the assessment of teenagers has drawn attention to the increasingly high degree of specialisation within child care field work disciplines such as family funding, juvenile justice, or child protection. Newly professionally qualified field workers very quickly find themselves developing their knowledge and skills within tightly defined and detailed working disciplines.

These realities may be advantageous to the profession in that they demand the extensive application of a knowledge base derived from research rather than a heavy reliance upon generic skills of engagement with clients which, although important, can be found seriously wanting if the worker lacks an authoritative, directly relevant knowledge base.

Although a reality to be lamented, the majority of new entrants to residential child care work will not be professionally qualified and will begin their careers within the framework of vocational qualifications. There is a distinction to be drawn between the employer expectations of vocationally and professionally qualified staff, but in residential child care this distinction cannot be tightly defined other than through the formal allocation of responsibilities of post holders. In residential child care there needs to be a clear route whereby staff can acquire accredited competencies first and then progress to gain professional qualifications and beyond.

We envisage that as NVQ and SVQ develop, the training and qualification acquired by staff pursuing careers in child care social work will, in future, move from the specialist to the generic rather than the other way round. Such a trend may carry with it a more rational use of training resources as much of the present content of the Diploma in Social Work is of much greater use later in the careers of newly qualified staff, whereas the vocational approach means that the skills and knowledge immediately necessary are available for application.

This trend is given force by the development of the Scheme of National Vocational Qualifications as a whole in England and Wales and their Scottish Equivalent, Scottish Vocational Qualifications. The NVQ/SVQ provide a system in which staff can have their existing knowledge and skills assessed and documented. This system of accreditation depends only upon evidence of a level of competence in aspects of the job. It is not associated with a training course and is not concerned with how competence has been acquired. Learning skills on the job, acquiring knowledge through private study or personal aptitude and flair can all contribute to gaining competence and can be duly accredited.

The proportion of qualified staff working with children and young people in residential settings has been low for many years. Nationally, a much greater emphasis has been placed, as already noted, on professional qualifications for field social workers whilst failing to address the needs of those working with children living in groups.

This has been in spite of the fact that children placed in children's homes, rightly or wrongly, have for many years been considered to be more difficult to work with than those in foster homes, many having, in fact, suffered a series of broken foster placements. There have been complex issues of low pay, working conditions and professional status at play in this phenomenon, but the simple fact is that professional qualifications, particular social work qualifications, have been disappointing in their relevance to the day-to-day work of staff looking after children and young people. Both the Utting and Warner Enquiries received evidence to this effect. Thus we have seen the phenomenon of staff in children's homes obtaining social work qualifications but subsequently and understandably using them, not to improve the quality of residential work, but as a passport to work in higher status, and often better paid, field social work posts.

Recognising the reality as described above, the question of a separate professional qualification for staff working in children's homes was raised by the Warner Committee in *Choosing with Care*. It was argued that this would effectively create a class of workers similar to the **social pedagogue**, a respected professional cadre formed in some European countries. Such a qualification, they argued, would also be transferable between settings such as those discussed in this book. However, the European relationship between teachers and residential staff is different from the UK situation and it has not been clear that the model could readily be transplanted. There are important arguments against constructing a system of qualifications which drive a wedge between residential and field work in child care. The merit of the European approach is that it recognises the primacy of child development as a synthesis of social, educational and health aspects. These are ideas which should inform our thinking about the training of staff in the personal social services who are professionally or vocationally concerned about the proper upbringing of children irrespective of whether they are residential, day care or field workers.

11.5.2   *Professional*

Although we stress the importance of qualifications at levels below those commonly considered to be 'professional' qualifications (ie. at higher education level or above) professional qualifications are nevertheless a vital piece in the training jigsaw. Nurses, teachers, social workers, and qualified therapists all have skills which are applicable to looking after children in groups. The Diploma in Social Work is an important qualification for many working in children's homes, partly because managers of children's homes need to share the broad background of knowledge and training which field workers and other allied professions bring to their tasks. This was the thinking behind Sir William Utting's recommendation in Children in the Public Care that heads of homes should, generally speaking, possess a professional social work qualification. Similarly, a teaching qualification will continue to be relevant – even when a member of staff in a boarding school is solely concerned with the pastoral care of pupils. It is particularly important that the leadership of the residential child care profession is perceived as qualified to a level which confers credibility and weight in the context of child development and care.

It is essential that in all residential child care settings there is professionally qualified leadership. The exact nature and level of that qualification will depend upon the needs of the children and the aims of the establishment. Managers will need to determine the appropriate balance between the numbers of professionally and vocationally qualified staff required to achieve or improve the quality of care, though the overall expectation in future would be that they were one or the other and not unqualified. Staff wishing to acquire professional qualifications should receive encouragement but it will be necessary for managers to provide this against the background of the establishment's requirements. If opportunities for capable staff to qualify professionally are unlikely to materialise, it will be better for them to make career choices with this knowledge rather than be allowed to become frustrated in consequence of vague promises. It is also crucially important that managers set the conditions and create expectations which provide rewarding work settings commensurate with the abilities of professionally qualified staff. In the hands of imaginative managers who know about child care there need be no unresolveable conflict between meeting the needs of children and the career ambitions of able staff.

11.5.3   Nationally Accredited Training

In our view, a system of training which covers the common core, partially outlined above, and options in the basic skills in the particular environments, needs to be established. The development of the NVQ/SVQ system of accreditation provides the framework needed. It could build on or replace the long standing In-Service Schemes (ISS) or the pre-professional courses provided in colleges of further education. Staff will have their existing knowledge and skills assessed and further training needs identified. NVQ/SVQ is intended to ensure comparability and compatibility of standards within, and between, all the sectors where children and young people are looked after in groups. In addition to geographical movement there is mobility between occupations and professions, health, education and personal social services; and between the various sectors – statutory, private and voluntary.

11.6   Delivering training

Once the appropriate knowledge and skills have been determined for different levels of competence and a system of accreditation and qualification decided, the issue of how best to deliver the necessary training remains. There is a particular problem in residential child care because the children still have to be cared for while staff are being trained. Even if it were always desirable, flexibility of staff numbers and time at the margins are often insufficient to allow for substantial training to take place away from the residential establishment. Training opportunities for staff embarking on a career in residential child care have often, of necessity, to be provided within the establishments or to be readily accessible locally.

Distance and Open Learning methods are now well tried and successful means of delivering education to individual students working in ways and at times convenient to themselves. These methods are particularly helpful for groups of people learning together or for staff who have common training needs such as those in children's residential care. Learning packs which combine video and audio technology with specially styled written materials and regular group development work with leaders/facilitators provide sophisticated and stimulating training. The training materials can either become the property of individual students or be used over again by successive students. There is already wide experience in the use of the Open University's courses *'Caring for Children and Young People'* (P.658) and *'Working with Children and Young People'* (K.254), the latter carrying credit within the Diploma in Social Work. Other courses commissioned by the Department of Health and specifically focused on the *Children Act 1989* and child abuse have been extensively used throughout the country. Yet others are increasingly available covering a wide spectrum of child care knowledge and practice.

Locally based training resources, such as local authority training units, are essential to supporting training undertaken within residential establishments. Although senior practitioners and managers need to play a significant role in training they cannot be expected to have all the skills required, nor is it always possible for staff in training to accept senior staff as teachers/trainers as well as being their line managers. External trainers can provide greater objectivity in helping to assess training needs and the best means of providing for them. They can also be valuable in providing personal tutoring or group facilitating in open learning groups.

Colleges are detached from the day-to-day activities of providing child care services. The detachment can also be used positively by providing a foil against too much emphasis on work place training which can hold the risk of being focused too narrowly on what may be insular ideas and practices. Colleges should see themselves as resource centres for academic knowledge based on research, specialist expertise and wider experience-based thinking. However, they are only likely to retain authority if they remain in touch with practical child care and the realities of everyday life in providing services. It is likely to be in their own interests to go out to homes, health units and schools and engage with staff in their work setting as well as receiving them into the academic centres.

They will want to help students expand the breadth of their knowledge and understanding in their area of work. In doing so it will be important to have regard to the utility of what they teach. It is in the interests of colleges to achieve a 'value added' factor in training staff who are experienced in their work place. Employers should then reciprocate by recognising a member of staff's enhanced knowledge and skills as a consequence of training. It should be possible to expect 'something extra' from a returning secondee and their return should not be soured by the not uncommon sentiment sometimes expressed by those who remained in the work place

> *'Well, you have had your holiday – it is time now to get back to the real work again'.*

Staff development is a responsibility of both employers and staff. This mutual responsibility has to be set within a framework. The various components are considered below.

11.7   Personal development

11.7.1   *The Personal Development Contract*

The concept of a Personal Development Contract was introduced to the social services child care world in *Choosing with Care*, the *Report of the Warner Committee*. It is a written agreement which both identifies the knowledge and skills a member of staff already has and the gaps or deficiencies which need to be closed or remedied to contribute to the aims and objectives of the establishment. In their report, the *Warner Committee* described the Personal Development Contract as

> '..... *a means by which staff and their managers consider the training requirements of the member of staff; plan how those training needs will be met over the next year, including who will meet them; and agree a written plan for training that is signed by all parties. The Contract should be linked to the statement of purpose and objectives for the home, so that the development of staff is linked to that of the home and organisation*'.

The Contract would spell out the activities within a training and development programme aimed at filling the gaps. The activities may be either formal training or simply opportunities to acquire particular experience. The Contract is normally held and maintained by the member of staff and is reviewed annually, usually at the time of their annual appraisal. It is a Contract because it forms a written agreement committing both the employer and the member of staff to the course of action proposed. It may be regarded as an additional component of the work place structures which support training discussed earlier in this chapter. It is portable. Should the staff member move to another job it would be a useful passport for engaging with the training and staff development opportunities in the new post.

It could be helpful to see the whole experience of training being held together for residential staff by the concepts of the Competent Work Place and the Personal Development Contract, as suggested in the following diagram.

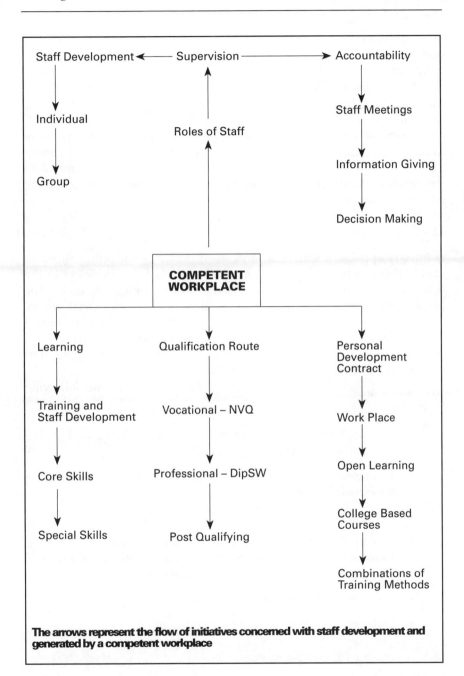

Staff Development ◄───── Supervision ─────► Accountability

Individual

Roles of Staff

Group

Staff Meetings

Information Giving

Decision Making

COMPETENT WORKPLACE

Learning

Qualification Route

Personal Development Contract

Training and Staff Development

Vocational – NVQ

Work Place

Core Skills

Professional – DipSW

Open Learning

Special Skills

Post Qualifying

College Based Courses

Combinations of Training Methods

The arrows represent the flow of initiatives concerned with staff development and generated by a competent workplace

Examples of the personal development contract provided in Choosing with Care can be found in APPENDIX 7. Both provide visible material which can be shared and reviewed with managers, peers and young people. A personal development contract provides tangible assurance that both staff and managers value training and see it as essential to achieving the aims of the establishment. It also provides members of staff concerned with evidence that they are entitled to training and are likely to receive it. Clearly the adoption of the Personal Development Contract in settings where staff do not already have an equivalent training/planning scheme would be a great improvement on many current situations.

11.7.2 Induction

All newly appointed staff need a planned period of induction aimed to enable them to become part of the staff team and to contribute to the establishment's aims, objectives, policies and working methods. The good sense of this is amply demonstrated in the commercial world. Induction should build on existing experience and skills identified during job selection. It should also list gaps in current experience and plan how these can be filled. A further product should be the creation or review of personal development contracts.

As part of their induction staff need information on the following subjects, at minimum:

- The problems and characteristics of the children and young people they will be looking after;

- The approaches and methods of care used, and records kept in the establishment;

- When and how to make reports to senior staff;

- The legal framework, for example the Children Act 1989 or equivalent legislation in Scotland and Northern Ireland and appropriate education and health legislation;

- The daily routine of the establishment;

- Links with families and the local community;

11.7.3 Training Through Supervision

Learning is implicit in staff supervision. Supervision is a primary source of direct training and regular and planned supervision should be provided for all staff by their managers. As discussed earlier, it may take place on an individual or a team basis. Effective supervision sessions, whether group or individual, should include the following which make explicit the link between the accountability requirements of supervision and the learning/teaching aspects of it:

- Identification of what has gone well in work with individual children and in the home generally;

- Examination of difficulties or problems and alternative ways of understanding and dealing with them;

- Development of the skills,knowledge, understanding and confidence required to work with children;

- Consideration of how the policies and standards of the unit and the organisation are being implemented, and identification of any difficulties in doing this which cannot be resolved either by the supervisor or the member of staff;

- Assistance for staff in understanding the impact of their work on themselves, and in devising ways of dealing with and assimilating this;

- Identification of any staff development needs.

Part of the importance of supervision is that it can assist staff to accept accountability without resentment because it demonstrates the link between verbal aspirations and practical reality.

Supervision needs to be a combination of 'management' supervision that is, checking that procedures have been followed, records are up-to-date and that the law is being applied correctly, and 'process' or practice supervision which can sometimes be lost at the expense of management. It needs to be protected by having, perhaps, a special status. In this type of supervision opportunities can be given to developing the capacity to 'understand' a child's problem, to learn about the fluctuations and frustrations which occur when change is being attempted and about the best way to enhance the therapeutic potential of an individual member of staff. It also gives an opportunity to pick up on 'inappropriate' relationships developing between child and worker which may not be evident if the supervisor concentrates mainly on procedural and organisational issues. It can thus combine aspects of management practice and staff development.

11.7.4   *Learning from each other*

The multi-disciplinary group which worked together to discuss the content of this book contained several members from education and social services who had also worked together in relation to the *Children Act 1989* and its application to boarding schools. They, and others in certain boarding schools, formed a group to consider what might be an appropriate framework of training which could particularly benefit those employed in boarding schools and residential education. The Holbrook Group, as it became known, produced a proposal for discussion by all associations which had boarding schools in membership, including ISJC, APS, and STABIS; by the Association of Directors of Social Services; by NCVQ and CCETSW; by the Department of Health, Department of Education and OFSTED. This has been widely accepted by organisations concerned with boarding and, because it seemed to us to be of considerable interest, we have included the Holbrook Group's proposal as APPENDIX 8. It is an example of the cross-fertilisation which can be achieved.

Under the heading of 'learning from each other' we suggest two other points which can be of great assistance to staff development. The first is about professional literature, books and libraries. Often, very little attention is given to on-site learning through the development of a culture which encourages staff to seek for information and ideas from available literature. All organisations and residential establishments need to develop resource libraries for their staff and encourage them to seek knowledge and new information when faced with unfamiliar problems. Such libraries do not need to be very large providing they contain stimulating publications. 'Journal clubs' which buy and share publications between members might also be helpful in fostering the sharing of new ideas and experience.

The second point is the desirability of encouraging and promoting the membership of professional associations, including backing or assistance for attendance at annual conferences, or workshops on specific topics of relevance to the work. Regrettably, opportunities for staff to meet colleagues from other parts of the country, even within their own local authority, and thus to feel part of a 'profession' of which they can be proud, are sadly lacking. They might also find valuable learning opportunities in meetings of local associations, for example, Child Psychology and Psychiatry (CPP), or the Association for Psychiatric Study of Adolescence (APSA). Such groups publish journals, and a cross section of professional tasks are represented in them. Membership of the Social Care Association offers access to a programme of seminars, as does membership of the National Children's Bureau but, for many of these, support from employers would be necessary both in cost and working time to attend them.

12   Management Issues: 'The Buck Stops Here'

12.1   Introduction

> 'It's much easier for an idiot to ask impertinent questions', declares Harvey Jones, who is master of the impertinent question (followed by penetrating analysis). 'Bluntness is a rare quality in Britain. Openness has to be cultivated'.
>
> The inimitable Harvey Jones was last week launching a series of BBC training videos based on his Trouble-shooter ' television programmes' [on management].
>
> *Sunday Times 27 June 1993*

Good management, the effective deployment of resources to achieve stated aims, is fundamental to the proper functioning of any residential setting. Although there may be efficient, well trained and motivated staff, a pleasant physical environment and adequate resources, good care still needs good management. Across all the sectors we have discussed, there is a range of management structures depending partly on the size of the particular establishment and the traditions of the organisation. The boarding school sector is characterised by large establishments, many of which are managerially self-contained; the children's home sector has smaller establishments usually managed by large organisations, local authorities or large voluntary organisations. In this chapter we try to suggest ways in which management of establishments could be strengthened and improved. We consider their aims; organisation of responsibility, accountability and care; staffing levels; supervision and appraisal; and staff selection. *The Utting Report 1991, The Howe Report 1991,* and *The Warner Report 1992* all addressed issues of management in residential settings and their recommendations could be of value in other locations besides social services.

12.2   Aims and Functions

Material presented in 1993 at a Social Services Inspectorate Seminar on Residential Care, for comparison of an official statement of purpose and function with the perception of the same establishment by a young resident:

'The Grange will continue to work with a mixed group of older adolescents, some of whom may have failed in other residential settings. As a group 1 unit it is understood that some of the residents may have more extensive problems. The home specialises particularly in working with young people who are emotionally damaged and while, inevitably given the ages and histories of the clients, there will be some involvement in delinquency this home does not specialise in delinquency management or youngsters whose central problem is criminal behaviour. Whereas the unit is mixed more recently the group has consisted of more young women than young men. This balance has tended to challenge some of the more aggressive behaviour of disturbed boys'.

(Taken from the official philosophy document of a children's home)

What does your home do?

'It gives you somewhere to stay'.

What do you think your home is meant to do?

'I don't know what it is meant to do, but I think they should help you with your problems'.

What do you think your home should do?

'I think they should be like parents and support you'.

(Comments from a young person currently being looked after in the same unit.)

If we accept the definition of management used at the beginning of this chapter, it is clear that effective management requires clearly stated and understood aims for every establishment. Arising from these **aims** will also be a statement of the **functions** of the establishment; that is, what action is taken to ensure that the aims are met.

The aims and functions of an establishment will underlie everything it does; the type and nature of the care provided; the physical environment; the process for recruiting staff; and training and development of staff. Staff who are recruited should have appropriate skills and qualities to help to support the aims. If there is not to be more than one version of the statement of aims and functions, the document will need to be written in language accessible both to children and families and to people who wish to use the establishment, such as managers of voluntary homes and boarding schools, who will want to see where the particular establishment stands within the overall range of services for children. It should include, amongst many other matters, policies concerning alcohol, smoking, drugs etc. This would also be of value to staff, parents of children and young people in the establishment and closely related other services such as schools, psychologists and general practitioners.

The statement of purpose and function provided by the *Children's Homes Regulations 1991* offers a good model, which can be adapted to most settings. It would address at least the following points:

- The purpose for which the home or school is established and the objectives to be attained for children and young people who are looked after;

- The name and address of the body responsible for the establishment – for example local authority, health authority or trust, board of governors, management board -and the person in day-to-day charge of the establishment;

- Details of the children and young people to be looked after, including at least the following;

  - age range, sex;

  - any special considerations which determine which children are to be looked after, for example educational aims or needs, children with physical or learning needs, children who have experienced particular traumas such as abuse, or children and young people who have behavioural difficulties;

  - the total number of children and young people looked after.

- The admissions policy of the establishment;

- The organisational and management structure;

- The philosophy and/or theory underpinning the education or care provided for children and young people;

- Care and development objectives for children and young people looked after;

- Arrangements for addressing cultural issues, religious observance and recognition of cultural and ethnic needs;

- Methods of control and discipline used, who authorises their use, and when they may be used;

- The physical environment the establishment is seeking to achieve;

- Arrangements for involving children and young people in decision making and in the daily life of the establishment;

- Details of relevant experience and qualifications of staff working in the establishment;

- The facilities and services to be provided within the establishment;

- Arrangements for protecting and promoting the health of children and young people;

- Fire precautions and other related health and safety procedures;

- Procedures for dealing with unauthorised absences of children and young people;

- Arrangements for contact with parents, family and friends, including overnight stays and returning home;

- Arrangements for dealing with complaints;

- Arrangements for providing education, including provision for children excluded from school;

- Arrangements for links with other services in the community, including social services, education, health, leisure and any local voluntary organisations;

- Arrangements for dealing with reviews under Section 26 of the *Children Act*.

Many of the above issues relate to procedures and legal requirements. A good statement of aims and functions will set these against the background of the overall aims of residential living, namely the care and social development of residents and their acquisition of independence and life skills.

It is particularly important that children's homes develop these statements because many of the recent inquiries and reports documenting failures in children's homes, most notably the *Pindown* and *Leicestershire Reports*, described how failure occurred because the homes involved were effectively out of the control of management. A statement of aims and functions provides a tool for monitoring a home, and for reviewing performance against objectives. Managers should use it to monitor individual homes, and governing bodies should use it to monitor the performance of managers. Careful thought should be given particularly to the process by which 'new' homes, or homes whose purpose has changed, set about producing their aims and objectives. The process should be one which encourages wide discussion.

The organisation with responsibility for a home should be involved as a whole in preparing and monitoring a statement of aims and functions. The head of home must be engaged in this process and, subsequently, should take overall responsibility for developing it. From the outset, the contributions of children, young people and staff in the home are crucial. Senior managers also need to be involved in the development, and the final version has to be agreed by the responsible body, whether local authority committees, board of governors, or other groups. In large homes which have more than one constituent house or unit, each needs its own statement of aims and functions, which accurately reflect the individual nature of each unit; these should complement each other so that adoption of different statements does not lead to differing standards within the home as a whole.

Line managers need to ensure that there is regular and thorough monitoring of homes, between annual reviews, to see that they are adhering to their stated aims and functions. This will help safeguard them from being constantly called upon, in emergencies, to take children for whom they are not properly equipped to care, and that where this does occur, the placement does not become long term simply because no-one has taken responsibility for finding a more appropriate placement. Senior managers and governing bodies need to receive periodic returns with details of admissions and discharges, including age, needs and reasons for the admission or discharge.

Annual reviews of statements of aims and functions by senior managers and governing bodies assess adherence to their terms especially in relation to numbers, ages, gender and reasons for children and young people being looked after. Homes should not have to take on tasks for which they are not equipped and for which their staff have not had appropriate experience or training. If aims and functions of a home change substantially, and new skills are required of staff in order to meet them, management should make sure that appropriate training is provided to enable them to meet the new demands, and that job descriptions of staff are altered accordingly. *The Warner Committee* commented that in some cases it may be necessary to consider closing a home for a short time to enable staff to receive appropriate re-training. Although the feasibility of this proposal will depend on its duration and method of funding, it is an option that senior managers and governing bodies should consider carefully.

12.3   Responsibility and accountability

All staff and all managers should be clear about who they are accountable to and what their responsibilities are. Even small homes and schools which may only have an officer in charge, or head teacher, and a small number of staff, nevertheless need a structure and someone to whom other people report and are responsible. Whatever the size of an establishment or its status, whether local authority, voluntary organisation, independent, or in the private (for profit) sector, it is advisable to have some form of appropriate outside 'management' as well as a clear internal structure of accountability. Being responsible for a residential establishment for children and young people can, at best, be quite a lonely and sometimes anxious job. To do it well, heads of homes must be committed to the home, involved in its life and therefore prey to subjectivity about what is going on. People who are heavily involved in any enterprise sometimes use the phrase *'I am too close to it'* to convey that they recognise they are not in the best position to judge whether it is good or bad. An outside management structure can provide not only monitoring with a degree of objectivity, but also support and, when necessary, advice and help. An establishment with no external points of reference can become inward looking, secretive and exploitative with little chance of problems being revealed until danger points are reached, or even passed.

It has to be said, however, that even when there is an external form of management/ accountability it is not always set up to provide the accountability and control (when necessary), or the support envisaged above. In some establishments, whether homes or boarding schools, managers/governors may attend regular meetings, even on the premises, but because their terms of reference are unclear and their duties ill-defined, they may be as ignorant of what is going on in the establishment as if they had never been there. The local authorities' associations have recently published guidance on visiting by elected members who, because of their legal responsibilities are seen as 'corporate parents', so that they can clearly identify their roles and functions and be confident in carrying them out. Although this guidance is not applicable in detail to establishments outside local authorities, its general stance is helpful and could be used as a model on which to build guidance for school governors and managers of voluntary and private homes. (*'Children in Our Care – Handbook for Members Visiting Children's Homes'*, Association of Metropolitan Authorities).

Many problems in children's homes in the past have occurred because managers and elected bodies have failed to take their responsibilities seriously enough, or arrangements for monitoring and oversight have been inadequate. In *'Choosing with Care'*, the *Warner Committee* listed what they saw as the prime tasks of members of governing bodies.

- 'Agreeing the strategic aims of residential child care, by making decisions on what is required of the sector, and its place within the strategy of the organisation.

- Approving the statement of purpose and objectives for individual homes, and reviewing and modifying them as necessary.

- Securing and allocating the necessary resources to do the job they have approved.

- Monitoring performance, by obtaining information about the performance of individual homes and taking remedial action where necessary through their managers'.

Carrying out these responsibilities may not always be easy, especially in relation to the dividing lines between the roles of elected members, governors, senior managers and line managers. It will be necessary for those concerned to discuss their roles and boundaries together and to work out in each local situation what best fits the task and the people concerned. Experience clearly demonstrates that both internal and external roles are necessary.

Managers and governing bodies are ultimately responsible for the home, school or health unit although they delegate the exercising of this responsibility on a day-to-day basis to the individual in charge. There must therefore be an effective system of communication, monitoring and review between the establishment and those who are ultimately responsible for its conduct. Those in charge of homes, schools or health units must know to whom they are responsible and who they should turn to for help and support; the situation outside the establishment reflecting that within. For effective monitoring, there must be both regular reports from the establishment to the managers or governing body, and annual appraisal of progress.

The *Howe* and *Warner Reports* both emphasised the need for delegation of decision making and budgetary powers to the lowest possible level in the organisation. Although the two reports were directed at the social services residential sector, this principle is also one which could, with benefit, be applied in other settings. It would mean giving heads of establishments greater responsibility for what goes on within a home, school or health unit; and greater power to decide where money should be spent. Budgetary and decision making responsibilities should be incorporated in the job description of the head of the establishment and, where there is further delegation within the establishment, it should also be in the job description of other staff who have these responsibilities. However, managers should build in safeguards to make sure that delegation within a home or school does not undermine required standards and that delegated responsibility is not abused. What should be aimed for is practical local autonomy, tightly externally monitored.

12.4 Line management outside the establishment

The head of a school, home or health unit does not act in isolation. He or she must be responsible either to a more senior manager, a board of governors or managers, or to a larger body such as a health authority, local authority, voluntary organisation, or trust. Again, the lines of responsibility and communication must be clear and understood by all. 'All' should mean parents and children in addition to staff both inside and outside the establishment. Within larger organisations such as social services departments,local education authorities or large voluntary organisations, this means that management structures should be easily understood and as simple as possible. As few levels of management as possible are desirable, commensurate with giving the task proper status and accountability within the organisation. There is nothing intrinsically wrong with hierarchies providing they are not too long or fragmented. They can clarify where responsibility lies and in the complex business of looking after vulnerable children this is an important requirement of management. Diffuse matrix structures of management may offer flexibility but there is a serious danger of their leading to confusion and muddle. Management needs, above all, to be functional and clear.

Heads of establishments, like other staff, need a clear job description. Those to whom a head of establishment is directly responsible should then ensure that the head is able to carry out his/her responsibilities. This means allocating appropriate resources and providing the necessary support. An important role for managers and governing bodies is ensuring that other services such as health, education and social services play their parts in supporting the work of the establishment. For example, we have already discussed in Chapter 4 how children and young people in children's homes are often disadvantaged because they have been excluded from local schools. It is the task of senior managers and governing bodies to ensure that there is proper support for excluded pupils, and to work closely with the local education authority and local schools to ensure that they receive suitable education. Heads of homes cannot be expected to operate alone at this level of inter-agency negotiation.

12.5   Management within – the hotelling function

Management of residential living situations is very different from managing an office, shop, or factory, and it is important in understanding the task to recognise its complexity. There are at least three major elements which have to be welded together. There is first the provision and maintenance of a setting in which people (adults and children), live, sleep, eat, experience social relationships, receive education, if it is a school, or treatment if it is a health unit. This can be called the 'hotelling' function. Secondly, there is a staff management task and, even in a small unit, the staff may include professional, vocational and ancillary staff; perhaps volunteers as well. In a large establishment there may be a variety of professional and other staff but all are needed to carry out their particular functions. The third element is provision of care for the individual and special needs of children and young people.[1] They may be there because of disability, or because they are specially talented; they may be there for education or treatment; for short or long periods; and may be of a range of ages from quite young children to young adults. In a large boarding school, boarding houses may be equivalent to the size of some special boarding schools, the responsibility of the house staff being commensurately heavy.

We all, at some time, experience residential group living in a hotel, a hospital, a camp, somewhere where the circumstances are different from small domiciliary style living in which the national average number of people, a 'family', is between three and four, or less. We are likely to have found that every residential experience has its own style, its own routines, disadvantages and problems. If you were in a hotel, were the beds comfortable; the water hot; did meals arrive when they were expected; was the place clean and fresh, orderly and attractive; were the other residents friendly or oppressive? If you were in a hospital, were the nurses friendly and informative, or did you feel you were losing your identity as your clothes came off and you got into bed? Whatever individual experiences have been like, what rapidly becomes clear is that getting meals to table on time and hot, keeping buildings clean and comfortable, creating a welcoming and non-threatening atmosphere, are not matters of chance. They are the achievements of a very complex job which requires considerable knowledge, many different skills and a lot of commitment to 'get it right'. In the hotel and tourist trade the complexity of this aspect of caring for people is recognised as requiring training and some people, particularly the managers, have often spent time learning all the various aspects of the task as well as training in overall management. Although there is increasing recognition that managers of residential care need specific training, few have been able to obtain it in the past and much available management training has been geared, not to the care model, but more to industrial and commercial models. With the support of the *Howe* and *Warner* Reports, and the consensus nationally on the importance of management training, it is hoped many more opportunities and more appropriate training will be available in future.

Management of the setting needs to take into account, as we have discussed elsewhere, not only the residents' needs, but also their rights. The children and young people are the reason for the residential establishment's existence; it is there to meet their needs, not something which has a life of its own. We have already mentioned the participation of the young people in choices of meals, furniture, soft furnishing, decoration, maintenance of a comfortable, homely place to live. In this, the care and sometimes treatment of children and young people, overlaps the management task leaving the manager with some fine

---

[1] 'The Management of Care' – Barbara Kahan, an audio tape produced by Social Information Systems Limited, 1985.

judgements to be made between the importance of the setting to the whole group, and the needs of individuals for special consideration at certain times.

Management of the setting also needs to take into account budgeting, daily, weekly, monthly and annually; care of the building, its fabric and surroundings; safety aspects in many respects, not just fire risks, but risks from electrical apparatus, wiring, faulty cooking utensils, plumbing problems, heating systems. Many of these issues also involve record keeping and paper work which needs to be up-to-date and accurate. These matters in homes or schools which are part of large organisations, are likely to involve interaction with other parts of the organisation's services, eg. finance, buildings, maintenance, estate management and catering services. Some of these may be staffed with professional people who are not concerned in any way with the care and/or education and treatment of children and young people. Their concern, because of their role, is likely to be related to what they perceive as cost benefits, lowest tenders, potential economies of bulk buying and standardised equipment, in some instances the exact opposite of what is seen as good practice in a children's home or a well run and child-centred boarding school. It will be part of the manager's job to avoid the financially preferred, but in children's establishments basically unsuitable, policies of bulk food buying, standardised equipment and always accepting the lowest tender. This may involve a lot of skilful argument, 'making friends and influencing people', gaining sympathetic support from senior managers and finding ways of letting the children and young people speak for themselves. *Utting, Howe and Warner* all supported greater devolvement of budgets and decision making to residential units and it is likely that similar devolvement, certainly in small scale expenditure, could be valuable in helping care staff to make boarding houses in schools individual and child-centred.

Occasionally very institutional practices arise, particularly in some local authorities, such as arranging for the school meals service to provide children's homes with all their main meals. In these circumstances, managers of homes will want to use every opportunity to persuade those concerned to think again. Diplomacy and patience are likely to be needed – but in the end the interests of the children must be promoted firmly and consistently. The order book for buying children's clothes has disappeared in many local authorities, but remains tenaciously in others. It can never be assumed that people whose first concern is **not** children and young people will necessarily understand the basic values in caring for them which underlie the work of residential care. Although a residential establishment is not a private household, it will be salutary to make a habit of asking whether there is really any need for long standing 'institutional' practices to continue. *Then the next questions should be 'Why is this being done? What would be as near as possible* *to what would happen in an ordinary household? What would make things more 'homely' for the children? Are we hanging on to it because it has always been done this way?'* The children may have useful suggestions about how some routines could be changed beneficially.

Children's need for privacy has been stressed in a number of contexts in earlier chapters. Individual privacy, with corollaries such as keys, supervision and trust, is part of it. Another part is the privacy of the establishment for everyone in it. The building may be seen by some people as a public building, part of a network of other services and therefore of official interest to a wide range of professional staff employed both inside and outside the responsible agency. These staff may, because of this, consider it to be within their ordinary working practice to treat the establishment as just another public building into which they can walk without hindrance instead of treating it as the home of the children to which they need to seek admission as they would to anyone else's home. It has not been an uncommon experience to find that staff from other services have entered a home or premises without giving notice, not through bad intent, but because of lack of appreciation of the differences between children's homes or schools and other public buildings. It is one of the skills of management to make clear the boundaries which must be observed and the professional principles involved in the right to privacy which children, young people and staff have in the setting in which they are living. The importance of appropriate buildings, in suitable localities and reflecting the importance of them being seen as the children's home is emphasised in Section III of The Quality of Care in *'Another Kind of Home'* (*The Skinner Report*).

The relationship between the manager and these outside services' representatives, and also with elected members or governors, can be a valuable means of informing and increasing understanding of the residential care task. Forecasting for a budget or revision of a current budget is an opportunity to consider and discuss more than just the financial costs of the care of children. If the recommendations of the *Howe* and *Warner* Reports in particular are implemented, the greater devolvement of budget preparation should increase these opportunities. Positive aspects of bulk purchasing, whether of food, furniture, soft furnishing, etc, need to be weighed against the loss of opportunity for staff and children to shape their environment and create a lively, homely setting in which to live. What could be more dreary than a house in which all the curtains were made from the same material, or the chairs all looked exactly the same? The reduced cost per head of bulk food buying can be challenged by the wastefulness of tins which may be too big for a single meal, drab uniformity of diet because of regular consumption of pre-prepared food, and loss of opportunity for independence training for young people through shopping locally and making the best of fresh food.

Shopping locally and being involved with the local community are aspects of the importance of local integration in the interests of the children. It is not, regrettably, uncommon for children's establishments, especially those which are believed to accommodate children and young people with problems, to encounter neighbourhood hostility. This may take the form of orchestrated campaigns, petitions and lobbying of politicians. It has also been known for homes to suffer vandalism, attacks on the premises and verbal aggression to children and staff. If a new establishment is being opened or a change of use being planned for an existing one, senior managers should make every effort to forestall hostility by careful consultation, good information services and public relations opportunities so that the establishment can start work from a good baseline. After that it will be a key responsibility for the head of an establishment to build up a continuing positive relationship with many local services and groups to ensure that the task being undertaken is understood and valued. This responsibility cannot easily be delegated. Churches, youth clubs, the police, local schools, voluntary bodies, neighbours, local groups such as women's institutes, rotary clubs, etc, even local traders, can all play a useful part in assisting the acceptance of residential care as part of the community, rather than an unwanted, stigmatised service.

12.6   Staff Management

12.6.1   Selection of Staff

Staff are the key to achieving a good quality of care and trouble taken in recruitment is an investment. Recruiting good care staff has never been easy, partly because of the demands of the tasks with their unsociable hours and heavy personal commitment. But it is likely that its image of being undervalued has been more significant than conditions of work, since other occupations such as nursing have equally stressful aspects. Turnover has also been a problem although the *Warner Committee* survey indicated that this no longer seemed to be so great. Some years ago, examination in a large county council area of staff turnover amongst residential child care staff demonstrated that turnover was more significantly related to how staff felt about the heads of homes than to the problems that the children and young people presented. Turnover of staff is a complex problem, low turnover occasionally being as problematic as high. It could be of benefit for managers to analyse this in some detail rather than to rely on average turnover figures.

Selection of staff must relate to the aims and objectives of an establishment and it is important that managers of residential establishments should be fully involved in drawing up job descriptions, person specifications, drafting advertisements, short listing, candidates' preliminary visits, and the whole procedure of selection. In this process the recommendations of the *Warner Report* are again of great significance and providing that suitably objective staff and methods are part of the process, managers should be invited to assist in designing the methods of selection which are additional to panel interviews. These could include exercises which test writing ability, judgement of priorities, functioning in a group, ability to give constructive feedback, and presentation of skills. Care should be taken that these exercises relate properly to the job description advertised and that racial and gender biases are excluded. If managers experience neglect of their involvement by personnel departments or staff, they owe it to the children and young people for whom they are responsible to make their views known. They must remind those concerned of their right to be involved in staff recruitment and selection and the knowledge they have which others lack.

Wherever possible, young people should be involved in staff selection. This suggestion is sometimes regarded as unrealistic or unfair on prospective candidates for jobs. Where it has been tried, however, as so often with the involvement of young people, their points of view and contributions have proved to be valuable and more realistic and fair minded than had been expected. They are, in fact, sometimes better than adults in identifying other adults who will not be suitable for the task of managing them.

'What were you looking for in the people who had come for a job?'

'We asked them all whether they would be good to us – but they needed to be able to manage us as well and to be dependable'

Adolescent boys in a Community Home with Education who had been involved in interviewing applicants for a job there in 1971

Amongst the general issues of staff selection, boarding schools staff are inevitably likely to be selecting for teaching requirements primarily. Increasingly, they may need to consider the feasibility of expecting teachers to be equally effective in the classroom and the group life of school houses.

The following is taken from an article in Community Care, 1 July 1993:

'Over five days in January and February five young people from Cleveland, who were either in care or had been in care, were engaged by the Children's Society to help interview candidates for appointments to its Independent Persons Project. The Warner Report had emphasised the need for vast improvements in recruitment methods when selecting staff for children's homes.

They were involved in interviewing 36 candidates, all of whom had completed a written case study before being short-listed. Their task was to assess each candidates's ability to communicate with and relate to young people. Other details about the type of person needed for the job were assessed by a traditional interview panel.

Prejudices

The process demonstrated the young people's ability to face up to their own prejudices. For example, before the interviews the young people were reluctant to consider that candidates over the age of 50 were suitable. They were able to voice their ageism openly in a way that adults have learned is no longer acceptable. It became clear, however, from their observations and conclusions after the interviews, that their attitude to age had not in any way influenced their assessment, and that they had responded to individuals regardless of age, race, or gender.The young people could give individual feedback as well as the consensus view of the group. They made comments such as 'this person never looked at me when he was talking -eye contact was very poor'; 'this person was very patronising – not only to us but to other candidates'. I didn't understand what he was talking about – he might have been very good but he used long words all the time'; or 'she was very sympathetic' and 'he seemed to understand what it's like being in care'.

The five young people agreed young people should be involved in deciding who should be fit to work in children's homes. They thought a candidate could too easily perform 'on the day' and could be 'giving all the right answers and it's only when they started that you found out what they were really like'. They all remarked on how they had seen staff 'act all concerned and caring when managers were around and then be totally different when they had gone'.

They observed that a few staff had limited ability or confidence in engaging young people in a discussion. Also they had found some staff were prone to make remarks which they regarded as disrespectful or patronising, and this had led them to doubt whether those staff actually understood, or even liked, young people. A common 'fault' which they observed was a failure to see young people as individuals with rights and not simply 'problems for them to solve or cope with'. As one young person put it: 'How can staff listen to young people when they already think they know best?'

The young people were undecided on the issue of whether it was better for them to contribute to staff recruitment by being part of the interview panel or, as in their experience with The Children's Society, to take part in group discussions and then feed views and impressions into the considerations at the end. The consensus appeared to be in favour of the latter. They appreciated being trusted to do their own separate interviews and appeared to thrive on the responsibility which inevitably went with this task.

Four young people were adamant that prospective staff should always be required to visit the children's home before the interview and spend some time in the company of young people. They added that young people ought to be asked their impressions and that any serious reservations or misgivings should be noted.

The young people felt their contribution to interviewing staff for the Society had made a significant impression and that their views had been taken seriously. This feeling had been reinforced by the fact that they had been paid for their work which reduced any sense that they had been either 'token' or 'exploited' interviewers. They accepted there ought to be a distinction between asking young people to volunteer their views and engaging the services of young people in a discrete piece of work for which they should be paid accordingly.

They were strongly critical of the practice of transferring staff from one children's home to another. In their opinion, this took no account of their feelings. They agreed with the suggestion from one young person that this gave the impression that 'it didn't really matter [to the SSD] who looked after them'.

Work experience

The young people contributed something valuable and gained useful work experience. They felt they had been listened to and treated as responsible people, an experience which they commonly contrasted with their interactions with social services. In particular, they prized highly the principle of being given a say in who looks after them.

They brought experience and insights to the interviewing process which could not have been matched within any conventional interviewing panel. They provided the employing agency with a critical opportunity to observe how well the candidates actually interacted and communicated with young people.

Each young person proved especially astute about, and sensitive to, whether candidates were genuinely interested in young people's interests and rights.

An additional advantage in involving young people in this way is the message it gives to candidates about the employing agency.

Hopefully it will introduce an element of self selection for those who are not prepared to work in partnership with young people, or, worse, those who have ulterior motives in seeking this kind of work'.

'Balanced Judgements' – Mike Lindsay, Children's Rights Officer, Cleveland SSD and Sue Rayner, Project Manager, Children's Society, Community Care 1 July 1993

The issue of the selection and recruitment of staff was addressed in a thorough and comprehensive way in *'Choosing with Care' (The Warner Report).* The proposals in that report are practical and constructive and those responsible for establishments other than the children's homes to which the report was addressed could derive much of use from the principles it embodies and the techniques it recommends. All establishments involved in selecting staff should have access to the report, and take account of its advice when recruiting staff. We do not wish to add to the report's detailed discussion of staff selection and recruitment but feel it is important to underline their concern, based on research, at the widespread use of the panel interview as the main method of selection. Its limitations and unreliability as a method are now so well established that managers need to explore the use of more penetrating and work-specific methods.

12.6.2   *Managing Staff*

Once staff are appointed it is the manager's task to organise and relate to them in ways which will enable them to give of their best and by so doing provide as much as possible of the care and help the children and young people need. Any enterprise that tries to help human beings must be flexible in its approach whilst being as clear as possible about its tasks, aims and objectives. We have already discussed these in the earlier part of this chapter. It is particularly relevant to managing staff since people are likely to become frustrated and disaffected if they are recruited, as they believe, to do one kind of job and then find themselves doing another. This has frequently happened to staff as the result of closures of homes and enthusiastic fostering policies which have changed the population in the remaining homes. Although originally recruited to care for younger children with family problems, they have found themselves faced with a mixed task of care for older adolescents, remand, outreach work and day care, all in the same premises and without any additional training or resources.

'Proposals for reorganising child care services..............

- (a)   all existing community homes to be discontinued in their current form;

- (b)   387 beds..... to be reduced by 164; (within a year)

- (c)   164 children and young people to be boarded out; (within 9 months)

- (d)   a family centre to be provided in each of..... nine areas with a range of new responsibilities in addition to providing residential care for 10-15 children and young people;

- (e)   observation and assessment to be carried out by family centre staff in cooperation with area social workers instead of by residential observation and assessment centres;

  Additionally they (family centres) would provide day care, overnight or weekend stay and full residential care for children and young people as required and for families for short periods if this would be of value'.

(Taken from a policy statement in Staffordshire)

The Pindown Experience and the Protection of Children, Paras: 3.40 and 3.41 – A Levy QC and B Kahan

---

12.6.3   Rights of Staff

As well as the rights of children we need to look at the rights of staff; in this context they are separate from those prescribed by employment law and embodied in contracts, pay agreements and conditions of work. The rights we are concerned with are those which enable staff to work to the best of their ability. Briefly we see them as follows:-

- Staff should be encouraged and given opportunity to develop their skills and knowledge as much as possible and to have their development assessed and reviewed;

- They are entitled to proper professional support from their managers, and also support from necessary services outside the home, school or health unit;

- They should be consulted about and involved in decisions concerning the establishment in which they work;

- The particular demands upon residential child care staff (who we require to work in a close and personal way with children) should be taken into account by managers and in any consideration of a disciplinary nature by managers;

- They should be able to make complaints to persons outside the line management system.

12.6.4   Welcoming New Staff

Reception and induction of new staff are likely to be tone-setting experiences which may colour their approach to their work for a long time. There are 'horror stories' about people arriving to take up a new post to be met by existing staff waiting to hand over the keys and records so that they can go on a much needed holiday. Regrettably, some of the horror stories are true. They may have resulted from delays in recruitment combined with under staffing and unexpected events like illness or accidents. Good staff reception practice needs planning and care. A welcoming letter or phone call; adequate preparation of the new staff member's accommodation, if living in; communication with existing staff; clarity about the new person's role and responsibilities are all important. On the day of arrival, if possible, someone already known to the new member of staff should be there to greet them. It is also a time for early discussion of the task and its setting and the way the establishment has been developing since the staff selection interviews.

Whether or not the manager of an establishment is involved in induction and training, it is certainly part of management responsibility to ensure that induction and training are provided. Preliminary discussion with new staff, as well as induction, will no doubt include such important items as staff meetings, staff supervision, appraisals, general communications and how personnel and disciplinary issues are dealt with.

12.6.5   Responsibilities Within the Establishment

It is important that the person responsible for the day-to-day running of the establishment, the officer in charge, head teacher, manager, director or nurse in charge of a health service unit, develops clear lines of responsibility within the unit. S/he must, in turn, be solely responsible to managers or governors outside the home, school or unit.

It has been recognised in schools that the care of children requires more than can be expected of teaching staff when classes are over, and specialist care staff are increasingly being employed. Care and teaching staff have distinct roles and specialisms and need to be line managed separately. The overall management of the school, however, should aim at achieving a good integration of care and education. The managerial crossover points between teaching and care functions are best when they are as close to the child as possible, provided it is consistent with proper professional support. In children's homes and other types of setting which provide only care, there may not be such a division of responsibilities, although many establishments which work in a therapeutic way with children and young people, or have education on the premises, may have a head of care who may also be head of treatment, and a head of education. Where such separation of functions can be identified, the management structure within the establishment must obviously reflect this.

The role of a deputy is likely to vary from one establishment to another. If there is a principal and separate heads of education and care, there may be no need for a specific deputy post, deputising when necessary being a function of one of the senior posts or both. In a smaller establishment, and in children's homes generally, the pattern will be different and may vary from home to home. It is important, however, that there is a clear delegation in the absence of the head of the home. During the *Pindown Inquiry* it became clear that responsibility for a home was assumed to change with every shift in the absence of the head. In consequence there was confusion and lack of accountability which undermined a sense of responsibility in those who shared the moving task. However the role of deputising is allocated it should be properly recognised and have clear responsibilities and accountability.

The statement of aims and functions is the starting point for determining the divisions of responsibility and accountability within the establishment. Managers need to look at the specific functions as described in the statement, and allocate responsibility for each element. Each element takes forward either the specific professional or caring aims of the establishment, and those responsible for a particular element then report to either a head of the specific professional task or a head of care. If the statement of aims and functions has been properly developed, lines of responsibility and accountability should merge as a matter of course.

Once the internal management structure of the home, school or unit has been developed and agreed, management are responsible for ensuring that all staff are aware of and agree to it. Staff need to be clear to whom they should report, who is reporting to them, who they can turn to for advice and support, who they should go to with complaints, or grievances, or when they feel something is going wrong. Failure by the head of a home, school or health unit to clarify these matters can lead to confusion in roles, lack of purpose among staff and, most importantly, failure to discover when something is going wrong, or failure to act when problems arise. Staff need to be told individually, as part of their induction, about their specific responsibility and accountability, and who they should report to for each aspect of their work. This information should also be included in job descriptions, and reviewed regularly to ensure that they are up-to-date and understood by both individual staff and managers.

12.6.6   Involving and Consulting with Staff

Staff working in residential child care expect to make use of their personalities and to call upon personal resources to an extent that is substantially greater than in most other forms of employment. For this reason employers have a duty to consult with staff as changes are anticipated in the course of working life. Consultation should not be extraordinary; it should be a regular feature, indeed a tool, of staff management. Decisions made without the knowledge of staff may be accepted only grudgingly, and morale and efficiency will ultimately suffer. When staff morale suffers the standard of care may also deteriorate. Of course, there will be times when decisions are made which are beyond the control of anyone in the agency including senior managers: legislative changes resulting from central government policy decisions, certain changes in local authority policies and, most commonly, decisions based on financial necessity. These are all for the most part **imposed** on homes, schools and health units, along with other staff in the agency. Even with these, however, there is often room for local interpretation and staff who fully understand the situation in which they are working may be able to help managers to implement decisions more sensitively.

The necessity to consult with staff means that autocratic styles of management are unlikely ever to be entirely successful in child care work. We know that poor leadership has resulted in poor standards, even in some instances, abuse. What is needed is a leadership style which naturally incorporates staff consultation and carries staff forward as a group. Within this there needs to be a degree of firmness which, while valuing consultation, ensures that decisions are made in the children's interests even when staff opinion is divided or ambivalent.

Staff involvement is essential to ensure that there is an open environment in which good practice can thrive. We constantly refer to the need to create such an atmosphere. The key to it is gaining the commitment of everyone, residents, parents, staff and managers, to the aims of the establishment. Staff are more committed to achieving the aims of the establishment if they are fully involved in devising, agreeing and reviewing those aims, and the means of delivering care most effectively.

The precise nature of the arrangements for consultation will need to be devised in partnership between staff and managers and will include the form of the consultation; whether staff meetings are the most appropriate way of hearing the voice of staff; should there be, for example, 'working party' arrangements, with staff working with managers and, where appropriate, young people, to address specific issues? The size of the establishment will be a factor. Would meetings of the whole staff group be feasible, or should there be meetings of staff from houses or health units within the establishment? How could staff meetings be fitted into the working day? Boarding schools may find that care staff can most conveniently meet during school hours when most of the children and young people are in classrooms. This will not be possible for teachers in boarding schools or staff in children's homes where some young people may have left school and are at home, or have been excluded from local schools. Should the meetings include managers for example, the head of home or head teacher of the school, or should staff be allowed to meet on their own before putting issues forward to their managers? Should all staff, at least occasionally, have an opportunity to meet managers who function outside the establishment? In children's homes, staff often feel that managers are kept away from them and that all decision making is done by a ruling elite. Should children and young people be involved in at least some staff meetings? There might well be an argument for involving older children, especially in a small establishment such as a children's home, where staff and residents live in a domestic 'family' atmosphere. In schools, where there are larger groups of children within a wide age range, older pupils might, from time to time, be involved in staff meetings where matters affecting the general welfare of boarders are being discussed. We suggest that even in large establishments all staff should come together periodically and notes or minutes of smaller staff meetings should be available to all, especially if they impact on their work.

How often should a staff group meet? It may be that regular, for example, fortnightly or monthly, meetings are best. Staff might, however, prefer to hold meetings only as and when issues arise. Both approaches have their dangers. Regular meetings may become a formality if there are insufficient issues to discuss, whereas occasional meetings may be bypassed by management because the importance of discussions with a staff group can be forgotten when they are pressed to make a quick decision. Some managers tend to become associated with crisis management and then make too many ad hoc decisions. Regular and scheduled staff meetings could be a useful check on this style of management and, on balance, are recommended. It is important that their purpose and frequency, and who is expected to attend, are clearly known. Staff contributions to the agenda, organisation, recording and subsequent action on decisions are also important elements. If meetings fall into an irregular pattern, perhaps with long gaps between them, and too much concentration on information giving and departmental instructions, attendance may drop off and they will not be as open, lively and creative as they should be. It can be hard work to keep good staff meetings going, but the alternative is likely to lead to poor communications, misunderstandings and even factions among staff. These not only diminish job satisfaction and effective working, but can also influence staff relationships with children and young people. Staff are likely to be most motivated by meetings which focus on children's needs and identify practical ways in which they can meet them. A child-centred focus is also more likely to protect from drifting into negligent or abusive practice, a point made in Chapter 8. It is also important, in involving staff, to have a reporting-back procedure. Again, it is for individual establishments to decide which system suits them best. If managers are directly involved in staff meetings, then formal mechanisms for reporting the group's discussions to them will be unnecessary, but notes of the meetings should be kept. If managers are not immediately involved, then there needs to be a system which passes on the staff group's views and proposals to managers, and also reports the managers' reactions back to the staff group. In small establishments this can all be done in an informal way although, again, brief written notes are desirable, not just actions, but enough information to indicate the reasons for action. In establishments with many staff there may be a need for formal mechanisms, such as circulating minutes to senior management, and a system of signing when they have been seen.

Staff meetings could take sections of national guidance as discussion targets and explore them, in relation to statements of aims and function, or school or home programmes. Similarly staff meetings might be used to try to define working objectives, for example, to identify all health problems amongst the children and get action in trying to meet them in the next month, term, or other defined timescale. Another target might be to involve each child in a new (to him or her) skill-based activity so as to acquire that skill within, say, six months. Setting measurable objectives as a group gives staff greater impetus to personal concentration on the children, their development and needs.

It is helpful for homes staff to discuss how tasks which are part of the job and part of the bureaucracy, can be achieved in a more humanly effective manner. A leaf out of the boarding schools' book may be helpful. For example, using house styles and small traditional ways of doing things can add interest and colour to life for both children and staff; for example, 'most helpful child of the week' award, news items before supper, bedtime cocoa, funniest event of the week! This may seem 'institutional', but not more so than some of the characteristic habits and personal routines which give structure and integrity to family life.

Staff meetings may also be used as explicit training opportunities, particularly in relation to the concept of the 'competent workplace'. as we have discussed in Chapter 11. It is necessary for staff to be familiar with guidance, for example, from the Department of Health or Department for Education, but not always easy for them to absorb it in working in their own time without help. It is important that there should be no limitations imposed on the process of staff consultation. No subject is 'off limits' if it affects the way the home, school or health unit is run or the way care is provided for children and young people.

12.6.7   Staff Supervision and Appraisals

Staff supervision and appraisals are core instruments of staff management in residential child care. The two activities are related but distinct both as regards purpose and the timescale over which they operate.

> 'The Government should require employers to introduce, within a year, arrangements whereby all staff have their performance formally appraised annually by their line manager; and an employee's personal file should contain a record of the appraisal showing the level of performance achieved and the agreed training needs to be met within the next 12 months as part of the individual's Personal Development Contract'.
>
> *Recommendation 45 – 'Choosing with Care', Warner Committee Report, HMSO 1992*

Supervision, which has also been discussed under training and staff development in Chapter 11, is about a member of staff's current performance. Volume 4 of the *Regulations and Guidance in the Children Act* series suggested that for care staff supervision should be individual, free from interruption for one to one and a half hours and be at a frequency of once every two to three weeks. *The Warner report* recommended that it should be at least fortnightly. Staff are required to account to their supervisor for the work they are doing. The supervisor is required to give feedback to the staff member on both good and unsatisfactory performance. Areas where performance requires attention are identified. The discussion is recorded concisely. The primary consideration throughout supervision is the quality of care provided for the children. It should nonetheless be experienced by staff as a positive and supportive part of the routine of work. It is about the competence of the workplace to deliver good child care.

Staff caring for children will have emotional demands made upon them and they will be obliged to respond. The demands of some children may be distorted, excessive or bewildering and a staff member may be only too conscious that a particular response was not entirely appropriate. These experiences will induce anxiety which need to be dealt with regularly in supportive supervision if cumulative anxiety is not to become debilitating. Some extreme occurrences will need immediate supportive counsel but staff should learn to hold on to reasonable anxiety until appointed supervision sessions. Supervisors must, of course, ensure that supervision is regular and reliable.

Appraisal is essentially about performance examined from the perspective of staff interest in training and development. It is a staff centred rather than a child centred activity, although clearly the impact of a member of staff upon children will be the central subject matter of an appraisal.

Appraisals will normally occur annually. Staff will be asked to assess their own performance over the period since the previous appraisal in a number of predetermined aspects of the requirements of the job. A proforma appraisal document facilitates this task. The supervisor will also make an assessment. These perceptions are then discussed and if differences are identified they will be reconciled as far as possible. Where there is disagreement then both perceptions of performance are recorded. Nothing the supervisor says in an appraisal meeting should be a surprise to a member of staff because strengths and weaknesses should have been identified in supervision as part of the routine of work. Appraisals are an opportunity to consolidate perceptions made over a period of time and to distil out enduring strengths and persistent weaknesses which need to be addressed. In addition to a record of performance, a key product of an appraisal is mutually agreed objectives for the coming working period. These objectives are the essential link between appraisal and staff development and will inform the personal development contract.

In both supervision and appraisal the skills of the supervisor are similar, and they derive from basic social casework training. Supervisors need to discover 'where members of staff are at' in their understanding, feelings and practical application to the task in hand. They need to help staff identify and accept both strengths and problem areas in their work; to reflect back to staff the impact they make on others in a way that is direct but not destructive; and to enable staff to tackle issues and effect positive change. The relationship between supervisor and staff member is, however, underpinned by the contract of employment and there are prescribed obligations which define expectations. Supervisors' engagement with staff should be confined to the staff's ability to do their job, and care should be taken not to intrude into the staff members' personal lives in ways that cannot be justified by the terms of employment. In supervision and appraisal the skills are similar to social work but the responsibilities are different.

12.6.8   *Getting It Right for Staff*

Those who care for children professionally elect to do a job which demands rather more than the application of knowledge and skill. They are obliged to draw on depths of emotional energy and apply their personality in a way which in most other forms of employment would be reserved strictly for the employee's personal life. The professional care of children intrudes into the most personal world of practitioners. Staff's encounters with children may challenge their feelings about their own parents, their family life, their sexuality, values, religious beliefs, racial tolerance and personal morality. They may challenge their intelligence, educational attainment and sense of personal achievement. There is undoubtedly clearly identifiable professional conduct to be observed but there is not the clinical distance that protects, for example, a doctor-patient relationship.

Staff who care for young people who have been profoundly damaged by their experience of adults may well find themselves the target for physical or verbal abuse by them. A member of staff may seem just another adult to distrust, test and possibly even despise and it may be a long time before a more positive relationship begins to take root.

It is increasingly recognised that some staff looking after children pay a price which cannot be compensated for by financial reward alone. Special forms of personal support are sometimes necessary and it is very much in the interests of those responsible for the supervision or management of care staff to spot those who need such special support. Failure to do so may lead to resignations, frequent or long term sickness or self-protective attitudes to the work, all of which can rebound in the form of poor care for the children.

The peculiarly intrusive nature of stress associated with residential child care and the difficulty of separating professional from personal, means that, at times, staff need confidential counselling from outside the employing organisation. This allows them the freedom to express their anxieties and the anger they feel towards children, staff or 'management' without the fear of repercussions affecting their employment. Employers may arrange for and meet the costs of such counselling as part of a package of staff benefits. They may well take the view that costs are more than recouped by reduced staff turnover, and lower sickness rates.

Such schemes clearly need careful design. Employers will need to decide whether staff should have direct access to a confidential counselling service without reference to line managers or whether access should be by agreement with a line manager in accordance with certain criteria. Thought has to be given to the need to distinguish between stress which is work induced and stress which has a cause unrelated to employment. Employers may reasonably wish to limit the number of counselling sessions for which they are prepared to pay.

For counselling schemes to be personally effective for staff and cost effective for employers, a balance has to be struck between the responsibilities of staff and employers. 'Getting it right for staff' means getting this balance right. Staff have a right to expect employers to recognise the particular stress of residential child care. Employers have a right to expect staff to be sufficiently robust to withstand the general rigours of residential child care and to be able to make responsible use of supervision, and confidential counselling when exceptionally required. Staff who become chronically dependent upon counselling support may need either to arrange this privately, if they feel that in so doing they can carry on with their work, or they may need to recognise that a change of employment must be considered. It is important for everyone's sake that some staff can acknowledge that they have run their course in this demanding work and move on to something else preferably at the stage when they can still feel positively that the experience has been worthwhile.

The special support needs of staff who look after children were recognised by the *Warner committee* in their report *'Choosing with Care'*. The principles and practice proposed in that report, reproduced below, could find application in settings other than children's homes.

General principles of a staff care scheme

- Each member of staff has a personal responsibility of care for other employees.

- Each manager has particular responsibility for ensuring that positive staff care is promoted in the team or unit they manage.

- All staff should have equal access to Staff Care services.

- Staff Care services should be well publicised so that all staff are aware of their existence, their purpose and how to access them.

- All staff with work related problems, or other problems which affect their work, should have access to welfare and counselling services without the need to disclose this to the division.

- Managers, in discussion with the staff they manage, should review working practices and conditions at regular intervals in order to reduce, as far as possible, factors which could give rise to stress or physical illness.

- Staff should be able to expect that staff care needs will be addressed by their manager and, if necessary, by appropriately trained staff or externally contracted specialists.

- Staff Care services should be able especially to assist staff who are:

  - experiencing uncertainty or change;
  - victims of assault or threatening behaviour;
  - experiencing personal problems that affect their work;
  - finding working relationships with colleagues are difficult;
  - subject to discrimination or harassment;
  - involved in disciplinary or grievance procedures;
  - having difficulties working with colleagues as a result of attention having been drawn to bad practices;
  - experiencing stress from the nature or volume of their work.

Annex 8A – 'Choosing with Care', The Warner Report 1992

12.6.9   Training and Staff Development

We have discussed training in some depth in Chapter 11. Although for many years policy in relation to training residential staff was inadequate to their needs, it is now accepted that they must receive training in order to develop the skills and knowledge which are necessary to enable them to do their job properly and that it is part of the responsibilities of managers to ensure that opportunities are made available. Training is not simply 'going on courses'. Training is also achieved through the medium of supervision, staff meetings, from more experienced colleagues, personal reading and distance learning programmes. As with all professionals, staff themselves have some responsibility to promote their own training and career development and they should therefore expect at least a little of their personal time to be spent in doing so.

Staff have a right to insist that their line managers discuss their training needs and develop programmes which meet them. This should form part of regular supervision sessions in which staff are able to agree what their specific needs are, how those needs should be met, and by whom. In planning budgets and child care strategies, managers really need to include the resources and time to allow staff to undertake training. The nature of residential child care is such that training and development needs to be viewed as an integral part of a care unit's working life and not an 'added-on extra'. External managers should understand the need, and create the conditions, for the ethos of a 'competent work place' within children's residential services.

12.7   Organisation of care

12.7.1   Child Care Information for Staff

No matter what the setting in which they work, staff will find it difficult to provide good care for children and young people if they do not have adequate and necessary information about them. A frequent complaint from residential staff, especially those working in children's homes, is that children and young people arrive at the home without staff being given any information, either before or at the time, about their particular needs, background or previous placements. Staff are then expected to start from scratch, inevitably proceeding by trial and error, because information which could have helped has not been made available to them. This is very poor professional practice and residential staff must insist, if necessary through senior management, that they are briefed in advance of children's admissions.

It is vital, except in unavoidable emergencies, that staff who have responsibility for a new arrival are properly prepared. For small establishments such as children's homes or hospital psychiatric units where residents may sometimes unavoidably arrive or leave at any time throughout the year, proper preparation is an integral part of the task of providing care. Even in boarding schools where there is a large annual intake, if new pupils arrive after the start of the academic year, information about them should be available to the house master, house mistress or care staff. We have discussed the importance of preparation for new arrivals earlier in the book, and need only add that if preparation has been inadequate, staff greeting new arrivals will have to be particularly helpful to them initially.

If information is not made available staff must insist that they have it. Managers, field social workers and other staff in the community have to accept that residential staff are entitled to full and thorough information about the children and young people they care for so that they can do their job properly. It is the duty of managers to ensure that information is available and that when reluctance or delay in providing it takes place those responsible are held to account. Regrettably, in spite of many years of training, professional statements and exhortation, there are still many instances of careless or unheeding attitudes in interaction between residential staff and other professionals. Senior management might constructively make it clear that, if they do not receive information, residential staff will have authority to visit the child and contact homes and schools to obtain for themselves what they need to know.

12.7.2   Staff Organisation

Managers must ensure that effective and high standard care is provided in the most appropriate and efficient way possible. The way in which care is organised is part of this. It involves ensuring that the organisation of staff and care is responsive to children's needs both as individuals and as a group, rather than to institutional convenience. Decisions must be made on staffing levels, staff shifts and deployment of staff to tasks for which they are most suited. Staff should be involved in these decisions and managers need their support when proposing changes to working patterns.

Volume 4 of the *Children Act Guidance and Regulations* provides guidance on the organisation of care in children's homes, and this guidance could be good practice in all settings. First and foremost, an appropriate level of staffing is needed. This is discussed in the next section. A named member of staff should deputise for the head of the home, school or health unit. This duty, as far as possible, should be performed by the same person whenever needed and should be part of that person's job description. Systems of rotation or ad hoc nominations are notoriously unreliable, and do not adequately acknowledge the responsibility involved.

Careful planning and structuring of staff rotas and shifts should ensure that, at all times, there are appropriate numbers of staff on duty. Thus, for example, more staff are needed in the evening when children and young people spend more time in social and domestic activity than during the day when most will be at school. This may seem self evident but SSI inspections still come across rotas which leave staff with little to do in the daytime, and over-stretched in the evening. However, there are responsibilities such as case conferences which require staff availability during the day and, regrettably, nowadays a number of children excluded from school need care and occupation at home.

Staff also need time for activities other than direct work with children and young people. Calculations of the time needed for these should be built into staffing rotas. It is vital in these areas that managers do not cut corners to keep costs down. The contemporary child care work cannot be done without training, development, supervision, appraisal and group discussions. In order to carry out their caring task properly, they must also have time to perform professional tasks which support it, planning, report writing and dealing with others who have an interest in the child, including parents. In boarding schools, planning staff deployment must also take into account any teaching duties. Managers must also be conscious of the need to plan for adequate staff to be on duty at night, whether sleeping in or on waking duty, and at times like school holidays in boarding schools if some children do not go home.

In order to achieve continuity of care and to minimise disruption in the lives of the children and young people, sufficient time is needed for handovers between staff coming on duty and those going off. This includes passing on information about significant events in the previous shift, for example, special activities undertaken with the group; aspects of individual behaviour which have caused or might cause problems, or medication which has been taken during the period. This process needs to be more than just a passing on of information and facts, important though these are. The shift going off duty should describe to the new shift the dynamic processes and interactions that they have been working with and which are perhaps still going on. If these care processes can be conveyed factual information will fall into place. On some occasions it may be helpful to involve children and young people. Staff also need sufficient time to complete their written reports covering their time on duty.

In most settings staff will be asked to take responsibility for particular children and young people; the 'key worker' role in children's homes and the personal tutor in boarding schools. Heads of units are responsible for allocation but should make their decisions in consultation with staff. Allocation of this responsibility must take into account individual children's needs, the skills and experience of staff members and the personal qualities of both staff member and child. Volume 4 of the Children Act Guidance states that:

> 'A child must not feel forced to form a special relationship with a certain staff member when that is not of the child's choosing'

and this rule should be applied in all settings. This means that children and young people need to be involved in decisions about which member of staff will be responsible for them. When they have been agreed, specific responsibilities for individual children should be recorded, and regularly reviewed in supervision sessions.

12.7.3   Staffing Levels and Deployment

Programming and use of time are important aspects of staff management and are crucial to management of the professional task, which is the reason for an establishment's existence. The thrust of the professional task must focus on the individual lives of children and young people, their day-to-day needs, inside and outside the establishment, their relationships with each other, with members of staff and with their families and friends. Deployment of staff to meet residents' needs is difficult to achieve because of the complicated logistics of working hours, time off, annual leave, sickness, training, meetings, case conferences, visits to outside agencies and the children's own homes. Yet proper matching of staff to individual children maximises development, rehabilitation, assessment, or whatever other function the establishment is intended to carry out. It also gives greater opportunities for children and young people to relate to staff, and greater job satisfaction for staff who will give better service in consequence. Events in each child or young person's life need to be carefully and sensitively supported, and deployment of staff and levels of staffing are more than just tidy management. They are the key to responding to crucial events in the lives of children and young people. Arrivals, departures, family events affecting them, illness, even impending death, may constitute a common pattern of events for members of staff. A sensitive manager will ensure that this familiarity does not cloud the importance for each child of the individual events as they happen in his or her own life. Just because they have to live away from home does not mean that personal events in their lives are of less importance. In fact they may assume greater importance because of the uncertainty, anxiety and often grief which accompany them in many instances and it is then that they need 'quality' time to be given them by a member of staff whom they can trust and rely on. The following example demonstrates the depth of feeling which these events can generate.

'On 22 September 1991 Jeffrey Horten hanged himself by using a shirt and hanging from a window (in Feltham Young Offenders Institution). He was 15 years old.....In 1990 he had been received into voluntary care and placed with short term foster parents. In March and April 1991 he spent a further period in care after being arrested for attempting to steal a car.

.....On 26 August Jeffrey's grandmother died. Jeffrey was informed three or four days later and was greatly upset. PO Smith found Jeffrey sobbing in his cell on 31 August. He wanted to buy flowers and attend his grandmother's funeral.

.....Feltham contacted...Jeffrey's social worker (about allowing him to attend his grandmother's funeral. Social services would have had to arrange transport and escort)..... Social Services decided not to collect Jeffrey.

.....At the inquest Mr M (the social worker) explained

'We considered the effect on Jeffrey. We knew him well and we believed that, although he might well be upset about his grandmother's death, missing the funeral would not have a very great effect on him. We also considered the obvious potential difficulties – it is nearly 200 miles (from the area to Feltham). .....There was also the cost to be considered'

At no stage did anyone from social services actually speak to Jeffrey to assess his emotional state in relation to his grandmother's death'.

Suicides in Feltham, 1993

Even joy and pleasure need a sympathetic environment and understanding from valued people if they are to be adequately enjoyed. Management skills in achieving all this include careful programming of time as well as deployment of staff. Daily, weekly, monthly and yearly programming should include consideration of children and young people's personal needs, and also special events, public holidays and community organisational necessities.

In ensuring that staffing levels are sufficient to satisfy the requirements of the statement of aims and functions, managers will need knowledge of individual children, and of the group as a whole, as well as the particular skills and experience of individual staff.

CASTLE PRIORY REPORT

A study first published in 1968, republished in the early 70s and known as the *Castle Priory Report* (*The Residential Task in Child Care*) was the result of discussions between all the professional child care groups at the time. It was accepted by the Home Office in 1970 as guidelines on staffing ratios in residential care and had considerable influence nationally in improving staffing provision. It postulated that:

'Neither good premises for the children, adequate accommodation for staff to lead a normal life of their own, training to fit the adults for their difficult task nor parity of salaries, status and esteem will produce residential work of the standard required if proper consideration is not given to the appropriate ratios of staff to the young people concerned'.

The report pointed out that staff who care for the children must have time and opportunity to do so. The best staff will defend themselves against mental, emotional and physical exhaustion caused by trying to look after too many demanding individuals at once. A member of staff

'will have to limit his 'giving' to his capacity and no-one's capacity is unlimited'.

Cutting corners on staff costs risks wasting the benefit of much of the work of the establishment. The report identified factors to be taken into account in the calculation of the total number of care staff required in a residential establishment. They included:

- The length of the waking day ie. the span of hours from children getting up to the approximate time the last child or young person goes to bed and settles down. These times may vary between schooldays and weekends or holidays, when the full day's waking span must be calculated for staffing needs;

- Number of children in that particular setting who can be given attention by one member of staff while on duty, for example, say, 3 younger children, 2 disturbed young people, or 4–5 stable long-stay young people;

- Annual leave allowance per staff member (including any relief staff);

- Allowance for sick leave;

- Length of working week ie. number of hours;

- Allowance for training purposes;

- Allowances for organisational responsibilities, including case conferences, staff meetings, board meetings, dealing with visiting social workers and parents, and supervision sessions;

- Allowance for managerial tasks, including involvement with agencies etc. outside the home;

Decisions which managers were asked to make would determine how many staff should be on duty at any one time. To do so answers were needed to the following questions, among others:-

- Will domestic help be additional to care staff to cover domestic duties of various kinds?

- Is the key worker/personal tutor system in place?

- Will staff be with children and young people while they are getting up?

- Will staff be preparing breakfast and eating it with the children and young people?

- Will all the children and young people be going into classrooms or out to school after breakfast? Will new arrivals be spending time with child care staff for settling in purposes? What about children who become upset in the classroom eg. in boarding special schools, or at school, and have to 'go home' (ie. back to care staff) for a time?

- Are there children at home who have been excluded from school and what arrangements are to be made to help them learn?

- Where appropriate eg. in boarding special schools, will care staff be joining teaching staff in classrooms for certain purposes and if so how much time is likely to be needed for this purpose?

- Who will deal with a child's social worker, parent, other interested person (eg. psychiatrist, psychotherapist) when they visit during school hours? How much time will need to be allowed for such responsibilities?

- Who will go with children to hospitals, doctors, dentists, opticians, etc?

- When will staff write up the records they are required to keep?

- Are staff required to prepare lunch and/or will they be eating lunch with the children and young people?

- When school is over, if it is assumed that staff will be with the children and young people until they go to bed, will they be having tea with them? Will they have had to prepare it? Will they be helping with homework? Will there be any homework? If not what will the children and young people be doing and who will be with them?

- If young people are being helped to prepare for independence or returning home, or helped with writing letters etc, who will be doing that and how will it be fitted in with the general care of the group?

- Will staff spend time with children settling them down for the night when they go to bed, reading to some of them, talking about their personal feelings and events of the day, and how late are staff likely to be occupied until the last child or young person settles down for the night?

- Will staff be fetching young people from outside activities or waiting up for adolescents to return? Until what time?

- Will someone be awake at night?

- Are the children/young people assessed as very disturbed. Have they had a foster home breakdown, many moves in care, or been abused in some way?

Although the detail of the *Castle Priory's Report* related to different hours of work and working conditions in some respects its basic principles provide examples of the many questions which need to be asked and answered in calculating how many people can adequately care for children and young people individually in an establishment. Merely to set a number of staff against a number of children without knowing in detail what will be required of staff is a meaningless exercise and can be misleading in relation to the quality of care. It is also important to ensure that adequate staffing allows staff members to 'recharge their batteries' by getting out of the residential environment regularly each week. It is all too easy for the conscientious to respond to shortages by becoming over committed and narrowing their horizons too much.

Providing answers to many of the questions needed to assess the number of staff required to care for the children will inevitably test the reality of how children and young people are going to be cared for. For example, managers must consider whether it is realistic to describe care as therapeutic, if in reality children and young people will receive little personal time spent with an adult because the ratio of staff to residents is too low to allow that to happen. Adults may have 'therapeutic' attitudes towards children in their hearts and minds, but if they have little or no chance to spend a little time every day with a child on his/her own, how will the child know, and what benefit will it be in his personal confidence and trust in adults?

A further issue which is relevant to staffing levels is one which, for managers in residential settings, can either be a nightmare or an opportunity for creative work ie. risk taking. Carefully considered risks have to be taken if children and young people are not to find their lives cramped, even fettered, and certainly unnecessarily institutional. Risk taking, however, needs to be based on the best information and thinking possible at the time and that means maximum use of knowledge, the manager's own and other people's, including the children and young people themselves who are entitled to know and contribute to what is happening.

Risk taking is one side of the coin; effective emergency backup systems are the other. Providing good residential care requires that managers have thought out and made careful provision for emergencies; not only fires, accidents and unexpected illnesses but emotional outbursts, aggressive behaviour, challenges to legal positions, sudden demands for help, sudden failures of normally reliable systems, whether human or material; a variety of situations by day or night. Who will be there? Who will know what to do? Who can be called on quickly? Will the system work? All of these questions are asked against a background of an agency's overall policy requirements and traditional approaches. Because the task of managing residential care well is amongst the most difficult tasks in the agency, it may be able to contribute to clarification, even to changes of departmental policy. For example, local authorities and others who still leave groups of children and young people in the care of only one person, either by day or, particularly, by night would do well to check with an experienced residential child care manager the dangers and risks of such a policy and the unreasonable expectations implied. It would not take long to demonstrate that the policy is dangerous and should be urgently revised.

A further important time commitment relates to essential communication tasks, keeping records, contacting outside consultants, interaction with other services and with other parts of the agency, dealing with emergencies and contributing both to the agency as a whole, whether school or home, and to professional work in a wider field. Communications, written and verbal, are important elements in good residential child care and involve many important processes such as daily journals, children's reviews, child care planning, monitoring of health and education, as well as different kinds of records such as accounts, staff reviews, diet sheets and, fire escape drills. Efficient record keeping is vital and it is necessary for senior managers to recognise the considerable overall time commitment which has to be available to achieve what is required.

12.7.4 *Professional Support*

The *Warner Committee* recommended that all children's homes should have support from psychiatric, psychological and psychotherapeutic services to enable them to do their job properly. It is likely that staff in other settings will have a similar need, if only from time to time. Many individual establishments may need to make their own arrangements for the provision of these services. Larger schools and homes may employ professional support; homes and schools which are part of a larger organisation, eg. local authorities, may be able to link into services provided by the parent body or by the National Health Service and local education services. Smaller, more independent units may need to seek advice as to where they should make their own contacts with organisations providing the services.

The *Warner Committee* also recommended that all children's homes should undertake an 'audit' of their need for professional support, and arrange for appropriate provision based on the results of the audit. This audit should analyse the strengths and weaknesses of the home's functioning with respect to its stated aims and objectives. Weaknesses should then be addressed according to whether they require action by managers, resourcing, staff training, professional support and personal support. This practice could, with benefit, become standard in all settings. Combining a review of support requirements with the review of the statement and aims of the establishment will enable managers to do their best to see that the home, school or health unit has all the resources necessary to carry out its functions properly. In doing so, two points need to be recognised. The first is that provision of these services is patchy geographically and neither the National Health Service nor the local education services always give the priority which is desirable to helping children's residential services. So some persuasion, even insistence, may be necessary if the importance of the need is to be fully appreciated. The second point is that provision of these outside support services, however good they may be, is no substitute for sound management and adequate staffing, resources and training. They are often of vital importance but it would be unrealistic to expect them to solve problems which have been made worse by poor management and lack of good staff and adequate resources. They cannot perform miracles and should not be expected to do so.

12.8   The outside world

12.8.1   *Official Visitors*

A school or home which tried to cut itself off from the outside world would be in trouble. Interaction with other services, whether schools or homes are involved, is of great significance in the effective running of an establishment. They include services such as police, education, health and welfare benefits, and also networks of people in related professional tasks, field social workers, training officers, accountants, architects, general practitioners, psychologists, psychiatrists, consultants in various aspects of the task.

Managers need particularly to ensure that links are developed with the local Area Child Protection Committee. All staff need to understand the role they would play in the local child protection procedures and managers should arrange for staff to receive training in child protection. They all have a role to play for the benefit of the children and young people and relationships with them will be most effective when managers understand their individual approaches and relate to them knowledgeably and positively.

Increasingly, there is need to welcome inspectors into residential establishments. There are three who have specific responsibility for inspection, local authority inspection units, members of OFSTED, and members of the Social Services Inspectorate all of whom, in their different roles, may be commenting on the work of a school or home. The nature of residential work with children and young people and some of the events which have sensitised its image, have led to a situation in which it is subject to considerable scrutiny from a variety of sources. Boarding schools which used to be subject to inspection by HMIs primarily for educational purposes but including some oversight of welfare are now, in the majority of cases, subject to educational inspection by OFSTED and for welfare considerations by social services departments. Children's homes and similar residential establishments are subject to inspections by local authority inspection units on a regular basis, and by the Social Services Inspectorate from time to time.

It could be argued that children in foster homes are at greater risk than those in residential care, because of their essentially isolated position. They are visited officially only by social workers, compared with the flow of people through residential establishments for children and young people. Currently, however, the law relating to foster placement only requires visits at certain times by social workers and residential care remains the focus of much greater attention.

It can be argued that there is also a necessary tension between a residential home and external management which, with thought and cooperation, can become a productive relationship. If the manager concerned spends time, not only with the manager in charge of the residential unit, but also with other members of staff and children, feeding back the observations and suggestions to the manager in charge as well as to senior external management, opportunities for development and greater understanding could arise. This, in turn, could also illuminate other visits by the local authority social services inspection unit and visits by the Social Services Inspectorate when they occur. One further idea might be helpful in considering these various 'inspectorial' tasks. Should monthly visits under Regulation 22 of *the Children's Homes Regulations* be shared between elected members and senior officers? It might be a productive collaboration in which elected members might see themselves as the children's political representatives!

'Hello, I am your local politician – I have come to carry out my surgery here!'

As mentioned earlier, valuable advice has been produced by the local authority associations entitled 'Children in Our Care' – *Commentary on Visiting Children's Homes and Handbook for Members Visiting Children's Homes*, Association of Metropolitan Authorities, Child Care Series No. 3, 1993. This helps define the task of 'corporate parenting' and not only indicates that the role of elected members (and senior officers) can be a valuable one, but also that it needs to be carried out sensitively. As representative of the 'corporate parent', the visitors need to be asking themselves, *'Are these children for whom I am responsible growing up as well as I would wish?'*. Such visits can be constructive or destructive. While bad practices need to be weeded out, it is important that the visits do not, in fact, increase feelings of helplessness amongst residential staff. Experience has shown that some visits can, because of the way they are carried out, undermine the authority of those who are responsible for the day-to-day work. Unless issues are very serious every effort should be made not to do this. It is also important to ensure that because residential work is more accessible and higher profile than some other forms of child care work, it does not become the victim of political controversy which may have little relevance to the children and their needs, but may distort the public image of work which is rarely clearly understood.

12.8.2 Flexibility and Structure

Flexibility is very important in providing child care services, but flexibility is more safely exercised when both formal and informal boundaries are clear. Otherwise performance of the task can become confused and unbalanced. Boundaries are needed, as we have discussed in several places in this book, in interpersonal relationships, both between adults, and between adults and children and young people. But boundaries are also needed in relationships with the neighbourhood in which an establishment is set; in accountability for equipment, food and money; in day-to-day decision making and in a variety of other issues. It is not always easy to draw the proper line between an easy, open, flexible, responsive, and at times, therapeutic approach to the task and the proper control of the environment with satisfactory group living for everyone's benefit. In fact it represents a very complex set of choices and decisions and is illustrated well by the use of volunteers.

Successful integration of a residential establishment into the neighbourhood may lead to volunteers being readily available. They can offer additional resources in time, relationships, skills, material assets and even, at various times, money. They can bring in fresh energy and stimulus and enrich the daily lives of children and young people, and staff. They can confer a valuable, additional flexibility on the home's or school's repertoire of child care opportunities. Their contribution, however, needs to be very carefully guided and absorbed at a rate which is appropriate for the residents' need and wishes and the capacity of staff to accept them. It is also important to assist them by clearly setting out the agency's requirements for vetting, training and organisation of volunteers. This will make the necessity of children's overall safety and protection of their welfare clear as the reasons for the safeguards. Publicity for events endangering children's welfare has been so great that most reasonable people are unlikely to be 'turned off' by explanations of the need for safeguards, particularly if they know that the same methods are used in checking staff applications.

12.9   A Complex Task – an Annual Review

It may help managers of homes and schools to hold firm in their minds the inevitably kaleidoscopic events which flow through a residential establishment for children and young people if they were to work within the framework of an annual review. This could involve a broad calendar with detailed timetables and events within it. An analysis might be included of residents admitted and discharged, including where they came from and where they went to; the range of children and young people looked after or educated; staff activities with achievements, failures and outstanding events. Such a record might not only give shape to a year, but also help to identify growth points, development trends, need for change and overall achievement. It would also be a way of helping other people to understand more about the task, including critics who often have little understanding of it.

Within all these and many other aspects of the task, managers will keep in mind the personal, human rights of the young people involved. We have talked elsewhere of their rights to privacy, their rights to confidential personal communications, issues of choice in food, need for space, time, clothes and complaints systems. We have discussed how their rights do not mean unlimited individual choice and freedom; nobody has that. For the manager the task is subtle and complex, juggling the requirements of organisation, resource constraints, legal provisions, public scrutiny and the needs of young human beings to be helped individually and personally to grow up and develop as best they can. It is a vital and indispensable task without which other staff cannot make their own contributions to the overall enterprise.

'In many ways management systems represent the nervous system of an organisation. Without information in the right form, in the right place and at the right time the best structure will not work and a strategy is unlikely to be soundly based....... The manager's task is to make the complex simple not to complicate it further'.

John Banham, then Controller of Audit in the Audit Commission for England and Wales – at a seminar in January 1985.

13   Conclusions

In this final chapter we draw together threads from the preceding twelve and some broad lessons from what they contain. We also suggest action which is needed to take practice forward in residential settings for children and young people.

During the period of preparation of the book health, education and social services all experienced major changes many of which had implications for the children and young people who were our concern. Change continues to affect the shape of services, their funding and organisational relationships within them and with other services. We believe, however, that the messages we offer are not affected by these changes. Children and their needs remain clearly identifiable and inescapable and, for some, life in a residential setting is 'a positive choice' in meeting those needs.

When the report 'A Positive Choice' (*Wagner Committee Report*) was published in 1988, residential child care in social services settings was still gravely undervalued. The belief of some local authorities was that in the near future it would no longer be needed and would diminish progressively until it would eventually disappear. Policies encouraging field social workers to rely entirely on foster placements or adoption were not uncommon. An alternative to using a local authority's children home was to rely on one off placements in homes provided by voluntary organisations, independent not-for-profit resources, or the private sector. Many of these agencies report increasing difficulty in sustaining good quality residential child care in a shrinking and uncertain market and so choice has diminished.

At the same time a belief that boarding special schools were accommodating children and young people who might otherwise have been in residential child care was sufficiently strong for this issue to be part of the terms of reference of a major research study ('*Closing Children's Homes: An End to Residential Child Care?*, Cliffe D and Berridge D, National Children's Bureau 1992) commissioned by the Warwickshire County Council soon after the *Wagner Report*. Although the research results were inconclusive in Warwickshire where it took place, there was widespread awareness that there might well be a connection nationally between a shrinking children's homes' population and a developing boarding special schools' population. This was supported by the fact that a significant proportion of the children in those schools were in the care of local authorities and that others were jointly supported by education and social services departments, some remaining in the schools 52 weeks of the year.

Reservations, sometimes amounting to prejudice against residential child care on the part of professional field social workers and often reinforced by the orientation of qualifying training courses and the attitude of senior managers in their employing departments were common. The *Barclay Committee* had commented adversely on this in their report *'Social Workers, Their Role and Tasks'*, 1982. *The Wagner Committee* drew attention to unhappy results for children and residential staff of the high foster home breakdown rates characteristic of some local authorities in the late 1980s.

Quite separate from the worlds of children's homes and boarding special schools, independent and maintained boarding schools continued to accommodate and educate very large numbers of children and young people routinely from 7 or 8 years old to 18, providing them with a substitute for their own homes for approximately 40 out of 52 weeks a year throughout their childhood and adolescence. In the late 1980s and early 1990s many children and young people in boarding schools were there, at least partly, because it was a solution to family problems caused by divorce, separation, long term illness, absence abroad, employment of both parents and high family mobility. Social workers were not required to be concerned about their welfare nor were they, in most cases, aware of their existence. Of social workers who considered boarding schools, many were likely to hold similar views about them as places for children to live as they did about residential child care. Meanwhile the families and children themselves, and the world of education, in the main regarded boarding as having many positive advantages including development of confidence, social skills, ability to be independent and concentrated educational opportunity.

Within children's homes standards varied widely. David Berridge's study *'Children's Homes'* (Blackwells 1985) and a report from an inspection of local authority community homes by the Social Work Service (now Social Services Inspectorate) in the same year, found many examples of good practice, as well as less good and sometimes poor. The most recent inspection by the Social Services Inspectorate (1993) of a national sample of children's homes found a similarly varied picture, with some good and others unacceptably poor.

Although the general climate concerning residential care had been so adverse, from about 1984 onwards government concern resulted in reviews of the services. *'A Positive Choice'* was one. Inquiry reports and new legislation had all been emphasising the need for reevaluation and changes of attitudes. This was so particularly from 1991 onwards when the *Pindown Inquiry Report*, the *Utting Report*, the *Howe Report* in 1991 and the *Warner Report* in 1992 all combined to take a positive approach to the contribution of residential child care in the scheme of national measures for those who could not live in their own homes. In addition, the *Children Act 1989* made a new link in England and Wales between social services departments and boarding schools which required the social services department to inspect the schools periodically in the interests of the welfare of the children living in them. We trace these developments in some detail in Chapter 3.

By 1991 we had already begun our discussions and thus we continued with the support of this changing climate and with the intention of attempting to promote a common core of good practice in residential settings for children and young people in health, education and social services.

A number of themes have run through the preceding 12 chapters. Some of the most important are openness, participation, continuity and children's rights and responsibilities.

Openness of climate sets the tone for much else which follows. In our view an open environment in which children, young people and staff are encouraged to talk about their problems, to speak out against perceived injustices and to express their fears and doubts, is essential to good child care. An environment in which staff and residents are afraid to speak out and cannot admit mistakes is one in which bad practice can flourish. Morale will fall and the standard of care will suffer. Many inquiries and reports have shown that it is also a climate in which abuse can take place and continue without detection or prevention.

We have discussed the importance of complaints systems, of staff being professional and courageous enough to 'blow the whistle' on abuse. Both of these are measures which will seldom be necessary if there is sufficient openness, trust and goodwill for people, staff and children to talk about what is going wrong, to be able to express their views without hard feelings and to know that what they have to say will be heard with respect and concern to help.

An open climate is also important for growth and development, both individually and in groups. It makes constructive suggestions possible. It allows for the sharing, not only of mistakes, but also achievements and the pleasure of success which in itself will provide encouragement and stimulus to further progress.

Participation becomes much more possible in such a climate too. Participation by both staff and children is an important factor in the production of good practice and its continuation. Managers who regularly involve staff in contributing experience and views and consult fully before formulating policy and making decisions, gain cooperation, avoid many difficulties and are likely to make wiser decisions. Similarly, the participation of children and young people is fundamental not only to openness in the daily life of an establishment, but also to their acceptance of the necessary structure and 'rules of the house'. We have given examples of how well young people respond to being involved even in matters as delicate as staff selection. When they are involved in discussion with staff of day-to-day organisational matters, measures of control, general disciplinary issues, leisure activities and many other common interests, staff will gain much greater commitment to what is decided because the children themselves have had a hand in it. They will have an investment in good standards for behaviour, for the environment and the development of 'their home'. This can also be a very effective way of ensuring that the establishment is child centred and not, as sometimes happens, run for the convenience of the organisation or the staff.

Continuity of Care is something the majority of children in their own homes take for granted. Children and young people in boarding schools, as we have seen, are generally assured of their future. If they abide by the school's rules and requirements, they will remain for a fixed length of time, often predictable from the beginning. They can thus have a sense of permanence and continuity which allows them to put down roots, plan from one term and year to the next, make long term friends, look ahead to achieving targets, whether academic or in sport, and become involved in school activities of a continuing nature. They will be able to become part of a tradition, part of a group and feel a sense of belonging which gives security and identity. The positive elements help when there are bad days, as there are in any setting.

Regrettably, too often for children and young people in children's homes the opposite is true. They are likely to have experienced many changes even before the local authority began to look after them. Some will be in the children's homes because they have already been placed in several different foster homes which have not provided secure care, for whatever reason. When they arrive in a children's home, therefore, they have been subjected to much insecurity, lack of certainty, even about where they will be next month, and inevitably feel troubled and anxious. Too frequently, just as they begin to settle down, this is taken as an indication that they are ready to try yet another foster home or similar placement.

This approach to children's needs should radically change, and senior managers, field social workers and staff in children's homes should all make every effort to allow the children in their care to **remain** and continue to develop **where they are seen to be thriving.** There are a number of accepted approaches which may need to change. One which we have already referred to earlier is the belief that a child cannot benefit by living in residential care and therefore placement in a family, even a lengthy sequence of family placements and breakdowns, is always preferable. Many young people do not want to accept someone else's family because of loyalties to their own. Many are at the age when, in the normal course of development, family ties are being challenged and resisted. They are also entitled to have their choice carefully considered under the *Children Act 1989*.

Another stance relates to the belief that the children and young people will become dependent and that dependency is bad. They must learn to be independent. This approach overlooks theory, knowledge and experience which teach us that it is necessary to have been able to experience safe dependency to be able to become properly independent. This is what happens in normal families. Because family life has not been as satisfactory as they needed it to be, it does not mean that these children can jump this stage and manage without it. They, like everyone else, need to experience stability and stable dependency, before moving on to the next stage.

A third approach which needs immediate review is the one which has expectations of these young people to become readily and safely independent several years earlier than is normal for the rest of the population. There are widespread practices which lead to 16 year olds, sometimes younger, being encouraged to move out of group living into what is described as 'independent accommodation'. This may be a bedsitter, lodgings, a flat, even bed and breakfast in which they will have to manage on their own and deal with adult living problems with totally inadequate preparation and inadequate income. The research of Mike Stein and colleagues, the work and studies done by Centrepoint, the Children's Society, National Children's Home – Action for Children and others, all demonstrate conclusively that this approach is not in the young person's interests. A very high proportion are not in the 'independent accommodation' long before finding themselves homeless, jobless, on the streets, at risk of drug dealers, prostitution, depression, pregnancy, illness, debt, depression, and even suicide.

Residential child care can be used more constructively to ensure greater continuity in the lives of these young people, more effective preparation for adult life, and the kind of care which more nearly approaches what a good parent would provide for late adolescents.

The theme of continuity is one of the most important. One of the points made to us by those who work in residential child care concerned the destructiveness of the approaches just identified. The argument went along the lines of:

> *'how can residential care make a satisfactory contribution in these circumstances? For God's sake give it a chance to succeed!'*

This prompts the suggestion that what is needed is a much more open-minded approach to the methods that might be used to meet a child's need and evaluation of outcomes. There is a need to take a leaf out of the doctors' book and to look more broadly at how a child's life chances might best be met. Probability is a difficult concept but the medical profession frequently uses it to inform decision making and put limits around people's expectations of them eg. *'one case in 10,000 has an adverse reaction to this drug'* or *'there is a 1 in 3 chance of a complete recovery'*.

Put in social work terms in relation to child care the comparison can be seen as balancing 'ideal' situations against individual situations in the reality of the 'here and now'. Some social workers place more value on finding the 'right' family placements than on continuity for a child in a certain set of circumstances. They tend to use residential care as a stop gap between family placements or an emergency receptacle when a family (natural or foster) breaks down. This approach imposes a definition of failure on residential care but does so on terms unrelated either to residential care as a method or to child development as the key factor in the child's welfare. The social worker's objective is 'a family' to which the rhetoric states 'every child is entitled' not to the development of the child to optimum advantage. Because residential child care is seen by definition to be looking after children whose life chances are seriously diminished, the contribution it can make to enhancing a child's life chances is not always appreciated or understood. Put in gambling terms some social workers reject residential child care because they feel that if they bet on the family placement fruit machine they have a chance, sometimes a very slim chance, of winning the jackpot – the family which will make everything right for a child. As they see it if they settle for residential care they have no chance of winning the jackpot.

However, even taking into account that, because of the way in which residential child care is often defined the chances of success may be low, to settle for residential care and work on some less ambitious improvements in the child's life conditions may be the rational decision. It may in fact be based on the balance of probabilities and work 'with the grain' of the child's own choice, the family's choice and the continuity of school, neighbourhood, friends, staff relationships and other important elements in the child's life pattern.

The concept of probability is not taught in social work as it is in medicine and the professional environment in which social workers are providing services does not generally understand or use the concept. It is not uncommon to learn that a child may have been 'waiting' for a foster home for a year or more. No one weighs the probability of finding the 'right' foster home. If they did and this was low, then rationally, perhaps, only a single attempt might be appropriate before deciding to use an alternative approach. This approach might address the issue of long term care in terms of probability. What are the developmental needs which can realistically be met? Which of them, if successfully pursued, are likely to afford the greatest advantage in the child's long term life chances – long after 18 years of age, as well as during the span of life until then.

Because social work makes little or no use of the probability concept, it tends to fall victim to simplistic absolute expectations. The disproportionate investment made in the 'permanency' policy has been an example of this. Because of this, a real chance of stability in group care may have been 'traded away' in favour of an 'ideal' foster home. A child may not have been able to settle down because she or he was 'waiting' for an ideal placement.

Residential staff in children's homes need to know about the probabilities of certain outcomes and strive to improve on this rate. Outcomes, probably most frequently the intermediate outcomes of the work carried out by Parker, et al, need to be recorded and by so doing create some awareness of the chances of achieving them. To do so would mean the task of care would be broken down into manageable chunks and success estimated in terms of the odds for or against rather than actual achievement or failure. It is also helpful to think in terms of positive inputs enhancing a child's life chances. This gives validity to a proactive planned approach to even short term care periods.

It might also be possible in this context to look more imaginatively at combining a set of resources ' a treasury of opportunities', which would meet a child's needs for several years because it would avoid some of the 'all or nothing' stresses which can develop in some circumstances and destroy a situation.

We would like to suggest that thought should be given to the combinations which might produce the following examples of arrangements for continuing care and education.

- Child's family in school holidays, boarding school in term time.

- Foster family in school holiday, boarding school in term time.

- Children's home for part of holidays, family for part of holidays, boarding school in term time.

- Children's home Sunday night to Friday during term time and school holidays, child's own home Friday to Sunday throughout the year.

- Foster home in school holidays, children's home in term time.

- Foster home in school holidays and weekends, children's home Monday to Friday.

With the greater understanding developing between social services and boarding schools, and the recognition by schools of the greater attention needed to children's overall care, a number of schools are likely to be able to be used in the kinds of combinations suggested above. The advantages for a child being looked after by a local authority could be continuity, stability, a good education, confidence building, increased self esteem. We hope that the length and diversity of experience brought to this discussion by the members of the steering group will at least ensure that consideration is given to these proposals.

Children's rights and responsibilities have been explored in national and international contexts in this book. The United Kingdom has underwritten the United Nations Convention on the Rights of the Child and legislation in this country embodies many of the rights which it articulated. The best interests of children, their right to be consulted on matters concerning them, freedom of expression, privacy, access to information, protection from abuse, a healthy environment, health, education, leisure, and protection from exploitation are echoed in legislation. Further rights under the Convention and in legislation concern young offenders and have become a major issue in Britain since changes in the law were proposed in 1993. Under these changes new establishments will be opened for 12 to 16 year old 'persistent offenders'. They would be secure and would hold the children for periods up to 12 months. The proposals heighten the importance of the common core of care which we have discussed in other contexts. While there is evidence that purely punitive regimes for the young often do not reform, nor deter for long after discharge, on the other hand there is also evidence[1] that factors such as quality and accessibility of staff, educational developmental programmes and positively caring attitudes can bring about changes for the better in young people whose behaviour has been problematic.

In discussing children's rights we have recognised not only that attention to them is an essential element in good care, but that both in the interests of children and staff, they need to be balanced with responsibilities. However badly treated children have been, if their own later life pattern is to be successful, they must be able to recognise and respect other people's rights and to contribute to the general well-being of those around them, if only through socially acceptable behaviour. We have suggested ways in which they can be helped to understand and incorporate these lessons. We have also suggested ways in which staff' rights and needs can be honoured and met, as an important part of good management of residential settings. It was very clear to us that the balance between children's and adults' rights had to be carefully adjusted whilst, at the same time, taking care not to curtail children's hard won rights in the interests of adult convenience or wish to retain traditional powers. The emphasis laid on children's rights by legislation and by international convention has not yet had totally enthusiastic support and it will continue to be necessary to be vigilant on their behalf.

---

1 See "Issues of Control in Residential Child Care" — Dartington Social Research Unit HMSO 1981

The relevance and application of the **rights of children** implicit in the Act to child and adolescent inpatient units were considered by Dr Mike Shaw, Consultant Child Psychiatrist, Queen Mary's Hospital for Children, at a conference in May 1993, organised for the Royal College of Psychiatrists, Child and Adolescent Psychiatry Specialist Section. Following discussion of restriction of liberty, other forms of discipline, partnership with parents and working with other agencies, some of the paper's conclusions were that:-

- it is essential for inpatient services to have a nationally accepted code of practice set in the framework of the Children Act 1989;

- the principles underlying the Act mostly coincide with what is already regarded as good therapeutic practice;

- health care purchasers are now responsible for assuring the quality of service and need widely respected standards to work from.

Dr Shaw's final comments could be applied in principle to many of the settings discussed in this book.

> '........ *good practice can only be achieved through painstaking effort. It is absolutely worthwhile, but places huge demands on time, manpower and skill. The young people we work with are amongst the most disadvantaged in our society, and we have a responsibility as clinicians to set standards which ensure that the resources necessary to do a good job are made available'.*

Increasingly, recognition of the importance of children's rights and Children Act requirements is also influencing boarding schools. As stated earlier in the book a number of

> '*prestigious establishments have positively embraced SSD inspections and rather than complain, resist or play down, they have seen the advantage and taken it..... They have seen that there are important things to be learnt from the world of child welfare'.*

(Observation made at a sub-plenary session at The Social Services Conference, 1993.)

Openness, participation, continuity and children's rights have been general themes which indicate the principles needed in the common core of good practice. They also relate closely to a further group of themes – the commonality of children's and young people's developmental needs; the importance of needs led care, including the special needs of certain children; shared care, particularly care shared with parents; and 'good parenting' care provided by residential staff.

The commonality of children's and young people's developmental needs was one of the key concepts which we kept before us in our work. There have been so many ways in which the importance of this concept has been hidden from view. As services have developed, labelling, categorisation, specialisation, separate budgets, separate central and local government departments, professional barriers, specialisms have got in the way of seeing a child as a child first and then as a child with particular needs. We have already shown how professional blinkers can narrow vision about ways to help a child. Departmental boundaries can be equally divisive and limiting. A new study carried out on behalf of the Children's Society by Mlemooda Malik entitled 'Passing the Buck' (1993) explores cooperation between agencies in providing services for young people in need of help.

> *'Manifesting one type of unacceptable behaviour -aggression – can lead to children being labelled in different ways .... If it is the juvenile justice system, the child is a 'young offender', while social services prefer 'beyond parental control'. Education services favour 'having a learning difficulty' or 'being disturbed'. Psychiatric professionals use 'mentally ill'. Despite these distinctions.......... three quarters of children studied had been in contact with more than one agency. A third had been in touch with three'.*

The 'serious implications' for the children, the study concluded, were that

> *'children [were] viewed as having a series of separate problems rather than being a complete individual'.*

In consequence, the emphasis placed on the child's problems is likely to match the focus of the service agency which deals with him/her rather than the individual's needs. These accidental factors have considerable influence on the style of care offered eg. as between a boarding special school, a psychiatric unit or a children's home practising 'good parenting' as far as possible. We believe that greater recognition of the importance of a common core of good practice would diminish these differences and emphasise the child's common developmental needs as the essential background of any special needs. As we have said earlier, a synthesis of policy in relation to children with difficulties is important in provision of services to assist their proper development.

Needs led care includes special provision for children with special needs. We advocate that care should, in general, be related to needs, not to observed behaviour. Staff may have to address particular aspects of behaviour (for example, if a child is harming him/herself or others) but day to day care should be grounded in meeting needs. This means that when a child first enters an establishment, staff must look at the whole person, not simply the behaviour which led to him/her being there, whether that behaviour is anti-social, the result of disablement, emotional trauma or prolonged neglect of adequate upbringing. It also means that special needs such as those of ethnic minority children, refugees, children from other countries, disabled children, must be carefully and sensitively assessed. Some special needs will require very special skills and resources which may be expensive, but others can be met by proper and sensitive use of existing resources.

A special need which may be common to may children, especially those looked after by local authorities, may be the need for care to be seen as an opportunity to compensate, even if only in a small way or only for a short time, for the major deprivations and disadvantages they have suffered.

Even in a short period of residential care, the values associated with long term care should be upheld. An episode in residential care might be an opportunity for compensation which could take the form of a careful and thorough approach to his/her health needs, extra educational opportunities including targets encouraging progress in basic important skills, but also development of individual gifts such as music, sport, art. Confidence for all of us is closely related to 'feedback' from other people. Small achievements or repair of some small physical blemish or overcoming a small disadvantage can make a huge difference to interpersonal capacity which, in itself, is the starting point for so much else. In addition, education is probably the most important determinant of a child's future success so that all or any small steps forward in achievement and social viability are important contributions to the child's adult life, long after the period when he is receiving help or care in public services. We have said earlier in the book that managers should see it as their duty to ensure every child receives maximum educational opportunity.

Shared care is a concept which has a firm place in the *Children Act 1989* in which residential care is identified as one of the means to be used to help families stay together. In some ways the limitations of residential care in being able to provide 'alternative parents' for a child can be turned to advantage in working with actual parents. The White Paper *'Scotland's Children – Proposals for Child Care Policy and Law'* takes a similar line. Under the heading 'Support' it speaks of local authorities' duty to care for any child whose parents are unable to provide proper accommodation.

> *'Such care has developed over the years to offer short term support to families.......*
> *Experience has shown that timely use of such care services can often alleviate*
> *stress and prevent a longer term breakdown of the family unit at a later date'.*

'Social Work Decisions in Child Care' published by the DHSS (now the Department of Health) in 1985 warned that social services departments might 'reap the whirlwind' as the result of having kept children out of care 'at all costs'. The report commented that family links were seldom given much consideration.

'The system itself is geared towards placing an emphasis on the justification for intervention rather than what intervention would achieve'.

(Linden Hilgendorf quoted in the report).

The *Children Act* built on many of the findings of research, including the studies summarised in *'Social Work Decisions in Child Care'*. It would be in line with the thinking behind the legislation for residential staff to work closely with parents in 'shared care'. Residential care staff and parents have a common interest in the child growing up well. Doing the right thing for the child can make them allies. Because of their experience of working with the children, care staff are well placed to understand and support the parents as well as the children. The relationships which could develop would not be dissimilar in essence from the parent/boarding school symbiotic relationship. Partnership with parents could have many benefits. It would avoid the rivalry and sense of inadequacy likely to be inherent in many foster placements. Children could feel safer about being away from home for a time if they were able to see staff and their parents working together to ameliorate a situation so that they could return. The residential staff could develop an aspect of their work which would add a sense of completeness to the task, provide opportunity for new challenges and give them greater understanding of the children for whom they care.

The last theme which is closely related to the others is what we have described as **'good parenting'**. It is discussed in Chapter 6 in the context of other approaches to care and in relation to the work of Parker et al on *'Assessing Outcomes in Child Care'*. The evaluative instrument devised by the authors was 'constructed around seven areas (or dimensions) of children's development and their social presentation'.

Outcomes for individual children would be evaluated by seeking to assess how a local authority fulfilled **ALL** rather than some of its parental responsibilities. The assessments are based on norms prevalent in the general population. Wherever possible, parents and children would be involved in the evaluations. The proposed measures were derived from the idea of what *'reasonable parents would consider a good outcome for their own children which in its turn was derived from the philosophy of the Children Act 1989'*.

As we have acknowledged clearly and firmly, residential staff are not and cannot take the place of parents, but like care staff in boarding schools and nursing staff in hospitals they have to, or should, fulfil many of the roles and tasks which parents would do if the children were at home. The work on assessing outcomes, in our view, clearly demonstrates the detailed concern which 'good parenting' care should involve. It is important that when a child or young person is not at home, the care which 'good parenting' involves should be carried on. This kind of detailed care, whether in the setting of a children's home, boarding school, therapeutic community or medical or health unit, will not only promote the child's overall welfare and development but will encourage the kind of relationship between adults and children which this book seeks to advance. In Chapter 6, where various psychological approaches to group care are discussed, 'good parenting' is set alongside them as an alternative to be considered. To use the model of what 'reasonable parents would consider a good outcome for their own children' could transform much of the work done with children looked after in groups, cause many decisions to be reviewed, and reduce the damaging 'turbulence' of frequent placement moves and educational fragmentation. A significant proportion of the disturbance some children exhibit may well be attributed to 'the system' they find themselves in which sometimes serves to increase, rather than meet, their need for special help.

There is much to be learned and gained from the psychological approaches we have described. We would, however, set them into focus by suggesting that the task of residential care is to interfere as little as possible with nature (another medical parallel) but to offer and try to get children to accept 'good parenting'. Then, if necessary, draw help from one of the psychological approaches most suited to the problem.

Staff are the most important element in the provision of care in any residential setting. The task which adults undertake in working with children and young people who live in groups is much more complex than is generally understood. To carry it out well requires adequate numbers of the right sorts of people, chosen with care, inducted into their jobs, and then supported in them by means of effective and sensitive management, supervision, training and staff development, as well as opportunities for regular self and managerial assessment. We have discussed these and related matters in several parts of the book.

In our conclusions we want to emphasise some important issues concerning staff. The first of these is **staff selection.** This is where everything begins. In spite of striking evidence in the *Pindown* and *Leicestershire* reports showing the very serious consequences of careless, ill informed and sometimes unethical methods used in filling staff appointments, much persuasion remains to be done. Complaints can still be heard about the cost of the careful and searching methods advocated by the *Warner Report.* Support is still given to the concept of using volunteers who can then become staff, once familiarised with the work. Anxiety is still expressed that candidates for posts cannot be expected to face stringent recruitment techniques which they might find too challenging. It cannot be stressed too strongly the need to think carefully, and without traditional prejudices which hinder the introduction of professional standards in staff selection. There are strong reasons for this. First, children have a right to be protected, as far as possible, against unsuitable and sometimes dangerous appointments. Their interests must have priority. Secondly, any analysis of the financial cost of advertising, the managerial, financial and human costs of dealing with trouble caused in consequence of bad appointments and the inquiries which can arise, readily shows the value of careful, detailed, objective and searching selection methods. It may be said that difficulties of obtaining staff are exacerbated by this approach. Experience shows, however, that establishments which are known to be looking for quality staff are respected and sought after because they are perceived as valuing the nature of the task for which they are recruiting and the people they wish to find.

Selection of staff is not a task for inexperienced, uninformed people, nor for those who believe they can assess in a panel interview all they need to know about a candidate. The whole process from drafting advertisements, job descriptions and person specifications, through selection procedures, references, police and other checks, requires experience and skill. It also requires full consultation and involvement of those with whom the staff will work, both adults and children.

The next important consideration is **training.** The proportion of trained candidates available for appointment will vary according to the residential setting, but even if they are qualified, training should be seen as a continuing part of employment. In fact, if children's homes are to meet the expectations of politicians, managers, placing social workers, (care managers!), other agencies, families and the children and young people themselves, training will need to be an integral part of life in the home. Training leadership will be called for from heads of establishments and the home as whole tapped into a training package geared to staff at different levels of experience and competence repeatable as required. In fact the establishment will need to be a centre for training in itself and not just a place in which certain people need training. It will also need to be linked into national accredition such as NVQ or Open University credits. Similar progressive development and practice improvement should also be an expectation in boarding schools, therapeutic communities and medical and health units.

Since common skills are needed in the task of caring for children and young people, wherever they are, some joint training is likely to benefit all disciplines. Some of this might well involve exchange visits between children's homes, schools and health units. They all have much to learn from each other and opportunities for informal meetings in which to share skills, experience and good practice are desirable. Career planning in the future is likely to benefit from widening the range of work which can be undertaken by individuals and, conversely but not in contradiction, there is a need for greater recognition of the specific professional task of working with children in various settings.

Professional practice within children's homes, boarding schools and therapeutic communities will need to reflect and be informed by an acceptable training package, understood and agreed not only by those within the establishment but by managers and consumers. Such training packages will not permit the idiosyncratic or 'home spun' methods and 'therapies' which have been the subject of inquiries in educational, social services and health care establishments from time to time.

Training has been under reconsideration as the group concerned with this book worked together. It has not adequately met the needs of staff or children in the past. As suggested in the *Warner Report*, consideration should be given to training for child care being more informed by such disciplines as nursing, paediatrics, psychology and teaching. At the same time nurses and teachers could benefit from their groups being more informed by some of the content of social work training. Greater concentration on the detail of child development and child care might benefit all disciplines. This, it could be argued, applies to the training of field social workers as well as residential staff. Child development is a stronger element in the educationalist' approach to children, and has links with the European concept of the social pedagogue or educateur advocated by the *Warner Committee.* It may be that the cultural split in the UK between education and social work is a factor in the difficulties contemporary residential child care has been facing.

One further point concerning training relates to more carefully informed professional practice. Homes, schools, therapeutic communities which are trying to offer remedial care should, in our view, be considering what they can do to measure their success. Perhaps, again, a model can be taken from medicine. Research is not limited in the medical world to full time or academic researchers. General practitioners, interested to pursue a small area of medical practice and enlarge the knowledge base a little, frequently carry out studies based on small samples which are then published. They may then be replicated or challenged from the experience of other doctors. In our view residential establishments, if necessary assisted by external support agents such as psychologists or psychiatrists, might carry out small follow-up or analytical studies in which some measure of the success or otherwise of what they are doing, might be seen. These studies could feed into the dissemination of good practice which should also be part of residential work's contribution to developing the common core of good practice. Studies of this sort would help strengthen team work, galvanise the common effort of staff and emphasise the real long term purpose of the residential unit. They will also help staff construct criteria for success which are more realistic and scientific than the often unreasonable or idealistic expectations of the general public and popular press.

Finally, we have to end this last chapter as we have the previous twelve – with management and policy issues.

The need for knowledgeable, understanding and appropriately experienced managers has been nationally accepted. These managers are at different levels from the most senior to the immediate line managers relating to individual establishments and those running them. It must no longer be possible for someone to be placed in such a role with no relevant experience and little relevant knowledge. The managers need to be confident enough to manage effectively and sensitively and not to feel obliged to rely on 'charismatic' figures who may abuse the power they hold by default. The managers must be able to support the staff accountable to them and recognise their need for help as well as incipient problems.

At national level our experience as a group led us to feel that there is a need, touched on several times in this concluding chapter, for synthesis between government policies involving children and young people living away from home in groups. The work we have done has shown that there are broad areas of common need and common skills. There is a need for a common core of good practice to be recognised and accepted by social services, education and health services. Much of the guidance published by the Department of Health in relation to the Children Act 1989 can benefit service provision in education and health establishments. Similarly, the recent Department for education circulars, notably those on the education of children with emotional and behavioural difficulties, exclusions from school, the education of sick children and the education of children being looked after by local authorities are relevant to social services and health establishments.

Children and young people are the common core of all these services and would benefit from greater unity of approach and policies both at Central and Local Government levels.

Appendix 1   Growing up in Groups

MEMBERSHIP OF THE STEERING GROUP

Ewan Anderson	*University of Durham*
David Berridge	*(then) Assistant Director (Research) National Children's Bureau*
Louise Bessant	*Young People's Forum, Birmingham*
Brian Bishop	*Assistant Director (Placement & Resources) Peper Harow Foundation*
Ben Brown	*Birmingham Action for Child Care*
Joyce Eyeington	*Rye Hill Family Care Centre, Newcastle upon Tyne*
Bob Jezzard	*Consultant Child Psychiatrist, Guy's Hospital, London*
Barbara Kahan	*Independent Child Care Consultant and Chair of the National Children's Bureau*
Paul Knight	*Representative of the Association of Directors of Social Services*
Dudley Roach	*Representative of the Social Care Association*
Richard Rollison	*Principal, Mulberry Bush School, Oxfordshire*
Alex Saddington	*Voice for Children, Wales*
Joan Sadler	*Former President of the Boarding Schools Association*
Sister Consolata Smythe	*Good Sheperd Centre, Renfrewshire*

Daphne Statham   *Director, National Institute for Social Work*

Jane Tunstill   *Representative of the National Council of*
                              Voluntary Child Care Organisations

OBSERVERS

Derek Brushett   *Social Services Inspector, Welsh Office*

Brian Fitzgerald   *(then) HMI, Department for Education,*
                              subsequently Office for Standards in Education

Denis O'Brien   *Social Services Inspector, Northern Ireland*

Wendy Rose   *Assistant Chief Inspector, Social Services*
                              Inspectorate, Department of Health

John Rowlands   *Social Services Inspector, Social Services*
                              Inspectorate, Department of Health

John Smith   *Social Work Services Inspectorate,*
                              Scottish Office

Peter Stone   *Social Services Inspector, Social Services*
                              Inspectorate, Department of Health

CORRESPONDING MEMBERS

Roger Bullock   *Dartington Social Research Unit*

Michael Little   *Dartington Social Research Unit*

Stephen Campbell   *Under Secretary Social Services*
                              Association of County Councils

Harriett Dempster   *Assistant Chief Inspector, Social Work*
                              Services Inspectorate, Scottish Office

Chris Payne   *Social Care Unit, National Institute for*
                              Social Work

Peter Westland   *Under Secretary Social Services*
                              Association of Metropolitan Authorities

Deirdre Wynn   *Convention of Scottish Local Authorities*

Appendix 2   List of HMSO Children Act 1989 and Other Related Publications

Children Act 1989 Guidance and Regulations

Volume 1:   Court Orders (ISBN 0-11-321371-9)

Volume 2:   Family Support, Day Care and Educational Provision for Young Children (ISBN 0-11-321382-7)

Volume 3:   Family Placements (ISBN 0-11-321375-1)

Volume 4:   Residential Care (ISBN 0-11-3214530-8)

Volume 5:   Independent Schools (ISBN 0-11-321373-5)

Volume 6:   Children with Disabilities (ISBN 0-11-321452-9)

Volume 7:   Guardians Ad Litem and Other Court Related Issues (ISBN 0-11-321471-5)

Volume 8:   Private Fostering and Miscellaneous (ISBN 0-11-321473-1)

Volume 9:   Adoption Issues (ISBN 0-11-321474-X)

Related Publications

Independent Schools with Boarding: An Induction Framework for Social Services Inspectors, Trainer and Managers (ISBN 0-11-321503-7)

Protecting Children: A Guide for Social Workers undertaking a Comprehensive Assessment (ISBN 0-11-321159-7)

An Introduction to the Children Act 1989 (ISBN 0-11-321254-2)

Principles and Practice (ISBN 0-11-321289-5)

Patterns and Outcomes (ISBN 0-11-321357-3)

Children in the Public Care (ISBN 0-11-321455-3)

Working Together (Revised) (ISBN 0-11-321472-3)

Registration of Childminding and Day Care (ISBN 0-11-321469-3)

Child Care Policy: Putting it in Writing (ISBN 0-11-321285-2)

Looking after Children: Assessing Outcomes in Child Care (ISBN 0-11-321459-6)

The Welfare of Children in Boarding Schools Practice Guide (ISBN 0-11-321477-4)

The Timetabling of Care Proceedings before the Implementation of the Children Act 1989 (ISBN 0-11-321487-1)

Children Act Guidance Volume 10: Index (ISBN 0-11-321538-X0

Social Work Decisions in Child Care (ISBN 0-11-321046-9)

School Life: Pupil's Views on Boarding (ISBN 0-11-321591-6)

A Sense of Direction: Planning in Social Work with Children (SSI) (Diana Robbins)

The Children Act 1989: An Introduction Guide for the NHS (DH)

Planning for Children and Young People (SSI)

Writing Child Care Policy (SSI)

Working With Child Sexual Abuse: Guidelines for Trainers and Managers in Social Services Departments (SSI)

Residential Care for Children, Report of a DH Seminar held on 30 October–1 November 1991 at Dartington, Devon

Appendix 3   Scottish Office Legislation and Circulars on Child Care, Education and Health Services

Social Work Services Group

SW1/1975   Non-accidental Injury to Children

SW4/1979   Release of Offenders Convicted of Offences Against Children in the Home

SW4/1982   Child Abuse

SW8/1987   Data Protection Act 1984 – Orders under Section 79(2) and 34(2)

SW9/1988   Child Abuse: An Action Programme

SW9/1989   Protection of Children: Disclosure of Criminal Convictions of those with Access to Children in Local Authorities

SW1/1989   Code on Confidentiality of Social Work Records

SW2/1989   Access to Personal Files (Social Work) (Scotland) Regulations 1989

SW18/1991   Protection of Children from Abuse: Coordination of Local Services

SWSG/1985   Report of a Working Group on Social Work Issues in Child Abuse *'Effective Intervention: Child Abuse Guidance on Cooperation in Scotland'*, HMSO19

Scottish Office Home and Health Department

NHS 1975 (Gen) 23   Non-accidental Injury to Children

NHS 1982 (Gen) 18   Child Abuse

Scottish Office Education Department

SED 1990   Protection of Children from Abuse: The Role of Education Authorities, Schools and Teachers

Scottish Office Home and Health Department

National Nursing and Wifery Consultative Committee: Child Protection – Guidance for Senior Nurses, Health Visitors and Midwives in Scotland 1989

Produced by Others but Issued by Scottish Office Departments

Physical Signs of Sexual Abuse in Children: A Report of the Royal College of Physicians 1991

Diagnosis of Child Sexual Abuse – Guidance for Doctors – Report of Standing Medical Advisory Committee HMSO 1988

Protecting Children – A Guide for Social Workers undertaking a Comprehensive Assessment. Department of Health HMSO 1988

Scottish Social Work Legislation
Social Work (Scotland) Act 1968
Criminal Procedures (Scotland) Act 1975
Children Act 1975
Health and Social Services and Social Security Adjudication Act 1983
Social Work (Residential Establishments – Child Care) (Scotland) Regulations 1987
Residential Care Order (Secure Accommodation (Scotland) Regulations 1988
Access to Personal Files Act 1987
Secure Accommodation (Scotland) Regulations 1983
Secure Accommodation (Scotland) Amendment Regulations 1988
Registered Establishments (Scotland) Act 1987
The Residential Care Order (Secure Accommodation) (Scotland) Amendment Regulations 1988
Adoption (Scotland) Act 1978
Adoption Agencies (Scotland) Regulations 1984
The Foster Children (Scotland) Act 1984 (as amended)
The Boarding Out and Fostering of Children (Scotland) Regulations 1985
The Foster Children (Private Fostering) (Scotland) Regulations 1985

Scottish Education Legislation
Registration of Independent Schools (Scotland) Act 1957 (As amended)
Education (Scotland) Act 1980 (Sections 98, 99)

Health Legislation
National Health Services Act 1978
Mental Health (Scotland) Act 1984
National Health Service and Community Care Act 1990

Appendix 4   Organisations and Addresses

ADVISORY CENTRE FOR EDUCATION
Unit 1B, Aberdeen Studios, 22-24 Highbury Grove, London N5 2EA
Tel: 071 354 8321

ALBANY TRUST (Counselling on sexual problems)
26 Balham Hill, London SW12 9EB
Tel: 071 675 6669

ALBERT KENNEDY TRUST (For young lesbians and gay men who have run away)
23 New Mount Street, Manchester M4 4DE
Tel: 061 833 2990

ALONE IN LONDON (For young single homeless people)
188 Kings Cross Road, London WC1X 9DE
Tel: 071 278 4224

ANOREXICS ANONYMOUS (Also other eating disorders)
24 Westmoreland Road, Barnes, London SW13
Tel: 081 748 3994

ASSOCIATION FOR CHILDREN WITH LIFE THREATENING OR TERMINAL CONDITIONS AND THEIR FAMILIES (ACT)
Royal Hospital for Sick Children, St Michael's Hill, Bristol BS2 8BJ
Tel: 0272 215411

ADVICE, ADVOCACY AND REPRESENTATION SERVICE FOR CHILDREN
C/O Childline
1 Sickle Street, Manchester M60 2AA
Tel: 0800 616101

BARNARDO'S
Tanners Lane, Barkingside, Ilford, Essex IG6 1QG
Tel: 081 550 8822

BLACK AND IN CARE (Bibini Project)
300 Moss Lane East, Mosside, Manchester, M14 4LZ
Tel: 061 226 9122

BRITISH PREGNANCY ADVISORY SERVICE
Austy Manor, Wootton Wawen, Solihull, W Midlands, B9S 6DA
(Other branches throughout England)
Tel: 056 42 3225

BRITISH YOUTH COUNCIL
57 Chalton Street, London NW1 1HV
Tel: 071 377 7559

BROOK ADVISORY CENTRES FOR YOUNG PEOPLE (Confidential
contraceptive and pregnancy advice)
153A East Street, London SE17 2SD
Tel(s):   071 708 1234
             071 708 1390

CARELINE (NATIONAL CHILDREN'S HOME - ACTION FOR CHILDREN)
Tel(s):   Birmingham – 021 440 597
             Cardiff   – 0222 29461
             Glasgow   – 041 221 6722
             Leeds   – 0532 456456
             Manchester – 061 26 9873

CENTRAL LONDON TEENAGE PROJECT (A 'half-way house' for young
runaways, including those under 16, run by the Children's Society
91–93 Queen's Road, Peckham, London SE15 2EZ
Tel: 071 639 1466

CENTREPOINT (Other direct access accommodation to homeless young people
in London)
140A Gloucester Mansion, London WC2 8HD
Tel: 071 379 3466

CHAR - HOUSING CAMPAIGN FOR SINGLE PEOPLE
5–15 Cromer Street, London WC1H 8LS
Tel: 071 833 2071

THE CHARTERHOUSE GROUP OF THERAPEUTIC COMMUNITIES
The Peper Harow Foundation, 14 Charterhouse Square, London EC1M 6AX
Tels: 071 251 0672
             071 251 6072

CHILD ABUSE SURVIVOR NETWORK
PO Box 7, London W7 6XJ
Tel: 071 723 5840

CHILDLINE
* 2nd Floor, Royal Mail Building, 50 Studd Street, London N1 0QW
* FREEPOST 1111 London EC4B 4BB
Tel(s)   0800 1111 (Helpline - 24 hours)
              0800 400222 (Helpline for deaf/hearing impaired children)
              0800 884444 (Helpline for children in care)

CHILDREN'S LEGAL CENTRE
20 Compton Terrace, London N1 2UN
Tel: 071 359 6251 (Advice line staff Monday-Friday, 2–5pm)

CHILDREN'S RIGHTS DEVELOPMENT UNIT (CRDU)
London   235 Shaftesbury Avenue, London WC2H 8EL
            Tel: 071 240 4449
Scotland   Lion Chambers, 170 Hope Street, Glasgow G2 2TU
            Tel: 041 353 0206
N.Ireland   Centre for Social Research, The Queen's University of Belfast, 105
            Botanic Gardens, Belfast BT7 1NN
            Tel: 0232 245133 Ext. 3580/3582

CHILDREN'S RIGHTS OFFICERS' ASSOCIATION
C/O Liz MacAuley, Press Officer
Liverpool Social Services, 26 Hatton Garden, Liverpool L3 2AW
Tel: 051 225 3881

CHILDREN IN SCOTLAND
Princes House, 5 Shandwich Place,
Edinburgh EH2 4RG
Tel: 031 228 8484

CHILDREN'S SOCIETY
Edward Rudolph House, Margery Street,
London WC1X 0JL
Tel: 071 837 4299

CHILDREN IN WALES
7 Cleve House, Lanbourne Crescent, Cardiff CF4 5GT
Tel: 0222 761177

THE COMPASSIONATE FRIENDS (An international organisation of bereaved
parents offering friendship and understanding to other bereaved parents)
6 Denmark Street, Bristol BS1 5DQ
Tel: 0272 292778

FIRST KEY (Advisory service on all aspects of leaving care)
First Floor, Oxford Chambers, Oxford Place, Leeds LS1 3AX
Tel: 0532 443898

INSTITUTE OF CHILD HEALTH
Royal Hospital for Sick Children
St Michael's Hill, Bristol BS2 8BJ
Tel: 0272 215411

JUST ASK (ADVISORY AND COUNSELLING SERVICE)
YMCA, 112 Great Russell Street, London WC1B 3NQ
Tel: 071 628 3380

LOCAL GOVERNMENT OMBUDSMEN
21 Queen Ann's Gate, London SW1H 9BU
Tel: 071 222 5622

MESSAGE HOME SERVICE (Runaways can leave anonymous messages to be relayed to their families)
Mothers' Union, 24 Tufton Street, London SW1P 3RB
Tel: 071 799 7662

NATIONAL CHILDREN'S BUREAU
8 Wakley Street, London EC1V 7QE
Tel: 071 278 9441

NATIONAL CHILDREN'S HOME - ACTION FOR CHILDREN
85 Highbury Park, London N5 1UD
Tel: 071 226 2033

NATIONAL COUNCIL OF VOLUNTARY CHILD CARE ORGANISATIONS
* Unit 4, Pride Court, 80/82 White Lion Street, London N1 0PF
Tel: 071 833 3319

NATIONAL COUNCIL FOR VOLUNTARY YOUTH SERVICES
Coburn House, 3 Coburn Road, London E3 2DA
Tel: 081 980 5712

NATIONAL SOCIETY FOR THE PREVENTION OF CRUELTY TO CHILDREN (NSPCC)
Curtain Road, London EC2
Tel: 071 825 2500

CHILD PROTECTION LINE
67 Saffron Hill, London EC1N 8RS
Tel(s):   0800 800500
               0800 181188

NATIONAL YOUTH AGENCY
17–23 Albion Street, Leicester LE1 6G1
Tel: 0533 471200

PICCADILLY ADVICE CENTRE (For young people newly arrived in London)
100 Shaftesbury Avenue, London W1V 7DH
Tel: 071 434 3773

POSITIVE YOUTH (For young people with HIV/Aids)
51B Philbeach Gardens, London SW5 9EB
Tel: 071 373 7547

SAMARITANS (London - Central)
46 Marshall Street, London W1V 1LR
Tel: 071 734 2800

SCODA (Details of local drug agencies)
1–4 Hatton Place, London EC1 8ND
Tel: 071 430 2341

SCOTTISH LAW CENTRE
Lion Chambers, 170 Hope Street, Glasgow G2 2TU
Tel: 041 333 9305

SEX EDUCATION FORUM
National Children's Bureau, 8 Wakley Street, London EC1V 7QE
Tel: 071 278 9441

SHELTER (National Campaign for the Homeless)
8 Old Street, London EC1V 9HU
Tel: 071 253 0202
Emergency Nightline: 0800 446441

SUZY LAMPLUGH TRUST (Helpline when someone goes missing)
14 East Sheen Avenue, London SW14 8AS
Tel: 081 392 1839
Helpline: 081 392 2000

TRUST FOR THE STUDY OF ADOLESCENTS
23 New Road, Brighton BN1 1WZ
Tel: 0273 693311

UK FORUM ON YOUNG PEOPLE AND GAMBLING
11 St Bride Street, London EC4 4AS
Tel: 071 353 2366

UNA
3 Whitehall Court, London SW1A 2EL
Tel: 071 930 2931/2

UNICEF-UK
55 Lincoln's Inn Fields, London WC2A 3NB
Tel: 071 405 5592

VOICE FOR THE CHILD IN CARE
Unit 4, Pride Court, 80–82 White Lion Street, London N1 9PF
Tel: 071 833 5792

YOUTHAID
409 Brixton Road, London SW9 7DG
Tel: 071 737 8088

YOUTH ACCESS
Magazine Business Centre, 11 Newark Street, Leicester LE1 5SS
Tel: 0533 558763

YOUNG HOMELESSNESS GROUP
2nd Floor, 10 Livonia Street, London WC1 3PH
Tel: 071 836 0494

YOUNG MINDS TRUST
22a Boston Place, London, NW1 6ER
Tel: 071 724 7262

'WHO CARES ?' TRUST
Citybridge House, 235–245 Goswell Road, London EC1V 7JD
Tel: 071 833 9047

NOTES:

(1)   Most organisations concerned with specific disabilities or conditions
      will give help and advice. Addresses are available from the National
      Children's Bureau's Information Service or from:-

DIAL UK (DISABLEMENT INFORMATION AND ADVICE LINE)
Park Lodge, St Catherine's Hospital, Tickhill Road, Balby, Doncaster DN4 8QN
Tel: 0302 310123

(2)   See: Social Services Yearbook (Available in reference libraries) for local
      branches of the CITIZEN'S ADVICE BUREAUX, SAMARITANS,
      RELATE, PREGNANCY ADVISORY SERVICE]

Appendix 5   The Race Relations Act 1976

Direct Discrimination (Section 1(1)(a)): What we would normally term discrimination ie. treating a person less favourably than another person is treated in the same or similar circumstances, on racial grounds. Racial grounds are those of race, colour, nationality (including citizenship) or ethnic or national origins. Mandla v Dowell Lee (House of Lords, 1983) extended this definition to include groups with a "long shared history" and a "cultural tradition" of their own, among other factors (Sikhs, Jews, Rastafarians and Gypsies are included). For example, refusing to admit a child to a school simply because he or she is black (or white) would be unlawful. Direct discrimination does not have to be intentional to be less favourable.

Indirect Discrimination (Section 1(1)(9b): This means applying a requirement or condition which is fair in form but adversely affects a particular racial group more than others because they cannot comply with it and which cannot be justified on non-racial grounds.

For example, allocating play group places to children whose parents are part of a circle of friends and acquaintances and have spread the word among themselves, (sometimes called "word of mouth" recruitment) could be unlawful if this method of filling places excluded a particular racial group and could not be justified. Indirect discrimination is important because it may not be intentional but be a result of long held practices which have the **effect** of discriminating.

Segregation (Section 1(2)): Segregating a person on racial grounds constitutes less favourable treatment within the definition of direct discrimination.

Victimisation (Section 2): If a person is suspected or known to be bringing proceedings under the Act, or giving evidence or information about such proceedings or alleges that discrimination had occurred and is given less favourable treatment than others in the same circumstances, that person is victimised. For example, refusing to put a child on a school waiting list, because their parents had previously complained about racial discrimination at the nursery, would be unlawful.

Allegations of racial discrimination can be taken up by individuals in industrial tribunals (in case of employment) and in the county courts (in all other cases). In addition, the Commission for Racial Equality has specific powers to conduct formal investigations into allegations, where there are grounds for belief that discrimination might have occurred. It has statutory powers to require evidence and has the duty to publish a public report of the investigation.

Appendix 6   Extract from Guidance on permissible forms of control in Children's Residential Care LAC(93)13 Department of Health

Section IX: General Principles Governing Interventions to Maintain Control

9.1 The following guiding principles provide a framework in which a residential social worker can make judgements about possible interventions. It is imperative that staff exercise sound judgement and act with discretion in deciding how to react in a particular set of circumstances.

(i)   A distinction must be maintained between the use of a 'one-off' intervention which is appropriate in the particular circumstances, and using it repeatedly as a regular feature of a regime.

(ii)   Staff must be able to show that the method of intervention was in keeping with the incident that gave rise to it.

(iii) The degree and duration of any force applied must be proportional to the circumstances.

(iv)   The potential for damage to persons and property in applying any form of restraint must always be kept in mind.

(v)   The failure of a particular intervention to secure a child's compliance should not automatically signal the immediate use of another more forceful form of intervention. Escalation should be avoided if possible; especially if it would make the overall situation more destructive and/or unmanageable.

(vi)   The age and competence of the child should be taken into account in deciding what degree of intervention is necessary.

(vii) In developing individual child care plans, consideration should be given to approaches to control that would be appropriate to that child's case.

Appendix 7   Personal Development Contract

EXAMPLE FROM "CHOOSING WITH CARE" – THE REPORT OF THE COMMITTEE OF INQUIRY INTO THE SELECTION, DEVELOPMENT AND MANAGEMENT OF STAFF IN CHILDREN'S HOMES – CHAIRED BY NORMAN WARNER, HMSO 1992

Personal Development Contract
Care Staff

For:_____

Date:_____

There are four parties to this Personal Development Contract:

The staff member

Name:_____

Signature:_____

The head of home

Name:_____

Signature:_____

The training department

Name:_____

Signature_____

The head of home's manager

Name:_____

Signature:_____

**BEFORE COMPLETING THIS DOCUMENT PLEASE REFER TO
THE GUIDANCE NOTES AT THE END**

1. What	2. How	3. When By	4. Result	5. Review	6. Comments
List here the skills/knowledge areas you want to develop in priority order	State how you plan to develop these skills/knowledge	Date(s)	How will you know when you have acquired these skills/knowledge?	Agreed review procedures and dates	

Guidance Notes

Column 1 Insert here one, two or three skills/knowledge areas that have been identified and jointly agreed as basic to your role (at two months), and (after one year) as necessary to qualify you as an officer in charge.

Column 2 Insert the chosen development options that you intend to use. Seek help from any colleague you feel is proficient in the identified skill area, or anyone who can help you to identify ways to meet your objectives.

Column 3 Insert a challenging but realistic target date for the attainment of the objective.

Column 4 Indicate how you will know when you have achieved the objective. How will others know when you have achieved your target? What will be different?

Column 5 Insert dates for your regular review meetings with your homes' manager and your officer in charge. Such meetings should cover progress to date, obstacles, new opportunities, etc.

Column 6 Jointly consider what, if anything, should follow the attainment of development objectives. How can these improvements be best transferred and utilised in the work situation? What next?

Personal Development Contract
Head of Home

For:_____

Date:_____

There are three parties to this Personal Development Contract:

The head of home

Name:_____

Signature:_____

The head of home's manager

Name:_____

Signature:_____

The training department

Name:_____

Signature_____

BEFORE COMPLETING THIS DOCUMENT PLEASE REFER TO
THE GUIDANCE NOTES AT THE END

Personal Development Plan

Identifying Needs What do I want to achieve?	Selected Learning Approach What learning methods will best meet my needs?	Projected Results What will be the effect of my applying learning experience and activities?	Timescales When will I be able to apply my learning

Guidance Notes (1)

The Benefits

Adopting a planned approach will help you to create opportunities for the kind of development you want to pursue, as well as taking advantage of experiences as they occur.

By developing yourself you make your contribution to the effectiveness of the Home and being leader of a team equipped with the skills required to fulfil its objectives.

Progression should be continuous, taking advantage of opportunities to learn as they arise, in whatever form, not limited by or timetabled to the availability of courses.

You should explore alternative ways of meeting your development needs. Recognising that, while your employer provides a range of learning resources and support, you can also create and manage your own learning.

Developing the Plan

You should have ownership of the plan and generate the content. Your manager should assist to ensure the plan is a balance of personal needs and activities, not just a list of technical knowledge and skill requirements. The plan should therefore cover three areas:-

Performance Improvement Needs – These will focus on skill and knowledge areas identified on an ongoing basis and required in order to perform your job to the agreed standards. In order to meet the current and future challenges of the home, these will require regular reviewing and updating.

Personal Development Needs – These should be identified to enhance existing skill and knowledge areas. This will help maximise your potential and growth now and in the future.

Additional Learning Opportunities – We are constantly confronted by new learning experiences both in and out of work. It is important to recognise these and take every opportunity to reflect upon and learn from each one. Whilst not planned, such opportunities can be equally valuable in helping you to meet the needs you have identified.

Guidance Notes (1)

Identifying your Neds

You may wish to consider the following questions before developing and discussing your plan

What are my main strengths and limitations?

What opportunities are there for me in the future?

What can give me more information on these opportunities?

What have I achieved in the last three months that I am most satisfied by?

What didn't I achieve? Why?

What would I like to be doing in two years' time

What are my six most important personal goals over the next 12 months?

What do I need to learn to enable me to achieve them?

How, when and where am I going to learn it?

What do I most want to change?

How am I going to change?

What resources are available to me?

Appendix 8   A Training Framework for Boarding and Residential Education and Care (Ewan W Anderson, University of Durham)

PART ONE: INTRODUCTION

Aim

In the light of the background and preparations described below, to develop a consultative document, which provides a basic framework for staff training in boarding and residential education and care establishments for children.

As a result of such an initiative the longer term aims are to produce, for at least the introductory awareness level, a common core course and to facilitate the recognition of boarding and residential education and care as a distinctive profession.

Background and Preparations

This initiative results from the following:

- Pilot studies in schools for the implementation of the Children Act (1989)

- Work with the Department of Health and Department for Education on the preparation of the *Practice Guide for the Children Act (1989).*

- Work with Social Services Departments, particularly North Yorkshire and Oxfordshire, on the development of inspection procedures.

- Pilot inspections and meetings in schools.

- Meetings of the Holbrook Group, members of which are drawn from across the full range of education and care.

- The Ellesmere College training conference.

- Research and development as a member of the Wagner Development Group.

- An analysis of relevant reports and publications, including the *Warner Report* and all publications concerned with the *Children Act (1989).*

- The production of a number of papers, including the *Implementation of the Children Act in Independent Boarding Schools: A Training Programme* (report for the Social Services Inspectorate, Department of Health, 1991).

- The coediting with Davison A J, of *Applying the Children Act (1989) in Boarding and Residential Environments* (London: David Fulton, 1993).

- Meetings of the Boarding Schools Association Training Group.

In all more than 70 people have made a direct contribution to this proposal.

To Whom Addressed

The proposal is addressed to the following:-

- All associations with boarding schools in membership, including Independent Schools Joint Council, Independent Association of Preparatory Schools and State Boarding Information Service
- The Association of Directors of Social Services
- National Council for Vocational Qualifications and Central Council for Education and Training in Social Work
- Department of Health, Department for Education and Office for Standards in Education

Proposal Outline

Three levels of course are proposed: an introductory 'awareness' programme, a certified course and an advanced course. The 'awareness' programme would provide a basic introductory coverage of all the subjects directly relevant to boarding and residential education and care. It would be provided as an **INSET** weekend within each establishment. Certain of the subjects would then be further developed during subsequent **INSET** days. For the first such course, all the staff having any connection with boarding or residents would be involved, but on later occasions, the focus would be on new members of staff. It is this level of course which it is hoped to develop as a common core throughout the whole field of boarding and residential education and care.

The certificated course would deal in greater depth with the subjects introduced during the 'awareness' course. The programme would comprise one year of full-time study, although it is assumed that most staff would take it on a part-time basis over two years. Staff would work together in clusters of neighbouring schools and the programme would involve contributions from external experts, possibly a pattern of day release and, almost certainly, an annual residential week. The course should be certified by a university which would also provide the advanced course and would, ideally, be a centre of boarding and residential education and care.

The advanced course would be at degree level and, for those without a first degree, would last three years. However, it may be possible, as with certain similar courses, to upgrade the certificate in a shorter period. There could also be a masters course, either taught or by thesis, for those already in possession of a first degree. Given the need for as much on-job training as possible, it is assumed that all degree courses could be taken part-time as well as full-time.

Course Providers

The 'awareness' course would essentially be in-house and the providers would be experienced members of staff, with the occasional leavening of visiting speakers. To ensure consistency, it would be necessary to produce guidebooks and teaching materials for this programme. Providers for the certificated course would be staff from the school cluster, external experts, relevant staff from local colleges and visiting staff from the award-making university. For the advanced course, the staff would be provided by the award-making university supplemented by national education boarding and care expertise. For the certificated course, the role of NCVQ would be important and, in parallel with the advanced course, elements on boarding and residential education and care might be introduced into relevant Bachelor of Education, Post Graduate Certificate in Education and social practice courses.

Timing

Social services departments began inspections of boarding schools in October 1992 and the results so far indicate that the lack of staff training is perhaps the major criticism. Therefore, it is considered vital that an 'awareness' course be agreed and introduced as rapidly as possible. As with the inspections themselves, it is confidently expected that the course would be improved with each iteration. Bearing in mind this necessity to introduce training as rapidly as possible, the Holbrook Group has already begun work on a training guide for the "awareness" course. This is being built round the subject areas identified in **Part Two** of this proposal. Additionally, initial approaches have already been made to more than one university.

PART TWO: PROPOSAL

Present Situation

Elements of training are already being developed and supplied by a multiplicity of providers, including Headmasters' Conference, Girls' Schools Association, Society of Headmasters and Headmistresses of Independent Schools, and Boarding Schools Association. On the social services side there are courses such as those provided by the Open University, together with a number of local initiatives.

Specifically related to the implementation of the Children Act (1989) and offering a complete course rather than discrete elements, there have been three initiatives.

(1) A proposed structure, combining boarding school and social service approaches: *The Implementation of the Children Act in Independent Boarding Schools:* A Training Framework, report for the Social Services Inspectorate, Department of Health, 1991.

(2) Training proposals to be published by the Wagner Development Group.

(3) As a result of various meetings, including the Ellesmere College Training conference, a structured proposal by the Holbrook Group previewed in *Applying the Children Act 1989 in Boarding and Residential Education Environments* (Anderson E W, Davison A J, 1993)

Need of Training

Very few members of staff,concerned with boarding and residential education and care, have received any formal training. Training, such as there is, amounts to on-job apprenticeship. For all staff involved, it would seem vital that there should be at least an introductory "awareness" training in which the key elements of residential life are introduced. For those intending to make a career in teaching and caring for children by living with them, training would offer a career structure, at present unavailable. In time, this would lead to the development of a recognised profession, the training for which would be applicable through boarding and residential education and care.

Client Groups
Boarding

- heads and deputy heads of boarding schools;

- experienced boarding staff;

- teaching staff new to boarding;

- other care staff, including matrons, sanatorium sisters, etc;

- ancillary staff with access to boarders, including secretarial staff, ground staff, etc;

- visiting staff, especially those with one-to-one access, such as doctors and peripatetic music teachers;

- short term untrained staff such as "GAP" students;

- senior pupils with boarding responsibilities, such as prefects.

It is felt strongly that all staff having contact with boarders (ie. those for whom List 99 needs to be consulted) should receive some 'awareness' training. Obviously, the appropriateness of a particular part of the course to a specific client group would need to be decided by the school.

Proposed Course Structure

There would be three levels of course designed to provide a natural progression from the non-certificated to the certificated and, finally, the advanced course. The starting point would be a consideration of the boarding or residential education or care ethos of the particular establishment.

1.   Non-certificated 'Awareness' Course

Initially, this would be provided as **INSET** training within each school but, once the established staff had completed the course, it would be provided by local school clusters for new members of staff as an induction course. The "awareness" course could also be used for management training for heads and aspiring heads of boarding schools and as a rapid introduction for 'GAT' students, senior prefects and interested non-boarding members of staff.

Course Content

Section 1 – Context

- The philosophy and ethos of the particular school/residential establishment in the total pattern of boarding and residential education and care.

- What is boarding?

- The ethos questioned and viewed from different perspectives.

- Bench mark questions to identify the ethos.

Section 2 – In Loco Parentis

- The Children Act: rights and responsibilities; legal perspectives; complaints procedures.

- Pragmatic guidance and reference material.

- Responsibilities and non-responsibilities.

- Confidential issues.

- Other important legislation.

Section 3 – Self-awareness

- Self-monitoring: development of questioning attitude; personal development; personal record keeping, etc.

- Practical experience and relevant dichotomies.

- Importance of open discussion.

Section 4 – Primary Care

- Health: Aids awareness; drug abuse prevention; safety aspects; sex education and appropriate relationships.

- Alcohol abuse and sexually transmitted diseases.

- Precautions.

- Staff coordination and responsibilities.

- Knowledge appropriate to age.

Section 5 – Child Protection Issues

- Local authority and police involvement; non-statutory guidance; abuse at home, outside school, at school.

- Bullying: definitions, actions to be taken.

Section 6 – Management

- Group management; time management; lines of communication; lines of management; resources; administration and record keeping; staff supervision; accountability; delegation.

Section 7 – Crisis Management

- Discipline and control; handling conflict; sanctions.

Section 8 – Child Development

- Personal, emotional and social development of children; monitoring; observation; reflection; social skills development; personal hygiene.

Section 9 – Relationships

- Between children, staff, parents, visitors; multicultural and gender issues; confidentiality; group work; personal dignity.

Section 10 – Communication and Counselling Skills

- Listening skills; advice-giving; ethics of counselling; counselling and therapy.

Section 11 – The Residential Environment

- Personal space; vertical and horizontal house systems; the external and internal environment; privacy and choice; symbolism.

2..   Certificated Courses
These courses would be run in clusters of neighbouring schools, using local and visiting expertise. They would normally be structured to include some day-release and almost certainly at least one residential week per year. The course would be completed in two years part-time and would be organised by the award-making institution. (Exceptionally, the course would be available over one year, full time).

Course Content
The following is an outline of the possible elements:

- Personal development
- Social theory techniques
- Child guidance
- Child care practice
- Child development theory
- Residential health and safety
- Residential legal responsibilities
- Residential organisation and management
- Group dynamics

The role of NCVQ would also be considered.

3. Advanced Courses

These courses would be at degree level and the structure would depend upon negotiation with the award-making institution.   Ideally, this would be a university which would also become a centre for research in boarding and residential education and care. The basic course would be for a Bachelors Degree and would be three years full-time or probably five years part-time. For staff with a first degree, there could be a Masters Degree, either by course work or by thesis. Additionally, elements on boarding and residential education and care could be introduced into the Bachelor of Education and Post Graduate Certificate in Education.

Course Content

The following is an outline of possible elements:-

- Psychology

- Organisational theory

- Guidance and counselling

- Philosophy and ethics

- Sociology

- Health care

- Law

- Social politics

- Social administration

Appendix 9   Publications referred to in the Text of
                'Growing up in Groups'

Accommodating Children: A Review of Children's Homes in Wales – Conducted by the Social Services Inspectorate, Wales and Social Information Systems Limited, 1991

After Grace – Teeth – A Comparative Study of the Residential experience of boys in Approved Schools, Millham S, Bullock R, Cherrett P, Human Context Books 1975

A Guide to Consent for Examination and Treatment – NHS Management Executive 1991

A Lost Generation – Abrahams A and Lobstein T, National Children's Home 1993

A Two Year Old Goes to Hospital – Film made by James Robertson, Concord Video and Film Council, New York University Film Library, 1953

An Evil Cradling – Brian Keenan, Vintage Books 1992

Another Kind of Home: A Review of Residential Care – The Social Work Services Inspectorate for Scotland, Angus Skinner, HMSO Edinburgh 1992

Answering Back: Report by Young People Being Looked after on the Children Act 1989, The Dolphin Project 1993

Applying the Children Act (1989) in Boarding and Residential Environments – Anderson E W and Davison A J (editors), David Fulton Publishers 1993

Aspects of Adoption – The Seventh Jack Tizard Memorial Lecture, Herzov L, Journal of Child Psychology and Psychiatry 1990

The Background of Children Who Enter Local Authority Care – Bebbington A and Miles J, The British Journal of Social Work, Volume 19, No. 5, October 1989, Quoted in Patterns and Outcomes in Child Placement, HMSO 1991

Balanced Judgements – An article on involvement of young people in interviewing staff for Children's Homes, Mike Lindsay and Sue Rayner, Community Care, July 1993

Bridges over Troubled Waters – Health Advisory Service, HMSO 1986

The Care of Children – Principles and Practice in Regulations and Guidance – Children Act 1989, Department of Health, HMSO 1990

Caring for People: Community Care in the Next Decade and Beyond – Department of Health, London HMSO 1989

Castle Hill Report: Practice Guide – Braman C, Jones J R, March J D, Shropshire County Council 1992

Charter for Children in Hospital – Action for Sick Children (formerly National Association for the Welfare of Children in Hospital) 1988

Charter of the Association for Children with Life Threatening or Terminal Conditions and Their Families – Institute of Child Health, Bristol, 1993

Child Care Now: A Survey of Placement Patterns – Jane Rowe, Marion Hundleby and Louise Garnett, British Agencies for Adoption and Fostering Research Series B, 1989

Child Psychiatric Perspectives on the Assessment and Management of Sexually Mistreated Children – Royal College of Psychiatrists, Bulletin of the Royal College of Psychiatrists 12 pp534–540 1988

Child Psychiatry and the Law – 2nd Edition, Wolkind S, Harris Hendriks J, London Gaskell 1991

Children Act News – Department of Health

Children in Care – House of Commons, Second Report from the Social Services Committee Session 1983–84, Volume 1, HMSO 1984

Children in Hospital – Peg Belsen in **Children and Society**, Thirty Years of Change for Children, National Children's Bureau 1993

Children in Our Care – Commentary on Visiting Children's Homes, Childcare Series No. 3, Association of Metropolitan Authorities 1993

Children in Our Care – Handbook for Members Visiting Children's Homes, Childcare Series No. 3, Association of Metropolitan Authorities 1993

Children Living in Long-Stay Hospitals – Maureen Oswin, Spastics International Medical Publications, 1978

Children Psychiatry and Social Services – Chapter 13 in **Seminars in Child & Adolescent Psychiatry**, Dora Black and David Cottrell (Editors), Published by the Royal College of Psychiatrists 1993

Children with Disabilities – Volume 6, Children Act 1989 Regulations and Guidance, HMSO 1991

Children in the Public Care: A Review of Residential Care – Sir William Utting, HMSO 1991

Children's Consent to Surgery – Alderson P, Buckingham Open University Press 1993

Children's Homes – Berridge D, Blackwell 1985

Choosing with Care – the Report of the Committee of inquiry into the Selection, Development and Management of Staff in Children's Homes, Chaired by Norman Warner, HMSO, 1992

Clinical Child Psychology: Social Learning, Development and Behaviour – Martin Herbert, published by Wiley 1992

Closing Children's Homes: An End to Residential Care? Cliffe D, with Berridge D, National Children's Bureau 1991

Containing Anxiety in Institutions, Volume 1, Isobel Menzies Lyth, Free Association Books 1988

The Core of Care: Essential Ingredients for the Development of Children Away From Home – Henry W Maier, Child Care Quarterly 8(3) Fall 1979

The Cost of Services – Knapp M and Robertson E, in **Child Care Research, Policy and Practice**, Edited by Kahan B, for the Open University, Hodder and Stoughton 1989

Decisions in Child Care – Parker R A, George Allen and Unwin 1966

European Convention on Human Rights – 1948

Family Placement for Children in Care – A Guide to the Literature, Shaw M, British Agencies for Adoption and Fostering, London 1988

Fit for the Future – Report of the Committee on Child Health Services, Chaired by Professor S D M Court, 1976

Going to Hospital with Mother – Film made by James Robertson, (in English and French), Concord Video and Film Council, New York University Film Library, 1958

Good-Enough Parenting: A Framework for Assessment – Adcock M, White R, British Agencies for Adoption and Fostering, London 1985

Growing up in Care: Ten People Talking, Kahan B, Blackwell 1979

Guidance on Permissible Forms of Control in Children's Residential Care – Department of Health 1993

A Home from Home: the experience of black residential projects as a focus of good practice – Jones A, Phillips M, Maynard C, Race Equality Unit (NISW) and Wagner Development Group, National Institute for Social Work 1992

Home Life – A Code of Practice for Residential Care – Centre for Policy on Ageing 1984

The Hurt and the Healing – John Fitzgerald on behalf of the Charterhouse Group of Therapeutic Communities, 1990

In Care: A study of Social Work Decision Making – Vernon J, Fruin D, National Children's Bureau 1986

Informed Consent – British Paediatric Association, 1992

Interprofessional Consultation – Steinberg D, Blackwell Scientific, Oxford 1989

Interviewing Children and Adolescents – Dr John Rich MD, McMillan 1968

Issues of Control in Residential Child Care – Report from the Dartington Social Research Unit to the DHSS Working Party on Control and discipline in community homes, Millham S and others, HMSO 1981

The Law on Child Care and Family Services – Cmnd 62 1987

Leaving Care – Mike Stein and Kate Carey, Blackwells 1986

The Leicestershire Inquiry 1992 – Andrew Kirkwood QC, Published by Leicestershire County Council 1993

Locking Up Children – Millham S, Bullock R, Hosie K, Saxon House 1978

Looking after Children: Assessing Outcomes in Child Care – The Report of an Independent Working Party established by the Department of Health, Edited by Roy Parker, Harriet Ward, Sonia Jackson, Jane Aldgate, Peter Wedge, HMSO 1991

Lost in Care – Millham S, Bullock R, Hosie K, Haak M, Gower 1986

The Management of Care – Barbara Kahan, on audio tape produced by Social Information Systems Limited 1985

The Mental Health Act 1983: Code of Practice, Department of Health and Welsh Office, HMSO Revised Edition 1993

The Needs and Care of Adolescents – Report of a Working Party set up by the British Paediatric Association, Published International Youth Year 1985

Not Just a Name – The Views of Young People in Foster and Residential Care, A Survey by the Who Cares? Trust and The National Consumer Council 1993

Nurse – I Want My Mummy – Pamela I. Hawthorn for the Royal College of Nursing and National Council of Nurses in the United Kingdom, 1974

The Quality of Care – Report of the Residential Staff's Inquiry Chaired by Lady Howe, published by the Local Government Management Board, 1992

The Physical and Mental Health of Children in Care – Kahan B, in **Child Care Research, Policy and Practice** Edited by Kahan B, for the Open University, Hodder and Stoughton 1989

The Pindown Experience and the Protection of Children – A Levy QC and Barbara Kahan, Staffordshire County Council 1991

Poor Starts, Lost Opportunities, Hopeful Outcomes – Christopher Beedell on behalf of the Charterhouse Group of Therapeutic Communities, 1993

Principles of Preventative Psychiatry – Caplan G, London, Tavistock 1964

Probation Hostels – Ian Sinclair, Home Office Research Study No. 6, **HMSO 1971**

Psychiatric Admissions – A Report on Young People entering Residential Psychiatric Care – Malek, Mhemooda – Children's Society, 1991

"Pupils with Problems" – DFE Circulars 8/94 to 13/94 27 May 1994

Removing Rights from Adolescents – Michael Freeman, Adoption and Fostering 1993 Vol. 17, No. 1, pp 14–20

Report of the Care of Children Committee – Set up by the Secretary of State for the Home Department, the Minister of Health and the Minister of Education, Chaired by Myra Curtis, Cmd 6922, HMSO 1946

Report of the Committee on the Education of Handicapped Children and Young People – Special Education Needs, Chaired by Lady Warnock Cmnd 7212, HMSO 1978

Report of the Committee Reviewing Provision to Meet Special Education Needs: Educational Opportunities for All? – Chaired by Fish J, Inner London Education Authority, 1985

Report on Hospital In-Patient Inquiry for the Year 1966 – Ministry of Health and General Register Office, HMSO

Report of the Inquiry into Child Abuse in Cleveland 1987 – Presented to the Secretary of State for Social Services by The Right Honourable Lord Justice Butler, Sloss **DBE 1988**

Residential Care – **Children Act 1989, Guidance and Regulations, Volume 4**

Residential Care for Children: A Review of the Research, Bullock R, Little M, Millham S, HMSO 1993

Residential Care: A Positive Choice – Report of the Independent Review of Residential Care, Chaired by Gillian Wagner OBE Ph.D, HMSO 1988

The Residential Task in Child Care (The Castle Priory Report) – Published by Residential Child Care Association on behalf of itself, The Association of Children's Officers and the Association of Child Care Officers – Kahan B & Banner G, 1968

The Review of Malcolm Thomson's Employment by Sheffield City Council, 1992

School Life: Pupils Views on Boarding – Roger Morgan, Chief Inspector, Oxfordshire County Council Social Services Department, HMSO 1993

Scotland's Children: Proposals for Child Care Policy and Law Cmnd 2286, HMSO August 1993

The Sex Distribution of Children in Care – Lawson C W, Lockhart D, Journal of Adolescence 8 pp167–181, 1985

Social Workers: Their Role and Tasks – The Report of a Working Party Set up in October 1980 at the request of the Secretary of State for Social Services by the National Institute for Social Work under the Chairmanship of Mr Peter M Barclay, Bedford Square Press 1982

The Spiritual Rights of the Child – John Bradford, published by The Church of England Children's Society for the International Year of the Child 1979

Suicides in Feltham – A Report by the Howard League for Penal Reform, Chaired by Anthony Scrivener QC 1993

Ty Mawr Community Home Inquiry – Gareth Williams QC and John McCreadie, Gwent County Council 1992

United Nations Convention on the Rights of the Child – 1989 (Ratified in UK 1991)

United Nations Declaration of the Rights of the Child – 1959

What is the Question You Need to Answer? – How consultation can prevent professional systems immobilising families, Dare J, Goldberg D, Walinets R, Journal of Family Therapy 12 pp355–369, 1990

The Welfare of Children in Hospital – Platt R (Chair), Report of the Committee on the Welfare of Children in Hospital, HMSO 1959

Welfare of Children and Young People in Hospital – Department of Health Guidance 1991

Who Cares?: Young People in Care Speak Out – Page R and Clarke G (Eds), National Children's Bureau 1977

Who Needs Care: Social Work Decisions About Children – Jean Packman with John Randall and Nicola Jaques, Blackwell 1986

Working Together – A Guide to Arrangements for Inter-Agency Co-operation for the Protection of Children from Abuse, HMSO 1991

Working with Child Sexual Abuse – Guidelines for Trainers and Managers in Social Services Departments, Department of Health 1991

Working with Children and Young People Who Sexually Abuse Other Children – **Chapter 4 in Child Protection: Practice Guidance for Social Workers**, Scottish Social Work Services Inspectorate (Draft), 1994

Young Children in Hospital, 1970 – Film made by James Robertson, Tavistock 1958

Young People in the Care System – John Fitzgerald, Director of the Bridge Child Care Consultancy Service, Paper given to the BAAF Conference, Swanwick June 1987, Published in Adoption & Fostering Vol. 11 Number 4 1987

Young People Leaving Care – Child Fact Series published by the National Childrens Bureau, June 1992

Appendix 10   Bibliography (additional to publications referred to in the text of 'Growing Up in Groups')

Research

A Home from Home – The experience of black residential projects as a focus of good practice, Adele Jones, Marcia Phillips (nee Richards), Charlie Maynard, (NISW) 1992

Black Children in Residential Care – Vivienne Coombe, in Race & Social Work, Coombe & Little

Boarding in Maintained Schools: A survey January 1986–March 1990 – A report by HMI, Department of Education & Science 1990

Care and Control in Children's Homes, Principles of Good Practice – British Association of Social Workers, BASW News, June 1993

The Chance of a Lifetime? – Royston Lambert, Weidenfeld & Nicholson 1975

Children's Homes – Child Facts No. 2, National Children Bureau

Education and Children in Need – Hampshire County Council Social Services Department and Education Department, Produced by the Social Services Educational Support Service 1993

Education for Disaffected Children – A report from the Office of Her Majesty's Chief Inspector of Schools, Office for Standards in Education 1990-1992

Education for Parenthood – Resource Pack, Published by The Children's Society 1994

English Girls' Boarding School – Weber M, Penguin 1971

A Framework for School Sex Education – Sex Education Forum, National Children's Bureau, 8 Wakley Street, London EC1V 7QE, 1993

The Hothouse Society – Royston Lambert, Weidenfeld & Nicholson 1968

Independent Schools, Vol 5 – The Children Act 1989, Guidance & Regulations, HMSO 1991

Institutional Abuse of Children: From research to policy – A Review, Helen L Westcott, NSPCC Policy, Practice, Research Series 1992

One Big Family – What Boarders Think of Boarding – Independent Schools Information Service for the Boarding Schools Association 1993

Passing the Buck – Institutional responses to controlling children with difficult behaviour, Mhemooda Malek, Children's Society 1993

Patterns of Residential Care – King R D, Raynes N V, Tizard J, Routledge & Kegan Paul 1971

Provision for Children in Need of Boarding/Residential Education – Anderson E, Morgan A L, Boarding Schools Association 1987

The Public School Phenomenon – Gathorne-Hardy J, Hodder & Stoughton 1977

Residential Care For Children: What we know and don't know – Roger Bullock, Dartington Social Research Unit, a paper given at an NCH Seminar in October 1991

Residential Education – Fraser W R, Pergamon 1968

Room for Improvement: (Disabled Children in Short-term Residential Care) – Carole Robinson, John Minkes, Clive Weston, Community Care 8 July 1993

Therapeutic Care and Education – The Journal of the Association of Workers for Children with Emotional and Behaviourial Difficulties

Varieties of Residential Experience – Tizard J, Sinclair I, Clarke R V G, Routledge & Kegan Paul 1975

The Welfare of Children in Boarding Schools – Practice Guide, Social Services Inspectorate, Children Act 1989, HMSO 1991

Health

The ACT Charter for Children with Life-threatening Conditions and Their Families – ACT (Association for Children with Life-threatening or terminal conditions and their families) 1993

Children and HIV: Guidance for Local Authorities and Voluntary Organisations – The Scottish Office, Social Work Services Group, Room 420, 43 Jeffrey Street, Edinburgh, EH1 1DN, 1992

Clinical Child Psychology: Social Learning, Development and Behaviour – Martin Herbert, Published by Wiley 1991

Code of Practice – Laid before Parliament in December 1989 pursuant to Section 118(4) of the Mental Health Act 1983, Department of Health & Welsh Office, HMSO

Mental Health Handbook – a handbook for parents and advisors, The Children's Legal Centre, Published in association with the Mental Health Foundation, 1991

Overview of Research on the Care of Children in Hospital, Update 1 – Sheila Roche and Margaret Stacey, University of Warwick, Review commissioned by the Department of Health 1990

Register of Adolescent Psychiatric Units – Published by the Association for the Psychiatric Study of Adolescents, 5th edition 1990

Report of the Working Party on the Needs and Care of Adolescents – published as the British Paediatric Association contribution to International Youth Year 1985

Setting Standards for Adolescents in Hospital – NAWCH Quality Review Series 1990, National Association for the Welfare of Children in Hospital

Setting Standards for Children in Health Care – NAWCH Quality Review, Christine Hogg, Jo Robin (advisor), Published 1989 by National Association for the Welfare of Children in Hospital, Argyle House, 29-31 Euston Road, London NW1 2SD

Towards a Combined Child Health Service – British Paediatric Association 1991

Children and Young People

Bully for You – National Coalition Building Association, published in CONCERN, National Children's Bureau, Spring 1993

Bullying – The child's view – An analysis of telephone calls to Childline about bullying, Jean La Fontaine, Calouste Gulbenkian Foundation 1991

Child Sexual Abuse: listening, hearing and validating the experiences of children – Blagg H, Hughes J A, Wattam C (eds), Longman 1989

Children Act 1989 – Produced by the School of Health, Welfare and Community Education at the Open University in association with the Department of Health 1993

Children and Trouble: A Study of Juvenile Justice Issues for Local Government – Child Care Series No. 2, Association of Metropolitan Authorities 1993

Gizza Say? – Reviews of Young People in Care – Mike Stein, Lecturer in Applied Social Studies, Leeds University and Shane Ellis, Development Officer, National Association of Young People in Care 1983

The Hurt and the Healing – John Fitzgerald for the Charterhouse Group 1990

Listening to Children: the professional response to hearing the abused child – Bannister A, Barrett K, Shearer E, National Society for the Prevention of Cruelty to Children, London Houghton 1991

Listening to the Silent Minority – Murray N, (Needs of Asian families with disabled children are not being addressed by social services and greater understanding is needed of the cultural, religious, and social values of these families) Community Care No. 929 20 Aug. 1992

Listening to the Unheard Voice – Bartlett N, (Young lesbian and gay people in care do not have their needs met) Community Care No. 780 14 Sept. 1989

Lothian Children's Family Charter – Lothian Regional council, Lothian, Scotland 1992

The Rights of the Child: a guide to the UN Convention – Produced by the Department of Health in conjunction with the Children's Rights Development Unit 1993

The Rights of Children in Institutions – Produced for the International Association of Child and Adolescent Psychiatry and Allied Professions, by Berridge D, Hollinshead L, Ind J, Lansdown R Consultant Psychologist, Department of Psychological Medicine, The Hospital for Sick Children, Great Ormond Street, London, 1992

A Statement on Principles and Practice in Work with Children, Young People and Families – Child Care, National Council of Voluntary Child Care Organisations

The Handbook of Residential Care – John Burton Routledge 1993

A Voice for All Children – Report of an Independent Committee of Inquiry under the chairmanship of Professor Nicholas Deahim for NCVO, Bedford Square Press 1982

Working with Troubled and Troublesome Young People in Residential Settings – A Directory of Training Materials, Compiled by Brian Dimmock with the assistance of Andrew Cornwell, Carol Johnson, Jill Reynolds and Wendy Stainton Rogers. Children Act 1989 produced by the School of Health, Welfare and Community Education at the Open University in association with the Department of Health 1993

Working in Group Care – Social Work in Residential & Day Care Settings – Adrian Ward Venture Press 1993

You and Your Rights – A guide for children and young people looked after by Leeds Social Services Department 1992

Minority Groups

Black Perspectives in Social Work – Bandana Ahmad, Race Equality Unit National Institute for Social Work and Venture Press 1991

Ethnicity and Child Care Placements – Peter M Smith and David Berridge, National Children's Bureau 1993

Sticks and Carrots – using the Race Relations Act to remove bad practice and the Children Act to promote good practice – Jane Lane, Commission for Racial Equality, Local Government Policy Making, Vol. 17 No. 3 December 1990

Sex Education

Aggleton P and others (1990)
AIDS working with young people. Warwick I, Horsham: AVERT (P.O. box 91, Horsham, West Sussex RH13 7YR) 162 pp. A collection of health education materials for use with young people aged 14 and over in youth clubs, youth centres and training schemes. The pack consists of a collection of fully piloted groupwork exercises and games which address issues related to HIV and AIDS. The exercises included cover areas of 1. Helping the youth worker prepare themselves for HIV/AIDS work with young people. 2. Creating a supportive structure for the group to work in. 3. Information about HIV and AIDS. 4. Attitudes to minority groups. 5. Sex and safer sex. 6. Drug use.

Ashdown R, Carpenter B, and Bovair K A (eds.) (1991)
The curriculum challenge: access to the National Curriculum for pupils with learning difficulties. London: Falmer Press 374 pp

BBC
BBC Sex Education Video. Three new programmes replacing the 'Merry-go-round' series for 8-12 year olds. Covers the physical and emotional changes of growing up; sexual intercourse; pregnancy and childbirth. A fourth programme for teachers discusses race, culture and single parent families.

Bremner J and Hillin A (1993)
Sexuality, young people and care: creating positive contexts for training, policy and development. London: Central Council for Education and Training in Social Work. 79pp (Aimed at professionals working in the residential child care field. Offers guidance on the issues of sexuality and HIV prevention work with young people).

Bristol YWCA (1991)
Teenage parenthood education pack. Bristol: Bristol YWCA. (Education pack focusing on unplanned, premature parenthood, to be used as part of a wider social and sex education programme. Issues covered in the pack include: a realistic understanding of teenage parenthood, information relating to health, education, housing, finance, young fathers, responsibilities of parenthood, sexuality and the right to say no. Also contains ideas for creative writing, role play and poster design, resource lists and suggested further reading).

British Film Institute (1990)
I'm British but ... London: British Film Institute. Video which looks at how young asians construct their identity.

British Film Institute (1990)
A nice arrangement. London: British Film Institute. Video which responds to British curiosity about arranged and traditional marriages. Looks at the experiences of a young woman faced with such a decision.

British Red Cross (1991)
Your Choice or Mine? Dunstable: Folens Publishers. Designed primarily for use with young people, although can be used with an adult audience. Video contains 50 'trigger' situations which are intended to promote class or group debate. The emphasis of this pack is on developing decision making skills in the area of personal relationships, sexuality and health whilst also providing up to date information on HIV and AIDS.

The Clarity Collection (1990)
Taught not caught: Strategies for sex education. New ed. Cambs: LDA. 216 pp. (British version of highly acclaimed Australian sex education book for young people (9-16+ years). Contains information relating to the current legal framework for sex education as well as a thorough introduction for the educator discussing values, techniques and evaluation. The exercises for young people contained in the book cover a range of issues including communication, relationships, sexual decision making, the body, puberty, menstruation, contraception, pregnancy, and STDs. Also contains a useful reference section containing lists of resources, organisations, etc.).

Cochrane James and Parris Sylvester (1993)
The Black male's sexuality and relationships social education pack. Mitcham. North East Mitcham Community Centre. 57 pp. This pack was developed as a response from a report called Undertaking work with a group of Black males around relationships and sexuality, by the same authors. This pack was undertaken to assist those working with males, more so Black males in various education settings. This resources pack, with workers' notes, contains a variety of exercises that can be used to explore a large number of issues around Black males, including topics to do with relationships and sexuality, image, racism and sex.

HEA PRIMARY SCHOOL PROJECT (1989) Health for life 1 – A teacher's planning guide to health education in the primary school. Walton-on-Thames: Thomas Nelson & Sons Ltd. Comprehensive teaching pack for primary school teachers. Provides many classroom activities, guidelines for policy making and relates to the health education curriculum.

HEA PRIMARY SCHOOL PROJECT (1989) Health for life 2 – Health education in primary school. A teacher's guide to three key topics: The world of drugs, keeping myself safe, me and my relationships. Walton-on-Thames: Thomas Nelson & Sons Ltd. A comprehensive teaching pack for primary school teachers. Provides many activities, guidelines for policy making and relates to the health education curriculum.

Laurenzi C (1988)
NDCS survey into sex education, AIDS and resources for young deaf people. National Deaf Children's Society, Leeds: NDCS. 5pp. Results of questionnaire sent to 200 parents of deaf children, 30 youth workers and 150 teachers of the deaf enquiring into the suitability of mainstream AIDS and sex education resources for deaf children. Findings indicate that deaf children need resources designed to meet their particular needs. This research formed the foundation for the development of the AIDS AHEAD video.

Lenderyou GILL (1993)
Primary school workbook: teaching sex education within the National Curriculum. London: Family Planning Association. 120pp. This practical guide to teaching sex education in primary schools has been developed in response to requests from teachers. It offers a varied range of classroom activities which relate to curriculum guidelines for teaching sex education in primary schools. The workbook provides: a discussion of the key issues; a brief summary of the legislation (pre Education Act 1993); guidance on doing group work; step-by-step exercises with illustrations and handouts; background notes for teachers; a resource list and useful addresses.

McCarthy G T (ed.) (1992)
Physical disability in childhood; an interdisciplinary approach to management. Edinburgh: Churchill Livingstone. 594 pp. (Includes chapters on specific disabilities).

Massey D (1988)
School sex education – why, what and how?: a guide for teachers. London: Family Planning Association. 78pp. Pack aims to help teachers implement sex

education in their schools for 4-16 years old. Contents include general background on the ethos of sex education, guidance on sex education at primary level, secondary level and for young people with special needs. Information on teaching methods, workshops for governors and staff members, guidance on creating a school policy. The appendices contain comprehensive lists of resources for teaching sex education as well as information on current research in this area. Written in the light of the 1986 Education Act, however not related specifically to the National Curriculum.

On the Road to Clarification: 'Good practice for child and adolescent in-patient units in the light of the Children Act 1989' – Dr Mike Shaw, Consultant Child Psychiatrist, Queen Mary's Hospital for Children, The Royal College of Psychiatrists Conference, Child & Adolescent Psychiatry Specialists Section, 11th May 1993

Riverside Health Promotion Service (1989)
Situations: A game for young people on issues around HIV and AIDS. London: Riverside Health Promotion Service Board game and accompanying guide for youth workers or teacher. Game is aimed at young people who are sexually active and/or those who are thinking about it. The situations included in the game address issues around sexuality, gender roles, peer pressure, contraception etc as well as HIV and AIDS. Helps young people consider the risks of HIV and AIDS in a way which is relevant and meaningful to them. The accompanying guide offers information on 'what you need to know' and 'points to think about' for all situations in the game. It also provides general information on HIV and AIDS for the teacher/youth worker and some ideas for follow up work. The game aims to develop young people's decision making skills.

Sanders P and Swinden L (1990)
Knowing me, knowing you: Strategies for sex education in the primary school. Cambridge: Learning Development Aids (Abbeygate House, East Road, Cambridge CB1 1D). 217 pp. Teaching resource for primary school teachers which not only provides 80 practical group exercises on a range of subjects relevant to sex education (including HIV/AIDS) but which also provides detailed and easily understandable information on the policy and legal situation re: sex education in schools. Contains ideas for a number of workshops for teachers and governors to enable them to develop clear policy and curriculum statements on sex education. Also has useful ideas for group work which involves parents. The book is written with an awareness of the National Curriculum, however the exercises are not directly related to key stages.

Sex Education Matters – Quarterly Newsletter of the Sex Education Forum, National Children's Bureau

Slonim-Nevo V, Ozawa M N, and Auslander W F (1991)
Knowledge, attitudes and behaviours related to AIDS among youth in residential centers; results from an exploratory study. JOURNAL OF ADOLESCENCE (USA), Vol. 14 pp 17-33. (Assesses the level of knowledge about, and attitudes towards AIDS amongst young people in residential care, and their propensity to engage in high risk behaviour. Assesses the impact of a short educational intervention).

Sone K (1992)
Truth or dare? COMMUNITY CARE, No. 923 (9 July) pp7. (Residential workers must ensure that young people in their care understand the risks of HIV and AIDS).

Tacade (1991)
Skills for the primary school child. (Teaching Pack) Re-Solv. TACADE. (Pack consists of a manual, schools' workshops, parents' workshops and lesson cards. Provides a positive, skills-based approach to preventing abuse and promoting the protection of children. Suitable for children aged between 4 and 10 years).

Thomas G (1990)
AIDS simulation game. Cambridge: Cambridge Resource Packs. 53pp. Materials for 4 experiential learning games designed for use in secondary schools or for training courses within health and caring professions. Pack could be part of a PSHE programme, or could stand alone as a cross curricular module. The games aim to inform students, assist them to look at their own behaviour and enable them to explore their own and others attitudes. Games do not presume sexual experience on the part of the participants. The games themselves are very ambitious and quite complicated. One aims to reveal to participants the exponential curve of HIV infection within a population, another addresses morality and honesty in a role play situation "will you marry me". In the knowledge based games participants are required to distinguish between fact and opinion and to consider the way in which facts can be distorted. No evidence to indicate that the pack has been piloted within a classroom context.

Thomson R (ed.) (1993)
Religion, ethnicity and sex education: exploring the issues. Sex Education Forum. London, National Children's Bureau. 120pp.

Thomson R with Scott L (1991)
An Enquiry into Sex Education – Report of a survey into Local Education Authority support and monitoring of school sex education. Sex Education Forum

Worthington A (1990)
Useful addresses for parents with a handicapped child. 6th ed. Sale: A. Worthington. 106pp, Council for Disabled Children, National Children's Bureau.

Who Cares Issue No. 20, Special issue on HIV/AIDS Summer 1992.

Who Cares Issue No. 18, Gay? Me? Winter 1991/2.

Printed in the United Kingdom for HMSO.
Dd.300249, C20, 2/95, 3400, 5673, 312903.